An Austro-Libertarian View, Vol. I

An
Austro-Libertarian
———— View ————

ESSAYS BY
DAVID GORDON

VOLUME I

ECONOMICS • PHILOSOPHY • LAW

MISESINSTITUTE

The Mises Institute wishes to thank Hunter Lewis
for his support in making these volumes available.

Mises Institute
518 West Magnolia Avenue
Auburn, Alabama 36832-4501
334.321.2100
www.mises.org

ISBN: 978-1-61016-671-3

Table of Contents
by Chapter Titles

Philosophy

Law

Table of Contents
by Review Titles

Preface

RALPH RAICO, THE GREAT EUROPEAN HISTORIAN who passed away this year, once said: "Who needs the Library of Congress when you have David Gordon?"

As the founder of the Mises Institute, I've had the good fortune to meet quite a few extraordinary minds over the course of many years. Yet David Gordon is unique. In fact, I'd go so far as to say that one of the great pleasures of my life with the Institute these past 35 years has been the opportunity to give David a platform and an outlet for his considerable (and important) output.

It's not simply that the depth and breadth of David's knowledge are so astonishing, though indeed they are: David is profoundly learned in history, economics, philosophy, and related fields, and can effortlessly summarize the scholarly literature on even the most abstruse debates within obscure corners of numerous disciplines.

It's also that his mind seems capable of feats that are denied to the rest of us. After speaking about Ludwig von Mises's discussion of Rome in *Human Action* at our annual Mises University summer instructional event in July, David (who always lectures without notes) casually added, "If you have the scholar's edition, it's around page 762."

That's typical David.

You can imagine what his book reviews are like. His vast knowledge equips him to ferret out errors big and small. His agile mind detects weaknesses and fallacies that escape other reviewers. Even books David likes rarely escape without the exposure of a minor error or two. Of course, a good review from David is especially meaningful: if someone of David's learning and intellect thinks you've made a valuable contribution, you surely have.

Who even knows how many book manuscripts David has received over the years, from authors hoping he might discover their errors before the book review stage? And David, as a kind and generous a scholar as anyone could ask for, has in so many cases gladly obliged.

So you can see why David's book reviews are worth collecting, studying, and cherishing, and therefore why we chose to highlight them in this form.

In fact, all the way back in 1979, Murray N. Rothbard was already marveling at David's extraordinary intellect, the likes of which he had never before encountered:

> I have been in the scholarly world for a long time, and it is my considered opinion that you are a universal genius unequalled in my experience.... The only flaw in your makeup is that you don't seem to have the slightest idea of what a genius you are. The fact that your talents have so far gone unrecognized and untapped is a horrible waste and injustice, and Ron Hamowy and I are embarking on a personal crusade to do something about it.

With that endorsement, you have a taste of the treat that awaits you in the pages that follow.

LLEWELLYN H. ROCKWELL, JR.
AUBURN, ALABAMA
JULY 2017

Foreword

SHORTLY AFTER MURRAY ROTHBARD'S lamented death in January, 1995, Lew Rockwell telephoned me. He asked me to write a book review journal for the Mises Institute, covering new books in philosophy, history, politics, and economics. Moreover, he wanted the first issue in one month. I managed to meet the deadline and continued to write the journal for a number of years. Articles from *The Mises Review* form the bulk of the material included in these volumes; but a few reviews from other sources are here as well.

My thinking tends to develop in reaction to what others have said; and this, I suppose, is why I have written so many reviews. If there is any original thought to be found in these books, it lies in the analysis of the arguments that various authors have put forward. To come up with a valid argument using sound premises is a difficult task, and I fear that many authors have underestimated its challenge.

For this reason, many of my reviews are critical, but I owe readers a word of explanation. As a humorous way to attract attention, I sometimes deliberately adopted a ferocious tone of voice. This has had its own "unintended consequences" and now there is no going back. To me, the greatest of all critical reviewers was the philosophical scholar A.E. Taylor, and it is his reviews, written in Mind and other journals, that I have adopted as models, though I am always conscious of how far I am below his standards

Ever since I first read *Man, Economy, and State* in 1962, I have been a convinced Rothbardian, and it is from this standpoint that I have written my articles. The articles in these volumes appear as written, aside from minor corrections.

I am most grateful to Lew Rockwell, for support for my work extending over many years, and to my friends and colleagues at the Mises Institute, including Pat Barnett, Jeff Deist, Peter Klein, Joe Salerno, Mark Thornton, Judy Thommesen, and Hunter Lewis. I am most of all grateful to my parents, to whom I owe so much.

DAVID GORDON
Senior Fellow,
Ludwig von Mises Institute

Economics

The Case Against The Fed[*]

Murray N. Rothbard

The Bankers' Cartel

April 1, 1995, *Mises Review*

MURRAY ROTHBARD begins this outstanding book by calling attention to a paradox. The Federal Reserve System enjoys virtual immunity from Congressional investigation. The few who propose to subject the Fed to even minimal scrutiny, such as Henry Gonzales of Texas, at once find a consensus arrayed against them (pp. 1 ff.). They threaten the stability of the market; since, it is alleged, only the Fed's independence blocks the onset of uncontrollable inflation.

Here lies the paradox. Inflation results from the infusion of new money into the economy, and it is the Fed that is responsible for its creation.

> The culprit solely responsible for inflation, the Federal Reserve, is continually engaged in raising a hue-and-cry about "inflation" for which virtually everyone else in society seems to be responsible. (p. 11)

How did this odd situation come about?

As one would expect from a top flight economist, Rothbard responds by tracing the problem to its roots. He briefly and clearly explains how money originated in a barter economy. Some commodities are much easier to market than others, and "[o]nce any particular commodity starts to be used as a

---

[*] Ludwig von Mises Institute, 1994.

medium, this very process has a spiraling or snowballing effect" (p. 13). Soon one or two commodities emerge into general use as a medium of exchange. And this, precisely, is money. Gold and silver have almost always been the commodities that win the competition for marketability. "Accordingly, every modern currency unit originated as a unit of weight of gold or silver" (p. 17).

Why has Rothbard gone to such pains to describe a historical process that seems very remote from the Fed? By beginning with a simple case he can elucidate the basic mechanism that underlies the Fed's operation. To explain a complex event by starting with a simple method and gradually complicating it is a basic procedure of modern science. Galileo termed this "resoluto-compositive" method and Descartes described it at length. Once one grasps how money has emerged, the key to understanding the mysteries of the Fed lies at hand.

We already can answer the following question; what is the optimum quantity of money? If one has understood the explanation of money's genesis, the answer is apparent. An increase in the supply of money does not increase real wealth, since money is used only in exchange. (The exception owing to non-monetary uses of gold and silver can for our purposes be ignored.) "Any quantity of money in society is 'optimal'" (p. 20). And, to add one complication, the answer remains the same when paper money has been introduced.

A problem now arises for the analysis so far presented. If an increase in the supply of money does not increase real wealth, why have governments continually resorted to inflation? Rothbard's response involves another fundamental insight of Austrian economics. Inflation does not affect everyone equally; quite the contrary, those who first obtain new money gain a great advantage, since they can purchase goods and services before most people become aware that the purchasing power of money has fallen. Inflation in is thus a form of counterfeiting (pp. 27–29).

But it is not the only form; another type of counterfeiting arose out of deposit banking. Because of the inconvenience of carrying gold and silver, people often deposited the metals in banks, obtaining in return a receipt. These receipts, since they are promises to pay gold or silver, soon began to circulate as money substitutes. But a temptation presented itself to the bankers. The receipts normally did not specify particular gold or silver coins to be returned to the depositor; they were rather entitlements to specified amounts of the money commodity. (Rothbard notes that the great nineteenth-century economist W. S. Jevons warned against these "general deposit

warrants" [p. 37]). Since they need only return the amount of money specified in the receipt, bankers might give out more receipts than they had gold
or silver on hand, trusting that not all depositors would demand redemption
at the same time. For those willing to assume this risk, the prospect of vast
profits called appealingly.

But is not this practice a blatant instance of fraud? So it would appear, and
so Rothbard firmly avers that it is. Unfortunately, several nineteenth century
British legal decisions held otherwise, and these verdicts were adopted by
the American courts as well. Rothbard describes the legal situation with the
sure hand of a master historian (pp. 42–44).

Our banker-counterfeiter, one might assume, can now proceed happily on
his way to illicit fortune. But an obstacle confronts him; should he issue more
receipts than he can redeem, the clients of other banks may ruin him through
demands for payment that he cannot make good. The solution is obvious; by
unifying the banks in a centralized system, this check to fraudulent wealth
creation would be ended. Hence the movement for a central banking system,
whose history in Britain and the United States Rothbard deftly summarizes.

The Federal Reserve System, as Rothbard makes crystal clear, was the cul-
mination of efforts that continued throughout the nineteenth century to
centralize banking.

> By the 1890s, the leading Wall Street bankers were becoming
> disgruntled with their own creation, the National Banking Sys-
> tem . . . while the banking system was partially centralized under
> their leadership, it was not centralized enough. (p. 79)

As he describes the movement to cartelize banking, Rothbard introduces a
dominant theme in his interpretation of twentieth-century American history; the struggle of competing groups of bankers for power.

> From the 1890s until World War II, much of American political
> history . . . can be interpreted not so much as "Democrat" ver-
> sus "Republican" but as the interaction or conflict between the
> Morgans and their allies on the one hand, and the Rockefeller-
> Harriman-Kuhn, Loeb alliance on the other. (p. 92)

In the agitation to establish the Fed, the House of Morgan was in the ascen-
dant; and Rothbard stresses the importance of the conference held at Jekyll
Island, Georgia, in November, 1910, under Morgan control (pp. 114 ff). The

entire section of the book (pp. 79–118) that deals with the origin of the Fed shows Rothbard's incredibly detailed historical knowledge. Though he was too modest to do so, he could had he wished have echoed the boast of Fustel de Coulanges: "It is not I who speak, but history who speaks through me." Rothbard brings the historical section of the book to a close with a discussion of the Fed's early years in which the Governor of the New York Fed, Benjamin Strong, guaranteed Morgan control (pp. 124–129). Only with the coming of the New Deal were the Morgan interests relegated to a lesser role, as the Rockefellers assumed leadership of the Eastern Establishment. Rothbard draws attention to the research of Thomas Ferguson, who has interpreted the New Deal as an anti-Morgan coup (p. 131, n. 40).

"Philosophers have only interpreted the world; the point however is to change it." For once, Rothbard agreed with his ideological antipodes, Karl Marx; and the present work is not only an academic study but a plan for action. And the plan in question is a radical one. If Rothbard is correct, the entire basis of modern deposit banking, the fractional reserve system, is a type of counterfeiting that must be abolished. Under present arrangements, "the Fed has the well-nigh absolute power to determine the money supply if it so wishes" (p. 144). In response, the Federal Reserve System must be liquidated and the gold standard restored "at one stroke" (p. 146).

Again and again, the reader will be struck by the way in which Rothbard's grasp of fundamental economic principles enables him to overturn conventional thinking. A brilliant example of this is his unmasking of the fallacy involved in deposit insurance (pp. 134–137). Wittgenstein says in the *Tractatus*, "Whatever can be said, can be said clearly"; but few have been able to live up to his exacting dictum. Murray Rothbard's writing always displayed the clarity of a first-rate mind. Those who wish to see this mind in action, as well as learn from someone in total control of the literature of American economic history, should immediately secure of *The Case Against the Fed*.

An Austrian Perspective on the History of Economic Thought, Volumes I & II*

MURRAY N. ROTHBARD

Rothbard's Last Triumph

July 1, 1995, *Mises Review*

Volume I: Economic Thought before Adam Smith

MURRAY ROTHBARD tells us that this gigantic work was first envisioned as a "standard Adam Smith-to-the-present moderately sized book, a sort of contra-[Robert] Heilbroner" (p. xv). When we see what has emerged from that plan, a parallel at once springs to mind. Cervantes began *Don Quixote* as a short story, according to Ramón Menéndez-Pidal; but he gradually expanded it into one of the great books of the world. Likewise, the "moderately-sized book" has become one of the great intellectual enterprises of our age.

For Rothbard, the history of economics has an unusually broad scope. To him it includes not only economic theory but virtually all of intellectual history as well. As he often did in conversation, Murray Rothbard here advances definite and well-thought out interpretations of major historical controversies.

---

* Edward Elgar, 1995.

As an example, Machiavelli was in his view a "preacher of evil"—not for him the fashionable portrayal of the Florentine as the founder of value-free political science (p. 189). With characteristic acuity, Rothbard asks:

> Who in the history of the world, after all, and outside a Dr. Fu Manchu novel, has actually lauded evil *per se* and counselled evil and vice at every step of life's way? Preaching evil is to counsel precisely as Machiavelli has done: be good so long as goodness doesn't get in the way of something you want, in the case of the ruler that something being the maintenance and expansion of power. (p. 190)

And he concludes his discussion with a stinging rebuke to modern political scientists, who "eschew moral principle as being 'unscientific' and therefore outside their sphere of interest" (p. 192).

Rothbard firmly rejects the Weber thesis, according to which the "inner-worldly asceticism" that Calvinism encouraged played a key role in the rise of modern capitalism. Capitalism began long before Calvinism; and the stress upon "God and profit" that Weber found distinctively Protestant was present in the Catholic Middle Ages.

For the Weber thesis, Rothbard substitutes another contrast between Catholics and Protestants, here following Emil Kauder. The Calvinist stress on the calling led to emphasis on work and saving and distrust of consumption: Catholic Europe, in the Aristotelian and scholastic tradition, found nothing wrong with consumption. This difference led to a crucial split in the growth of economics, between utility and cost-of-production theories of price.

I fear that readers will have become impatient because I have yet to treat economic theory. But one last topic before doing so, covered in what to my mind is the single most brilliant page in Rothbard's two volumes. With a few bold strokes, Rothbard demolishes oceans of misinterpretation about the quarrel between the ancients and moderns.

> The pitting of "tradition" vs. "modernity" is largely an artificial antithesis. "Moderns" like Locke or perhaps even Hobbes may have been individualists and "right-thinkers," but they were also steeped in scholasticism and natural law. (p. 314)

Further, on the same page our author strikes at another theory of vast but unmerited influence.

> Neither are John Pocock and his followers convincing in trying to posit an artificial distinction and clash between the libertarian concerns of Locke or his later followers on the one hand, and devotion to "classical virtue" on the other ... why can't libertarians and opposers of government intervention also oppose government "corruption" and extravagance? Indeed, the two generally go together. (p. 314)

I wish that everyone interested in European history would study this marvelous page.

Rothbard firmly opposes the Whig view of the history of economics, in which "later" is inevitably "better," thus rendering the study of the past unnecessary. In his view, much of economics consists of wrong turnings; and the present volume ends with a tale of decline that will surprise many readers. Yet paradoxically, Rothbard's own method is in another way Whiggish itself. He has his own firmly held positions on correct economic theory, based on his surpassing command of Austrian economics. He accordingly is anxious to see how various figures anticipate key Austrian themes or, on the contrary, pursue blind alleys.

The dominant theme in Rothbard's appraisal of economics is the nature of value. Economic actors, endeavoring to better their own position, guide themselves by their subjective appraisals of goods and services. The pursuit of an "objective" measure of value is futile: what influence can such an alleged criterion have, unless it is reflected in the minds of economic agents?

Rothbard especially emphasizes, in this connection, the so-called paradox of value. How can it be that water costs little or nothing while gold is extraordinarily expensive? Life cannot exist without the former, while the latter is the merest luxury. The answer, fully developed by the Austrian school, depends on the fact that subjective appraisals of particular units of a good, not the supposed value of the whole stock of the good, determined price. Since water is abundant while gold is scarce, there is no anomaly at all in the greater price of the latter.

Our author never fails to praise those who reach or approach this insight. The scholastics fare especially well: Pierre de Jean Olivi, e.g., realized that the "important factor in determining price is *complacibilitas*, or subjective utility, the subjective desirability of a product to the individual consumers. . . . Utility, in the determination of price, is relative to supply and not absolute" (p. 61). Again, he lauds Jean Buridan for extending the subjective utility analysis to money (p. 74).

A key corollary of the subjectivist position is that an exchange does *not* consist of an equality: each party values more highly what he obtains than what he surrenders. Those who miss the point arouse our author to protest. Even Aristotle, whom he much admires as a philosopher, does not escape censure:

> Aristotle's famous discussion of reciprocity in exchange in Book V of his *Nicomachean Ethics* is a prime example of descent into gibberish. Aristotle talks of a builder exchanging a house for the shoes produced by a shoemaker. He then writes: "the number of shoes exchanged for a house must therefore correspond to the ratio of builder to shoemaker. . . ." How eh? can there possibly be a ratio of "builder" to "shoemaker"? (p. 16)

Those who knew Murray Rothbard can almost hear him asking this.

The subjectivist insight by no means died with the close of the Middle Ages. On the contrary, the School of Salamanca upheld it in the sixteenth century; and in the eighteenth, Cantillon and Turgot considerably extended it. But the path of economics was not one of continued progress. Theory suffered a major setback through the work of one of Rothbard's main villains, Adam Smith.

Far from being the founder of economics, Smith in the eyes of Rothbard was almost its gravedigger. Although Smith in his classroom lectures solved the paradox of value in standard subjectivist fashion, "in the *Wealth of Nations*, for some bizarre reason, all this drops out and falls away" (p. 449). Smith threw out subjective utility and instead sought to explain price through labor cost. Because of Smith's mistake, the "great tradition [of subjectivism] gets poured down the Orwellian memory hole" (p. 450).

Rothbard's discussion of utility constitutes only one strand in his powerfully argued case that Smith derailed economics from the analytical achievements of the scholastics and their French and Italian successors. And even in the discussion of utility, I have had to omit much. (The brilliant dissection of Daniel Bernoulli's mathematical approach to utility [pp. 380–381], e.g., should not be missed). But no review can do justice to the scores and scores of insights and scholarly discoveries in this volume.

Volume II: Classical Economics

THE READER OF this volume will at once face a puzzle: how was one person able to unify so vast a mass of material into a tightly organized narrative? I cannot pretend to provide a full answer, but one part of the solution lies in the fact that Rothbard follows a few main themes with iron consistency.

One of these central themes emerges in the book's initial chapter: "J. B. Say: the French Tradition in Smithian Clothing." Jean-Baptiste Say, far from being a mere popularizer of Adam Smith, "was the first economist to think deeply about the proper methodology of his discipline, and to base his work, as far as he could, upon that methodology" (p. 12).

And what is the procedure that Say advocated? One starts from certain "general facts" that are incontestably known to be true. From these, the economist reasons deductively. Since the beginning axioms are true, whatever is validly deduced from them also is true. Here, in brief compass, Say discovered the praxeological method that came to full fruition in the work of Mises and Rothbard himself.

To understand praxeology, a key point about the initial axioms must be kept in mind. The starting points are common sense, "obvious" truths, e.g., that people engage in exchange in order to benefit themselves. The economist should not begin from oversimplified hypotheses about the economy as a whole, chosen because convenient for mathematical manipulation. To adopt this wrong method was the besetting vice of the economics of David Ricardo, the main impediment, in Rothbard's view, to the development of economic science in the nineteenth century.

This conflict of method had a fundamental effect on the content of Say's and Ricardo's economics. Say began from the individual in action, the subject of the common sense propositions he took to be axiomatic. Thus, Say placed great emphasis on the entrepreneur. One cannot assume that the economy automatically adjusts itself: only by the foresight of those able and willing to take risks can production be allocated efficiently. "It seems to us that Say is foursquare in the Cantillon-Turgot tradition of the entrepreneur as forecaster and risk-bearer" (p. 26).

Again, Say's stress on the individual underlies his analysis of taxation, which Rothbard rates among his greatest contributions. Some, including notoriously Adam Smith, consider taxes a way to benefit the public; but Say would have nothing of this nonsense. Taxation, in essence, is theft: the government forcibly seizes property from its rightful owners. If the powers-that-be then condescend to spend some of their ill-gotten gains for the "public benefit," they are in reality purchasing people's goods with the people's own money. Taxation, accordingly, should be as low as possible: the search of Smith and his followers for "canons of justice" in taxation must be rejected. Rothbard characteristically adds: why have any taxes at all?

As any reader will discover after a few pages, Rothbard spurns the desiccated neutrality of much contemporary pseudo-science. He has his heroes and villains, chosen not by arbitrary preference but according to his carefully reasoned conception of economic principles. Yet he is no uncritical partisan of his heroes: he is a master of the fine discriminations that Dr. Leavis has taught us characterize the great critic.

When, we turn to Rothbard on Ricardo, the atmosphere is entirely different. Once again, our author reverses conventional opinion. Say was not a popularizer, but a great economist; likewise, Ricardo was not the first truly scientific economist. His much-praised logic is "verbal mathematics" that fundamentally misconceives economics.

> Ricardo was stuck with a hopeless problem: he had four variables, but only one equation with which to solve them: Total output (or income) = rent + profits + wages. To solve, or rather pretend to solve, this equation, Ricardo had to "determine" one or more of these entities from outside his equation, and in such a way as to leave others as residuals. (p. 82)

Rothbard explains with crystal clarity the path by which Ricardo sought to escape. He simply held fixed as many of his variables as he could: by oversimplified assumptions, he could "solve" his equations. In particular, he adopted a theory of rent based on differential productivity, which Rothbard neatly skewers; and he made price largely a function of the quantity of labor time embodied in a commodity's production.

Ricardo's labor theory of value had a consequence that would no doubt have shocked its author: it paved the way for Marxism.

> Marx found a crucial key to this mechanism [by which the cap-
> italist class would be expropriated] in Ricardo's labor theory of
> value, and in the Ricardian socialist thesis that labor is the sole
> determinant of value, with capital's share, or profits, being the
> "surplus value" extracted by the capitalist from labor's created
> product. (p. 409)

And with his stress on the Ricardian roots of Marxism, Rothbard begins a devastating assault on "scientific socialism," the like of which has not been seen since Böhm-Bawerk.

As Rothbard notes, Marx's economics falls into error from the start. Marx assumed that in an exchange, the commodities traded have equal value. Moreover, he took this postulated equality in a very strong sense: both of the goods must be identical to some third thing. This, by spurious reasoning that Rothbard deftly exposes, he claimed could only be labor.

But the flaw in Marx's derivation does not lie in the details of his argument. A *leitmotif* of Rothbard's work is that an exchange consists not of an equality, but rather of a double inequality. Marx's whole edifice thus rests on a spurious assumption, and the three volumes of *Das Kapital* constitute an elaborate attempt to conjure a solution to a non-existent problem.

But the difficulties of Marxist economics are not confined to its starting point. Rothbard points out that Marx's theory of wage determination really applies not to capitalism but to slavery.

> Oddly, neither Marx nor his critics ever realized that there is one
> place in the economy where the Marxist theory of exploitation
> and surplus value *does* apply: not to the capitalist-worker rela-
> tion in the market, but to the relation of master and slave under
> slavery. Since the masters own the slaves, they indeed only pay
> them their subsistence wage: enough to live on and reproduce,
> while the masters pocket the surplus of the slaves' marginal prod-
> uct over their cost of subsistence. (p. 393)

Rothbard does not confine his assault on Marxism to an exposure of its economic fallacies. Behind the economics of Marxism, he finds a hereti-cal religious myth, the goal of which is "the obliteration of the individual through 'reunion' with God, the One, and the ending of cosmic 'alienation,' at least on the level of each individual" (p. 351).

One might at first think that abstruse theosophical speculations that date back to Plotinus have little to do with Marxism. But Rothbard convincingly shows that Marx, through the intermediary of Hegel, presented a secularized version of this witches' brew in the guise of "scientific socialism." In the course of doing so, Rothbard makes Hegel's philosophy seem amusing; his remarks on the "cosmic blob" are worthy of Mencken (p. 349). Rothbard's analysis of Marx's philosophy re-enforces the pioneering investigations of Eric Voegelin; this parallel between the conclusions of these two great scholars is all the more remarkable in that Rothbard, though familiar with Voegelin, was not deeply influenced by him

So filled with material is the book that one could easily write another detailed review stressing entirely different parts of it, such as the long and learned account of the bullionist controversy. I shall, with regret, confine myself to two final items. In his discussion of utilitarianism, Rothbard's philosophical turn of mind is evident. He notes that according to that system, reason

> is only a hand-maiden, a slave to the passions.... But what, then, is to be done about the fact that most people decide on their ends by ethical principles, which cannot be considered reducible to an original personal emotion? (p. 57)

Rothbard has here rediscovered an objection to utilitarianism raised by Archbishop Whately: how can utilitarianism accommodate preferences based on competing ethical systems? John Stuart Mill, though familiar with the objection, never answered it in a convincing way.

I cannot resist ending with Rothbard's assessment of Mill:

> John Stuart was the quintessence of soft rather than hardcore, a woolly minded man of mush in striking contrast to his steel-edged father.... John Stuart Mill's enormous popularity and stature in the British intellectual world was partially due to his very mush-headedness. (p. 277)

You will not elsewhere encounter an intellectual historian who writes like that. Murray Rothbard's two volumes are a monument of twentieth-century scholarship.

A Future For Socialism[*]

John E. Roemer

A New Socialism?

October 1, 1995, *Mises Review*

JOHN ROEMER IS A BRAVE MAN. Few American economists today are prepared to defend full-fledged socialism; after the Soviet Union's collapse, even Robert Heilbroner, that quintessential leftist, had words of praise for Ludwig von Mises. Roemer, an economist of unquestioned technical competence, breaks with the current consensus. His book has already won praise from academics saddened by the fall of the Worker's Paradise.

Roemer does recognize that "the Soviet model of socialist society is dead" but, stalwart in his faith, he does not despair. "[T]hat does not mean that other, untried forms of socialism should be buried along with it" (p. 1).

To abandon socialism because of so temporary a setback as Communism's collapse would be to ignore a basic truth. "The Bolshevik revolution was, I think, the most important political event since the French revolution, because it made real to hundreds of millions or perhaps billions of people, for the first time since 1789, the dream of society based on a norm of equality rather than a norm of greed" (p. 25).

Faced with so eloquent and moving a defense of a regime based on cold-blooded mass murder, I was reluctant to subject Roemer's inspiring vision to analysis. But duty calls.

Roemer has had a bright idea. Why not save socialism by abandoning what that term usually designates? Thus, socialists need no longer support

[*] Harvard University Press, 1994.

public ownership of the means of production. If public ownership has failed, and public ownership is equated with socialism, then socialism has failed. But this would end the dreams of millions, if not billions. Instead, since the pursuit of "equality" defines the "dream of society" even the once hated market may be used in the struggle.

But equality of what sort? As Roemer sees matters, socialists aim at "equality of opportunity for: (1) self-realization and welfare, (2) political influence, and (3) social status" (p. 11). He glides quickly over his three desiderata, evidently taking their goodness to be self-evident. Self-realization, we learn, "is a specifically Marxist conception of human flourishing" (p. 11). Under it, people develop their talents in a way that gives meaning to life.

So vague a goal seems hardly suitable for a political system which determines which abilities are to be realized, and by whom, but minor matters such as this do not faze Roemer. He does not bother to characterize welfare in any specific way, nor does he explore possible conflicts between self-realization and welfare. What if some people would be happier *not* developing their talents in the fashion the Commissars specify? Judging by his praise for the wisdom of Zhou Enlai, one of our century's foremost mass murderers (p. 130), I rather suspect that individual preferences would not count for much.

But this, admittedly, is speculation. Giving Roemer the benefit of every doubt, however, his principles strike one as radically implausible. His first principle mandates nothing at all about self-realization or welfare, even putting aside the vagueness of these terms. What his rule requires is *equality of opportunity to attain* self-realization and welfare. A slave society in which all were equally oppressed, then, would outrank one with a hereditary aristocracy, even though in the latter everyone had a high level of self-realization and welfare. The *actual* level of self-realization does not matter: all that counts is that everyone have the same chance at this vague and impalpable goal. Given this principle, Roemer's pining for the glorious days of economic growth under Comrade Stalin becomes understandable (p. 43).

And just why should everyone have the opportunity for equal political influence and social status? Roemer does not tell us, although, commendably, he recognizes that conflicts may arise among his three principles. He does not specify a ranking for the rules in case conflict does arise, but that of course would be asking too much.

Roemer's principles raise a more fundamental question. Why is equality (of welfare, self-realization, influence, or whatever) desirable at all? As must never be forgotten, Roemer is a high-powered intellectual, "brilliant" in the opinion of the eminent Warren Samuels; so he is not without resources. He notes that "political philosophers [working] on egalitarian theories of justificationism" have established the truth of the egalitarianism on which socialism rests. In particular, John Rawls's *A Theory of Justice* "accomplished the feat of convincing a large number of social scientists that egalitarianism was not simply a value judgment that people might or might not hold according to their taste but was, rather, a view of what social arrangements were right, a view that any rational, honest person had to accept" (p. 27).

Here then is the scintillating argument offered by our talented author to support egalitarianism. Political philosophers, especially Rawls, have established it. Period.

Incidentally, he does not even succeed in getting right his account of Rawls. Rawls does not claim that any "rational, honest person" would adopt his theory; on the contrary, his theory proceeds from what he terms a reflective equilibrium among certain moral intuitions. Rawls does not go so far as to make holding these intuitions a criterion of rationality. But accuracy is of little account; after all, the future of socialism stands in the balance.

Some backwards people may prefer to found political philosophy on the right of self-ownership. This principle, however much it may offend egalitarian sensibilities, has at any rate the merit of clarity. But to adopt it, Roemer thinks, would be to fall victim to a drastic mistake. "Libertarians use the postulate of self-ownership to deduce the injustice of redistributive taxation; those Marxists for whom self-ownership is the foundation of the attack on capitalism must therefore explain why they reject libertarianism's animosity toward the welfare state" (p. 16). Self-ownership must thus exit the scene: were it to be accepted, it might lead to the rejection of socialism, which is of course absurd. QED.

Perhaps, though, I have been overly harsh in assessing Roemer. He is by training an economist, not a philosopher; so whatever the problems of his forays into political theory, his book may have value for its contributions to economics. And indeed, Roemer makes some useful points. Surprisingly for a socialist, he maintains that Friedrich Hayek got the better of Oskar Lange in their famous debate over socialist calculation. Lange endeavored to solve the challenge posed by Mises: lacking a price system, a socialist economy cannot allocate resources efficiently. Lange ingeniously suggested that a socialist economy could mimic the market. Why not use the market to achieve socialist goals?

To this, Hayek had in Roemer's view a convincing reply:

> To the extent the planners would require anything (other than
> profit maximization) of the firm managers, the managers could
> not then be held responsible for losses the firms incurred; thus,
> any interference with the market by the CPB [Central Plan-
> ning Board] would let the managers off the hook and, in effect,
> place all responsibility on the planners for the outcome. This
> point brilliantly foreshadows the political sociology of the soft
> budget constraint as developed by Janos Kornai ... some thirty
> years later (pp. 31–32).

Further, Roemer usefully criticizes socialists who propose that firms be
managed by the laborers who work in them. As Roemer notes, firms of
this type may be reluctant to take risks that threaten the discharge of some
of these managers. "Indeed, it is possible that adopting the form of labor
management for all firms in an economy could have the result that everyone is worse off than they would be in an economy with mixed management firms" (p. 123).

If the socialist calculation argument of Mises and Hayek works, and if
worker management is not the pearl of great price, why not abandon socialism altogether? Oh, but this would be to ignore the surpassing philosophical merits of egalitarianism, which we have already had occasion to examine.
What, then, is Roemer to do? His philosophical views mandate socialism,
but economic analysis speaks against it. How can he restore consistency to
his beliefs?

He does so by advocating a new version of market socialism, which incorporates even more market features than Lange's plan. In Roemer's scheme, firms
receive capital from publicly controlled banks. Each bank would monitor the
firms in its group; by withdrawals or increases in the supply of capital, it would
impose economic discipline on its firms. Thus, the problem, in Roemer's view,
that has plagued hitherto existing market socialism at last is solved. No longer
are the firms in a market socialist order subject to arbitrary interference from
the state: instead, they are subject to publicly controlled institutions whose
independence is constitutionally guaranteed. If stockholders can control managers in a capitalist market, Roemer asks, why cannot banks do so as well under
market socialism?

Roemer, as it seems to me, errs in thinking that the "agency problem" poses the principal difficulty for market socialism. Suppose that he is right that in his system firms will do as bankers dictate. What in his system channels money from banks unskilled at meeting the wishes of consumers to those better able to do so? He asks: how do investors in a capitalist economy get managers to do their bidding? But he does not ask: how does the stock market promote efficiency in investment?

And what Roemer grants with one hand he withdraws with the other. In his view, the state ought to play a large role in directing investment. But does this not bring back exactly the problem that, Roemer agreed, fatally flawed Lange's system, the "soft-budget constraint"? As he says himself: "A basic challenge to any model of investment planning is that some political process must be used to choose the investment targets, and this opens up the Pandora's box of rent-seeking, the wasteful use of resources for the benefit of interest groups who aim to influence the outcome of that process. It is beyond the scope of this essay to engage this challenge" (p. 106).

Yet we have not yet reached the most incredible part of Roemer's argument for socialism. As mentioned earlier, Roemer is a technically accomplished economist; and he constructs a model of a market socialist economy which outperforms a rival capitalist model (pp. 60 ff). But his "argument" simply assumes the key points he needs to establish.

He postulates that the rich are more likely to generate a "public bad" than the poor: hence a system that restricts the growth of the former will promote the general welfare.

Suppose, using Roemerian tactics, one wishes to show that socialism fails. One need only construct a model, one of whose assumptions is that the socialist planners are a gang of homicidal maniacs, while capitalist entrepreneurs are decent and economically rational. One could quite easily "prove" the capitalist regime superior; but I hardly think Roemer would find *this* argument convincing. And yet its assumptions are considerably closer to reality than those of the models our author has devised.

Roemer's technical tools thus avail him little in his endeavor to promote socialism. He offers a "future" for socialism only in an Orwellian sense.

The Philosophy and Economics of Market Socialism: A Critical Study[*]

N. Scott Arnold

What Remains of Socialism?

July 1, 1996, *Mises Review*

N. Scott Arnold's outstanding book makes a vital contribution to the debate over socialism; but Arnold has in part misconceived his own achievement. Since the collapse of socialism in the Soviet bloc, the world has had to recognize a fact long known to students of Mises. Centrally planned socialism is not, as its proponents imagined, a system vastly more efficient than the "anarchy of the market." Far from it: socialism cannot solve the calculation problem and thus cannot function at all.

Absent a price system, socialist planners cannot determine which resources should be directed to the consumer goods they wish to produce. Faced with the collapse of their dream, what can socialists do? Oskar Lange offered the most popular socialist response: why not a socialist system that uses market pricing? The schemes that have drawn inspiration from Lange's idea have been many and various; but the main instance Arnold wishes to investigate may be simply described. (Incidentally, Lange was not, as Arnold states, Mises's first opponent in the calculation debate [p. 39].)

---

[*] Oxford University Press, 1994.

The type of socialism Arnold considers relies heavily on workers cooperatives. Firms are not owned by capitalists—these the socialist regime has banished to outer darkness—but by the workers who labor in them. But like capitalist firms, cooperatives buy and sell on a free market: no central authority directs them to set certain prices. The state does not remain totally idle: its policies largely determine the rate of investment. With this plan, market socialists hope, the advantages of socialism can be retained and the problem posed by Mises avoided.

What is one to think of this system? Arnold establishes, with immense skill at careful argument, that market socialism is far inferior in economic efficiency to the free enterprise system. But he thinks that he is doing something else as well. I propose first to describe the main lines of Arnold's criticism of market socialism and then to explain how he misconceives his own project.

Our author has seized hold of a key point in his assessment of market socialism. In order to function, a market socialist system cannot allow capitalist enterprises in any significant number to exist. Put otherwise, market socialism can be seen as a list of prohibitions: it forbids certain "capitalist acts between consenting adults," in Robert Nozick's famous phrase. By contrast, a free enterprise economy does not forbid workers cooperatives: they, just as much as firms owned by capitalist entrepreneurs, stand free to face the test of market competition.

Does it reduce economic efficiency to ban capitalist firms? If it does, the market socialist system collapses, if judged on economic grounds. And just what Arnold shows is that market socialism drastically interferes with rational conduct of the economy. In doing so, Arnold relies heavily on the "new institutional economics" of the Berkeley economist Oliver Williamson.

To show the superior efficiency of free enterprise a simple argument appears to suffice. In a capitalist economy, as we have said, people are free to form workers cooperatives as they wish. If, then, such cooperatives promoted efficiency, why would they not supplant capitalist firms through the force of competition? If market socialists correctly judge the benefits of their system, efforts to establish it appear unnecessary: the market will accomplish the task by itself. If, on the contrary, capitalist institutions flourish in a free economy while cooperatives occupy only a minor role, is this not *prima facie* evidence that market socialism fails to work? Legislation to establish market socialism is either unnecessary or harmful.

This argument, which threatens to undermine market socialism with one blow, applies the "evolutionary hypothesis" used by the new institutionalists. On this view, the very existence of an institution on the free market provides evidence of its superior efficiency. Were it not efficient, why would it exist? Though this argument impresses me as a strong one, Arnold does not make use of it. He essays a more difficult task: he endeavors to show in detail the superior economic efficiency of capitalist institutions.

Under capitalism, workers characteristically do not own the firms in which they work. Why do workers consent to such arrangements? Surely workers wish to control their own labor; if they do not do so, have they not been forced by the imperatives of the system to work for others? Arnold uses pioneering work by the economist Armen Alchian to show that the working arrangements of capitalism make eminent good sense.

In "team production," in which workers must coordinate their activities on a joint endeavor, a tendency is present for each individual to shirk. Why not, to the extent that one can get away with it, turn to other things and let one's fellow workers bear the brunt of the task? To deter this, monitoring is necessary. And the question at once arises: what form of monitoring is most efficient? Alchian gave strong reason to think that monitoring works better if the monitor has interests independent from those of the workers. From the workers' own viewpoint, it makes sense for them to hire themselves out rather than to manage their own work. They are likely to be more productive, and hence earn more money, if they do so.

But what of the competing Marxist claim that workers labor for capitalists because they are forced to do so? Arnold deals in an especially effective way with one variant of this claim. Sometimes, it is contended, workers are forced into capitalist employment because they lack bargaining power. If they do not accept the jobs offered to them, they face starvation. The capitalist, by contrast, can readily find a replacement for those who find his terms not to their liking. Arnold responds: "The problem with this is that as an explanation, it is a non-starter; it simply restates the allegation to be proved" (p. 156).

To return to Arnold's use of the new institutional economics, the institutions of capitalism can quite readily be shown to make sense from an economic point of view. In particular, Arnold shows that the two forms of organization most characteristic of a free enterprise economy, the classical capitalist firm and the open corporation, have strong advantages over workers' cooperatives.

It is here that Arnold relies most heavily on the work of Williamson. The Berkeley economist places great stress on what he terms "asset specificity." This inelegant phrase designates an inescapable fact: many assets are tied to very specific uses, and lose much of their value in alternative employment. The skill of a champion baseball pitcher may be worth millions; in its next most valuable use, the players athletic ability might gain him next to nothing. Given asset specificity, it is important for market participants to build close relations with particular suppliers and consumers; they become tied-in to firms whose production is exactly suited to their needs.

But this raises a further problem. If two firms become closely tied together through repeated transactions, what are they to do should they arrive at an unexpected situation that neither contemplated? No contract can anticipate all contingencies, since human beings have only "bounded" or limited rationality. The chief theme of Williamson's career has been to discover how institutions are shaped to cope with the situation just described.

Arnold's application of Williamson's analysis proceeds in intricate detail, but his results admit of little doubt. The classic capitalist firm, in which one person owns the business and directs production, efficiently deals with the problems to which Williamson calls attention. The open corporation, though it separates ownership from control of production, preserves many of the efficiency advantages of the classical firm. In addition, it enables vast sums of money for investment to be raised.

I fear that my account of Arnold's book has so far been misleading. I have presented matters as if his principal contention was this: capitalist firms are much more efficient than workers' cooperatives; thus market socialism is not a viable alternative to the free enterprise system. I shall not conceal my belief that it would have been better had Arnold offered his results in just this way.

But he does not. Arnold is a philosopher, not an economist; and what principally concerns him is the justice of free enterprise and market socialism. More specifically, he concentrates on the Marxist claim that under capitalism, workers are exploited. Using his efficiency results, he turns the tables on the socialists: it is socialism, not capitalism, that exploits workers.

Arnold at first crisply disposes of the Marxist charge of exploitation. The Marxist contention rests on the labor theory of value, and "[t]he fatal flaw in this account is that the labor theory of value is not true" (p. 58). But the failure of the Marxist claim should not, Arnold thinks, lead us to cast exploitation entirely aside.

Economic value, as economists now see it, is a subjective affair; but it does not follow from this that it is senseless to say that someone does not receive the value of his services. To receive less than one is worth is to be subject to exploitation; and Arnold thinks he has an account of this fully consistent with the modern understanding of value. An advantage of his analysis is that it applies generally to any transaction: exploitation is not confined to relations between employers and workers.

Put briefly, the "value of something" is "what it would fetch in an ideal market" (p. 72). If something exchanges at its value, the exchange is fair. (Arnold's account does not require that a fair exchange take place in an ideal market: the requirement for fairness is that the price be the same as what would be obtained there.) If this condition is not met, the exchange is unfair, but this does not suffice for exploitation. The victim of the unfair exchange must have no better alternative available to him; if he can secure his value in another exchange, he is not exploited. (I have here simplified a rather involved definition that Arnold presents on p. 86.)

I admire the ingenuity and care with which Arnold develops his definition; but I cannot see that his notion of unfair exchange has the slightest moral significance. Why has someone any cause for complaint at all if the price he receives differs from that found under conditions of an ideal market? (By "ideal market" Arnold means, roughly, a perfectly competitive market.) Why should one call the perfectly competitive price a good's value? Prices are determined by values, but are not values themselves. Contrary to Arnold, the subjective theory of value does indeed render senseless the notion of someone's failing to receive the value of his services in a free exchange.

Arnold's rejoinder is obvious. Are we to rule out, by a stroke of the pen, exploitation in the free market? Surely an argument from definition will avail little in a clash with market critics. But I have not ruled out exploitation by definition. It does not follow from the fact that exploitation cannot be defined in terms of the subjective theory of value that no account of exploitation is legitimate. All that follows is that the theory of value is the wrong place to look for one.

If Arnold's account of economic exploitation were correct, he would indeed have contributed in a major way to the dispute over the justice of capitalism and socialism. Since exploitation, in his analysis, depends on deviations from competitive market prices, his demonstration of the superior efficiency of capitalism at once has an important consequence. Because market socialism is less efficient than capitalism, the conditions for exploitation are more readily met in the former system. But, once more, I am not sure why this matters, where justice is concerned.

Even if this criticism is correct, Arnold's discussion is a first-rate achievement. He has provided the best and most carefully worked out account of market socialism that I have read. His book is a model of how philosophers can use economic theory in their work—and in this department there can be no doubt of Arnold's efficiency. As if this were not enough, the book contains a superb assortment of sarcastic remarks about lawyers.

Making Economic Sense[*]

MURRAY N. ROTHBARD

Up from Statism

October 1, 1996, *Mises Review*

URRAY ROTHBARD had a remarkable ability to ask fundamental questions that others, even those within his own free-market camp, missed. After Rothbard touched an issue, it could never remain the same. This quality emerges in the present outstanding collection of his articles for *The Free Market*, written between 1982 and 1999.

Many economists have noted that in a free market, consumers have much greater freedom of choice than in an economy run by government coercion. But here a misstep threatens. Because consumers have greater choice in a free market, it is easy to jump to the conclusion that whatever promotes choice is a free-market measure. Thus, Milton Friedman, in some circles "the very essence of a modern major general" of free-market forces, has supported vouchers so that parents can send their children to the schools they choose for them.

Rothbard at once penetrates to the heart of the matter in his analysis.

> [B]y fatuously focusing on potential "choice," the voucher revolutionaries forget that expanding the "choices" of poor parents by giving them more taxpayer money also restricts the "choice" of the suburban parents and private-school parents from having the sort of education that they want for their kids. (p. 159)

---

[*] Ludwig von Mises Institute, 1995

The focus, he argues, should not be on the abstract notion of "choice," but on money and income. The person who earns more money necessarily has more "choices" on how to spend that money. A simple point: a free-market society rests on a system of property rights, not on a futile effort to maximize choices, of whatever sort. Yet who before Rothbard saw the point so clearly or so well?

Rothbard was ever alert to mistaken arguments for capitalism that, in an effort to be value free, lack a sound foundation in ethical theory. He brilliantly illustrates the fallacy of the so-called Pareto criterion, taken as the sum and substance of welfare economics, in a comment on a proposal for population control:

> A grotesque example of a "free-market" "expert" on efficiency slightly moderating totalitarianism was the proposal of the anti-population fanatic and distinguished economist, the late Kenneth E. Boulding. Boulding proposed the typical "reform" of an economist. Instead of forcing every woman to be sterilized after having two babies, the government would issue each woman . . . two baby rights.

The mother could have two babies, or if she wanted more, she would purchase a baby right from a woman who wanted to trade hers in. "If we start from the original ZPG [Zero Population Growth] plan," Rothbard comments, "and we introduce the Boulding plan, wouldn't everyone be better off, and the requirements of 'Pareto superiority' therefore obtain" (p. 149)?

If the key to a free society cannot be found in economic theory, neither is resort to that contemporary shibboleth, democracy, sufficient. The mere fact that the majority of a society supports some measure tells us very little about that measure's desirability:

> What, in fact, is so great about democracy? Democracy is scarcely a virtue in itself, much less an overriding one, and not nearly as important as liberty, property rights, a free market, or strictly limited government. Democracy is simply a process, a means of selecting government rulers and policies. It has but one virtue, but this can indeed be an important one: it provides a peaceful means for the triumph of the popular will. (p. 41, the essay from which this quotation comes was a Confidential Memo here made available to the public for the first time in *Making Economic Sense*)

With Rothbard, you can rarely predict what is coming next. No matter how carefully you may think you have grasped his thought, he was always several steps ahead. Thus, what follows from the passage I have just cited? You might think that, given his view of democracy, he would call for us sharply to deemphasize democratic reforms. Quite the contrary, he demands more democracy.

It does not at all follow from the fact that democracy is theoretically inessential that moves in a democratic direction cannot be the order of the day. Rothbard was especially concerned to strip from the judiciary its power to overturn popularly supported initiatives. In a highhanded way, our judicial lords and masters find in the Constitution the leftist values that they have imposed on that document. Rothbard would have none of this: he proposed measures that would "effectively crush the power of the Supreme Court" (p. 413).

As should be by now sufficiently obvious, Rothbard was no conventional economist. His economic analysis was always embedded within a careful account of politics and ethics. Thus, many "free-market" economists, when considering NAFTA, saw only that some tariffs would by its terms be lowered. Was this not a move toward free trade, that deserved the support of libertarians? Rothbard's analysis penetrates much deeper:

> The worst aspects of NAFTA are the Clintonian side agreements, which have converted an unfortunate Bush treaty into a horror of international statism. We have the side agreements to thank for the supra-national commissions and their coming "upward harmonization." The side agreements also push the foreign aid aspect of the establishment's "free trade" hoax. (p. 309)

Rothbard's treatment of the politics of economic issues covers a vast field, but one theme perhaps stands uppermost. Whatever advances the power of the state was to him a deadly danger. And even worse than an increase in the power of a single state was the rise of an imperial power that sought world domination.

Here he saw a prime danger of NAFTA, a vital step to a New World Order. Politically, it suggests that the United States is "totally committed" to a form of global government. Economically, it means not free trade but a "managed, cartelized trade and production, the economy to be governed by an oligarchic ruling coalition of Big Government, Big Business, and Big Intellectuals/Big Media" (p. 312).

Rothbard locates here the root failing of Keynesian economics, which he numerous times does battle with in this volume. Lord Keynes and his disciples spurned the gold standard, which Rothbard sees as the only basis for a sound currency. Instead, the Keynesians endeavored to establish a worldwide fiat currency, under the control of an international bank. To achieve this, the Keynesians thought, would eliminate a principal obstacle to their economic plans.

As everyone knows, the Keynesian system almost always prescribes inflation. But if one country inflates and others do not, or do so only to a lesser extent, it will lose gold or income to them. A Keynesian World Bank would permit all countries to inflate together: gone would be the check that independent monetary systems impose on radical Keynesianism.

Of course, there is the minor matter that a world Keynesian monetary system spells disaster. "At the end of the road would be a horrendous worldwide hyper-inflation, with no way of escaping into sounder or less inflated currencies" (p. 254). Fortunately, Keynesians have been unable to put their schemes into full operation; but the manifest failure of their system has not deterred them, and they must ever be combatted anew. Rothbard's unique combination of political with economic analysis is an indispensable weapon in this struggle.

But if Keynesianism leads to disaster, wherein lies salvation? One false step, appealing to many, is to cast away theory altogether. The National Bureau of Economic Research has famously attempted to study the business cycle through strict reliance on fact. The Bureau's

> proclaimed methodology is Baconian: that is, it trumpets the claim that it has no theories, that it collects myriads of facts and statistics, and that its cautiously worded conclusions arise solely, Phoenix-like, out of the data themselves. (p. 232)

Rothbard subjects the alleged scientific approach of the Bureau to devastating scrutiny. Rothbard, although of course firmly committed to Austrian economics, had a detailed knowledge of statistics, at one time his college major (p. 38); and he could meet the measurement devotees on their own ground.

The section "Our Intellectual Debts" strikes me as especially appealing. Here Rothbard pays tribute to W. H. Hutt, F. A. Hayek, V. Orval Watts, and Margit von Mises, all of whom, incidentally, lived to be at least eighty-nine. Rothbard's obituary on Hayek raises issues of major importance. He fully recognizes Hayek's outstanding contributions to Austrian business-cycle theory and to the socialist calculation argument, as well as the impact of his anti-statist classic, *The Road to Serfdom*. But after World War II, Rothbard maintains, Hayek strayed from the path of righteousness. "To the extent that Hayek remained interested in cycle theory, he began to engage in shifting and contradictory deviations from the Misesian paradigm" (p. 378).

And worse was in store. Hayek, "radically scornful of human reason" (p. 379), rejected natural law arguments in support of classical liberalism. Instead, he championed a murky doctrine of social evolution. Rothbard, both here and in "The Consequence of Human Action: Intended or Unintended?" makes crystal clear his aversion to undue stress on Hayek's leitmotif, the unintended consequences of human action.

Rothbard's measured response to an eminent name in the Austrian tradition may at first evoke surprise. But one of Rothbard's great strengths was his ability to adopt an independent intellectual outlook. Even the great Mises himself is, elsewhere in Rothbard's work, subjected to criticism. Rothbard's willingness to engage in frank criticism of bad ideas from any source only underscores his insistence on honesty and independence of mind.

Expectations and the Meaning of Institutions: Essays in Economics*

LUDWIG LACHMANN

EDITED BY DON LAVOIE

The Other Side of Lachmann

December 1, 1996, *Mises Review*

I N PAST ISSUES OF THE *MISES REVIEW*, I have sometimes criticized Don Lavoie in harsh terms: in fact, some of what I have said about him has been quite horrid. On this occasion, I am happy in part to redress the balance. Lavoie has performed a genuine service in bringing together twenty-one essays by Ludwig Lachmann, written over a span of some fifty-five years.

The collection reveals Lachmann's considerable strengths, as well as what seem to me some more questionable elements. Lachmann comes forward at his best in "Austrian Economics Under Fire: The Hayek-Sraffa Duel in Retrospect." Here Lachmann applies to good use his considerable knowledge of the history of economics.

The influence of Friedrich Hayek at the London School of Economics was rudely interrupted, if not permanently frustrated, by Piero Sraffa's savage review of Hayek's "Prices and Production" in the *Economic Journal* for March 1932. Sraffa seemed to score some devastating blows against Hayek; but his own standpoint was obscure. He declined Hayek's request to specify that standpoint, holding that Hayek's confusions made this unnecessary.

---

* Routledge, 1994.

In fact, Lachmann points out, Sraffa rejected the "subjectivist revolution" in the explanation of value; he wished instead to return to the views of Ricardo. Had Sraffa's real agenda been generally known, his criticisms of Hayek might have had less effect, since few of his contemporaries would have heeded the call, "Back to Ricardo."

How did Lachmann arrive at his important insight? There runs throughout his long career, like the proverbial red thread in the ropes of the British Navy, a concern, almost an obsession, with the nature of equilibrium. It is this concern, I suggest, that enabled him to detect Sraffa's hidden assumptions:

> For Sraffa real-world market prices are determined by supply and demand. But behind them, as a centre of gravity, there lies the equilibrium position. Equilibrium prices are determined by the objective, partly technical, conditions of production and distribution, while demand determines equilibrium quantities of goods produced. (p. 162)

Here concern with equilibrium led Lachmann to a penetrating dissection of an episode in the history of thought; but the results were not always so fortunate. Unlike Mises, Lachmann took a radically restricted view of the ability of the market to coordinate production.

In markets with a "steady flow of supply," adjustment readily takes place. "Variable stocks are held, but as a matter of convenience, and their size depends on the flow. For good reasons all participants take the flow as their main point of orientation" (p. 271).

But in markets where large stocks of goods are held and the flow is not constant, difficulties arise. Speculative markets, with no constant pattern of supply and demand, cannot readily be gauged. "In such markets every transaction is a departure for the unknown, but buyers and sellers depart in different directions" (p. 272). Where speculative markets are concerned, the market is not a discovery procedure. "One can discover only that which is, not that which might or might not be" (p. 273). (Incidentally, Lachmann's first published article made use of the stock-flow distinction.)

This is not the place for an analysis of Lachmann's claim; but prima facie, his argument appears vulnerable at one point. Granted that it is harder to anticipate future prices in a "speculative" market than one with goods in constant flow, how does it follow that this cannot be done? Why will the market not bring to the fore, through the usual process of selection, entre-preneurs who can cope with speculative conditions?

In his excellent "The Flow of Legislation and the Permanence of the Legal Order," Lachmann himself seems to acknowledge the point just made. He criti-cizes a German law of 1976 under which workers received places on the supervi-sory boards of industrial corporations. The law, he contends, ignores a basic fact:

> the Stock Exchange "monitors" the performance of managers. Brokers, investment analysts and others devote time and effort to this purpose. The daily fluctuations of market prices reflect continuously the results of this activity by specialists. The share-holder watches these prices and draws his conclusions. (p. 256)

Perhaps speculative markets need not always be a venture into the unknown! Unfortunately, this passage is not elsewhere followed up.

Lachmann was certainly no Keynesian, but his stress upon the problems of speculative markets led him at times to quasi-Keynesian conclusions. It "became obvious" during the Great Depression "that pessimistic expecta-tions may not only prevent recovery when its other conditions are present, but actually set in motion multiplier processes of contraction" (p. 245).

Professor Lavoie is no doubt right that Lachmann did not think "eco-nomic reality completely chaotic," much less deny the existence of a real world altogether (p. 2). But he does emphasize disequilibrium much more than other Austrians, owing to his view of speculative markets.

But this of course raises a new question. Why was his view about specu-lative markets so oriented toward the limits of knowledge? I suggest that Lachmann was in the grip of a dubious philosophical view. As he says over and over: "The future is unknowable though not unimaginable." This phil-osophical dogma, hardening his skepticism about anticipation in specula-tion markets, then led him to a complete rejection of equilibrium.

But why did Lachmann think that the future is unknowable? What exactly is the argument that shows this? Perhaps Lachmann believed that G. L. S. Shackle, upon whom he lavishes praise numerous times in the book, had found the argument; but, if so, I do not know what it is supposed to be. Profes-sor Lavoie, or one of Lachmann's other admirers, would do us all a great favor if he would make the argument explicit. Set it out on paper so that we can have a look at it. The constant repetition of the phrase "the future is unknowable" does not suffice for a proof.

Getting It Right:
Markets and Choices[*]

ROBERT J. BARRO

In Defense of Secession

April 1, 1997, *Mises Review*

F ONE PASSAGE in Robert Barro's excellent book attracts notice in the wrong quarters, he is liable to find himself in serious trouble. Our author, a free-market supporter in the inhospitable climate of Harvard, has previously given evidence of a penchant for nonconformity. But now he goes one step farther: he challenges one of the most entrenched taboos of the American Establishment.

As Barro points out, the United States has tended to react with suspicion toward secessionist movements:

> if the US government had supported the right of secession in some other parts of the world, such as the Soviet Union, then it would have indirectly challenged the basic premise of the Civil War. Why was it desirable for Soviet republics to have the right to secession and undesirable for US states to have the same rights? (p. 27)

Surely Barro knows that the sanctity of the Union cause is a given. How can he dare to challenge it? Against the conventional wisdom, Barro adduces some simple facts.

---

[*] MIT Press, 1996.

> The US Civil War, by far the most costly conflict ever for the
> United States . . . , caused over 600,000 military fatalities and
> an unknown number of civilian deaths, and it severely damaged
> the southern economy. Per capita income went from about 80
> percent of the northern level before the war . . . to about 40
> percent after the war. . . . It took more than a century after the
> war's end in 1865 for southern per capita income to reattain 80
> percent of the northern level. . . . Instead of being the greatest
> of American presidents, as many people believe, Abraham Lin-
> coln may instead have presided over the largest error in Ameri-
> can history. (pp. 26–27)

One can easily conjecture how defenders of Father Abraham will
respond. Was not the cost of the war justified to free the slaves? To this,
Barro has an effective rejoinder. "Everyone would have been better off if the
elimination of slavery had been accomplished by buying off the slaveown-
ers as the British did with the West Indian slaves during the 1830s instead of
fighting the war" (p. 28).

And if this suggestion is dismissed as unrealistic, our author is still not
defeated. If the North had accepted Southern secession, what would have
become of slavery? Other nations in the Western hemisphere, most notably
Brazil, abolished slavery without war: why would matters have been any different in an independent Confederacy? The spirit of the times was against
indefinite continuance of the "peculiar institution."

Barro's aim extends beyond making a historical point, however important.
He maintains that economic considerations do not mandate large nations:
the much-vaunted efficiency advantages of vast national size are spurious.

> There is no relation between the growth or level of per capita
> income and the size of a country, measured by population or
> area. Small countries, even of populations as little as a million,
> can perform well economically, as long as they remain open to
> international trade. (p. 28)

Secession by no means stands alone among the political issues that Barro's
economic analysis illuminates. He finds economic benefits in having a "relatively homogeneous population within a given state" (p. 30). Diverse ethnic
groups pent up in a single state will tend to devote resources toward securing

state patronage. The temptation to benefit at the expense of a rival race often proves too much to overcome, with great losses to economic efficiency. (Barro's argument, incidentally, was anticipated by Ludwig von Mises in *Nation, State, and Economy*.)

Given Barro's contention, it is surprising that he opposes "curbs on immigration" (p. iv); but even if he is unwilling to accept the implications of his own analysis, others will readily see where the argument leads.

I have so far emphasized Barro on political issues, since his remarks are here especially compelling; but he covers many other topics in this wide-ranging collection. The author, a leading member of the "rational expectations" school, has little use for Keynesian economics. According to Keynes, an

> increase in aggregate demand due to the government's higher expenditure supposedly leads to so much utilization of underemployed labor and capital that output expands by more than the rise in government spending that is, by a multiple greater than one. Thus, if the economy is operating at less than "full employment," then government programs are even better than a free lunch. (pp. 110–111)

This famous hypothesis, Barro points out, cannot cope with a most inconvenient fact. Not a single instance of the so-called demand multiplier has been shown to exist. Contrary to the claims of many historians, the vast spending by the American government during World War II did not rescue us from the depression: "the data show that output expanded during World War II by less than the increase in military purchases. . . . No multiplier showed up in the United States during World War II, and none has been observed in other times and places" (p. 111).

I fear that I have so far disappointed my readers. I have had hardly a word of criticism of the book. A favorable notice of a non-Austrian economist in the *Mises Review*? Unthinkable! At best I can give only partial satisfaction. Some points in the volume indeed stand open to objection; but the book nevertheless is outstanding.

But, enough of praise: let's get on with what we have all been waiting for. Barro is most famous among economists for his defense of "Ricardian equivalence." Against claims that a budget deficit crowds out investment, our author demurs. Faced with a budget deficit, taxpayers will realize that taxes must eventually be raised to pay the bills.

This being so, they will, if rational, set aside money to pay for the tax increases they anticipate. What counts is not only current taxes, but the present value of future taxes. "[E]ach person subtracts his or her share of this present value [of taxes] from the present value of income to determine a net wealth position, which then determines desired consumption" (p. 93). Since anticipated future taxes affect consumer spending in the present, "taxes and budget deficits have equivalent effects on the economy" (p. 94).

The objections to Ricardian equivalence are many and various, a fact of which our author shows himself well aware. For one thing, people cannot be sure what the government will do in the future. "Eventually" the bills must be paid; but eventually may be a long time, and perhaps taxpayers will not wish fully to take account now of a bill that may be indefinitely deferred. In the extreme case, it will not be they who pay, but a future generation of whom they know nothing. And (a point Barro does not here mention) a deficit can hardly always be equivalent in economic impact to taxes. Otherwise, a deficit might always be substituted for a tax; and no tax bill would ever fall due.

The case against Ricardian equivalence seems to me strong, but the point here is not principally an assessment of this hypothesis. Rather, the issue I wish to address is the way in which Barro confronts the objections to his view. He does not, surprisingly, respond by an endeavor to refute the counter arguments. Instead, he readily admits that "some of the objections to Ricardian equivalence are formally valid" (p. 94).

If so, why does he not abandon the thesis? Because "the quantitative implications of these points are unclear ... the Ricardian view that budget deficits are unimportant may serve as a theoretically respectable first-order proposition" (p. 94). Put crudely, Barro is saying that it does not matter whether his hypothesis is false. All that counts is that it generate predictions that do not depart very much from the data.

For Barro, the pursuit of statistical significance is a categorical imperative. In contrast to Mises, for whom historical evidence can only illustrate economic theorems established by deduction, Barro directly derives supposed economic laws from statistical correlations. Thus, he endorses a supposed "iron law of convergence" that about two percent of the gap between a rich and poor country disappears each year. An Austrian would inquire of Barro why we should take this supposed "law" as more than a summary of past facts. Why need the law hold in future?

In another area, Barro seems also vulnerable to objection. Readers will, I trust, not be unduly surprised that this area is another departure from the Austrian approach. Barro's contention, if in my view mistaken, is characteristically ingenious. The wages of professional athletes in major sports, it seems, are "too high." What matters to fans in sports performance is not the absolute level of skill but how a performer does in comparison with his rivals.

> The relative performance feature means that each team has too much incentive to hire the best athlete and each athlete has too much incentive to raise his or her level of performance . . . each time a player gets more skillful, he or she effectively reduces the skill of the other players. (p. 154)

The technical details of Barro's argument do not for our present purposes matter. Rather, what is of interest is the implicit standard Barro uses to condemn athletic salaries as "too high." It is the familiar model of completely efficient resource use, in which all "externalities" have been subjected to correction. But why should this model be taken as an ethical ideal by which to assess market performance? With their insistence on full awareness of presuppositions, Austrians know better than to assume without argument that this criterion should be accepted.

But, much as it goes against the grain, I shall not end on a negative note, because Barro does not deserve it. His fine book abounds in insights. The author's commendable skepticism about the economic benefits of democracy and his keen dissection of the "endangered species" regulations are especially compelling.

I have space for only one sample.

> Most puzzling is the determination of the level of spending on a species once it has been listed [as endangered]. . . . The key matter appears to be whether the animal has charismatic qualities. . . . Basically, people like bald eagles, and that is why they get so much attention. (p. 153)

Essays on Capital and Interest: An Austrian Perspective*

ISRAEL M. KIRZNER

Puzzles for Economists

July 1, 1997, *Mises Review*

SRAEL KIRZNER has achieved greatest renown as an Austrian economist for his work on entrepreneurship. But he is also a distinguished capital theorist; the present volume usefully collects several of Kirzner's essays in this field, most notably his 1966 "An Essay on Capital."

A central theme stands out in Kirzner's essays. For Austrians, capital is not a disembodied abstraction. Instead, the decision to invest in capital goods must always be traced to individual actions. The significance of capital is not its "physical characteristics or physical history" (p. 44), but its ability to allow individuals to more readily realize their plans. This characteristic proves much more illuminating than the classical notion of capital as "produced means of production."

In the high point of the book, Kirzner deploys his thesis to great effect in criticism of the capital theory of Frank Knight. According to Knight, capital, like Topsy, "just growed." It is a self-perpetuating fund, which replenishes itself as if by magic.

Kirzner will have none of this. Knight's fanciful notion of permanent capital merely reflects the undoubted fact that if a decision is made constantly to replace used-up capital goods, these goods will be maintained indefinitely.

* Edward Elgar, 1996.

But Knight fails to see that there is nothing automatic about the decision to replace a capital good.

As always, the individual actor is primary, and his decision to replace a capital good is far from automatic. Kirzner dismisses Knight's fantasy of "Crusonia," an economy in which all capital is derived from a perpetually growing plant, as useless for understanding how capital functions in the real world.

Kirzner's demolition of Knight is first-rate. But at times in the present work he advances views that strike me as puzzling or mistaken. Though our author is a devout disciple of Mises, he unfortunately does not resemble the great Austrian in clarity of writing. Rather, he appears to have adopted the clotted style of David Ricardo as a model; and his remarks often prove difficult to elucidate.

A prime example occurs in Kirzner's defense of the pure time preference theory of interest. Incidentally, though our author rightly sees that this theory is central to Mises's thought, he does not expound it in the precise form held by Mises. He writes: "This theory solves the interest problem by appeal to widespread (possibly universal) positive time preference" (pp. 137–138). For Mises, time preference is an a priori category of action.

But this is not the issue that I find puzzling: if Kirzner retreats from Mises's *ipsissima verba*, that is his own affair. Rather, the problem on which I wish to focus arises from Kirzner's comments on a rival theory of interest. As he rightly notes, the pure time preference theory differs entirely from the view that ascribes interest to the productivity of waiting. In this view, waiting is a productive input that commands a price.

One might expect Kirzner to challenge the rival theory; but he fails to do so. He remarks: "As a matter of logic, the Fisher productivity-of-waiting theory deals with the interest problem" in "an impeccable manner. The only way through which the validity of the productivity-of-waiting view (at least as we have presented it thus far) can be challenged, is by disagreeing with the concept of 'waiting' as a productive factor service" (p. 136).

Very well then: one would now expect Kirzner to show why waiting is not a productive factor service. He begins by delimiting the field of inquiry: the dispute between the pure time preference view and its rival is "strictly a noneconomic 'philosophic' one" (p. 137).

Now comes the surprise. Kirzner does *not* argue in favor of the philosophic view of time which he believes lies at the base of the Austrian position. He confines himself to declaring the pure time preference view a possible option. By the close of his discussion, he claims to have shown that PTPT refusal to recognize any physical productivity role in the explanation for the existence of interest income, rests on (*the admittedly arbitrary*) view that time and waiting are not to be seen as productive agents. (p. 152, emphasis added)

If Kirzner's conclusions do not go very far, he displays one contrasting intellectual virtue: he tackles the most difficult questions in capital theory. Among these stands that nerve-wracking conundrum, the reswitching controversy. According to the Austrian theory of capital, lowering the rate of interest leads to longer, more roundabout methods of production.

But sometimes, it is alleged, "capital reversal" may occur. In such a case, lower interest induces the capitalist to switch to a shorter, less capital-intensive technique. Piero Sraffa, Joan Robinson, and other neo-Ricardians used examples of this sort to assault the neoclassical theory of capital; but, as Kirzner rightly notes, they threaten the Austrian view as well for the reason we have seen.

A formidable challenge. Kirzner maintains that the examples of reswitching rest on a dubious premise. They assume that "each technique of production involves a simple, unidimensional 'quantity' of time" (p. 9). But this premise cannot stand. "The cases that yield the capital-reversing paradoxes all arise from production processes involving more or less complex dating patterns for inputs and outputs" (p. 9). These complex patterns cannot readily be unified into a single quantity: hence the crucial premise on which reswitching depends collapses.

Kirzner's treatment strikes me as suggestive but inconclusive. Suppose that every case of reswitching involves a complex pattern of dating. (Must this be true or does this arise from the choice of example?) Does it follow that we can never say that one complex pattern takes less time than another? I do not see that it does.

He escapes criticism if his point is only that the reswitching advocates have not proved that one complex pattern *can* be ranked as longer than another. But, as with the pure time preference theory, he has arrived at a very modest defense of the standard Austrian view.

If Kirzner is right, neo-Ricardians can no longer claim that the Austrian view fails because lower interest may lead to a shorter production technique. But neither can Austrians claim that lower interest always leads to more roundabout methods of production. Kirzner's point, if valid, tells against both Sraffa and Mises. "Unreconstructed" Austrians should not rush uncritically to embrace it.

From the onset of his long career, Professor Kirzner has been alert to the normative dimension of economic theory. Even if one agrees with Hume that an "is" does not logically imply an "ought," surely judgments of fact are often very relevant to value judgments. If you know that a glass contains poison, you have a very good reason not to offer it as a drink to a passing stranger.

To Kirzner, the pure time preference theory of interest has just this sort of normative relevance. Opponents of the free market often condemn interest as unjustified by considerations of efficiency. By contrast, neoclassicals defend interest as the reward to a productive service.

Market sympathizers who are inclined to think that the Cambridge critics of capitalism have the better of the neoclassicals may find solace, Kirzner thinks, in the pure time preference theory of interest. Austrians agree that interest does not constitute a productivity return. "On the other hand, PTPT very definitely sees market interest as expressing a market-determined rate of intertemporal exchange" (p. 151). A defender of capitalism can thus use the pure time preference account to justify interest without assuming that it rewards productivity.

Here, once more, I am puzzled as to how much Kirzner's point shows. Certainly, there is something to it: but why must an opponent of capitalism accept that capitalists should derive financial gain because time preference exists? If he thinks that only productivity justifies income, he will remain unconvinced. If, however, he condemns interest not because it is unproductive, but because he thinks it fulfills no function, then Kirzner's point may indeed induce a change of heart. Like much in this book, this is a modest result, but not for all that, without value.

Perfect Competition and the Transformation of Economics[*]

FRANK M. MACHOVEC

No Contest

October 1, 1997, *Mises Review*

DOCTORAL DISSERTATIONS seldom make good books. Even the most trivial assertion in a thesis must be footnoted; and the author, much to the reader's discomfort, must demonstrate his control of his subject in excruciating detail. But occasionally, the virtues of the form triumph over its limitations; and Frank Machovec's excellent work is one of these happy exceptions. His extraordinarily thorough research illuminates many areas of economics.

Machovec's choice of topic manifests his courage. The mathematical formalism favored by Léon Walras has come to dominate modern economics. Elaborate models of perfect competition are the prime topic of contemporary microeconomics; and newcomers to the subject often think that they have walked by mistake into a seminar of the mathematics department.

Like other Austrians before him, Machovec contends that models of perfect competition do not adequately account for the characteristic features of competition in the real world. Our author is not an Austrian of the strictest observance, and he does not renounce the use of these models altogether.

---

[*] Routledge, 1995.

> As one who holds undergraduate degrees in mathematics and
> meteorology, I am an equivocal supporter of the of formalism
> in economics. I fully concur with Jevons's observation that, in
> a discipline devoted to the study of small marginal effects, the
> widespread employment of calculus is inescapable. (p. 9)

But the dominant theme of his book is not the benefits of formal models,
but their limitations.

When formalists face attack, they are liable to respond with derision. "Who
are you," they will say, "to challenge the way economics is done? If you do not
like our mathematics, found your own discipline." Machovec neatly turns the
flank of this rejoinder. The mathematical economists are themselves interlop-
ers. They falsely contend that their models develop the insights of the great
classical economists of the nineteenth century. In fact, our author contends,
they do not do so: formalistic analysis neglects the process approach to competition favored by the classicals. The Austrian critics of perfect competition,
not its latter-day proponents, carry on the study of economics as it has been
historically conceived.

But what exactly is wrong with mathematical models? For one thing, they
assume that the market price cannot be changed by the actions of an individual producer: prices are parametric. Further, individuals operate with perfect
information. "Since Knightian perfect competition assumes perfect knowledge by all producers and consumers, a market populated solely by price-
taking firms will have only one price charged to all buyers" (pp. 101–102).
And of course if the law of one price obtains, mathematical analysis gains a
firm foothold.

Machovec's argument must confront an objection. Perhaps, it will be
claimed, the models of past days rested on overly restrictive assumptions; but
we have overcome all that. Do we not now have models that allow for imperfect information?

Our author is not to be put off this easily. These models, he contends, fail
to take account of genuine uncertainty.

> The equilibrium theorist assumes that the decision-maker is al-
> ready drilling in the right field, whereas the process theorist em-
> phasizes that recognizing the appropriate place to start digging
> is the big hurdle. In equilibrium theory, the probabilistic outline
> of the unknowns is already known, thereby enabling a Stiglerian

marginal benefit, marginal cost analysis to reap an optimal outcome. Equilibrium theory simply cannot address the real problem: where to search and what to search for. (p. 171)

This response gives rise to a new objection. What if the mathematical economist says: All right, we do use unrealistic assumptions. So what? They work.
Have you never read Friedman's "The Methodology of Positive Economics"?

Machovec directly confronts this counterargument, and to my mind his
answer is the best feature of the book. He shows that adoption of the mathematical model leads to serious mistakes, especially when the model is taken
as a welfare ideal by which to judge the actually existing market.

Our author's account of the socialist calculation debate impresses me as
especially insightful. When Ludwig von Mises demonstrated in 1920 that
a socialist economy could not rationally allocate production goods, he left
socialists in disarray. What were they to do? Oskar Lange, a Marxist who
was also a leading neoclassical theorist, found what he took to be an escape.
Whatever the market could do, so could socialist planners: they had merely
to allow the managers of socialist enterprises to compete for resources.

Lange concluded that the problem of socialist calculation can
be solved, theoretically, through a series of trial-and-error prices.
Producers react to shortages (or surpluses) by raising (or lowering) their prices until general equilibrium is reached. (p. 53)

Mises, in Lange's view, was hoist with his own petard: his demonstration that
the market worked efficiently by that very fact showed that socialism also is
efficient. The equations of equilibrium are the same in both systems. Lange's
argument won over most of the economics profession, until the collapse of
communism made it clear that Mises was right.

What blinded so many eminent economists for so long to the validity of
Mises's argument? For our author, the culprit is equilibrium analysis. Wrongly
taking the perfect competition model to be a picture of an economy as it ide-
ally ought to work, economists saw no reason a socialist system could not allocate resources according to the model's requirements. Had they grasped that,
for actors in the market, uncertainty is rampant, they would have realized that
their models of efficient socialism were useless.

Machovec uncovers a surprising fact about the debate over Lange's model.
One of Lange's sharpest critics was Maurice Dobb, a Cambridge University

economist who was a committed Communist. Lange's system allowed considerable governmental redistribution of income; and here Dobb found a fatal flaw.

> By moving toward a more equal distribution of income, the socialist state buys more equality only by inducing inefficiency. This wrote Dobb, "is the central dilemma" faced by socialism. (p. 54)

I hasten to add that Dobb did not agree with Mises that socialism was inefficient. He favored full-scale central planning and failed to confront Mises's argument at all.

Our author devotes considerable attention to showing that economists before the mathematical revolution had a much more accurate conception than their successors of how the market works. They realized that, in a world of uncertainty, the entrepreneur's role is vital. Prosperity depends on enterprisers whose judgment enables them to anticipate the wishes of consumers and shift resources accordingly. The linchpin of the economic system is that information is not perfect.

Among the nineteenth-century figures who clearly saw this, I was surprised to learn, was Jeremy Bentham.

> Every thing which is routine today was originally a project . . . ; and when new, it was the production of that mischievous and bold race . . . of projectors [Bentham's term for entrepreneurs]!
> (p. 115, quoting Bentham)

Bentham's views, though innovative, were by no means anomalous in the nineteenth century, as Machovec abundantly shows. But readers who wish to study the historical details should consult the book directly. I found especially valuable Alfred Marshall's warning against too much reliance on static models (p. 243).

Inevitably, at least when I am the reviewer, a few details arouse misgiving. While Machovec has conclusively shown the falsity "of the neoclassical claim that the classical theory of the market was entrepreneurless" (p. 2), he has not shown false the claim that mathematical models formalize particular aspects of the classical view. I doubt that his claim that Bakunin was influenced by "the practices of early communal Christians" is correct (p. 327, n. 12). He seems to me to allow too much scope for the state to regulate monopoly (p. 303). And the claim that "[I]f I already know the consequences of each available course of action open to me, then the ultimate path is, in effect, given, not chosen" (p. 72) seems dubious. To know that something will happen does not fix how one values it.

I'm sorry I had to insert that last paragraph. The remarks in it do not detract from the fact that Machovec has made an outstanding contribution to economics.

Dynamics of the Mixed Economy: Toward a Theory of Interventionism[*]

SANFORD IKEDA

Between Freedom and Socialism

December 1, 1997, *Mises Review*

L UDWIG VON MISES'S DEFENSE OF THE FREE MARKET against its rivals extended far beyond the proof of the impossibility of socialist calculation for which he is best known. As Sanford Ikeda reminds us in this important and erudite book, Mises advanced an argument designed to undermine a supposed third economic system interventionism alleged by its supporters to combine features of capitalism and socialism. Ikeda does us all a service with his careful analysis of Mises's argument, although some of his modifications and extensions of it seem to me questionable.

Mises exposes interventionism for the pipedream it is, as the example of price control best illustrates. The direct result of a price ceiling, as everyone except bureaucrats knows from elementary economics, is a shortage. Sellers of a good offer less quantities for sale at the imposed lower price than consumers wish to purchase.

What is to be done? As Mises saw matters, the interventionists have two alternatives. They may repeal the ceiling and return to the free market. But then what of the poor unable to buy at the higher price?

---

[*] Routledge, 1997.

If the temptation to intervene proves irresistible, the planners may decide to assist retailers to sell enough to meet the quantity demanded at the lower price. How may they do so? By imposing further price ceilings on the products retailers must purchase in order to carry on their business. Given lower costs, retailers will lower their prices.

The results of the new initiative will come as no surprise. The new price ceilings will cause shortages in the goods on which they are imposed, for the same reason as before. Once more the planners confront a choice: return to the free market or press on with yet more controls. Should they continue along the path of regulation, they will soon arrive at a system in which the government sets all prices. And this is socialism, not capitalism.

Mises endeavored to show that any attempt to interfere with the working of the free market would fail of its intended purpose. That being so, there is no third, interventionist system on the agenda: the choice confronting society is restricted to socialism or capitalism.

Ikeda explains Mises's argument in painstaking detail. I found especially valuable his distinction between several different senses in which an interventionist measure may fail, from the viewpoint of its supporters, to achieve its aims (pp. 110–112). Further, our author carefully delineates areas to which Mises's argument does not directly apply, such as nationalization of industry. As he notes, Mises directed his principal attention to measures that aimed to regulate the market, rather than redistribute wealth and income.

Though Mises's critique of interventionism was centered elsewhere, he does adduce a vital point that bears on redistributionist policies, as Ikeda ably brings out. Redistribution depends on a "reserve fund" of assets which the planners can plunder. Should interventionists radically upset production, there will be no funds to redistribute. To cite Mises himself:

> An essential point in the social philosophy of interventionism is the existence of an inexhaustible fund which can be squeezed forever. The whole system of interventionism collapses when this function is drained off: The Santa Claus principle liquidates itself. (pp. 125–126, quoting Mises, *Human Action*)

Our author's aims extend far beyond the task of expounding Mises's case against intervention. He notes a problem in Mises's argument, which he terms the "Misesian paradox." Intervention, according to Mises, is an unstable system.

But are not all the economies of the world interventionist to some degree? Even the Soviet system, of blessed memory, was more accurately viewed as a mixed system rather than a full-scale socialist one. How could it have been the latter, given the soundness of Mises's calculation argument?

We may press the point further. Not only does price control lead to shortages, it does so quite obviously. Why then do interventionists persist in butting their heads against the wall? One would think that even a leftist would eventually see the error of his ways.

Ikeda's principal aim is to explain this persistence in error. In his quest to do so, he imposes on himself a severe methodological constraint. He wishes to explain the growth and contraction of intervention "in terms of endogenous economic forces," i.e., using forces internal to the economic system (p. 14).

This constraint leads him to put to one side the most popular way among public choice economists to explain support for seemingly irrational intervention. Richard Wagner and other "public choicers" point to self-interest: tariffs and minimum wage laws, for example, are very much to the advantage of certain groups, who manipulate the political process to their benefit and everyone else's loss.

Ikeda does not reject this view as false far from it. But it fails to explain what, within the system itself, induces actors to institute greater or less intervention. Once more, it is the endogenous explanation that he seeks.

He finds the answer to his quest in Hayek and Kirzner and accordingly embeds Mises's argument in the framework of the "knowledge problem." As Hayek and Kirzner see matters, actors in the economy continually face consequences of their actions which they did not anticipate. In Kirzner's phrase, they constantly confront "radical ignorance."

Here precisely, according to our author, lies the key to the Misesian paradox. Because of the large numbers of events taking place in the economy, and their complicated connections, planners cannot adequately assess the results of their interventions. Hence, in a way that Ikeda describes in elaborate detail, they may continue with their policies in spite of what strikes the informed Austrian observer as manifest absurdity.

But has not Ikeda proved too much? If the economy is that complex, why should we expect capitalism to work either? Ikeda has a ready response. Though the price system never reaches perfect equilibrium, its signals alert entrepreneurs that misallocation of resources is present, enabling continual improvement in satisfaction of consumer wants.

In the course of his account of interventionism's progress, Ikeda makes an especially insightful point. As the economy approaches more closely to socialism, Mises's socialist calculation argument becomes ever more relevant. That is to say, the calculation argument applies not just to full socialism. Rather, if an economy becomes significantly socialist, to that extent chaos takes the place of the market. This argument strikes me as excellent, but here for once our author's remarkable erudition fails him. Murray Rothbard made an analogous point in *Man, Economy, and State*. He there noted that "islands of calculational chaos" restrict the size of firms. Ikeda fails to note this adumbration of his own argument.

What is one to make of Ikeda's modification of Mises? Ikeda's ingenuity commands our admiration, but he argues with a Rube Goldberg abundance of qualifications, making evaluation of his claims difficult. Planners would do thus and so, unless of course such and such circumstances arise, in which case perhaps. No doubt the fault is my own, and I do not presume to assess him badly owing to my own lack of acuity.

On a few points I venture to think our author mistaken. He uses H. A. Simon's notion of "bounded" satisficing rationality to explain in part the mistakes that interventionists make (see, e.g., pp. 100, 160). But Simon thinks that the process he describes is a rational method of choice. If Ikeda disagrees, he should explain why the use of bounded rationality is liable to eventuate in error.

Further, in his argument for the instability of the minimal state, he claims that "since the minimal state is currently providing only those services essential to the operation of the catallaxy, a reduction in the supply of governmental services would not be feasible" (p. 205). This seems to me to ignore the possibility of downward revisions in the quantity of these essential services. Incidentally, Anthony de Jasay advances an argument about the minimal state quite similar to Ikeda's in *Social Contract, Free Ride* (Oxford 1989).

More fundamentally, I wonder whether the entire search for endogenous explanation is on the right lines. Why must we seek an account of this type, if an appeal to "outside" causes is simpler? I suspect that Ikeda has, through his rigid adherence to an ideal of explanation, made complicated what is after all in Mises a very simple argument. But even if this criticism is right, Ikeda has given us a great deal of importance to think about.

Interventionism: An Economic Analysis[*]

LUDWIG VON MISES

Edited by

BETTINA BIEN GREAVES

Mises on War and Conscription

July 1, 1998, *Mises Review*

INTERVENTIONISM, though written nearly sixty years ago and published now for the first time, expertly dispatches a scheme popular with a few contemporary conservatives. In the view of these professed nationalists, the free market is not good enough. Foreign trade threatens the jobs of American workers. For the good of the nation, tariffs must rise.

But does not elementary economic analysis show the fallacy of trade restrictions? What of the international division of labor? Our new protectionists are not ignorant of economics; but, they aver, economic arguments must take second place to the national interest. If a nationalist explicitly places his ideological convictions above market prosperity, what can be said against him?

Mises offers a ready response. At the time he wrote this short book, arguments of the type just canvassed were very much the order of the day. Nationalist nostrums roused great interest among conservatives in the 1930s and 1940s. Mises was thus thoroughly familiar with the "higher" non-economic argument for protection.

---

[*] Foundation for Economic Education, 1998.

In response, Mises makes a vital distinction. Tariffs, and similar measures designed to strengthen the nation, "should not be considered as measures of production policy." They aid some citizens at the expense of others; they do not help the economy as a whole.

> One might differ as to the advisability of protecting the Prussian Junkers by a tariff on grain imports against the competition of the Canadian farmers who are producing on more fertile soil. But if we advocate a tariff to protect Prussian grain producers, we are not recommending a measure in favor of the production of the supply of grain, but a measure designed to assist the owners of German land at the expense of the German grain consumers. It will never be possible to base an economic system on such assistance privileges. (p. 20)

Mises here completely explodes the nationalist argument for protective tariffs. Since these measures do not benefit the totality of the nation, they cannot be unambiguously endorsed from a nationalist point of view. Commitment to free trade, then, need not rest on utopian commitment to internationalism, as some suppose. Given the goal of nationalism, protection does not follow.

But does not the tariff supporter have here a counter to deploy against Mises? He may grant Mises's point: a tariff will benefit some citizens at the expense of others. Nevertheless, he may say, the national interest dictates that the tariff be instituted. Aid to certain groups, it may be contended, *is* in the national interest.

Mises appears to concede something to this rejoinder, but his concession does the protectionist little good.

> Whether such an expenditure is justified or not is of no concern for economic evaluation. . . . There are undoubtedly cases in which restrictive measures appear justified to most or all of our citizens. But all restrictive measures are fundamentally expenditures. They diminish the supply of productive means available for the supply of other goods. (p. 20)

Mises's "admission" is in fact a devastating counterargument. Tariffs are *never* defended by their proponents on the grounds that they privilege some at the expense of others within a nation. Quite the contrary, they are alleged to benefit the nation at the expense of foreigners. Absent an account of the national interest with explicit arguments that justify largesse for special interests, the nationalist defense for tariffs fails utterly.

The case Mises advances against tariffs illustrates the book's dominant theme, one that all readers of Mises will meet as a familiar friend. The proposals advanced by interventionists fail to achieve the goals their advocates have in mind for them, and they thus stand self-condemned. As an example, an

> attempt by government forcibly to give the national credit money or paper money a value higher than its market price causes effects which Gresham's Law describes. A condition results which generally is called a shortage of foreign exchange. (p. 44)

Should the government attempt to remedy its intervention by further interference, disaster soon impends. The new measure will also fail to achieve the goals of its supporters. Again, the interventionists must confront the basic choice: more intervention or return to the free market. Should the former course entice them on, the result will soon be full-scale socialism. Mises concludes that no third system exists intermediate between the free market and socialism.

Since so many refuse to learn its lesson, Mises's argument against interventionism merits continual repetition. But the details of Mises's case have been often presented in his other works; and Sanford Ikeda has gone over the whole argument at length. An unkind reader of the *Mises Review* (if such exists) might inquire: must we have this argument repeated once more?

There is justice in this imagined complaint (not, of course, distributive justice, for there is no such thing). With this in mind, let us then turn to a topic that I have found nowhere else in Mises: his analysis of how a free society should wage war.

For one thing, conscription is out. The use of compulsion to man the military characteristically does not stand by itself. Rather it has formed part of an interventionist scheme to subject the economy to control. As such, it must be rejected for the reason earlier stated: interventionism cannot endure as a stable system.

Mises states the essential point in this way:

> The first step which led from the soldiers' war back to total war was the introduction of compulsory military service. . . . The

> war was no longer to be only a matter of mercenaries—it was
> to include everyone who had the necessary physical ability. . . .
> But when it is realized that a part of the able-bodied must be
> used on the industrial front . . . then there is no reason to dif-
> ferentiate in compulsory service between the able-bodied and
> the physically unfit. Compulsory military service thus leads to
> compulsory labor service of all citizens who are able to work,
> male and female. (p. 69)

But what is the alternative to total war with total state control? Mises's
response will surprise no one: he favors reliance on the free market. To support his view that a market economy can effectively wage modern war, Mises
advances a surprising claim about the early part of World War II.

He ascribes the fall of France to anti-capitalist views. Because of campaigns in the 1930s against "war profiteering," the French (and to a lesser
extent the British) refused to rely on the market to provide them with the
arms they needed to withstand the German onslaught.

> On the basis of such [anti-capitalist] reasoning the [Léon] Blum
> government nationalized the French armament industry. When
> the war broke out and it became imperative to place the produc-
> tive power of all French plants into the service of the rearmament
> effort, the French authorities considered it more important to
> block war profits than to win the war. (p. 72)

Mises's contention is at once exposed to an obvious objection; but he
knows this full well and has his counter ready. The German army in 1940
ranked second-to-none as a fighting force; yet it was hardly a free-market
army in the style favored by Mises.

But Mises does not deny this. On the contrary, he acknowledges that the
"German army has an enormous superiority in every type of equipment that a
fighting army requires" (p. 71). Mises's contention is that, given German power,
interventionism and anti-capitalism are paltry and insufficient responses. Only
capitalism, not half-hearted socialism, can defeat a total state.

We may readily grant Mises's point that a hampered market economy is a
poor bet during wartime. But how does Mises know that an arms procurement policy of the sort he wants would have led to French victory in 1940?
Does he not go too far in this self-confident judgment?

No doubt Mises has not proved his case: his suggestion is merely that of a well-informed contemporary observer. But his contention provides us with a stimulating hypothesis for future research. What was the effect of French restrictionist policies on armaments production during the 1930s? Here is a question that cries out for historical research. And we have Mises's unique combination of mastery of economics with historical insight to thank for it. Though written in 1940, this book is essential reading for all Misesians.

The Logic of Action[*]

MURRAY N. ROTHBARD

The Rothbardian Turn of Mind

July 1, 1998, *Mises Review*

T IS BOTH ESSENTIAL AND IMPOSSIBLE to review these two volumes. Essential, because they include the bulk of the scientific papers written by a great Austrian theorist. But also impossible, because of the incredible variety of topics covered, ranging from the nature of human action to the influence of gnostic thought on Marxism.

As one reads these disparate essays, however, a common quality comes to the fore. Murray Rothbard again and again challenges an assumption that everyone else takes to be obviously true. Once Rothbard poses his question, our view of the relevant topic is at once turned upside down.

Everyone knows that the free market is the most efficient economic system; Milton Friedman *et hoc genus omne* build their defense of the market largely on this consideration. One might expect that Rothbard, second to none as a champion of the market, would join in lauding its efficiency. Instead, he asks a fundamental question: does the concept of efficiency mean anything?

> Let us take a given individual ... in order for him to act efficiently, he would have to possess perfect knowledge of the future. But since no one can ever have perfect knowledge of the future, no one's action can be called "efficient." ... [I]f ends change in the course of an action, the concept of efficiency—which can only

---

[*] Edward Elgar, 1997.

> be defined as the best combination of means in pursuit of given
> ends—again becomes meaningless. (I, pp. 266–267)

And if efficiency can be given no clear characterization for an individual, it fares even worse when the ends of more than one person are considered.

Murray Rothbard viewed the logical positivists with alarm; but as the example just discussed shows, he used with great skill a favorite tactic of theirs. He asks: what is the operational definition of a concept under discussion? If none can be provided, the concept must be eliminated from science.

Another instance of this technique occurs in the essay, "Toward a Reconstruction of Utility and Welfare Economics." Our author will have no truck with James Buchanan's attempt

> to designate the State as a voluntary institution. Buchanan's the-
> sis is based on the curious dialectic that majority rule in a democ-
> racy is really unanimity because majorities can and do always shift.
> The resulting pulling and hauling of the political process, because
> obviously not irreversible, are therefore supposed to yield a so-
> cial unanimity. The doctrine ... must be set down as a lapse into
> a type of Hegelian mysticism. (I, p. 252)

Rothbard's procedure is a simple one. He asks: what does the voluntary state amount to? And given Buchanan's characterization of it, Rothbard goes on to ask: is this what we ordinarily mean by "voluntary"? As it obviously is not, this conception of the voluntary state cannot stand. (Another instance of the same technique may be found in the search for an operational definition of monopoly price in *Man, Economy, and State*.)

As the same essay illustrates, Rothbard took nothing for granted in ethics. Much of conventional welfare economics rests on the detection of positive externalities. Our author, with his characteristic jump to the essence, inquires, why are positive externalities a social problem?

> A and B decide to pay for the building of a dam for their uses;
> C benefits though he did not pay. . . . This is the problem of the
> Free Rider. Yet it is difficult to understand what the hullabaloo is
> all about. Am I to be specially taxed because I enjoy the sight of
> my neighbor's garden without paying for it? A's and B's purchase
> of a good reveals that *they* are willing to pay for it; if it indirectly
> benefits C as well, no one is the loser. (I, p. 25)

Let us once more pause to grasp the revolution involved in Rothbard's query. Before him economists assumed without much thought that beneficiaries of positive externalities ought to pay for them. Once Rothbard has raised the question, you cannot help but wonder, why should this controversial premise be assumed without argument?

When Robert Nozick made a similar point in *Anarchy, State, and Utopia* (1974), philosophers were quick to take notice. But Rothbard was there long before. (Incidentally, the response that it maximizes efficiency for beneficiaries to pay is blocked by the earlier Rothbardian analysis discussed above.)

In the second volume of this monumental collection, where issues of the application of Austrian theory feature prominently, Murray Rothbard continues his pursuit of the revolutionary question. People have usually looked at an issue in a certain way; but why should we do so?

Thus, an influential approach to welfare economics endeavors to minimize transaction costs. In "The Myth of Neutral Taxation," Rothbard is ready with an iconoclastic query: "What is so terrible about transaction costs? On what basis are they considered the ultimate evil, so that their minimization must override all other considerations of choice, freedom, or justice?" (p. 88). If one responds that reducing these costs has some, though not overriding, importance, Rothbard's question compels one to specify exactly how much, and why, they are to count.

Fortunately for our society, support among economists for the free market is widespread. For almost any government activity, you can find an economist to argue that the market will provide the service in a better fashion. Yet who but Rothbard would think to ask, why should the government be allowed to collect information?

He makes a simple and devastating point: absent statistical data, the government could not interfere with the economy.

> [S]tatistics are, in a crucial sense, critical to all interventionist and socialistic activities of government. . . . Statistics are the eyes and ears of the bureaucrat, the politician, the socialistic reformer. Only by statistics can they know, or at least have any idea about, what is going on in the economy. . . . Cut off those eyes and ears, destroy those crucial guidelines to knowledge, and the whole threat of government intervention is almost completely eliminated. (II, pp. 182–183)

As you might expect, my favorite section of the volumes is "Criticism," in which Rothbard annihilates adversaries in unique fashion. Again, he always grasps the essential.

As an example, deconstructionists claim that texts lack a fixed meaning. The apparent meaning of a text is always accompanied by countervailing patterns. A reader must then "deconstruct" a text rather than take it to have coherent sense. Rothbard raises the key point: why bother? "If we cannot understand the meaning of any texts, why are we bothering with trying to understand or to take seriously the works or doctrines of authors who aggressively proclaim their own incomprehensibility?" (II, p. 277).

Rothbard, in philosophy as elsewhere, insisted on clear definitions: without this, nonsense inevitably ensues. He found a prime instance of philosophical nonsense in what he termed "reabsorption theology." He maintained that this bizarre view lies at the heart of both Hegelianism and Marxism.

I cannot do better than to end with Rothbard's hilarious account of the reabsorption doctrine.

> Stage One is the original state of the pre-creation cosmic blob, with man and God in happy and harmonious unity, but each rather undeveloped. Then, the magic dialectic does its work, Stage Two occurs, and God creates man and the universe. But then, finally, when the development of man and God is completed, Stage Two creates its own *aufhebung*, its transcendence into its opposite or negation: in short, Stage Three, the reunion of God and man in a "ecstasy of union" and the end of history. (II, p. 340)

After you read about the "cosmic blob" it is difficult to take Hegel and Marx entirely seriously. And this, I suspect, is exactly the effect Rothbard wished to achieve.

Economics of Income Redistribution[*]

&

On Voting: A Public Choice Approach[†]

Gordon Tullock

The Master Doubter

April 1, 1999, *Mises Review*

ORDON TULLOCK is a difficult author to review. His books are filled with an almost unlimited profusion of ideas. It is enough that Walter Block has defended the undefendable: I cannot endeavor to summarize the unsummarizable. Instead, I shall pick out a few points that readers not specializing in public choice are likely to find valuable.

Almost all political philosophers, and most economists, favor income redistribution to the poor. But do any good arguments justify this? Is it that we wish to eliminate or alleviate poverty? But in that case, why do we give aid to the poor in our own country rather than to much more poverty stricken inhabitants of the third world?

> My point is simply that there is a contradiction in saying that a program is intended to eliminate poverty when it gives only very

---

[*] Kluwer, 1997.

[†] Edward Elgar, 1998.

> small amounts of money to the Third World. If we wish, we can
> ignore the poor in the Third World, but if we do ignore them,
> we should not talk about our deep desire to take serious efforts
> to help the poorest of the poor. (*Economics*, p. vii)

It would not be an adequate response to Professor Tullock to say that just
what we want is to help the poor in our own society, rather than worldwide.
Precisely the question under discussion is whether there are good arguments
for our current policies or redistribution.

Perhaps resort will be made to the relative deprivation hypothesis. The
poor in our own country are unhappy with their status, because they can
readily see others in better circumstances. Not so the poor in Bangladesh
and Ethiopia.

Professor Tullock is not buying it.

> In other words, the poor mother in the Sahel watching her child
> starve to death is not really made terribly unhappy about it be-
> cause it is a very common event there and she does not feel dis-
> criminated against. . . . I have invented an unkind, if accurate
> aphorism for this: "if everybody in the village has a toothache,
> it does not really hurt." (*Economics*, p. 83)

The strategy that underlies these arguments strikes me as a major contribution to moral philosophy. The general scheme of Tullock's argument is: "If
you really favored A, as you say you do, then you would do B. But you don't
do B: therefore, you don't really favor A."

In a further example of this technique, our author overturns another
familiar argument for income redistribution to the poor. Owing to the
declining marginal utility of money, isn't a dollar to a poor man worth
much more than the same dollar to a rich man? If so, will not redistribution to the poor increase total utility? (Of course, Austrians will reject
the argument on grounds that interpersonal comparisons of utility are not
allowed. But somehow in questions of redistribution economists often
turn a blind eye to this elementary point.)

Tullock ingeniously responds by an application of the argument scheme
already discussed. Those who wish to maximize total utility should favor
an increase in population since new people, at least up to very large numbers, add to total utility. When the leading proponent of the redistribution

argument, A. P. Lerner, confronted Tullock's point, he replied "that he had proposed maximizing utility as a goal when discussing income redistribution. He did not think it was a suitable goal for population policy. This would seem to indicate that he does not really value maximizing total utility very much" (*Economics*, p. 7).

Further, what if some people are much more efficient generators of utility than others? Would not someone who wished to maximize total utility have to favor redistribution to such people? "From observation of human behavior it is apparent that some people get a great kick out of things and others do not" (*Economics*, p. 7). But Professor Tullock finds that supporters of Lerner-style redistribution almost never endorse redistribution to the happy. Thus, he once more concludes that the redistributionists really do not support maximizing total utility.

At one point, I venture to suggest, our author's approach misfires. John Rawls famously supports inequality only to the extent it benefits the least well-off class in society. But, Professor Tullock asks, shouldn't Rawls support on his own principles even greater equality than he in fact does? The really worst off are the dying and those with terrible illnesses such as multiple sclerosis. Should not the difference principle be applied to benefit them? In that case, we would require immense transfers of income to raise the utility of those unfortunates. But Rawls does not support this sort of redistribution. Does he then genuinely support the difference principle?

By now, you no doubt recognize Tullock's usual argument scheme in action. This time, though, it does not work. Rawls explicitly confines his theory to those who mutually contribute to increasing the social product. Self-interested choosers behind the veil of ignorance would have no reason to take Tullock's class of badly off people into account. Fortunately, there are abundant other arguments sufficient to overthrow Rawls's egalitarian concoctions.

Readers influenced by Murray Rothbard will, I am sure, note that the two economists have very different casts of mind. Rothbard had a theory of the rights people actually have. Tullock advances no ethical principles of his own: instead, he probes the principles held by others and endeavors to find inconsistencies in them. Though Rothbard's approach reaches further, Tullock's Socratic inquiries are a very useful supplement.

I fear that Professor Tullock applies his argument scheme to Rothbardians as well as egalitarians. If you accept a Lockean theory of property acquisition, might it not turn out that you are now a trespasser? Perhaps the area on which you now stand was once unjustly taken from an Indian tribe that had acquired it in proper Lockean fashion. For the reasons stated in my review of *The Ethics of Liberty* found in in Volume 2, "Political Theory," I am inclined to think that Rothbardians have successfully responded to Tullock here.

Professor Tullock is no more inclined to accept the pieties of democracy than he is those of egalitarianism. Most people profess belief in majority-rule democracy as the best method of making governmental decisions; but (Tullock's familiar question) do we really believe this? Do we favor abolition of jury verdicts by unanimous vote, the presidential veto, a Senate in which the states are represented equally without regard to population and similar non-majoritarian institutions? If we are not prepared to jettison these institutions, then we are not the majority rule democrats we claim to be.

Tullock's style of argument is unsettling. I shall in conclusion suggest a very speculative replay to the argument he advances. He says: "If you support A, then you should support B. But you do not. Therefore it is questionable whether you support A." Can an escape be found by saying this?:

> I acknowledge that if I support A, I ought to support B. If in fact I do not, this is an interesting psychological peculiarity about me; but it does not suffice to show that I don't in fact support A. Neither does it show that it is irrational for me to continue to support A. Perhaps it is irrational of me instead not to endorse B.

Revenons sur la terre. Tullock is a thinker from whom all classical liberals can learn a great deal. With Nietzchean force, he summons us away from hypocrisy.

Market Socialism:
The Debate Among Socialists*

Edited by
BERTELL OLLMAN

The Socialist Asylum

July 1, 1999, *Mises Review*

ONE QUESTION ABOUT SOCIALISTS has for many years puzzled me: how can they exist? The Soviet Experiment, the Chinese Great Leap Forward, etc. are now "one with Nineveh and Tyre"; but how can they have deceived a rational person for more than a moment?

The question can be made more pointed. Whatever the blindness of Western intellectuals before 1989, surely, one might think, no one can now be a socialist. Given socialism's manifest failures, the position seems about as plausible as the presidential candidacy of Harold Stassen.

Nevertheless, socialism is alive and well in the American academy, and this book helps us understand why. It consists of debates on market socialism conducted by four socialists in good standing. Two of them, David Schweickart and James Lawler, support market socialism; Hillel Ticktin and the editor, Bertell Ollman, oppose it.

I shall not hold readers in suspense any longer. The answer to the question posed above is a simple one: the socialists are stark, raving lunatics. They embrace socialism because they cling to the empty shibboleths of Marxism.

---

* Routledge, 1998.

Only Mr. Schweickart earns partial clemency from this verdict: he is at least acquainted with the rudiments of economic thought. In his principal essay, he ably summarizes the standard Misesian and Hayekian case against socialism. A centrally planned economy "faces four distinct sets of problems: information problems, incentive problems, authoritarian tendencies, and entrepreneurial problems" (p. 12).

Mr. Schweickart's statement of the first of these problems, as set forth in the Mises-Hayek calculation argument, is excellent:

> Production involves inputs as well as outputs, and since the inputs into one enterprise are the outputs of many others, quantities and qualities of these inputs must also be planned. But since inputs cannot be determined until technologies are given, technologies too must be specified. To have a maximally coherent plan, all of these determinations must be made by the center, but such calculations, interdependent as they are, are far too complicated for even our most sophisticated computational technologies. Star Wars, by comparison, is child's play. (p. 12)

Of course, no socialist in good standing can say an unqualified good word about the great Austrians. And so Mr. Schweickart feels impelled to add:

> It is absurd to say . . . that Ludwig von Mises and Friedrich Hayek have been proven right by events, that a centrally-planned socialism is "impossible." To cite only the Soviet Union: an economic order that endured for three-quarters of a century . . . should not be called "impossible." (p. 12)

I cannot help but suspect that Mr. Schweickart really knows better. Mises and Hayek did not doubt the existence of Soviet Russia. Rather, they contended that a world socialist economy could not engage in rational economic calculation, for reasons well stated by Mr. Schweickart himself. The Soviet Union (as the contributors to this volume never tire of reminding us) was not fully centrally planned; further, it had available capitalist prices as set on the world market. The existence of Soviet Russia posed no threat to Mises's and Hayek's case.

Although a confirmed socialist like Mr. Schweickart cannot help but on occasion wax nostalgic over the Workers' Paradise, nevertheless, in his sober moments he acknowledges the force of the argument.

What then is he to do? Will he overcome his inclination in favor of central planning and embrace capitalism? Perish the thought! Our ingenious author redefines socialism so that it no longer entails central planning. Instead, he favors a system he grandiloquently terms Economic Democracy. In it, production takes place in firms owned by workers. The state coordinates these firms through its control of investment, but there is no central planning of the sort that Mises and Hayek have refuted.

The problems of this scheme are well brought out by Hillel Ticktin. But before turning to his comments, I shall add a difficulty of my own. This problem, one may be sure, would not appeal to Messrs. Ticktin and Ollman, despite their opposition to cooperatives, since it strikes at the heart of socialism. Suppose that Mr. Schweickart were right that cooperatives greatly exceed in efficiency standard-model capitalist firms. Nothing prevents cooperatives from developing on the free market and (if Mr. Schweickart's view about their superior efficiency is right) supplanting firms owned by capitalists. The fact that this has not happened suggests that cooperatives are not the paragons of efficiency that Mr. Schweickart imagines.

Mr. Schweickart's response (besides calling me a mean-spirited reactionary) is obvious. He will counter that the capitalist-controlled state and banking system would strangle an incipient cooperative commonwealth in its cradle. In point of fact, precisely the opposite is the case. In spite of large tax advantages cooperatives have never succeeded in making much headway in capitalist economies. It is not necessary to confront fantasies of capitalist resistance: cooperatives characteristically fail to rise to the level at which such resistance would have a point.

Suppose, though, that one ignores this argument, as I am sure Mr. Schweickart will be happy to do. The question remains: why does he think that cooperatives are desirable? Mr. Schweickart has a reason, but it is one that most readers will I suspect find unappealing.

The reason in question is the great economic success of China under a system controlled by worker-owned firms. "This 'incoherent' market socialist economy has been strikingly successful, averaging an astonishing ten percent per year annual growth rate over the past fifteen years." (p. 8). Mr. Schweickart does find one fly in the ointment: "China is not inspirational now the way Russia was in the aftermath of the Bolshevik Revolution, or as China was for many on the Left in the 1960s or as Vietnam or Nicaragua or Cuba have been" (p. 8). Well, you can't have everything.

Our author has not managed to think of a ready-to-hand explanation for China's "astonishing" growth rate. China under Mao made such a mess of things that any move toward normality will generate substantial growth rates. (If you blow up your house and then rebuild it, your growth rate will be very high.) I hardly think this is much of a point in favor of the Chinese economy.

Even if Mr. Schweickart's case for cooperatives is weak, his arguments have not been theoretically refuted. What can be said against them? Here Mr. Hillel Ticktin, a Trotskyite and an expert on the history of Bolshevik economics, contributes something of value. Like Mises, though from an opposite perspective, Mr. Ticktin argues that socialism and capitalism do not mix.

> The Marxist answers that market socialism cannot exist because it involves limiting the incentive system of the market through providing minimum wages, high levels of unemployment insurance, reducing the size of the reserve army of labor, taxing profits, and taxing the wealthy. As a result, the capitalists will have little incentive to invest and the workers will have little incentive to work. Capitalism works because, as Marx remarked, it is a system of economic force. In market socialism, that force is insufficient to provide an incentive to make the system work. (pp. 60–61)

Mr. Ticktin goes further in his apparent Misesianism. He remarks that in a socialist economy, "any privacy would be purely artificial. In this respect ... Mises was correct against Lange, in their well-known debate on calculation in a socialist society" (p. 160).

Given Mr. Ticktin's insights, a question will no doubt have occurred to you. Why did I include him among the crazies? Is he not entitled to exemption, along with his market socialist opponent Mr. Schweickart? Do we not have here another example of my usual meanness of spirit?

I venture to hope that further exposure to Mr. Ticktin's profundities will reinforce my original verdict. True enough, he thinks, a socialist system cannot calculate; but so what? Calculation through prices is needed only under capitalism, where the law of value obtains. (By this he means that in capitalism, the value of a good is the socially necessary labor-time needed to produce it.) Socialism abolishes the law of value, and abundance now comes into being.

Scarcity, contrary to bourgeois purveyors of pessimism, is not a permanent feature of the world. Socialism means abundance; and where scarcity does not exist, the lack of a rational method of pricing works no harm. Everyone can have as much of everything as he wishes.

With the other two contributors we may be more brief. Mr. Lawler wishes to show that, although sympathetic to market socialism, he remains a simon-pure Marxist. Not for him the blandishments of revisionism! To prove his orthodoxy, he endeavors to prove that the Master Himself thought that a system of market socialism would prevail during the first stage of socialism. With considerable success, Mr. Bertell Ollman argues that Mr. Lawler has misread his Marx. Both authors are fond of invoking dialectics, and I leave their debate to those interested in such matters, or amused by them.

Post-Socialist Political Economy: Selected Essays[*]

JAMES M. BUCHANAN

Myth of the Voluntary State

July 1, 1999, *Mises Review*

PROFESSOR JAMES BUCHANAN, the 1986 Nobel Laureate in Economics, has achieved fame through public choice economics, which he, together with Gordon Tullock, invented. According to this discipline, economic analysis does not stop with market participants. The state consists not of impartial arbiters, but of agents anxious to advance their own interests. Professor Buchanan applies his insight into politics to great effect in one area of American politics. Unfortunately, he fails to develop this insight, and several others almost as important, to the fullest extent possible.

If politicians avidly pursue their own interests, what are the rest of us to do about this? One response, that of libertarian anarchists such as Murray Rothbard, suggests getting rid of the state altogether; but this is entirely too radical for the public choice school. Rather, it suggests that the malign effects of self-seeking politicians can be considerably alleviated through a federal system.

If political power is decentralized into small units, and a country's citizens enjoy the right to move freely among these units, then competition limits governmental abuses. If, for example, a state imposes high taxes on corporations in its jurisdiction, they will flee to more congenial climates.

---

[*] Edward Elgar, 1997.

All this is hardly news, but Professor Buchanan applies the federalist point in a way that illuminates a crucial period in American history. He writes:

> We know now that the Madisonian enterprise [of federalism and limited government] failed. The great American Civil War removed forever the threat of secession by the states. This basic constitutional change more or less insured that, eventually, the United States would be transformed into a centralized majoritarian democracy with few, if any, checks on ultimate political authority. In this modern setting, democracy dominates society. (p. 220)

Well said! But if one adopts this perspective, will not the Rothbardian position soon follow as a reasonable extension? If states may secede from the Union, why may not individuals secede from the state? I do not suggest that there is a logical contradiction in defending state secession but rejecting an individual's right to secede. But does not the same reasoning that sees secession as a deterrent to oppression by the central government also suggest that the right of individual secession limits the power of the states to do bad? If not, why not?

And if individuals may secede, have we not in effect arrived at a Rothbardian position, in which individuals do not surrender their natural rights to a state at all? But this view Buchanan rejects as extreme. Or does he?

In one brilliant essay, he seems to transcend his customary perspective of "constitutional political economy." He speaks favorably of self-ownership, the key theme of Rothbard and his followers.

> We can refer to private ownership in person, in the individual's own capacities to produce economic value. Such property-in-person exists when the individual is at liberty to choose when to submit to the direction of others concerning the use of his or her own labor services and when there exists also freedom to choose among locations, occupations, and professions, both as offered by the market and as potentially created by the individual's own entrepreneurial initiative. (p. 193)

Our author, I fear, is no master of English prose, but it is the thought that counts. He takes the second crucial Rothbardian step also, as the passage just quoted suggests. He recognizes that individual self-owners may acquire rights to property. These rights are valued by the individuals as a means of enhancing liberty. Unlike Chicago school economists, Professor Buchanan does not view property titles solely as a means to maximize efficiency.

> [P]ersons desire ownership of property in order to secure and maintain liberty over the disposal of resources, without which liberty there could be no hope of bettering the conditions of life. (p. 192)

Before I go on with the line of argument Mr. Buchanan's defense of liberty and property suggests, allow me a digression. (After all, this is my publication.) The Canadian political philosopher C. B. Macpherson once raised an interesting objection to the free market. Proponents of the market, Macpherson noted, claim that individuals in a laissez-faire economy are free to make any exchanges they wish. All voluntary transactions, then, take place only if all participants expect to benefit. Perhaps so, said Macpherson, but are individuals free to leave the market altogether? How many people can become fully self-subsistent farmers? And if you are not free to exit the market, is your freedom to exchange as significant as advocates of capitalism think?

Professor Buchanan does not mention Macpherson, but several of his remarks enable us to construct a reply to the objection. He points out that ownership of long-term assets reduces direct dependence on the market.

> Consider ownership of a house. As the owner of this asset that yields services over time, the individual is producing these particular services for himself or herself. To the extent that self-production is made possible, the owner is insulated from direct dependence on the market. (p.194)

Macpherson failed to see that exit from the market need not be total. The force of his objection to the market is thus blunted.

But this is by the way. Although Professor Buchanan travels a good deal down the road with Rothbard, he stops short. He rejects complete laissez-faire because of that dread specter—public goods. As our author sees matters, individuals must be coerced, in some cases, to do what they themselves recognize as in their own collective interest.

An example will clarify what Professor Buchanan means. If I hire a policeman to protect my house, his presence also helps you, if you are my neighbor. Prospective burglars who see him will probably avoid your house as well as mine. An externality results: any neoclassical theorist worth his salt can readily show that the market outcome is "inefficient."

Is there not available an easy escape? Why not an agreement by the concerned individuals to produce the public good—in our example, protection—at the optimal amount? Unfortunately, matters are not so simple. Individuals who make such an agreement might find it rational to break their word. If I can get a public good without paying for it, will I not be better off than I would be if I had paid the share agreed upon? Unfortunately for me, everyone else is in the same position. Since each of us foresees that it will be rational for each of us to renege on an agreement to produce a public good, no such agreement will be made in the first place. The result will be, *horribile dictu*, a nonoptimal supply of public goods.

Here, in Mr. Buchanan's view, the state comes to the rescue. By forcing people to adhere to their agreements, public goods are produced in amounts most beneficial to all. Optimality is at hand: all is for the best in this best of all possible worlds.

What is one to make of this? Arguably, self-owners in Rothbard's sense can voluntarily agree to establish an agency to compel them to observe an agreement. But unless someone actually joins in such an arrangement, force against him cannot be justified. To claim that he would have entered into an agreement, had he been rational, does not suffice. Nor does it suffice if the majority of people in someone's society accept an arrangement: so long as a person has not explicitly consented, an attempt to compel him to contribute to a public good violates his rights.

So, at any rate, a consistent supporter of self-ownership will argue. The upshot, of course, is that no actually existing state respects people's rights, since there has never been the explicit agreement on coercion that self-ownership mandates.

Professor Buchanan, I regret to say, wants to have it both ways. Even though he recognizes that in existing states, there has been no actual agreement by everyone to use the state as a coercive agent, he nevertheless retains the agreement or exchange model.

> At this point, those who defend contractual or exchange models find it useful to introduce conceptual as opposed to actual agreement as a device for retaining some explanatory value.... Could the existing rules that define the overall operations of the polity have been agreed upon by all citizens if, indeed, there could have been some imagined initial dialogue? At this point, the potential conflict among the separate interests of persons

and groups is mitigated by resort to constructions that introduce a veil of ignorance or uncertainty. (p. 176)

To his credit, Professor Buchanan recognizes that hypothetical consent
poses problems, and he also finds attractive a Hobbesian view of the state
as a predatory agency. Yet at the end he refuses to abandon the "exchange"
model; and he is left with the nonsense-concept of a state that is coercive but
nevertheless voluntary.

A History of Economic Thought: The LSE Lectures[*]

LIONEL ROBBINS

Edited by
STEVEN G. MEDEMA
& WARREN J. SAMUELS

The Return of Lord Robbins

October 1, 1999, *Mises Review*

AUSTRIANS HAVE SOMETIMES been very hard on Lord Robbins. He at one time embraced the views of Mises and Hayek; and in the Great Depression, he presented a resolutely Austrian theory of the business-cycle. But, sometime during the 1940s, he fell from grace. He repudiated his book on the depression and loudly proclaimed the greatness of Lord Keynes. Although by the standards of the 1950s he remained a classical liberal, he was anxious to let everyone know that he was not a fanatic who favored laissez-faire.

After reading *A History of Economic Thought*, I incline to think that Austrians ought to view Lord Robbins with much greater favor than they customarily do. (I cannot believe it—am I saying that others have been too severe?) The book, which consists of transcripts of lectures that were recorded between 1979 and 1981, is filled with insights, many of strongly Austrian character. Before turning to the substance of the book, I must say

[*] Princeton University Press, 1998.

a few words about its style. The editors, in order to retain to the fullest the inimitable flavor of Robbins's personality, have wisely not tidied up the text.

With regret, I shall confine myself to one example of Robbins's humor and charm:

> I recommend in my bibliography a book by a man called Father Divine [1959]—not that rather brash man who used to make terrific broadcasts in the interwar period, but a man who studied for a PhD at the London School of Economics. (p. 34)

I should explain to younger readers that the Father Divine not recommended was an American leader of a religious cult who thought he was God.

A central theme that emerges in Robbins's lectures is the conflict between subjective utility and cost of production theories of value.

Like Murray Rothbard and Raymond de Roover, he stresses the importance of the fourteenth-century writer San Bernardino of Siena. He clearly recognized that the economic value of a good is determined in large part by its desirability.

> Well, to continue with San Bernardino, the usefulness or the desirability as a deciding factor is not absolute. "Otherwise," he says, "a glass of water would be almost priceless," but it's "abundant." ... He doesn't actually solve the so-called paradox of value as you get it in Adam Smith and some of the classical economists, but he gets pretty near to it. (p. 30)

Incidentally, our author, a scholar of enormous erudition, was well aware that San Bernardino borrowed heavily from Pierre Olivi.

Unfortunately, economics in the line that began with Adam Smith and continued through Ricardo and John Stuart Mill approached value in a different way. Adam Smith, in a famous passage of *The Wealth of Nations*, argued that in primitive conditions, quantity of labor determines price. Concerning this, Robbins remarks:

> Well, I hope that that's obvious to all of you. When you have an economy in which the only scarce factor service is unskilled labour, then the ratio of the quantities of labour expanded provides a key to what Adam Smith calls the natural, and what we should call the normal, price. (p. 136)

Here Robbins concedes too much. No doubt Robbins is right that under the indicated conditions, price can be directly correlated with the quantity of labor. But it does not follow the quantity of labor causes price. Rather, a subjectivist would say that the quantity of labor is allocated to each good in a way that corresponds to the subjective valuations consumers give the goods in question. True enough, the figures come out the same whether one adopts the labor theory approach or its subjectivist rival. But for the Austrian School, the issue of causation is crucial.

If Robbins elides this point, he is nevertheless no partisan of the labor theory of value. He neatly skewers the theory in this way:

> Then Adam Smith goes on to discuss differences of skill. And he doesn't really solve the problem, but he thinks that in the advanced state of society allowances must be made for superior hardship and superior skill. Those allowances, of course, are in value terms, and Adam Smith has begged the question by just casually treating it that way. (p. 137)

David Ricardo, with great expenditure of labor, produced a labor theory of value much more rigorous than that of Smith. But, as Robbins ably brings out, he too failed to solve the problem that defeated Smith:

> Well, so far as differences of quality of labour are concerned, they were for the most part ignored. It was said that labour is determined by the higgling of the market, but that, of course, is circular reasoning. If you are trying to explain value by something other than value, by quantity of something, it's no use invoking value to explain value. (p. 189)

With beautiful concision, this argument demolishes the labor theory.

Robbins has not yet finished with Ricardo. He dismisses Ricardo's attempt to eliminate rent from the cost of production by going to the rentless margin. To do so is to take a specialized situation as the norm: what if an area of land has alternative uses? Then rent surely cannot be dismissed from the calculation of costs. The problem of opportunity costs "just evaded" Ricardo (p. 191). Though Robbins treats Ricardo's system with much greater respect than does Rothbard, he razes its foundations.

Karl Marx no more than Smith and Ricardo met the problem of differences in the types of labor. Like them, he invoked the market to explain these differences and thus argued in a circle. "And in Marx you find that this is rather more pretentiously attributed to a social process which goes on behind the backs of producers, but what he meant was indeed the market" (p. 236). At one point, I venture to suggest, Robbins misses a key weakness in Marx's theory. He rightly notes that Marx had a "cost of production theory of labourers" (p. 237). But, contrary to Marx's argument, his own labor theory of value does not entail this theory of wages. Without the cost of production theory of wages, Marx's entire analysis of capitalism crumbles, since he cannot show that labor for capitalists necessarily creates surplus value.

Robbins entirely supports the alternative that has supplanted the labor theory: he is a confirmed devotee of the marginal utility theory. Although he, like most English economists, bows low in worship of Alfred Marshall, he fully appreciates the genius of Carl Menger. Robbins is at great pains to emphasize the care with which Menger developed his account of value. "Whatever one may think of the virtues of brevity, he goes very deep and he's very thorough" (p. 271). Menger spurned the beguiling elegance of mathematics in favor of a causal account of how value arises from human action.

In their rush to algebra, the competing marginalist schools were less thoroughly subjectivist than Menger. William Stanley Jevons held that cost of production determines value; the Austrian account, especially as Philip Wicksteed developed it, avoids this regression to old mistakes. I am not at all sure that our author shares this opinion of Jevons's theory, but he ably sets forward the basis for a more consistent Austrian verdict.

It is good to see that he recognizes the great importance of Mises's *Theory of Money and Credit*. It "probably provides a more detailed linking up of the cash balance approach with the general marginal utility theory as developed by the Austrians than is to be found anywhere else in the literature" (p. 316).

The editors deserve high praise for making these fine lectures available. I have noted a few mistakes: on p. 37, two Latin words are misspelled; and on p. 82, the last lines should read "not only that which is necessary." *Ignis fatuous*, I assume, is a joke.

Rewarding Work: How to Restore Self-Support to Free Enterprise*

EDMUND S. PHELPS

Rethinking Intervention

October 1, 1999, *Mises Review*

EDMUND S. PHELPS is no right-wing extremist. Quite the contrary, he stands at the center of Keynesian orthodoxy in economics. Often termed an "economist's economist," he is most famous for his work on the natural rate of unemployment and for his structural account of business cycles.

In *Rewarding Work*, Mr. Phelps risks his reputation as a guardian of the establishment: he almost, but not quite, kicks over the dogmas of the welfare state. Fortunately for those of an Austrian bent, his proposals can easily be fixed so that they conform entirely to classical liberalism.

As free-market advocates see matters, the welfare state cripples market incentives. Why work, if you can get as much, or in some cases more, by idling on welfare? From Herbert Spencer and William Graham Sumner to Henry Hazlitt, classical liberals indict welfarism as a subsidy for voluntary unemployment.

The conventional wisdom brushes aside this view as extreme and hardhearted, but our author views things differently.

---

* Harvard University Press, 1997.

> [T]he welfare programs that are not work-related, such as Med-
> icaid and food stamps, devalue work and thus reduce job attach-
> ment. Means-testing intensifies the impact.... Wage earning
> and job holding are now dwarfed by the welfare system. Wel-
> fare pays more than work for the mothers eligible for Aid to
> Families With Dependent Children (AFDC) and the train of
> benefits that follow from it. (p. 99)

But, defenders of the present system will allege, what is so bad about this?
Surely the United States is a rich society: can we not afford to provide for
the less fortunate? Only reactionary ideologues could object. Do not such
benighted figures as Mises and Rothbard, who condemn welfare, elevate
property rights above human rights?

Mr. Phelps, amid a few disclaimers, allies himself with the reactionaries.
Work is essential to a person's well-being: absent gainful employment, one's
life is liable to be dreary and futile.

> One of the most important rewards in most jobs is mental
> stimulation. They present a continual series of exercises in
> problem-solving.... Of course mastering the simplest jobs
> will generally be less of a learning experience than a career in
> the most complex and demanding jobs. Jobs do not all have
> to provide a mental workout, though, to sustain the main
> point.... The reflections of people in humble lines of work
> show that they learn much from their work and from its school
> of hard knocks. (p. 11)

This passage, by the way, is an excellent short rebuttal of Marxist cant about
"alienated labor."

To a classical liberal, the indicated course of action is simple—eliminate the welfare state. Then, those formerly on welfare will be able to attain
the benefits of work which our author has so ably described. Absent a premium for idleness, what alternative do they have to the bracing discipline of
employment?

No, says Mr. Phelps, people who argue in this fashion overlook a key
point. You gain the advantages for living which a job provides only if the job
pays adequate wages. Unless you have enough money to support yourself
and your family in a decent manner, employment will not end the futility

of your life. Precisely here arises the point at which Mr. Phelps dissents from the views of classical liberals.

Mr. Phelps holds that there is no reason to think that, in present circumstances, the free market will provide a living wage for unskilled workers. During the nineteenth century, land was readily available. "Labor was so scarce that all hands were of considerable value in gaining a foothold on the new land" (p. 2). But this fortunate situation no longer obtains, and the lot of the contemporary unskilled is not a happy one.

Our author offers a wide range of data to support his claim that the unskilled do not earn enough for a decent life. These data I shall lazily leave to readers to evaluate for themselves. But my failure to discuss this part of Mr. Phelps's case is not entirely due to laziness. Rather, as it seems to me, a crucial wrong assumption invalidates much of his argument.

Mr. Phelps purports to be arguing that unskilled workers do not earn enough for a decent life. But much of his discussion concerns whether the wages of the unskilled have kept pace with the pay of abler workers. To show that they have not does not suffice to establish what Mr. Phelps needs for his argument against the market. Inequality and lack of wages adequate for a decent life are two very different things.

But suppose that Mr. Phelps is right: what can be done? Our author is too good an economist to recommend an increase in minimum wages. An increase of the minimum wage to

> a sufficiently high level is bound to decrease employment: all the affected workers would be priced out of the market. No economist I know of has suggested that wage rates of $4 an hour might be pushed up to $7 by means of a hike of the minimum wage without causing a major decline in employment among low-wage workers. (p. 146)

Although this argument is too deep for the likes of Robert Reich, it is of course elementary and hardly news. Much more significant, to my mind, is that Mr. Phelps also rejects governmentally sponsored job-training programs to "educate" the unskilled to a higher calling.

> It shows a profound lack of understanding of capitalism to suppose that outsiders can anticipate the training that entrepreneurs can make use of before the entrepreneurs have decided what goods

> or services they will try to sell and what methods of production they will try. Decisions about most training are best made by the entrepreneurs. (p. 150)

So much for what Mr. Phelps thinks will not be successful. His own proposal has the merit of simplicity: he favors wage subsidies to employers who hire the unskilled.

At first glance, this sounds like just another interventionist panacea; but closer examination shows, I think, that our author's proposal may readily be taken in a way consistent with the free market. Mr. Phelps is perfectly willing to have the subsidy take the form of a remission of payroll taxes. Further, though he himself favors a graduated program of subsidies—the higher your wage before the subsidy, the lower your subsidy—he also thinks that subsidies for all workers would be beneficial. This cuts out governmental efforts to direct the proportion of skilled to unskilled work.

Translating this latter version of the proposal into a payroll tax remission, what our author says comes to this: if the government reduces taxes on wages, wages will tend to rise. Mr. Phelps has, with a roundaboutness that would do credit to Rube Goldberg, arrived at a free-market position.

It would, of course, not do to end on a note of praise for an economist who rejects laissez-faire. Let us note, then, that like John Rawls, whom he here follows, Mr. Phelps gives no argument for his view that fairness demands that the surplus generated by economic cooperation benefit the least well-off to the greatest extent possible.

Human Action: The Scholar's Edition*

LUDWIG VON MISES

The Great Treatise at 50

December 1, 1999, *Mises Review*

THERE ARE TWO WAYS TO READ Mises's great treatise. Most readers will, I fear, find the book too much to attempt to grasp systematically. Not everyone feels like reading a nine-hundred-page book straight through. If you shrink from a full confrontation with the book, you will, as I hope to show, miss out on a great deal. But all is not lost. You can open the book almost anywhere and come away with new insights.

As an example, Mises demolishes the central core of Marxist economics in a few brilliant pages. Marx famously claimed to have discovered the "laws of motion" of capitalism. How does the capitalist transform his initial monetary investment into a larger sum of money at the close of production? For Marx, the answer did not lie in trickery.

Quite the contrary, Marx claimed to show that the capitalist could extract profit even if all commodities exchanged at their value. The capitalist buys labor and raw materials at their value and sells the product manufactured with their aid at its value. Why does it turn out that the second sum is greater than the first? Why, in other words, are not the prices of the factors of production bid up to absorb anticipated profits?

---

* Ludwig von Mises Institute, [1949] 1998.

The answer, Marx thought, lies in the exploitation of labor. By the labor theory of value, which Marx professed, all goods exchange at the value of the labor required to produce them. Labor, then, obtains as wages what is required to produce the laborer. In brief, labor earns a subsistence wage.

Once the capitalist has purchased labor, his fortune is made. He now gets whatever value the labor he has purchased adds to his raw materials. (Remember, in Marx's theory labor is the source of economic value.) In the usual case, this value exceeds the subsistence costs of labor. The result of this surplus, which Marx terms the rate of exploitation, is profit, and our pretended Newton on economics has here unveiled his new scientific law.

I have gone on at some length about labor exploitation, as this notion is vital to Marxism. Destroy it, and the whole of Marxist economics collapses. And this is just what Mises proceeds to do. He at once locates the central fallacy in Marx's argument.

Even if one accepts the labor theory of value, Marx's explanation of wages fails. Except under special conditions, the price of labor is not determined by the costs of subsistence.

> The "iron law of wages" and the essentially identical Marxian doctrine of the determination of "the value of labor power" by "the working time necessary for its production" ... are the least tenable of all that has ever been taught in the field of catallactics. ... [I]f one sees in the wage earner merely a chattel and believes that he plays no other role in society, if one assume that he aims at no other satisfaction than feeding and proliferation ... one may consider the iron law as a theory of the determination of wage rates. (p. 602)

The conditions required for Marx's view to hold practically never obtain, as Marx himself had to admit. Workers' wages under capitalism rise far above subsistence. Rather than acknowledge that his theory failed, Marx changed its terms. He now contended that what constitutes subsistence is a question of history: for workers in a given society, "subsistence" may mean relative luxury. As Mises mordantly notes, this is to abandon completely the attempt at a theory of wages.

> What he [Marx] has in mind is no longer the "indispensable necessaries," but the things considered indispensable from a

traditional point of view. . . . The recourse to such an explanation means virtually the renunciation of any economic or catal-
lactic elucidation of the determination of wage rates. (p. 603)

Let us turn from Marx to the fall of the Roman Empire. (As we shall later
see, the topics are linked.) Why did the Roman Empire, long able to contain
barbarian assaults, eventually fall victim to them? Mises finds the answer
in an unexpected place: economics. By the second century CE, the Roman
Empire had developed into a complex economy. "The various parts of the
empire were no longer economically self-sufficient. They were mutually
interdependent" (p. 761).

Unfortunately, governmental interference crippled the economy, thus
opening the way for invaders. Price control and currency debasement were
the chief culprits: "The Roman Empire crumbled to dust because it lacked
the spirit of liberalism and free enterprise. The policy of interventionism . . .
decomposed the mighty empire as it will by necessity always disintegrate
and destroy any social entity" (p. 763). Mises's account extends the analysis
of Michael Rostovtzeff, whom he cites.

I have so far imagined a reader who dips into the book sporadically and
tried to show how he can expect to find insight after insight. But such a
reader will miss much. *Human Action* is unified by a central theme, which
Mises always bears in mind.

Mises saw human beings as faced with a fundamental choice. Nature provides man with no automatic sustenance; and, if confined to living in small
groups, human beings will find life hardly worth living. But the situation is
not entirely bleak.

To escape from Darwinian struggle, man must take advantage of social
cooperation through the division of labor. Here, in Mises's view, lies the veri-
table key to civilization. But how can human societies best take advantage of
the division of labor?

In the answer to this question lies Mises's central point. Only if a method
of calculation exists can human beings in a complex society take full advantage of the division of labor. Alternatives must be compared with one another,
if people are to know how best to fulfill their desires for goods and services; and this can be done only if the alternatives can be reduced to a common denominator for assessment. This, in turn, can be accomplished only
through market prices.

Now it is apparent that the two insights discussed above, far from being random remarks, fit exactly into Mises's central strategy. The Marxist system proposes the destruction of capitalism—hence it must be rooted out and destroyed. Even more directly, Mises's comments on the Roman history illustrate his principal thesis-interfere with economic calculation, and you are sunk.

Once you have grasped Mises's leitmotif, everything falls into place, and the book takes on a relentless quality as Mises hammers home his case. Another illustration of the way in which Mises elaborates his theme of capitalism and calculation must here suffice.

Controversy over the effects of the Industrial Revolution on the standard of living of the working class has been a staple of modern historiography. Such eminences as E. P. Thompson and Eric Hobsbawm paint the plight of the working class in somber hues. (I do not think it altogether a coincidence that both of these writers once found a welcome haven in the British Communist Party.)

Mises refuted these supposed authorities in advance, with a simple but devastating point. Population in eighteenth-century Britain increased greatly. Unless the new industrial system was indeed more able than its predecessor to supply the wants of the workers, no such increase in numbers could have taken place.

> But let us not forget that in 1770 . . . England had 8.5 million inhabitants, while in 1831 . . . the figure was 16 million. This conspicuous increase was mainly conditioned by the Industrial Revolution. (p. 617)

The *Scholar's Edition* of *Human Action* reprints the first edition of Mises's great work. As Jeffrey Herbener, Hans Hoppe, and Joseph Salerno make clear in their excellent introduction, this edition is superior to the later redactions—second thoughts are not always best. Its treatment of monopoly price includes important passages later dropped, and only this edition contains Mises's brilliant account of the Nazi barter agreements (pp. 796–799). The *Scholar's Edition* is even better than the original 1949 printing since it includes the aforementioned introduction comparing the various editions. Further, the book has been beautifully printed, as befits a work of this stature.

Luxury Fever: Why Money Fails to Satisfy in an Era of Excess[*]

ROBERT H. FRANK

Miscalculating Human Interest

April 1, 2000, *Mises Review*

I N 1958, JOHN KENNETH GALBRAITH assailed American spending patterns. Consumers, he told us in *The Affluent Society*, spend too much on such fripperies as large tailfins on cars. As the result of this wasteful spending, the government was starved of the money it needed to provide essential services. Not content to leave ill enough alone, Professor Frank has some forty years later given us an updated and theoretically sophisticated version of Galbraith. Fortunately, a useful idea can be salvaged from his effort.

Mr. Frank spends a great deal of time belaboring the obvious point that the rich have extravagant tastes. The Calibre '89 Patek Philippe wristwatch sold for a minimum of $2.7 million. For the less financially secure, bargain Patek Philippes can be had for $17,500. In Beverly Hills, California, 17 mansions with more than 10,000 square feet of living space were sold in 1997 (p. 21). Yachts can cost over $1.5 million per year to maintain (p. 23). And so on and so on.

All no doubt fascinating, if you are interested in this sort of thing, but why is luxury spending a problem? If rich people spend their money in a

---

[*] The Free Press, 1999.

way Mr. Frank considers wasteful, is that not their business? No, our author replies: to take consumer preferences as givens not subject to rational criticism is to ignore important issues.

Those who pay $50 for a cigar are, by hypothesis, increasing their utility: otherwise they would not buy the cigar. But do these purchases, and others like them, really make consumers happy? Economists uncritically assume that preference satisfaction makes for happiness, but psychologists know better.

> Unlike economists, psychologists and other behavioral scientists tend to have few preconceptions about the extent to which free-market transactions promote human satisfaction. Their approach is an empirical one that attempts to measure human satisfaction and identify the factors that influence it. (p. 67)

By "happiness," Mr. Frank means "life satisfaction," and the point he is concerned with is this. Even if you get what you choose, so your utility as economists define it increases, you may not find your life more satisfying. How does Mr. Frank know this?

The assured results of modern psychology, he replies, tell us. "[W]hat the psychologists call subjective well-being is a real phenomenon. The various empirical measures of it have high consistency, reliability, and validity" (p. 71). These measures bring bad news for luxury spenders.

> One of the central findings in the large scientific literature on subjective well-being is that once income levels surpass a minimal absolute threshold, average satisfaction levels within a given country tend to be highly stable over time, even in the face of significant economic growth. (p. 72)

This appears paradoxical but in fact is not. How can it be that if you get the goods you want, you do not feel subjectively better? The answer, our author thinks, lies in the fact that people quickly adjust to a higher standard of living. If you sell your 3,000 square feet home and purchase one twice as large, you may at first feel elated. Soon, though, you will treat the new conditions as normal, and the extra space will give you no special thrill. You will have gone to a good deal of trouble and expense to wind up about as happy as you already were.

Mr. Frank has resolved his paradox only to raise another in its stead. If the pursuit of material wealth beyond a certain point does not lead to greater happiness, why do people continue to seek more and better things? If "the more we have, the more we seem to feel we need" (p. 74), will not at least some people after a while realize that the quest for more leads nowhere? If so, will they not rest content with what they have?

A further fact explains our getting and spending. People become happier by improvements from their position in the recent past. To an even greater extent, they dread a reduction in their standard of living.

> The economist Richard Thaler coined the term loss aversion to describe this tendency. Loss aversion means not just that the pain of losing, say, $1,000, is larger, for most of us, than the pleasure of winning that same amount. It means that it is much larger. (p. 105)

Once more, our author has resolved a difficulty only to confront an even more formidable obstacle. If he is right, he has explained luxury spending: people wish to beat out others in the battle for prestige and power. They may find, once they have gotten their Patek Philippe watches, that these items evoke no long-lasting spasm of delight. Nevertheless, the struggle counts more than the arrival, and people always act to increase their happiness.

But here precisely is the problem for our social-reformist author: there appears to be no problem that requires tinkering with capitalism. If people did not have rivalrous impulses, maybe they would find it much easier to be happy. But Professor Frank cannot suggest a program to extinguish these desires, since he holds that evolution has implanted them firmly within us. Our author has explained the world, but what room has he left to alter it?

At last we are in a position to see Frank's major innovation: he has found a way to come to a Galbraithian conclusion without casting himself as a stern moralist who presumes to tell others what they "should" want. He argues that the struggle of rivals for material goods generates negative externalities. If these "public bads" can be reduced, people can seek superiority at less cost. This will free resources for projects that will genuinely increase happiness. Suffice it to say that these projects, including expanded public education, food inspection, and highway maintenance involve heavy government spending.

The negative externalities that concern our author can best be understood through an example. Among offensive linemen in professional football, it is an advantage to weigh more than one's rivals.

[O]ther things being equal, the job will always go to the larger and stronger of two rivals. Because size and strength . . . can be enhanced by the consumption of anabolic steroids, individual players confront compelling incentives to consume these drugs. Yet if all players take steroids, the rank ordering by size and strength—and hence the question of who lands the jobs—will be largely unaffected. (p. 154)

Given the danger of steroids, would not players all be better off if the drugs were banned?

Mr. Frank generalizes the point of his example. A progressive tax on consumption will cut out much of the wasteful spending that rivalrous luxury spending involves. Once more, the spending is wasteful not because our author disapproves of it but because people engage in it only to forestall their rivals.

I cannot think that Mr. Frank's ingenious analysis gives us a good reason to institute the consumption tax he favors. He has made without evidence a crucial and questionable assumption. Let us return to his football example. He assumes that the rank order of players remains the same, whether or not they take steroids. Resources devoted to steroids are then a deadweight loss.

But why assume this? We have no grounds to assume that the ban leaves everything besides access to the dangerous drug as it otherwise was. Like our author, we may generalize our conclusion. Frank has not shown that a consumption tax will affect all rivals equally. Absent this showing, he has failed to show that rivalrous consumption generates pure waste. His argument collapses.

Further, Mr. Frank provides no support whatever for another key assumption. He devotes much attention to spending by the super-rich, who constitute only a minute part of the population, for what seems to him a compelling reason. If those not among the fortunate few learn of the extravagancies of Bill Gates *et hoc genus omne*, they in turn will spend more than they otherwise would have done. The cancer of wasteful luxury spending thus spreads through the economy.

A pretty theory, you may think. But, so far as I can see, Mr. Frank gives not one word of evidence that this demonstration effect exists. His "argument" is a mere free-floating fancy.

Our author does however have one excellent idea, though this has little to do with the book's central thesis. He points out the great value of saving and growth in capital goods. Through the "miracle of compound interest" deferred compensation now can give savers the means for much greater consumption in the not-too-distant future.

One application of this point is especially insightful:

> The Social Security system . . . takes no advantage whatsoever of the miracle of compound interest. . . . Unlike private savings, our Social Security tax payments are spent almost immediately, and therefore do not draw interest over a period of many years. And this simple fact makes Social Security vastly more expensive than private savings as a means for financing retirement. (p. 103)

Well said! Why did he have to write the rest of the book?

Power and Prosperity: Outgrowing Communist and Capitalist Dictatorships[*]

MANCUR OLSON

New Light on Socialism

July 1, 2000, *Mises Review*

M ANCUR OLSON'S NEW BOOK resolves for me a major mystery. As all readers of the *Mises Review* know, socialism is an unworkable system. Mises conclusively demonstrated that a centrally planned economy cannot calculate rationally; and the collapse of communism in 1989–1991 enabled even the invincibly ignorant, such as Robert Heilbroner, to grasp Mises's point.

But if socialism cannot calculate, why did it take so long to collapse? Part of the answer is easy to understand. The Soviets had the help of the capitalist market in setting their prices; they did not abolish free enterprise altogether; and they received vast sums in aid from the West. Indeed, Anthony Sutton has made a strong case that much "Soviet" industry was directly imported from abroad.

Nevertheless, a question remains. Whatever external aid it may have received, the Soviet socialist economy was manifestly inefficient. And yet, under Stalin the Soviets built up a substantial industrial base. Further, they raised and supplied an army that, albeit with a great deal of lend-lease aid from the United States, held off and then defeated the German Army during World

---

[*] Basic Books, 2000.

War II. How did the Soviets achieve such feats, when one might reasonably have thought that they could at best limp along for a few years?

Olson has given us much of the answer: Stalin developed an ingenious system of wages and taxation, which turned the bulk of the Soviet population into hard working slave laborers. In essence, everyone had to work for a subsistence wage, during his or her primary hours of labor. Everything that one produced above subsistence went to the state, for "investment" as it saw fit. Much of this investment, of course, took place in armaments.

So far, though, we have mere garden variety tyranny. Stalin's master-stroke was to allow, with unparalleled generosity, workers to labor overtime and keep most of what they earned for themselves. The chance to earn even small increases over basic subsistence set the skilled avidly to work.

As Mr. Olson explains the point:

> All that is needed is to set the base or inframarginal wage of the jobs that require more ability at almost the same levels as those of unskilled workers. A far higher implicit tax rate is put on the more able people in the more productive roles. Only the tiniest premiums, if any, are needed to provide an incentive for the more able people to accept the jobs that require higher ability, because the system of placing little or no tax on marginal or "bonus" income means that the more productive are able to keep most of their higher output for extra work. (p. 120)

Stalin had other "brutal and cunning innovations" (p. 129) as well: those interested in details must consult the book. Combined with the tax exploitation scheme just explained, the military and industrial prowess of Soviet Russia becomes much less mysterious.

But of course the calculation argument tells us that the Soviet system was eventually doomed. Olson does not appear aware of the Misesian version of the argument: his own account of Soviet decline stresses difficulties in gathering information and bureaucratic inefficiencies and corruption. His points are valid so far as they go, but Austrians cannot help thinking that Mr. Olson has here missed the central point.

Paradoxically, though, our author's avoidance of Austrian economics in one respect enhances the value of his contribution. He often arrives at Austrian, or near-Austrian insights through his own arguments: in doing so, he casts unexpected light on standard points.

All Austrians, and most non-Austrians, for example, realize the futility of price control. Prices set below the market rate will result in shortages; minimum prices, by contrast, generate surpluses. In the most familiar instance of the latter phenomenon, minimum wage rates cause unemployment.

So far, so familiar. Olson points out that because price controls prevent people from making the exchanges they desire, an incentive toward corruption arises. Under a maximum price, it will

> be the case that there can be a mutually advantageous trade—
> one with both a buyer and a seller gaining—at a price that is
> higher than the controlled price and lower than the market
> clearing price. Both parties gain by violating the law and . . .
> neither has an incentive to report the offense. Essentially all of
> the private-sector incentive is to undermine the law. Of course,
> the same thing holds true if the government sets a price above
> market clearing levels. (p. 106)

If some people wish to violate the law, room is created for bribery, so long as the prospective gains from trade are substantial enough.

> When caught in violation of the rule, those on both sides of
> the market have the same incentive to persuade or bribe the of-
> ficials not to enforce the law. Sooner or later, the government
> becomes corrupt and ineffective. (p. 107)

Mr. Olson here offers a very useful, and so far as I am aware original, supplement to the Austrian analysis of interventionism. And this is not the only area in which Olson, going his own way, arrives at views of great value to Austrians.

One of the most interesting of these is Olson's assault on a key tenet of the Chicago luminaries George Stigler and Gary Becker. Actors on the market aim to benefit themselves: all and only those exchanges tend to be made that both parties find beneficial. The Chicagoites perversely apply this point to government. Will not government programs also be the most efficient possible?

The complex logic by which Becker justifies his roseate view of government is best left to those interested in such things. Our author readily locates the fallacy in the "whatever is, is optimal" school. His way of putting the point sounds as if it had come from Murray Rothbard.

When we drop the assumption that all interactions are voluntary, the implication that social outcomes are necessarily efficient disappears. The party with power gains from threatening
to use or using the power . . . the thief need not care whether a
fence would pay him as much for what he is taking as it is worth
to the victim . . . Similarly, there is nothing that ensures that a
government will necessarily confiscate the property of its subjects only when the government can use this property more efficiently than its previous owners could. (p. 61)

Here precisely is Rothbard's central criticism of the Public Choice School.
Governmental action cannot be equated to the enforcement of voluntary
contracts: those who think otherwise, such as James Buchanan, foolishly
take the myth of the social compact literally. Both the Public Choice School
and Becker and Company fail to grasp that force is the essence of the state.

Mr. Olson shies away from libertarianism: the very mention of laissez-
faire makes him recoil. What of public goods? Is not governmental action
to produce them necessary? I do not propose to analyze Olson's case here:
rather I shall confine myself to one simple observation. Suppose that Olson
is entirely right: the free market cannot generate an optimal supply of public
goods. (Sound Rothbardian that I am, I of course reject the entire line of reasoning that leads to this conclusion.) Given the coercive essence of the state,
so much stressed by Olson himself, is it not the path of wisdom to abandon
altogether tinkering with the market in order to arrive at a chimerical optimal provision of public goods?

But I prefer not to stress Olson's deviation from Austrian orthodoxy. Rather,
much more significant is that he meets Austrians most of the way on the
most vital contemporary economic issue. He fully recognizes that the key
to prosperity lies in secure individual property rights. Except for "on-the-
spot" trades, exchanges cannot take place unless individuals have clear and
enforceable titles to property. Why make a bargain that involves future performance if you cannot rely on the other party to honor a contract?

Olson parts company with those in the Rothbardian tradition in thinking
that governmental action is needed to secure this key to prosperity. (Once
again, a "public good" is involved.) But is it not remarkable how far this eminent political economist travels with Rothbard?

Public Finance and Public Choice: Two Contrasting Visions of the State[*]

JAMES M. BUCHANAN &
RICHARD D. MUSGRAVE

The Limits of Public Choice

July 1, 2000, *Mises Review*

IN MARCH, 1998, a series of public discussions between James Buchanan and Richard Musgrave took place at the University of Munich; these along with questions from the audience and an Introduction and Conclusion by Hans-Werner Sinn, are transcribed in this valuable book.

I found by far the most enlightening aspect of the discussion the portrait of Richard Musgrave. Now approaching ninety, he is the "grand old man" of public finance and was vastly influential during the New Frontier and Great Society, of blessed memory. He embraces nearly every statist fallacy in existence to a point approaching self-parody.

Both of our authors display the expected concern with "public goods" which, it is alleged, the unhampered market cannot optimally supply. Musgrave happily quotes David Hume as a precursor of this doctrine. But faced with Hume's suspicion of government, Musgrave is much less appreciative:

> I do not join Hume's proposition that in viewing government
> "everyone ought to be considered a knave." . . . I would rather

---

[*] MIT Press, 1999.

> draw on people's capacity to serve as responsible members of
> the community, so that government may do its important tasks
> and do them well. (p. 82)

Professor Musgrave's faith in governmental beneficence, though initially star-
tling, readily falls into place if one reviews his life. As Hans-Werner Sinn notes:

> Musgrave has a social democratic background. He ... has grown
> out of the German public finance tradition. His thoughts can
> be traced back, and often developed in opposition, to pub-
> lic finance economists like Schäffle, Sax, and, in particular,
> Adolph Wagner, one of the *Kathedersozialists* [sic].... A con-
> sistently favorable view of the beneficial functions of the gov-
> ernment sector has characterized Musgrave's work through-
> out his life. (p. 6)

Readers who recall Mises's withering scorn in *Omnipotent Government*
for Wagner's statism and militarism, characteristic of the Socialists of the
Chair in Wilhelmine Germany, will view Sinn's characterization of Musgrave with foreboding. Nor can one take solace in the hint that Musgrave's
opinions in part developed in opposition to Wagner.

It quickly becomes apparent that in the crucial respect, Musgrave is the
perfect Wagnerite. Explaining his beneficent view of government, he rejects
the theory that the malignant growth of the public sector during the twentieth century stems from

> a self-aggrandizing Leviathan. Budget growth, or much of it,
> is seen in pathological terms, reflecting the fallacies of ma-
> jority voting, the usurpation of power by self-serving poli-
> ticians and bureaucrats, and fiscal illusion. I am skeptical of
> that model. (pp. 64–65)

Quite the contrary, Musgrave tells us, the budget can easily be too small.
Government spending is good for you! In support, Musgrave appeals to—
you guessed it—the renowned Socialist of the Chair Adolph Wagner. The
share of GNP going to the public sector in the industrialized countries of the
West now ranges from 30 to 60 percent, a vast increase from the situation
at the beginning of the twentieth century. The growth, Musgrave alleges,
can be explained by Wagner's law of public expenditure growth. The law is

"traceable to major factors: structural changes in the economy, democratization of society, and an increased concern for social justice" (p. 64).

One might at first suppose that Musgrave could be readily refuted. No fancy theories need be adduced: one has only to glance at the record of the dismal twentieth century, with all its appalling wars and massacres. Given the manifest invidious consequences of the modern state, how can our Harvard eminence be so blind? Can any reasonable person, faced with the historical record, think government a beneficent force?

Musgrave's response is for me the highlight of the book:

> The twentieth century has been marked by two terrible wars, made more deadly than those of the past by the advancing technology of destruction.... It is true that there have been unthinkable episodes of brutality, such as the Stalinist terror and the Holocaust. But many of these terrible events occurred during the first half of the century, and I would suggest that the second half has been a success. (p. 227)

How unfortunate that the victims of Mao's massacres in China, or Pol Pot in Cambodia, are not able to learn these glad tidings.

The man is really unbelievable. He simply cannot grasp why anyone would wish to restrict the state. In one discussion session, William Niskanen asked him, "What type of institutional arrangements do we need to assure time consistency? . . . How do we prevent each generation from treating the future as a commons?" (p. 235).

I should have thought obvious the purport of Niskanen's incisive question. How do we limit the government so that it will not leave future generations with a crushing burden of debt? How do we prevent inflationary booms that have later disastrous consequences? Would not these, and similar issues, leap to one's mind in assessing Niskanen's comment?

Musgrave actually takes the question to indicate the need for greater governmental activity. "I agree [!] that equity across generations is not something that the market can handle, so government is needed" (p. 235). He calls for a properly funded Social Security system, to make sure that the benefits of future retirees do not fall. The burden of the taxes required to pay for these benefits goes unmentioned.

But I have laughed at Musgrave enough: it is time to get down to arguments. He maintains that the government must decide questions of distribution by computing the "social welfare function." That is to say, we must compare the gains and losses to particular people from proposed schemes of redistributive taxation.

But hold on a moment. Has not the social welfare function long since been cast out of economic theory? Did not Arrow's Impossibility Theorem kill it? Yes, our author admits, if you mean "a Bergson-Samuelson social welfare function, [which] requires interpersonal and cardinal utility comparison" (p. 45), then the social welfare function has not been successfully derived.

This by no means settles the matter, our author avers. Why not use a social contract to determine the function? Musgrave regrettably does not explain his favored procedure in detail, but he does sketch out its main features. Each person has equal worth: thus, individuals "start out with equal inputs and equal voice into what is to be considered fair in society" (p. 56).

What results from these deliberations? Musgrave supports a combined principle of fairness. Like Rawls, he inclines to think that "inequality is fair only where it is to the benefit of everyone" (p. 86). This however must be modified by Lockean rights of entitlement, to which he would give "one-quarter weight with three-quarters of the Rawlsian concept" (p. 56). (Incidentally, this does not mean that people may hold one-quarter of their income exempt from confiscation. Rather, it requires only that the government give entitlements some weight in its deliberations.)

Whether Musgrave deserves his reputation in public finance is not for me to judge: what I can say is that as philosophy, his remarks are incompetent nonsense. For one thing, there appears no connection between his starting point and his conclusion. He begins with people who, it is alleged, have an equal voice in determining the principles of justice. How does he know that people under conditions of equal voice will arrive at his peculiar formula—take _ Rawls, ¼ Nozick, mix, and serve? He does not tell us.

However one may deplore Rawls's difference principle, one must at least give its distinguished author credit: he gives reasons for the principles of justice he advocates. Musgrave, in one of his best insights, rejects Rawls's argument:

> Reasoning in terms of risk aversion (the basis for Rawls's derivation of the difference principle) is attractive to the economist's penchant for maximization but I question its usefulness as a principle of justice. (p. 46)

But he puts nothing in its place.

Readers will have noticed a glaring omission in my review. I have so far said nothing about Musgrave's antagonist, James Buchanan. This failure is not one of my ever-increasing fits of absentmindedness. Buchanan confines himself to reiteration of his well-known views, and breaks no new ground.

It would be uncharacteristic of me to let an author off scot free, so I shall conclude with a few critical remarks about Buchanan. In his pursuit of the mirage of "pure procedural justice," the view that justice consists entirely of rules of decision, Buchanan accomplishes an amazing feat. In one place, he is less in favor of property rights than Musgrave. "I [Buchanan] don't buy at all into Nozick-type entitlement claims" (p. 85).

Further, he essays no reply to Musgrave's criticism of his social contract approach:

> Why should self-interested individuals, when knowing of their superiority, agree to an impartial choice, even though still in a Hobbesian setting they could secure a better bargain? (p. 45–46)

But Buchanan's contractarianism, whatever its failings, is at least better than Musgrave's rehash of tired social-democratic clichés.

Economics and the Good Life: Essays on Political Economy*

BERTRAND DE JOUVENEL

Edited by

DENNIS HALE & MARC LANDY

The Quantitative Delusion

October 1, 2000, *Mises Review*

MANY PEOPLE HAVE WONDERED why modern intellectuals hate capitalism. In "The Treatment of Capitalism by Continental Intellectuals," one of the essays included in Professors Hale's and Landy's excellent collection, Bertrand de Jouvenel asks a more original question: why should we trust intellectuals? On historical grounds, de Jouvenel tells us, they should be viewed with suspicion.

Contemporary intellectuals who oppose capitalism profess their concern for the poor and downtrodden. But no necessary connection binds intellectuals to the poor. Beginning in late medieval times, secular intellectuals attacked the Church for "wasting" money on the poor.

> During the Middle Ages the church had amassed immense wealth from pious gifts and foundations for charitable purposes. From the Renaissance to the eighteenth century these accumulations were returned to private possession through

---

* Transaction, 1999.

> far-reaching confiscation. In this process the intellectuals played
> a major role. The lay intellectuals took little account of the so-
> cial needs fulfilled by the institutions they sought to destroy.
> Beggars should be rounded up and led to forced labor; this was
> the great remedy. (pp. 145–146)

But has not de Jouvenel here fallen into fallacy? Why should the willingness of intellectuals hundreds of years ago to push the poor aside have any
bearing on their present proclivities? Do they not declare in fervent tones
their devotion to the least well-off?

De Jouvenel does not deny this, but he locates a common pattern of thought
in today's intellectuals and their early modern precursors. Intellectuals, our
author maintains, tend to reduce all values to quantity. Whatever does not fit
their preconceived schemes of measurement must be swept away. Early modern writers thought that the poor blocked the growth of efficiency: hence
they were dispensable. Contemporary intellectuals view the poor otherwise,
but the quest for quantitative reduction continues.

In a brilliant critique, de Jouvenel shows that modern welfare economics
has been infected by the quantitative delusion. A society should be judged,
welfare economists contend, by the extent to which it maximizes individual
satisfactions. But of course we cannot in practice compare the satisfactions
of one person with those of another. Is welfare economics then doomed?
(Attempts to avoid the problem, e.g., through appeal to the Pareto criterion,
have only very limited use in practice.) Here the quantitative temptation
proves too strong for many economists.

Since we cannot directly assess satisfaction, why not use money as a proxy
for utility? To increase a society's wealth more than any available alternative
becomes the goal of policy. (In sketching this view, de Jouvenel anticipated
the precise position advanced by Richard Posner, of "law and economics"
fame, in his voluminous works.)

Our author finds this position deeply mistaken. Not all goods can be measured in money.

> Let me first attend to the drawback of emphasizing those ser-
> vices obtained from money as against those which are not. Any-
> thing people are willing to pay for is an addition to welfare. And
> things are contributions to welfare only in such proportion as
> people do pay for them. . . . Those things which are free, such

> as an excellent climate, are not counted and do not figure . . .
> while the production of waterproofs in the country in which
> they are necessary does figure in welfare. (p. 29)

The last sentence of the passage just quoted indicates another way in which
de Jouvenel thinks the monetary criterion inadequate. If people spend money
to correct a problem in order to restore themselves to the *status quo ante*, the
funds spent count as additions to welfare. But is this not absurd?

A situation in which people do not have a problem requiring correction
counts as worse than one that does.

> For instance in a country where people are very careful that no
> fires break out few firemen are needed. Stupid pictures now
> induce an outbreak of arson . . . but the fires which break out
> now call for a vast increase in the number of firemen and the
> fire machinery: this is also an increase in welfare. Thus an evil
> and its correction bringing things back to the former situation
> both come out as additions to welfare. (p. 29)

Libertarians may at this point be inclined to object, but de Jouvenel
shows himself well prepared to meet the line of attack they are likely to
pursue. Is not de Jouvenel merely attempting to substitute his preferences
for those of free actors in the market? Who is he to say that people should
prefer trips to the Parthenon to the "stupid pictures" on which they choose
to spend their money?

De Jouvenel thinks this objection has considerable weight: "It is fully in
keeping with our ideas of freedom that the position of individuals is improved
every time they willingly alter it: doing the best for themselves in their behavioral world" (p. 31).

Has not de Jouvenel here painted himself into a corner? He first criticized
the monetary criterion for its failure to consider certain classes of goods.
But, in response to the counter that he wishes to interfere with individual
choice, he admits that persons act to maximize their welfare as they see it.
How can he maintain both those positions?

Exactly at this point lies the seminal insight of de Jouvenel's essay, and
here he converges with the central thrust of Murray Rothbard's "Toward a
Reconstruction of Utility and Welfare Economics." If by welfare we mean
individual choice, nothing beyond the actions of free individuals counts. If

one challenges these preferences, one has shifted to a new notion of welfare. Thus (and here at last is the point) the "choices" of the State cannot be assessed by the criteria used in individualist welfare economics.

De Jouvenel is a master of the example that clarifies a difficult concept. Suppose that a

> society spends so much on education. Now its government deems this not enough and increases expenditure on education, obviously through taxes. The previously ideal distribution of resources is thereby *distorted*.... If we adhere to the subjectivist conception of welfare, we must maintain that welfare has decreased. Consumers have been moved away from their chosen position. (p. 32)

Thus, de Jouvenel and Rothbard are in perfect accord. The coercive acts of government do not increase welfare. By a masterly feat of creative destruction, statist welfare economics has been reduced to rags and tatters.

Have I not, though, left out a vital point of difference? De Jouvenel allows, while Rothbard does not, certain acts of state intervention. Rothbard argues that since state action does not increase welfare, it should be curtailed; de Jouvenel's point is rather that other criteria than individual welfare maximization must be used to judge state policy.

Though I think that this objection misreads Rothbard's essay, it calls attention to something that is true enough: de Jouvenel, unlike Rothbard, was not a libertarian of the strict observance. In practice, though, he raises trenchant criticisms of government intervention in the economy.

If, from de Jouvenel's point of view, the free choices of individuals can be called "good" or "bad" from some standpoint not their own, it does not follow that the *State* is a fit agent to operate by these criteria. As an example of state ineptitude, de Jouvenel cites the French policy of rent control in the years after World War II.

Because the French government thought that workers needed cheap housing, a severe system of rent control was imposed. In 1948, "a dollar a month will pay a wage earner's rent in Paris" (p. 157). The result will be no surprise to any student of elementary economics: "rents are very low but there are no lodgings available" (p. 159).

Here I confess I have a trick up my sleeve. I anticipate this comment: "Of course, de Jouvenel is right about rent control. But why make such a fuss over so obvious an issue? What is supposed to be the remarkable display of insight?"

I have, I fear, so far concealed de Jouvenel's most important argument about the rent control case. De Jouvenel notes not only the bad effects of rent control, but also that everyone realized these bad effects. Why, then, did the program continue? In part, the answer is obvious: special interest groups favored it.

But de Jouvenel adduces another factor. Although legislators knew that the existing situation was deplorable, they feared the effects of an immediate return to the free market. Instead, they followed a gradualist path that did very little good. "No systematic view inspired this policy. It just grew from the fear of a sudden return to liberty which seemed ever more dangerous as prices rose" (p. 161).

Lacking the courage to trust the market, the policymakers were doomed to futility and drift.

Many people understand what is wrong with rent control and similar misguided measures; but few possess de Jouvenel's willingness to accept the consequences of what they grasp in theory: the government programs must be immediately ended. For his clear view of this point, and for his penetrating criticism of applying welfare economic criteria to the state, de Jouvenel deserves the attention of everyone interested in Austrian economics.

Selected Essays by Frank Knight
Vol. 1: What is Truth in Economics?
Vol. 2: Laissez-Faire: Pro and Con*

Edited by
ROSS B. EMMETT

Frank Knight's Mixed Legacy

October 1, 2000, *Mises Review*

FRANK KNIGHT COMPLICATES THINGS in interesting ways. He first argues for a free economy in a way that Austrians can only applaud. After making an incisive case for classical liberalism, he next raises objections (in my view mostly wrongheaded) that threaten to undermine his own case.

But he is not yet finished. After setting forward his objections to the market, he in turn raises problems about attempts to respond through state action to these same objections. Knight ends up, to an extent difficult to specify exactly, as a chastened supporter of the market. It is not the "best" social system: rather it is the "least bad" arrangement.

Knight succinctly presents the basic principle on which classical liberalism depends:

> [A]ll relations between men ought ideally to rest on mutual
> free consent, and not on coercion, either on the part of other

---

* University of Chicago Press, 1999.

> individuals or on the part of the "society" as politically orga-
> nized in the state. The function, and the only ideally right
> function, of the state . . . is to use coercion negatively, to pre-
> vent the use of coercion by individuals or groups against other
> individuals or groups. (vol. 2, pp. 4–5, emphasis removed)

The principle, *prima facie*, has considerable force. Why should you not be allowed to act, as you think best, so long as you do not violate the rights of others? Who among us qualifies as a moral dictator, able to coerce people into doing what he deems best for them?

Further, the principle seems desirable on grounds of utility. If two or more persons freely consent to an exchange, we know that, as each sees matters, his utility has risen. Freedom of exchange guarantees an increase in welfare. With coercive exchange, by contrast, we can make no such claim. The utility increase of the supporter of coercion cannot be measured against the decrease to the loser.

But is not this happy picture vulnerable to objection? If external economies or diseconomies exist, voluntary action by individuals in the market, it has been alleged, does not maximize utility. Knight has little patience with this argument. The claim that a market inefficiency exists assumes that the external good (or public good, as we would now say) is not owned.

But why make this assumption? In his classic article, "Some Fallacies in the Interpretation of Social Cost," Knight demolishes an example, devised by A. C. Pigou, of "excessive" investment in roads. Professor Pigou's assumptions, Knight charges,

> diverge in essential respects from the facts of real economic sit-
> uations. The most essential feature of competitive conditions
> is reversed, the feature namely of the private ownership of the
> factors practically significant for production. If the roads are as-
> sumed to be subject to private appropriation and exploitation,
> precisely the ideal situation, which would be established by the
> imaginary tax, will be brought about through the operation of
> ordinary economic motives. (vol. 1, p. 97)

Knight's article, incidentally, anticipated by some thirty-five years the famous article by R. H. Coase, "The Problem of Social Cost," which makes a similar point.

Nor were Knight's arguments confined to arcane issues of high theory. He had no patience with attempts to raise wages beyond the free-market rate.

> There is no sense in minimum-wage laws apart from provision for supplying the prescribed income in some other way, and this would make any prohibitive measures superfluous. And the only discoverable reason for existence of large national unions is to coerce the public, rather than the employers.... It is simply impossible for all labor to benefit significantly at the expense of all employers. (vol. 2, p. 354)

On yet one more issue, Knight's position resembles Austrian doctrine, though here his views have often been misunderstood. According to the standard picture, Knight rejected Mises's calculation argument against socialism. By contrast with Mises, Knight viewed socialism as a purely political issue.

Closer examination shows that Knight fully agreed with the vital core of Mises's argument. A socialist economy faces exactly the same problems as a capitalist system, and these it can attempt to solve only through managers of firms. But socialist managers cannot adequately cope with changing conditions. In a neglected footnote, Knight makes his position entirely clear:

> Thus the contention of Professor von Mises... that there would be no objective rationale for the organization of production under socialism, while adequately refuted by Professor Lange (and others) for the routine operations of a stationary economy, is after all essentially correct for the really serious problem of organization. This is the problem of anticipating substantial changes in the given conditions of economic life. (vol. 2, p. 105)

Knight has failed to note that Mises did not intend his argument to apply to a stationary state: in *Human Action*, he dismisses attempts to solve the calculation problem via differential equations, just because these equations hold true only in a stationary state (Mises Institute, 1998, pp. 706–711). Knight, then, contrary to his own belief, is a full Misesian on the argument.

One can thus quite easily construct a full-fledged Knightian defense of the free market. Unfortunately, Knight himself did not know when to call a halt to an argument. He thought that various considerations weakened, if they did not rule out of court altogether, the case for laissez-faire.

One of these difficulties has a familiar ring. The rewards individuals obtain in the market depend, to a large extent, on their natural abilities. Since I lack the talent Michael Jordan has to shoot baskets, or talents that the market values comparably, I am doomed to make far less money than he. Is this situation unfair?

Knight answered yes. We do not gain our talents because we morally deserve them: we are born with them, or somehow acquire them through our environment. To make our fortunes depend on such arbitrary affairs as talents, Knight holds, offends against both morals and aesthetics.

Any student of political thought who hears this argument will at once say to himself, "John Rawls." An entirely Knightian argument lies at the heart of *A Theory of Justice*. And, indeed, if one turns to that fabled tome, one encounters the following:

> No one supposes that when someone's abilities are less in demand or have deteriorated (as in the case of singers) his moral deserv-ingness undergoes a similar shift. All of this is perfectly obvious and has long been agreed to ... it is one of the fixed points of our moral judgments that no one deserves his place in the distribution of natural assets. (J. Rawls, *A Theory of Justice*, Harvard, 1971, p. 311)

A footnote to this passage cites Knight.

I regret to report, then, that Knight bears at least partial responsibility for the principal antimarket argument of our time. But unlike his epigone Rawls, Knight continues to raise complications. Although, in terms of ideal justice, we do not deserve the rewards we get in the market, it does not follow that the state should alter matters through a principle of radical social reconstruction.

If the market is imperfect, the state is even worse. What grounds do we have to think that power-hungry politicians can achieve a more equitable outcome than the free market? Knight puts the essential point eloquently:

> I mistrust reformers. When a man or group asks for power to do good, my impulse is to say, "oh, yeah, who ever wanted power for any other reason? And what have they done when they got it?" So I instinctively want to cancel the last three words, leaving simply "I want power"; that is easy to believe. And a further confession: I am reluctant to believe in doing good with power anyhow. (p. 390)

Knight has thus, by a circuitous route, returned us to a location near the free market: how near, I should not care to hazard a guess. If the journey has taken some unneeded detours, it remains a valuable one that teaches us much—in part by opposition.

From Subsistence to Exchange
and Other Essays *

PETER BAUER

The Poverty of Envy

December 1, 2000, *Mises Review*

P ETER BAUER POSSESSES A RARE ABILITY: he can see the obvious.
Several philosophers discussed in this issue—Rawls, Dworkin, and
Cohen—rail on and on about equality. Capitalism must be condemned, they tell us, because of inequality. However productive the system,
it fails the test of ethics.

Bauer makes two points about equality which have eluded the thinkers just
mentioned. Taking a Nietzschean turn, Bauer asks: what is the basis of the
demand for equality? Is egalitarianism ethically required? No, he responds, it
is not: the ideology of equality rests on envy. According to egalitarian dogma,
the rich possess at least a good part of their wealth unjustly, having gained it
by exploiting the poor. Will not the poor, if convinced of this, seethe with
rancorous hatred of those who have taken what should be theirs?

Our author writes: "Insistence on politically-organized redistribution
within and between countries also fuels envy and resentment. . . . Envy and
resentment are soul-destroying sentiments liable to corrode people afflicted
by them" (p. 104). Bauer does not shrink from challenging Pope Paul VI,
who sympathized to a degree with egalitarianism, on the ground of theology.

---

* Princeton University Press, 2000.

"What the Pope asserts, in common with so many other modern clergymen, serves to encourage one of the seven deadly sins" (p. 104).

To this there is an obvious rejoinder. Does not Bauer's argument presuppose that capitalist ways of distributing wealth are just? If they are not, then is not the resentment of the poor fully in order?

Our author has of course anticipated this point; he devotes the bulk of the book to showing how inequalities between nations arise. But I wish for now to put this issue aside. Let us suppose that Rawls's or Dworkin's theory is correct: income and wealth should be distributed much more equally than at present. Would it follow that Bauer's point about envy can be dismissed?

I do not think so. Would it not be better for the poor to concentrate on productive means of raising themselves? Even if a philosophical theory correctly shows they are entitled to more than they have, it does not seem obvious that their time is best spent in agitation for redistribution.

It is not hard to guess what an egalitarian would answer. Is not the line of thought I have suggested mere capitalist apologetics, designed to ensconce the rich in their ill-gotten gains? Readers must judge for themselves.

When Bauer warns of the malign effects of envy, he speaks from a rich background of historical experience. Envy of productive minority groups has been widespread and has often led to brutal outrages that slake popular passion at the expense of morality and economic progress. Bauer notes an example:

> In Malaysia, for instance, Chinese economic performance has for many years been far superior to that of Malays in spite of long-standing discrimination against them. In recent years, indeed, attempts to combat by political means the results of their superior economic performance have become the cornerstone of official economic policy. (p. 101)

Envious discrimination against the productive is not the only bad consequence of egalitarianism our author discerns. Pursuit of equality leads necessarily to the growth of the state. Not equality, but tyranny of the government over the rest of us, arises from following the siren song of egalitarian justice.

Bauer places great stress on the contemporary importance of this point.

> In an open society, attempts to eliminate, or even substantially to reduce, income differences extend coercive power, that is, inequality of power between rulers and ruled. This also implies

politicization of economic life.... Extensive politicization of life enhances the prizes of political power and thus the stakes in the fight for them. This in turn exacerbates political tension, at least until opposition is forcibly suppressed or effectively demoralized. Politicization of life, often pursued in the name of equality, has in many countries brought about a situation in which the question of who controls the government has become a matter of overriding importance, even a matter of life and death to millions. (p. 144)

Emphasis on historical example is not the most common way of doing economics today; an economics article that does not consist largely of equations or econometric time-series has little chance of attracting attention in elite circles. Bauer is thus at great pains to defend his method, and his criticism of the dominant approach is of great value to Austrian school supporters.

Bauer applies his method of historical case study to respond to a query posed earlier. Why are some countries much richer than others? Have the gains of the rich come from exploiting the poor? Rather than resort to complicated theorizing, Bauer adduces a simple fact.

The poorest and most backward countries have until recently had no external economic contacts and have often never been Western colonies. It is therefore obvious that their backwardness cannot be explained by colonial domination or international social stratifications. (p. 54)

Another obvious point—obvious that is, once Bauer has brought it to our attention—supports his attack on the exploitation theory of poverty. The countries most often accused of exploitation, such as Britain and the United States, themselves started as poor nations. Since they were the first developed economies, their earlier poverty cannot have resulted from economic exploitations by more advanced economies.

What then does explain the poverty of nations? The most popular answer appeals to the "vicious circle of poverty." (This view often goes together with the exploitation theory, but it need not do so.)

On this account, suppose that a nation, whether through exploitation or otherwise, is now poor. Once in this state of affairs, it is claimed, it will be unable to extricate itself.

> There is a distinct model behind the hypothesis of the vicious circle: the growth of income depends on investment; investment depends on saving; saving depends on income. The model pivots on the notion that the low level of income itself prevents the investment required to raise it, hence a zero or negligible rate of economic growth. (p. 45)

As one would by now expect, Bauer's refutation consists of citing an obvious fact.

> The volume of investible funds is not a critical independent determinant of economic advance. If it were, millions of people could not have advanced from poverty to prosperity within a few years ... capital formation was a minor factor in the progress of the West since the eighteenth century, a period particularly congenial to productive investment. (p. 45)

The theory just mentioned falls into a materialist fallacy: it equates material resources with economic assets. In doing so, it ignores the ability and enterprise of the people alleged to be inevitably sunk in poverty.

> Poor people can generate or secure sufficient funds to start on the road to progress. ... They can save modest amounts even from small incomes to make possible direct investment in agriculture, small-scale trading ... and for many other purposes. (p. 451)

The importance of the internal market runs as a constant theme in the book, and Bauer assaults with vigor those who dismiss middlemen as unproductive.

On only one point of the carefully structured argument of this book would I venture a criticism, and it is one that arises from the author's virtues. He deems it obvious that the more productive and talented deserve to profit from the increases in consumer welfare their activities generate. Thus, once he can show that wealth arises from superior talent rather than from exploitation, he thinks he has refuted the egalitarian case. He does not imagine, owing to an excess of common sense, that some egalitarian theorists could acknowledge and then dismiss his point. They claim that superior talent does not merit reward. Bauer would no doubt dismiss this view as obviously absurd; unfortunately, this absurdity dominates contemporary political theory.

Unintended Consequences: The Impact of Factor Endowments, Culture, and Politics on Long-Run Economic Performance*

Deepak Lal

Tie the Hands of Governments

December 1, 2000, *Mises Review*

D EEPAK LAL, a distinguished development economist, might have entitled this book *The Rise and Future Decline of the West*. In his view, the nations of Western Europe first discovered the secret of economic prosperity. But precisely what enabled them to discover it now threatens them with doom. Asia lacks the fatal flaw our author stresses. It now is in good position to supplant the West. Our author seems to me at his best when he confines himself to economics. He poses a plausible explanation of prosperity, but to understand it, we must first specify his question more exactly. He distinguishes between Smithian and Promethean economic growth.

For much of history, until the rolling Industrial Revolution allowed a substitution of a mineral for an organic economy, the only hope of getting intensive growth was through the increasing division of labor associated

---

* MIT Press, 1998.

with the capitalism of Adam Smith. This I label *Smithian* growth, as contrasted with the "technologically" based, more modern form I call *Promethean* growth. (p. 20)

Lal asks: how did the West, unlike any other culture in history, attain Promethean growth? He finds the answer in large part in a simple fact. The economic transformation

> in part stemmed from the political changes that accompanied
> the slowly rolling Industrial Revolution. Briefly, these tied the
> hands of governments, stemming if not stifling their predatory
> instincts. Intensive growth followed. [The economic historian
> Eric] Jones, for one, believes that intensive growth was always
> bursting to bubble through but was snuffed out by the "rent
> seeking" of predatory states. Political changes in the West constrained this predatoriness and unleashed the unbound Prometheus that has transformed the world. (p. 18)

Our author does not go so far as to think the state unnecessary: he uses the familiar "public goods" argument to show that a society requires an agency having monopoly control of violence. But the state does not confine itself to this function. Quite the contrary, the state seizes people's resources through taxation and outright confiscation. Absent secure and stable property rights, economic growth can occur only within rigid limits.

What Lal has in mind is illustrated by the history of China. During the Sung dynasty in the eleventh century, "China had intensive growth, and for the first time population exceeded 100 million" (p. 40). Conditions seemed set for Promethean progress.

> But the really extraordinary aspect of this medieval Chinese spurt
> was that it was also associated with remarkable scientific and
> technological advances such that it had all the technical ingredients . . . [for] the Promethean form of intensive growth. (p. 42)

The Confucian mandarinate stifled this potential development. It despised business; and the very prosperity engendered in the Sung period gave the mandarins the resources to clamp down on the economy. A predatory state of this type will not destroy economic activity entirely; that would be to kill the goose that lays the golden eggs. But its damping effect sufficed to prevent Promethean growth.

Lal, here echoing Mises, notes that attempts by the state to prey on the economy now face a formidable obstacle: the integration of the world capital market. Countries attempting to impose economic controls will provoke a flight of capital. Mises emphasized the other side of the coin: he stressed that governments intent on intervention would be driven to control foreign exchange.

Our author comments:

> But it was not until the growing integration of world capital markets . . . that the hands of national governments were tied in the pursuit of various forms of enterprise. In the new LIEO [liberal international economic order] full-blooded Keynesianism is dead . . . when even Sweden has to abandon its "middle way" because Swedish companies fight shy of holding their country's debt instruments, the public-borrowing route to financing government activism is closed. (p. 123)

But our author is not yet satisfied. So destructive is the predatory state of continued economic progress that Lal wishes to constrain it further. Why should government involve itself in the money supply at all?

> But the hankering after some form of Keynesian tinkering is likely to persist—as Hayek clearly saw late in his life—as long as there is a government monopoly of money in a world unable or unwilling to accept the rigors of the nineteenth century gold standard. (p. 122)

Those in the Mises-Rothbard tradition will disagree with Lal's preference for Hayek's denationalization scheme over a return to the "rigors" of gold. It is clearly cause for celebration, though, that this eminent economist shows himself ready to sever the link between money and the state.

Now for the bad news. Our author, remember, has left us in a quandary. However enterprising people may have been, predatory states always blocked them from achieving Promethean growth. Somehow, though, Britain, followed by other Western European nations, managed to free themselves in the eighteenth century of state control. How were they able to do this, when others before them had failed?

Lal offers us a convoluted answer, the essence of which is this. To develop industrial capitalism, people had to break from economies totally dominated by close kinship ties. Persons had instead to think of themselves as inner-directed individuals. So far, you may say, Lal echoes Max Weber; but he thinks that Weber got the dates wrong. Inner-directed individualism did not stem from John Calvin, as Weber thought: it was the product of the early medieval church.

Our author stands on solid ground in his stress upon the church as a power independent of the state:

> The primacy of the church over the state allowed it to acquire temporal power in the West in the eighth century.... This claim to an inherent right to political power changed the relation between the secular and the divine. With the divine now claiming to rule the world through the church, the church becomes in-worldly. This was the crucial step in transforming the outworldly into an in-worldly individual, a process completed by Calvin. (p. 78)

Unfortunately, Lal embeds this excellent point in an elaborate and forced distinction between shame and guilt cultures. As he says, many anthropologists, and some philosophers such as Bernard Williams, have made a great deal of this supposed distinction; but I am unable to see that there is much to it. Readers should judge Lal's discussion (pp. 13ff) for themselves.

One gathers that guilt-ridden people live in a near-constant state of anxiety; they fear that they have transgressed the will of God. Shame, by contrast, is a social affair: one is ashamed when one is "seen, inappropriately, by the wrong people, in the wrong condition" (p. 13). I quite fail to see the contrast at which Lal is driving. Is he saying that the Greeks, and others who lived in supposed shame-cultures, did not feel upset at doing wrong unless they were caught out? If he is not saying this, why would there not be a fear of being seen by others that would act as guilt does? Is the contrast supposed to be that guilt cultures believe in judgment by God? But did not at least some of the Greeks believe in this also?

Lal's distinction, however impalpable, is vital to the book's argument. In his view, Western morality is based on guilt, and guilt rests on belief in God. But belief in God collapsed in the nineteenth century.

> The death of God announced by Nietzsche in 1881 is now apparent in the lives if not the words of most people in the West. This ... has had enormous consequences for the major socializing

     force—guilt that the Church has used to check the individual-
     ist passions its greed had unleashed. (p. 102)

(By "greed" Lal alludes to his odd theory that the Church inaugurated a
"family revolution" in order to attract bequests.)

    With guilt gone, the West can no longer sustain the internal discipline
essential to economic growth. Fortunately, the East is now ready to take the
baton of leadership. Eastern culture has never been based on guilt, so the
Nietzschean death-of-God leaves it unscathed. Before the eighteenth century, the East's tight kinship networks impeded individualist enterprise; but
now that the West has developed capitalism, the East can do so as well.

    Lal's account fails to grasp the depth of Nietzsche's assault on morality.
Lal assumes that, absent belief in God, some sort of morality based on self-
interest can function perfectly well without further foundation. But just this
Nietzsche denied. He thought that atheism collapses the whole notion of
moral obligation. Lal is at best a halfway Nietzschean. And if he replies that
Nietzsche was wrong and that an independent morality based on nothing
but social cooperation is exactly what he does wish to affirm, a new problem
arises. Why cannot the West also practice such a morality? Lal wishes to use
Nietzsche to destroy Western values, while leaving the East immune to his
critique. This hardly seems plausible. Lal needs to set forward his philosophical argument much more carefully than he has done. In the meantime, he
should stick to economics, at which he is excellent.

Capital in Disequilibrium: The Role of Capital in a Changing World*

PETER LEWIN

Overvaluing Uncertainty

April 1, 2001, *Mises Review*

ETER LEWIN here undertakes a difficult task and carries off his mission with notable success. He studied with the late Ludwig Lachmann, by whose thought he has been greatly influenced. But to carry on the work of his mentor, as Dr. Lewin in this book endeavors to do, *prima facie* raises a difficulty.

Lachmann famously argued that uncertainty pervades economic action. Action aims to achieve a result in the future, and future knowledge is by definition now inaccessible. Our author succinctly states Lachmann's central theme:

> He [Lachmann] considers it axiomatic that the passage of time cannot occur without the arrival of new knowledge. Each moment in time is unique and time is irreversible. "As soon as we permit time to elapse, we must permit knowledge to change." ...
> I have referred to this as Lachmann's axiom. (p. 24)

Here the difficulty arises. If economic actors always act in the face of radical uncertainty, can the theorist say anything useful about action at all? Is he not reduced to playing endless variations on the theme of uncertainty?

---

* Routledge, 1999.

Lachmann's critics have not hesitated to speak in this connection of theoretical nihilism. Is economics in the style of Lachmann possible?

Dr. Lewin decisively meets this challenge. He convincingly shows that
stress on uncertainty, far from dissolving economics, often promotes theoretical insights. To support his contention, he adduces a wide variety of topics in capital theory, including Hicks's view of capital and time and Becker's
concept of human capital. One example must here suffice to show the power
of our author's approach.

He argues that in the battle of the Cambridges, both sides relied on a false
premise. The celebrated controversy pitted Joan Robinson and her acolytes
at Cambridge University against Robert Solow and Paul Samuelson of MIT
(located in Cambridge, Massachusetts). Mrs. Robinson devised ingenious
counterexamples to the capital and growth theory that Solow and Samuelson had set out. This theory took capital to be part of a "production function"; like land and labor, it earns a fixed rate of return.

> Because capital, like any other input, is subject to diminishing
> returns, it will be accumulated up to the point where the value
> of its marginal product just repays the opportunity cost of its
> employment. (p. 81)

The critics found this growth model beset with indeterminacy. How can
one assume a fixed rate of return to capital, when the amount of capital cannot be measured apart from prices and the distribution of income? "It is not
possible to separate the *value* and the quantity of capital" (p. 81). The thrusts
of the Cambridge Neo-Ricardians forced Solow and Samuelson to execute a
strategic retreat. They admitted some of the enemy's points but claimed that
these were of dubious relevance to the actual world.

Dr. Lewin, putting to good effect what he has learned from Lachmann,
indicts both groups for a common failing. Both assume equilibrium conditions; but this is precisely to ignore Lachmann's foremost lesson. Because
economic actors face radical uncertainty, equilibrium models distort reality.

> Neither side in the debate raises any questions relating to the availability
> or use of knowledge or expectations regarding production techniques. . . .
> Neither side wondered about the relevance of their framework to the market
> process as we know it. (pp. 82–83)

Our author's stress on time and uncertainty leads him to adopt the pure time
preference theory of interest, and he brings to light a convincing argument from

Lachmann against the possibility of negative rates of time preference (p. 106). But in one respect his laudable desire to convey the insights of his mentor betrays him. So anxious is he always to bring uncertainty to the fore that he advances fallacious arguments against Mises and Rothbard for daring to derive time preference as a pure category of action.

He charges Mises with logical contradiction:

> he assumed the absence of uncertainty in order to "prove" the necessity of time preference as an implication of action, where action in a world without uncertainty is, by his own definition, logically impossible. (p. 104)

But action under conditions of certainty *is* possible.

The argument to the contrary proceeds in this way: if you knew with certainty that something would happen, action would be pointless. Why attempt to bring about the inevitable? But suppose that you know both that an event will occur if and only if you act and that you will act. I know that I shall take in the mail if and only if I go to the mailbox and I know that I shall go there. Here action and certainty are quite compatible, Dr. Lewin to the contrary notwithstanding.

No more convincing is another argument to show that time preference depends on uncertainty. He asks us to consider a familiar thought experiment:

> The teacher takes out a ten-dollar bill and asks the class which they [sic] would prefer: (1) the ten dollars right now or (2) the same ten dollars this time next week. He adds that the students may not earn any interest on the ten dollars. Of course, everyone opts for (1). (p. 105)

The experiment aims to bring home to the student the reality of time preference, but Lewin maintains that it works only if uncertainty is assumed.

> [I]f we assume that (2) and (1) are equally and completely certain, then a priori it does not seem to be possible to say that one will be preferred to the other. The knee-jerk preference for (1) over (2) seems to be crucially bound up with the fact that the students automatically realize that the passage of time brings with it unexpected events. (p. 105)

Dr. Lewin has not asked himself a basic question: why does the subject in the experiment want money? If the money is not to be spent but simply held, then given complete certainty it does not matter whether the teacher or student holds the money. All that is on offer is the certainty, either way, that the student will have available to do with as he wishes ten dollars next week. No real difference exists between the two options. If, however, the student is allowed to spend the money as soon as he gets it, will he not prefer to have it now rather than next week? Otherwise, he must wait to satisfy his desires. Uncertainty has nothing to do with the case.

Our author here falls into a fallacy that at times ensnared Lachmann. Rightly seeing how important uncertainty is for economics, Lachmann and his followers press their point too far. Uncertainty lies everywhere around them; and they often concoct bad philosophical arguments to elevate their favored concept into a metaphysical necessity. Why, e.g., should one accept Lachmann's axiom? Granted that the future does not now exist, how is it supposed to follow that we cannot now know what will happen? Is the argument supposed to be that we cannot know what people will freely choose to do, since their choices are by hypothesis undetermined by law? It is not apparent, though, that one cannot know when someone will freely choose. I know that Dr. Lewin will not endorse minimum wage laws tomorrow, but he is free to do so.

Lachmann and his school merit praise for their concern with the philosophical foundations of economics; but I venture to suggest that they do not always grasp the difficulty of the subject. With becoming modesty, Dr. Lewin tells us that he makes "no claims to expertise in the field of epistemology" (p. 221, n. 4). Perhaps he should have then steered clear of controversial pronouncements about it. Fortunately, this flaw does not much mar his excellent book.

The Driving Force of the Market: Essays in Austrian Economics *

Israel M. Kirzner

Discovery in the Balance

April 1, 2001, *Mises Review*

I N A MASTERLY ESSAY included in *The Driving Force of the Market*, Israel
Kirzner asks whether Hayek can best be seen as a hedgehog, who sees
one big thing, or as a fox, who sees many things. If the same question is
posed about Kirzner himself, the answer admits of little doubt. The distinction that Isaiah Berlin adapted from Archilochus seems made for our
author. He is a hedgehog among hedgehogs, developing throughout his
work a central insight.

The insight in question can at once be explained if we turn to "Rationality, Entrepreneurship, and Economic 'Imperialism,'" a penetrating discussion of the work of Gary Becker. Professor Kirzner finds in the analysis of
the famed Chicago economist a fundamental flaw. Becker's entire apparatus
assumes that equilibrium is at hand.

> An examination of Becker's work in applying the economic ap-
> proach to areas usually reserved to other social sciences, indeed
> reveals that the assumption of universally attained equilibrium
> is taken very seriously and quite self-consciously. (p. 266)

---

* Routledge, 2000.

(I digress to point out that Kirzner mildly upsets *my* equilibrium by placing a comma between subject and verb. I fear that he quite often thus lapses into grammatical sin.)

Here lies Becker's error and Kirzner's central insight. The market cannot accurately be characterized by the equations of equilibrium, which assume that actors, relying on perfect knowledge, always choose optimally. To make this assumption flies in the face of reality. Actors in fact operate in the midst of uncertainty, a circumstance that inevitably gives rise to errors and offers a chance to correct them.

Kirzner criticizes without mercy economists who see optimality everywhere. How can they fail to grasp that the market is a process, not a static state of equilibrium? Some Chicago economists go so far as to extend the assumption of universal optimality to governmental intervention.

> The late George Stigler, pursuing this logic to its bitter end (an end many are likely to consider a *reductio ad absurdum*), argued that . . . [t]o declare a public policy to be economically "wrong" is . . . not to assert a scientific conclusion: it is merely to engage in "preaching." The world, according to its own lights, is always in an optimal state. But all this seems, surely, abundantly perverse. (p. 261)

We have not yet reached the core of Kirzner's work—the center of the center, as it were. Because economic actors make errors, entrepreneurs have room to operate. An entrepreneur alertly recognizes that prices somewhere are out of line. He can, by his perception of error, "buy low and sell high," thus earning a profit. Each correct act of entrepreneurship brings production to greater accord with consumers' demands and thus moves toward equilibrium. But of course the data constantly change and equilibrium never arrives.

As our author sees matters, the entrepreneur is in essence an arbitrageur. Kirzner campaigns for his view with all the skill of a great general, but at one point he overextends himself. On the arbitrage theory, "the emphasis . . . is on the ability of the superior entrepreneur to identify, more correctly than others are able to do, where today's market undervalues future output" (p. 118). So far, so good; but now Kirzner falls into error.

It does not follow from Kirzner's arbitrage theory that the successful entrepreneur corrects a misallocation of resources, as he more than once suggests. He states, on one occasion:

> The market process consists . . . in the continual correction of
> false prices that occurs in the course of entrepreneurial compe-
> tition. . . . False prices are false in that they incorrectly reflect the
> urgency of consumer demand for the various alternative pos-
> sible products that can be created with these factors. It is this
> discoordination between what might be produced and what in
> fact is being produced, which offers alert entrepreneurs oppor-
> tunities for pure gain. (p. 153, emphasis mine)

But if the error that the entrepreneur perceives is that future prices will
exceed future costs, why need there be any present misallocation of resources?
Even if all goods were produced in the exact quantities consumers now
demand, estimates of future prices might still be out of line. Hence, the entrepreneur need not detect something that is now being produced in the "wrong"
quantity; it is enough that he foresees an error in futures markets.

It would be folly further to do battle with so distinguished an economist
in his own specialty. Prudently, then, I turn to another topic. Our author,
ever the hedgehog, endeavors to extend his insights about the entrepreneur
to ethics: and here I cannot think the result is entirely successful. He contends that entrepreneurs, as they profit from perceived errors, bring about an
increase in the extent that people's plans are coordinated. Of course, entrepreneurs often err, but still the tendency toward coordination dominates.

> For although entrepreneurs can . . . make errors, *there is no* ten-
> dency for entrepreneurial errors to be made. The tendency which
> the market generates toward greater mutual awareness, is not off-
> set by any equal but opposite tendency in the direction of dimin-
> ishing awareness. (p. 31, emphasis and grammatical sin in original)

The tendency toward coordination never completes itself in equilibrium,
but nevertheless is a pervasive feature of the market.

From this tendency, our author generates an ethical criterion. Plans of
action are coordinated, he contends, if each actor takes account of everyone
else's action. And not just what each person *in fact* does must be considered:
each must bear in mind everyone else's alternative actions. As an example,
"were two airplanes to collide, we would say that the actions of their respective pilots were not mutually coordinated. Each pilot failed to take into
account what the other pilot was doing" (p. 136).

We have not yet reached Kirzner's criterion. It is not, as you might have guessed, the extent to which actors in the economy have their plans in coordination. Rather, it is the extent to which a dynamic tendency exists to bring about this happy state of affairs.

Our author, with his customary precision, exactly specifies the sense in which he claims that his criterion is objective. To accept it as a goal, he readily admits, involves a judgment of value. But whether the criterion is met is a pure matter of fact. "What is needed for an objectively-based normative economics, is a criterion which . . . can be unambiguously identified by economic science" (p. 134, grammatical sin in original).

You might at first think that Professor Kirzner has landed himself in a quandary. Even if the extent to which the criterion is met can be objectively determined, how does this help him if *accepting* it involves a value judgment? Does he not at once fall back into subjectivity? But I fear that I have thus far been unfair to him.

With his customary sagacity, our author has anticipated our objection, as would be evident had I not truncated the quotation just given. Kirzner goes on to say that the criterion must seem "likely to be able to serve as a norm for goodness in the light of independently established, widely shared or otherwise assumed moral principles" (p. 134). Our author thinks, then, that although accepting his criterion involves a value judgment, it is one that bears its truth on its face.

And this is exactly what I question. No doubt each person is usually better off if he knows what other relevant actors will do, though not always. (Suppose, e.g., that you would not have undertaken a risky but beneficial action had you not been ignorant of someone's possible response.) It does not follow from this that everyone is better off if Kirznerian coordination prevails. Let us return to our author's favorite, the entrepreneur. He can hardly rate it an improvement if others become aware of his intention to buy low and sell high. If they do, they will block his moves and he will gain no profit.

I suspect Professor Kirzner will respond that this objection misfires. He does not claim that his criterion measures an increase in aggregate social utility. Quite the contrary, he denies that such a thing makes scientific sense. Why, then, do I judge his criterion by a standard he explicitly disclaims?

But if the criterion is not a measure of welfare, what is its purpose? Why is the mere spread of knowledge taken to be a good in itself? Kirzner wants a criterion that relies on commonly accepted ethical principles, but he does not come close to providing that. One can easily think of cases such as his pilots example in which an increase in knowledge is noncontroversially good. I venture to suggest, though, that these examples will be ones where knowledge increases welfare. Absent this, the criterion rests on nothing.

Our author of course dissents. He claims, if I have understood him, that anyone "morally concerned that members of society undertake their actions in a way that does not inevitably spell disappointment and/or regret (such as must ultimately ensue from patterns of action which incorrectly anticipate and depend upon the actions of others in the system)" (p. 145) should endorse the coordination criterion.

By no means has he shown this. Why is it taken as obvious that the more people can achieve the goals they anticipate, the better? Perhaps in other circumstances, more people will fail to achieve their plans, but at the same time will face alternatives that they judge more desirable than those they would face under coordination. You might well prefer an even chance of being hanged to the certainty of execution, even though you can much more readily anticipate the actions of others in the latter situation.

However much one may disagree with Professor Kirzner on various points, one cannot but admire the painstaking skill in conceptual analysis he displays in this outstanding book.

Time and Money: The Macroeconomics of Capital Structure*

ROGER W. GARRISON

Garrison vs. Keynes

July 1, 2001, *Mises Review*

ROGER GARRISON'S LONG-AWAITED BOOK compares and contrasts Austrian business cycle theory with a number of other approaches, including Monetarism, New Classicism, and New Keynesianism; but I propose to concentrate on only one strand in this rich volume. Professor Garrison has given us an outstanding account of Keynesian economics; after reading his comparison of the Austrian model with that of Keynes, I understood much more clearly than ever before what is at stake in the conflict between the two schools.

Suppose that in an economy, spending on consumer goods falls. Must depression inevitably ensue? Not at all, say the Austrians. Resources can shift into the production of capital goods. As Hayek in particular stressed, following Böhm-Bawerk, production can be divided into several stages, depending on the distance of the product from consumption goods. Mining iron ore takes place at a much higher stage than inserting a steel plate in a gunshot victim's head.

---

* Routledge, 2001.

So long as resources can freely shift from lower to higher stages of production, "capital-based macroeconomics" contends that a fall in consumer spending need not occasion disaster.

> Capital-based macroeconomics is designed to show that quite independent of any movements in the general price level, the adjustment of relative prices within the capital structure can bring the intertemporal allocation of resources in line with intertemporal consumption preferences without idling labor or other resources. (p. 53)

But all is not for the best in this best of all possible worlds: We must cope with the malign hand of government. Should the financial authorities, in a misguided attempt to spur production, increase the supply of bank credit, dire results may impend. If the interest rate is driven below the "natural rate," primarily determined by people's preferences for present over future goods, investors might be misled.

They may shift unduly to higher stages of production, not realizing that lower interest rates reflect, not a genuine decrease in time preference, but rather financial manipulation. When interest rates rise again to their "true" level, overly optimistic investments face collapse. The process of adjustment to the actual preferences of consumers is precisely, in the Austrian view, the downturn phase of the business cycle.

Garrison skillfully parries a major objection to this approach. Why should investors be misled by the expansion of bank credit? Will not experienced investors tend to treat with caution the new influx of money? As our author notes, so long as businessmen fail to adjust their expectations perfectly, the interest rate will fall; and the prospect of a boom-bust cycle impends.

> The notion that the central bank cannot, even for a short period, reduce the rate of interest is as implausible as the notion that it can fool the economy—permanently— into behaving as if market participants are more future-oriented than they actually are. (p. 78)

Incidentally, I do not understand why Professor Garrison calls "glib" Mises's response to Ludwig Lachmann's article (p. 17) on expectations in *Economica* (1943). I should have thought that Mises's main point was identical with Garrison's: The severity of the cycle depends on the extent to which businessmen have elastic expectations.

Lord Keynes had an entirely different view. A sharp decrease in consumption spending would lead, not to a shift of investment to higher stages of production, but to a general economic downturn. Because of lowered consumer spending, businessmen's expectations will tend to the pessimistic. Far from shifting their funds to a different stage of production, they will shrink from investment altogether.

As Garrison makes clear, the problem for Keynes does not lie in wage rates that do not adjust downward to decreasing demand.

> The stickiness or flexibility of the wage rate, then, is not at all essential to our understanding of the problem identified by Keynes. The behavior of the wage rate has implications only for the particular way that the problem manifests itself. (p. 149)

The primary problem, once more, is expectations: on the market, these are governed by "animal spirits" and are in essence irrational. If business investors fear the worst, the economy will face partial or total collapse.

Here we confront a clear choice. In the Austrian view, investors will meet changes in patterns of spending by shifts in the structure of production. Unless misled by governmental high jinks, they need encounter no major obstacles to these changes. To Keynes, in contrast, investment is volatile and irrational. Gripped by an attack of pessimism, investors will unintentionally cause economic collapse. How can we decide between these conflicting visions?

Our author has uncovered an issue vital to a rational response to our query. Why was Keynes so concerned with irrational expectations? Why, in brief, was he so much in fear of fear? Did Keynes simply generalize too readily from the exceptionally bad conditions of the 1930s? Garrison shows that the primary focus of Keynes's concern lay elsewhere.

To Keynes, the business cycle was of secondary significance. He denied

> that counter-cyclical policies narrowly conceived can save the market economy. Its flaws are too deeply rooted for that. The decentralized decision making, which is heart and soul of the market economy, must be eliminated or at least severely restricted. (p. 180)

When Keynes spoke of a permanent tendency to unemployment under capitalism, he had principally in mind a different issue from that which concerned his critics.

Even a prosperous capitalist economy would not meet Keynes's extravagant demands. Because the capitalist economy rests on the expectations of investors, production and employment fall far short of what they could be. Suppose investment were centralized under control of the government. No longer would we be at the mercy of evanescent animal spirits. The interest rate would fall to next to nothing, capital would be available without limit, and prosperity would rise to undreamed-of heights. Keynes argues

> from the belief that in a society with ideal economic institutions the rate of interest would be zero to the conclusion that in our society, with its less than ideal economic institutions, the rate of employment is too low. (p. 185)

Once one sees Keynes's underlying premise, his system loses its plausibility. He, like many critics of the market, has constructed for himself a utopia "that never was, on sea or land," and has used this to find capitalism deficient. Judged by ordinary standards, capitalism has not been shown to stand in danger of "unemployment equilibrium." Only on the basis of his unsupported claim that a radically better economic system is in the offing does his indictment of the free market make sense. Small wonder that Mises mocked Keynes's pretensions to perform the miracle of turning stones into bread.

But what if Keynes abandoned these far-flung claims? If one restricts his theory to ordinary business cycles, how should we choose between it and the Austrian account? Here I wish that Professor Garrison had been clearer as to the criteria for choice we should adopt. Does the bare existence of the Austrian theory suffice to refute Keynes's claim that an attempt to save more by reducing consumption "will necessarily defeat itself" (p. 160, quoting Keynes)? Suppose Keynes admitted that Hayek's model defines a possible course of the economy. Might he not still contend that his system was preferable? I am not altogether clear how our author thinks Austrians ought to respond.

Professor Garrison's analysis of Keynes provides me a welcome occasion to mount a hobbyhorse. G. L. S. Shackle, Ludwig Lachmann, and others who stress the radical uncertainty of the future often appeal to Keynes to support their skeptical doctrine. But Garrison makes evident that the uncertainty that troubled Keynes was a specific difficulty with market conditions. Investment under socialized control would in his conception not be uncertain. Thus his system does not rest on some mysterious philosophical argument that rules out knowledge of the future.

Professor Garrison addresses a great many other topics in this outstanding book. I commend to readers especially his attempt to show that Austrian theory is compatible with monetary disequilibrium theory in the style of Leland Yeager.*

---

* The characterization of Henry Hazlitt's *The Failure of the "New Economics"* as "the work of an unreceptive and hostile eavesdropper" (p. xi) seems to me much too harsh.

Capitalism: A Treatise on Economics*

GEORGE REISMAN

A Masterful Treatise

October 1, 2001, *Mises Review*

PROFESSOR REISMAN centers his enormous book about a key insight: It is capitalists who run the capitalist system. (He has been greatly influenced by Ayn Rand, and I suspect that his claim is in part inspired by *Atlas Shrugged*.) This insight enables him to bring out a vital aspect of Austrian economics, essential to a grasp of that system of thought.

Our assertion, though, at once seems vulnerable to attack. Far from vindicating Austrian economics, does not Reisman contradict it? He was a student of Mises, for whom he has the greatest admiration; yet he also tells us that he wishes to combine Austrian views with the classical economics of Ricardo and his school. "[B]ecause of the profound influence of the classical economists on my teaching, it would be more appropriate to describe my views as 'Austro-classical' rather than as 'Austrian'" (p. 11, n. 2). Is this combination tenable?

The case that it is not may be put in this way: According to Mises, the consumers in a capitalist economy are sovereign. Their decisions to buy determine what goods will be produced. As Mises never tired of asserting, modern capitalism is a system of mass production for the masses. And the sway of

---

* Jameson Books, 1998.

consumer sovereignty is not limited to the goods that consumers purchase themselves. Far from it.

Given the prices of consumer goods, the prices of all other goods in the economy can be determined. As Austrians phrase this, the prices of production goods are imputed to them from the prices of consumer goods. But according to our author, capitalists run the economy; if so, one assumes, they determine at least some important economic magnitudes. Does he not then reject a principal thesis of the Austrians?

We may locate more precisely the apparent contradiction between Reisman's system and Austrian economics. Our author takes pains to inform us

> that the demand for *A* is the demand for *A*—that is, that the demand for any concrete good or service is simply and only a demand for that concrete good and service.... The plain fact is that in buying a loaf of bread, one buys neither a quantity of flour, nor a quantity of wheat, nor the labor of a baker, nor the labor of a miller ... nor anything else but a loaf of bread.... Well over a century ago John Stuart Mill advanced the essentially similar proposition that "demand for commodities is not demand for labour." (p. 683).

Can the rejection of Menger's doctrine of imputation be put any clearer?

I hope that readers will allow me to build suspense by digressing for a moment, before I endeavor to dissolve the apparent contradiction. Professor Reisman holds that to embrace the view he repudiates is to adopt what he terms "a Platonic-Heraclitean view of the nature of entities" (p. 674, emphasis omitted). If one claims, say, that the price of bread includes the price of flour, then one must hold that bread can be both itself and flour at the same time. But to hold this is to claim that entities are the "creation of the human mind in the form of abstractions which can be put together and taken apart at will to form different entities" (p. 674).

Enough suspense. Our author does not reject consumer sovereignty, and he remains an Austrian in good standing. He explains:

> When the Austrian theory of value declares that the value of consumers' goods determines the value of the means of producing them, it is always on the assumption ... that the relationship between the value of the products and the value of the factors of production can be ignored. (p. 689)

More simply put, Reisman readily acknowledges that consumers, by their spending, determine which consumer goods will be produced. Their decisions in turn bring about shifts in spending on factors of production. Our author denies, however, that consumers decide the balance between capital and consumer goods in the economy.

But does Reisman, in fact, remain true to Austrian economics? It might be claimed that he does not. What, according to Austrians, determines the balance between total spending on consumer and capital goods? Clearly, it is the rate of interest. But to say this seems to reintroduce exactly what Reisman wishes to repudiate. Time preference determines the rate of interest; if so, then it appears that consumers, who determine the rate of time preference, do set the balance of spending in the last analysis. And if the consumers do not settle this, who does?

Here, at last, we reach the heart of Reisman's system. He acknowledges that the rate of interest determines the relative shares of capital and consumer goods, but he maintains that this rate depends on the rate of profit, itself determined by the producers' demand for consumption goods. Is this not in effect to say that the time preference rate of businessmen, rather than consumers, principally sets the rate of interest? (I am not sure our author would accept this way of putting his point.) If businessmen have high time-preference rates, the rate of interest will likewise be high; if, on the contrary, they are willing to settle for less consumption, the rate of interest will be low.

Reisman holds this view because, as he sees matters, business spending controls the economy. He wishes to show

> the enormous role of [business] saving and productive expenditure in the generation of aggregate demand—a role which far exceeds that of consumption expenditure in size and is more fundamental than that of consumption expenditure. (p. 683)

Our author takes great pains to work out a new concept, Gross National Revenue, that reflects these realities better than the customary measures of national product.

Our author's difference from the "standard" Austrian position comes to this: On the usual view, time preference determines interest. On Reisman's modified Austrian view, "the connection between the rate of time preference is not direct, but indirect" (p. 743). Time preference determines interest only through its effect on the rate of profit. This "give" in the system permits Reisman to deny the unlimited scope of consumer sovereignty. Reisman thus adopts a "weak" concept of imputation.

Even if I am right that Reisman remains within the Austrian ambit, why does all this matter? Our author's innovation permits him to deal a death stroke to one version of Keynesianism. On this view, prosperity largely depends on the level of consumer spending.

> [W]ith such an exaggerated view of the role of consumption spending as constituting virtually all spending, there is nothing left for the view of saving except to regard it as hoarding. (p. 683)

For Reisman, prosperity depends mainly on business saving and spending, not the vagaries of consumers.

But, one might object, Keynesianism easily makes a comeback. Another variant of that doctrine, perhaps truer to Lord Keynes himself, blames depressions on erratic investment, governed by "animal spirits," and takes swings in consumer spending to be of only secondary significance. What good will it do Reisman, as a defender of capitalism, to ascribe autonomy to capitalists, if their actions are characteristically erratic?

To this our author has a ready response: He maintains that capitalist investment in the free market easily sustains continued growth. In particular, there is no long-term tendency for the rate of return to capital to decline. (His argument for this is long and complex.) If he is right, Keynesianism of this variety fails as well.

I should like to suggest a further advantage of Reisman's innovation, one not explicitly stated in the book. The rigid view of imputation that he opposes threatens to undermine Mises's socialist calculation argument. (Our author provides a superb exposition of that argument. He shows that it is a generalization of the standard refutation of price control.) Suppose that spending on consumer goods directly determines all other economic magnitudes. Then, if a socialist economy could establish a set of prices for consumer goods, Mises's problem would dissolve.

Here disaster looms. Mises posed the calculation argument as a difficulty about capital goods; he conceded that a socialist economy could set prices for consumer goods. But this concession, combined with extreme imputationism, "solves" the calculation problem for socialism. (This, incidentally, was Schumpeter's reason for dismissing Mises's argument.) Unless one adopts Reisman's view, or devises another alternative to the imputationist view, the socialist calculation argument must be abandoned.

Mises, with characteristic insight, fully grasped this issue. In a passage of *Human Action* which has not received the attention it deserves, Mises refers to

> Professor Schumpeter's dictum according to which consumers in evaluating consumers' goods "ipso facto also evaluate the means of production which enter into the production of these goods." It is hardly possible to construe the market process in a more erroneous way. (*Human Action*, *Scholar's Edition*, p. 354)

Our author shows himself ever alert to defend capitalism against objection, and I found especially impressive his demolition of Marx's argument that profit derives from exploiting labor.

> According to Marx, the capitalist expends a sum of money M in buying materials and machinery and in paying wages. A commodity C is produced, which is then sold for a larger sum of money, M, than was expended in making it. The difference between the money the capitalist expends and the money he receives for his product is his profit or surplus value. (p. 478)

Against Marx's argument, Reisman deploys an argument that I have not previously encountered. He contends that Marx's theory rests on a fundamental mistake. If, under capitalism, profits are deducted from wages, then wages must be the original source of income. But, our author contends, this is false:

> In the precapitalist economy, only workers receive incomes, and there are no capitalists and no money capital. But all the incomes that the workers receive are profits and none are wages. (p. 479)

Profits come first, and the prior existence of wages does not explain them. A Marxist might respond, I suppose, by claiming that even if precapitalist income is entirely profit, matters alter once capitalism is in place. But this seems an unpromising line to pursue.

The book contains what seems to me a few questionable points. The brief remarks on the history of economic thought neglect the contributions of writers before Adam Smith, most notably the Spanish scholastics (p. 1); "Louis Bodin" should be "Jean Bodin" (p. 6); Lynn White was not "the leading environmentalist theologian" but a historian of medieval technology (p. 114); and Murray Rothbard's views about the Cold War did not ever make him "an admirer of the Soviet Union" (p. l, n. 15, emphasis removed).

Nevertheless, Professor Reisman has written one of the outstanding treatises of modern economics. It is immensely long; its double-columned pages make it, in my estimation, twice the length of *Human Action*. Tennyson's line, "But I go on forever," will, I fear, sometimes come to the reader's mind; but time devoted to this masterly work is well spent.

Ludwig von Mises: The Man and His Economics[*]

Israel M. Kirzner

The Student and His Professor

December 1, 2001, *Mises Review*

PROFESSOR KIRZNER'S OUTSTANDING BOOK "aims to present, in briefest outline . . . the story of Mises in his role of economist" (p. xi, emphasis removed). In this task, it is eminently successful. But Kirzner achieves much more than this. Owing to his profound grasp of Austrian economics, he clarifies Mises's views in a number of important areas.

As everyone knows, for example, Mises regarded the German Historical School of Schmoller and Wagner with unremitting hostility. But our author raises, and then dissolves, a paradox about Mises's opposition.

> What rendered the controversy between the Historical School and the Austrian School particularly fascinating, perhaps, was the circumstance that both schools appreciated the subjective dimension of social phenomena. It was of course Menger, who, in almost revolutionary fashion, stood classical economics on its head by insisting on the subjective character of economic phenomena and the primacy of individual choice. But the German Historical School, too, recognized that social phenomena cannot be understood apart from human motives and interests. (p. 76)

---

[*] ISI Books, 2001.

Given this agreement on this fundamental issue, why was Mises so opposed to the historicists?

For Mises, subjectivism was not enough. Economics claims to discover laws that hold universally, and this the Historical School denied. "From Mises's perspective, the propensity of the German Historical School to deny the universality of the conclusions of economic theory led the school to deny the essential contributions of economics" (p. 77).

Kirzner's argument may be extended to the hermeneutical school of Austrians that many years ago generated considerable sound and fury, now somewhat abated. (I hasten to add that Kirzner bears no responsibility for where I take his argument.) The hermeneuticians, like both Mises and the Historical School, stressed the need in economics to grasp the meaning of human action. But they sought philosophical support for their stress on meaning in the convoluted prose of Hans Gadamer, and in doing so they fell into a trap.

The nature of the snare is adumbrated in the title of Gadamer's principal book, *Truth and Method*. Gadamer ardently defends the importance of meaning in understanding human action: from the Austrian perspective, so far, so good. But he contrasts meaning with scientific knowledge that endeavors to find universal rules. Hence his book's title; the truth of understanding opposes the method of the sciences. An "Austrian" economics that relies on Gadamer cannot adequately show how we can discover economic laws. It thus falls in danger of transformation into its opposite, historicism.

For Mises, opposition to the Historical School was much more than a recondite philosophical dispute. Schmoller and his colleagues not only thought universal economic laws impossible; they had a very practical reason for refusing to recognize their existence. Such laws threatened the statist policies that the group favored. If, for example, economics shows that price controls cannot achieve the goals their proponents intend, do we not have an excellent argument against instituting them? But that, for the "socialists of the chair" would never do. Far better to close one's eyes to the relevant economic law.

As Kirzner makes clear, Mises thought the policies of the Historical School disastrous.

> Mises also traced the cataclysmic twentieth-century events for which Marxism and Nazism have been responsible to the teachings of the German Historical School. He reports that Menger had ... foreseen that the policies pursued by the European powers would "lead to a horrible war that will end with gruesome

revolutions, with the extinction of European culture and the destruction of prosperity of all nations." (p. 160)

Mises, Kirzner tells us, early established his reputation as a monetary theorist; and the errors and bad policies of the Historical School in financial matters naturally occupied his attention. In particular, he directed a withering polemic against the "state theory of money" devised by Georg Friedrich Knapp, a member of the Historical School. In Knapp's view, the "institution of money was essentially an invention of the state; and it is the state which determines which commodity is to serve as money" (p. 134).

This of course flew in the face of Mises's contention than money, no less than other economic phenomena, falls within the scope of economic law. Further, Knapp's theory played into the hands of supporters of inflation, who denied the connection between increases in the supply of money and rising prices.

Mises's defense of monetary theory against Knapp formed part of a larger assault on the policies of the Historical School. His principal line of attack has already been mentioned; but I have so far omitted a vital part of Mises's argument. As suggested above, Mises thought that interventionist measures, such as price control, favored by the Historical School would fail to achieve their goals. But what would happen when the interventionists grasped this failure?

The interventionists would then face a choice. They would either have to abandon their interference and return to the free market or attempt to remedy their failure through further intervention. Should they adopt the latter course, the new measures would fail in their turn, and the same choice would again arise. The continued choice of intervention would soon eventuate in full-blown socialism. According to Mises, this was precisely the course of events in Germany during World War I, when interventionist war-planning measures quickly led to total government control over the economy.

Mises saw the influence of this pattern of socialism in surprising places. Kirzner in this connection draws attention to Mises's review of Hayek's *Constitution of Liberty*. Though he found much in the book to praise, Mises

> pulled no punches in expressing disagreement with Hayek's treatment . . . of a number of features of the welfare state. "In fact," Mises wrote, "the Welfare State is merely a method for transforming the market economy step by step into socialism. . . . What emerges is the system of all-round planning, that is, socialism

of the type which the German Hindenburg plan was aiming at in the first World War." (p. 181, quoting Mises)

Economic law, then, rules out interventionism: but how are the laws relevant to it, as well as others, to be discovered? Mises had a famous and controversial answer. Economic laws are a priori true; that is to say, the laws can be known to be true just from a grasp of their meaning. Kirzner clarifies in an illuminating way Mises's position on the a priori by a comparison with Hayek's views on method.

Hayek, in Kirzner's rendition, thought that a priori economics was confined to a "pure logic of choice." The logic in question concerned equilibrium states: the learning processes needed to approach such states could only be analyzed with the help of empirical information. Mises disagreed:

> Mises really did believe that the same a priori insights which permit us to understand how individuals behave in market situations permit us also to understand—at least at the most general level—those powerful tendencies toward equilibration which markets generate. (p. 85)

Kirzner seems to me right as far as he goes, but I do not think he has fully penetrated to the essence of Hayek's position. Hayek, in speaking of the pure logic of choice as consisting of "formal propositions," indicated that he accepted the views of the logical positivists and his friend Karl Popper about a priori truth. In the positivist view, all a priori truths are tautologies; they can teach us nothing new about the world. Mises dissented from this dogma, and here lies the nub of the dispute between him and Hayek.

Our author relies on a personal conversation with Mises to clarify his teacher's view on a related matter.

> This writer [Kirzner] once asked Mises how a person can know that human beings other than himself are indeed purposeful.... Mises's answer surprised me greatly: it may perhaps soften the image of Mises as an extreme a priorist. Mises answered my query by saying, in effect, that we become aware of the existence of other human agents through observation. (p. 88)

Kirzner's remarks are valuable, but I am surprised at his surprise. Why would he expect Mises to think otherwise? Mises thought that economics was an a priori science: he expressed no such view about epistemology. Was Kirzner likewise surprised that Mises did not advocate an a priori ethics?

Of course Mises did not confine his discussion of economics to questions of method, and much of Kirzner's book is devoted to Mises's views on prices, entrepreneurship, and capital. Rather than summarize Kirzner's treatment of them, I propose in the space remaining to stress one topic where Kirzner strikes me as especially insightful.

In fact, his remarks on the topic in question are for me the best part of the book. Mises famously contended that time preference is always positive. People always prefer a good now to the same good in the future; in like fashion, they would rather have a good in the near future than the same good in the far future. But are there not exceptions? Critics often note that ice in winter is less valuable than ice in summer; is not a future good here preferred to a present one, if it is now winter?

Kirzner dissolves the puzzle with a brilliant insight:

> For Mises, time preference refers not to dates, but to future distance from the moment of evaluation. Of course, the date at which ice is available . . . may affect its subjective evaluation. But for Mises, that kind of influence upon valuation is not what he understood by the notion of time preference. Time preference, for Mises, refers to the *sense of futurity*. (p. 159, emphasis in original)

The higher value of ice in summer than in winter does not depend on the fact that it is not now summer.

Unusually for me, I was able to find only one serious disagreement with the author; and it does not concern a central issue. He remarks that Murray Rothbard "did not subscribe to Mises' insistence on the need for (and possibility of) a sharp separation between the *wertfrei* propositions of economic science and the value-laden statements of political-philosophical discourse" (p. 217, n. 7). I do not think this an accurate account of Rothbard's position. He, like Mises, thought that economics was value-free; he differs with Mises on whether ethics is objective. But in the present book, this is a point of minor importance. Professor Kirzner has written an indispensable work for all students of Austrian economics.

Economics as Religion: From Samuelson to Chicago and Beyond*

ROBERT H. NELSON

Faith in Mammon

April 1, 2002, *Mises Review*

PAUL SAMUELSON has been called many things in his long career, but never before to my knowledge a theologian. But according to Robert Nelson in this excellent book, modern economics is bound inextricably with religion; and he takes Samuelson, the most influential American economist of the years after World War II, as a prime example of his thesis. By no means, though, does he confine his analysis to Samuelson. Frank Knight's work, much more to Nelson's liking, emphasized different theological themes. At first sight, Nelson's view seems paradoxical to the point of absurdity: is not modern economics in essence scientific and mathematical? How then can it be religious?

One answer is to say, like Cornelius Van Til, that all disciplines are religious; but Nelson does not adopt this view. Is not Nelson, then, flying in the face of patent facts? Samuelson explicitly aimed at an economics modeled on the physical sciences:

> Like most other professional economists, Samuelson presents his work, as he states in the first edition [of his textbook] in 1948, as a "science" in the same category as "physical or biological sci-

* Penn State Press, 2001.

> ences." ... Samuelson believes that "there is only one valid real-
> ity in a given economic situation" and professional economists
> are uniquely capable of revealing it. Ethical questions, however,
> belong in a separate realm, where subjective factors may domi-
> nate. (p. 49, quoting Samuelson)

What could possibly be less religious than this? If physics is not religious, why is economics?

Nelson does not deny that Samuelson and his many neoclassical follow-ers have devised elaborate mathematical models. But they do not stop with these. Quite the contrary, they believe that these models enable experts to guide a nation to prosperity; and here is where religion enters the scene. Nel-son uses "religion" in a broad sense, so that any use of fundamental value judgments counts as "religious." The models cannot be applied in the way Samuelson and his cohorts wish, absent certain value-impregnated assump-tions, and Samuelson's economics thus qualifies as religious.

A typical neoclassical economist would at this point leap up in anger. True enough, he will say, economists make, in practice, innocuous value judg-ments—e.g., "unemployment is bad" and "prosperity is good"—but these hardly affect the scientific character of their discipline. Nelson dissents, and shows to great effect that the neoclassical school cannot easily escape contro-versial "religious" views. We shall see later, though, that the imagined reply can be used by Austrians to deflect Nelson's critique.

Nelson sets the stage for his account of Samuelson by calling to mind the economists of the Progressive Era. Like Murray Rothbard, he thinks that post-millennial Christianity influenced economists such as Richard Ely to think that they could help bring about the Kingdom of God on earth through ratio-nal planning.* But even the more secularly minded economists of that time saw themselves as leaders of a new world order.

Our author finds Thorstein Veblen a perfect example.

> Thus, as Veblen would write, control over the productive system
> should be assumed by "Production Engineers" and "Production
> Economists." ... As the "keepers of the community's material wel-
> fare," they would be motivated not by a "commercial interest," but

---

* Nelson cites Rothbard on the secularized messianism of Marxism, but misses his work on postmillennial pietism (pp. 24–25).

by a "common purpose." . . . Professional groups were thus to be
the new priesthood of progressive religion. (p. 45)

A problem thwarted these economists' ambitious aims. Central planning,
far from having quasi-divine virtues, must inevitably fail. Would not economists who shared the grandiose ambitions of the progressives have to give
up in despair? Samuelson found an escape. In his view, the elite could incor-
porate into their plans much more of the free market than had been previously thought possible or desirable. But to do this did not entail abandoning the goal of a directed society, since elite economists remained necessary.
They had to fine-tune the economy, in Keynesian fashion, to prevent undue
unemployment and inflation.

Nelson includes some excellent pages showing that Keynes himself fully
shared the messianic mindset of the progressives. "Like the early followers of
Jesus in biblical times, Keynes thought that the arrival of the kingdom of heaven
on earth was near at hand, to occur in perhaps one hundred years or so" (p. 31).

But our objection recurs. Even if Nelson has correctly identified Samuelson's social goals, how does this show that his economic theory is in any
way religious? Why is the analysis of more than biographical interest? Nelson responds that value judgments lie at the heart of neoclassical economics.

Basic to Samuelson's fine-tuning plans is the use of deficit finance, which
involves paying interest from one group of people to another. For Samuelson, internal debt has little importance.

> Thus, most students were left with the simple idea that the national
> debt need be no concern because it is simply transferring money
> from one part of society to another. . . . This vision again is best
> regarded, not as an economic argument of substance, but an im-
> plicit value statement, another metaphor in the progressive poetry
> of *Economics* [Samuelson's textbook]. Samuelson was implicitly
> saying that all Americans are united in one organic whole. (p. 95)

In support of his view, Nelson notes that, "tucked away in an appendix,"
Samuelson notes "major technical problems" with deficit finance (p. 94).

Nelson locates another, and much more pervasive, value judgment involved
in Samuelson's account of the economy. Samuelson maintains that the market,
if adequately fine-tuned, best promotes efficiency, and is for that reason desirable; but here, surely, is no value-free, purely descriptive statement.

> In the implicit theology of *Economics*, that which is good is now
> that which is efficient; conversely, evil is defined to be that which
> is inefficient. Samuelson is the heir to the progressive value system,
> often characterized by historians as the gospel of efficiency. (p. 76)

But has not Nelson here pressed his point too far? Is it really controversial to think efficiency better than its negation? If Nelson wants to call this a value judgment, so be it; but Samuelson's resort to it hardly makes him a theologian. Our author is not yet defeated; he maintains that "efficiency" is a much more value-loaded concept than at first sight appears.

In their calculations of efficiency, Nelson claims, neoclassicals tend to take for granted that psychic costs and benefits are small. Thus, free trade earns high marks from economists for transfer of resources from less to more efficient uses. But what about those driven out of their jobs by requirements of efficient markets? Even if the "winners" can in good Pareto fashion compensate them for their financial losses, what about the psychic costs to them of the transition to new jobs? Why should these be ignored? And do not so-called "existence values" complicate the matter further? These concern the psychic benefits that some people gain from items in the environment. If these are included in one's calculations, Nelson thinks it much less evident that Samuelsonian policies always promote efficiency. (I believe that Austrians have the resources to answer this point, but of this more later.)

If Nelson's account of Samuelson hits the mark, what should be our response? Should economists endeavor to purge judgments in essence theological from their science? Not at all, our author says. Instead, they should become aware of their religious assumptions; and one economist serves him as a model of the required self-awareness. Frank Knight did not long for a utopia without scarcity, in the style of Keynes, nor did he think prosperity unproblematic, like Samuelson.

Though Knight supported the free market, he did not do so because of the abundance of material goods it generated.

> Ascetic discipline rather than the pursuit of happiness should
> guide conduct. [Don] Patinkin recalled from his classroom
> lectures "Knight's commenting that from the long-run viewpoint . . . denial of wants was the only way that a definitive
> adjustment of wants to resources could be achieved." (p. 131)

Nelson maintains that here Knight embraced a secularized version of Calvinism, in spite of his overt opposition to Christianity.

If Knight held the pursuit of wealth in lower esteem than did Samuelson and his school, was not his support for the free market anomalous?* After all, socialism has no problem in generating a dearth of consumer goods. Knight's line of reasoning, in Nelson's view, exhibits his theological sophistication. In a way parallel to the Christian doctrine of original sin, which strongly influenced him, Knight maintained that human beings inevitably come into conflict over values.

Faced with such conflict, what can be done? Groups will be tempted to impose their wills on one another, and we seem fated to a perpetual struggle for power. Our best hope out of the impasse, according to Knight, was compromise; and here the free market was the essential instrument.

> Rather than seeing competition as a benefit, Knight argues that the advantages of the market should be understood in terms of promoting a "pattern of cooperation" among people who come together on a non-coercive basis for mutual advantage . . . the market minimizes the role of power in human interactions because in a market "there are no power relations." The market enables each person "to be the judge of his own values and of the use of his own means to achieve them." (p. 136, quoting Knight)

Nelson seems to me right to prefer Knight to Samuelson, but I think he has not shown the intriguing general thesis of his book to be true. As he sees matters, economics fundamentally reduces to a matter of competing value judgments; we face what Thomas Sowell has called "a conflict of visions." Must economists simply choose the view of the world they prefer, e.g., Knight's application of original sin over Samuelson's millenarianism?

The author's thesis rests on an insufficient diet of examples. Had he taken into account the Austrian School, he would I think be compelled to recognize that the case for scientific economics is stronger than he has made out. When I first presented his analysis of Samuelson, I suggested a possible

---

* Nelson points out that Milton Friedman and other members of the Chicago School were much closer to Samuelson than to their teacher Knight in their uncritical advocacy of efficiency as a goal.

line of reply for the neoclassicals: the value judgments that the economist uses are noncontroversial. The defense fell short when we undertook a more detailed account of Samuelson's system. It proved crucially dependent on value judgments very much disputable.

Exactly this defense, as it seems to me, succeeds admirably for Austrian economics. Misesian economics incorporates none of the controversial value judgments so ably exposed by our author in his treatment of Samuelson. Obviously, Austrians do not assume that society is a single organic entity; to the contrary, methodological individualism is a prime tenet of the school.

But does not Mises, like Samuelson and Friedman, assume without argument that wealth maximization is the supreme test of any economic system? No, Mises assumes only the hardly controversial claim that most people prefer a decent standard of life to extreme asceticism or death. In Mises's view, capitalism is the only viable economic system; its main rivals, socialism and syndicalism, collapse into chaos. Neither is there available any intermediate system between socialism and capitalism, since interventionist measures fail from the standpoint of their own advocates. All this Mises claims to show by strictly scientific reasoning.

Thus, unlike Samuelson, Mises does not assume that psychic benefits or existence values are of little importance, as compared with material goods. He takes for granted only that people want a reasonable minimum of wealth; and one can hardly view this judgment as captive to a theological vision.

Machine Dreams: Economics Becomes a Cyborg Science[*]

PHILIP MIROWSKI

Games Economists Play

July 1, 2002, *Mises Review*

ROBERT NELSON TELLS US in *Economics as Religion* that modern economics is a branch of theology.[†] In a book that shows his immense learning, Philip Mirowski presents an altogether different story of post-World War II economics. As he sees matters, economics faced a crisis at the end of the 1930s. The standard model of economic theory, based heavily on nineteenth-century science, encountered problems it could not solve.

Developments in military research during World War II offered a way out of the crisis. In particular, John von Neumann, a mathematician of surpassing intellect, wished to reconstruct economics on new foundations. At first, he invented a new branch of mathematics, game theory, as a tool with which to accomplish this task. But he quickly moved on to another project.

In his new view, economics was to be subsumed in a general science that investigated the nature of artificial intelligence. The new theory of automata blurred the distinction between human and machine operations—thus the "cyborg science" of the book's title. (A cyborg has both human and machine properties; sometimes, Mirowski uses the term to describe scientists who study these devices.)

---

[*] Cambridge University Press, 2002.

[†] See my review found in Volume 1, "Economics."

Unfortunately, economists proved unequal to the task von Neumann had set them. Mirowski concentrates his attention in this regard on the Cowles Commission, an influential group of economists that benefited heavily from military funding, and on the RAND Corporation, for which many noted economists worked. Instead of developing a new science along the lines von Neumann suggested, the economists in these two groups attempted to salvage as much as they could of the old general equilibrium model.

Two factors especially limited their progress. Their version of game theory stressed the importance of Nash Equilibrium, a concept that von Neumann dismissed as having little importance. To Mirowski, the progenitor of this concept, the brilliant but mentally unstable mathematician John Nash, is the antihero who has misdirected modern economics. Further, the Cowles Commission and its allies failed adequately to use cyborg science, owing to their bewitchment by the *fata morgana* of equilibrium.

Not content with being a historian, our author also dons the prophet's mantle. He sketches a new way of practicing economics that he regards as more responsive to the cyborg revolution. Those inclined to an Austrian perspective will see many things differently from Mirowski; nevertheless, his vast tome has much to teach us.

As already noted, Mirowski sees much of modern economics as dominated by the general equilibrium construct. The elaborate attempt to work out the mathematical details of equilibrium was not simply an attempt to carry out the program of Léon Walras. Instead, a key purpose was to counter Mises's calculation argument.

Mises maintained that a developed modern economy could not function without economic calculation; and only the price system of capitalism can fulfill this task. If he was right, the entire socialist project lay in ruins: hence the imperative necessity for true believers in socialism to answer him. A popular solution endeavored to enlist the equations of general equilibrium in support of socialism. If socialist planners could solve these equations, Mises had not destroyed socialism—so at any rate it was claimed. To make good their contention, these socialists needed to develop an exact account of equilibrium.

> It has yet to be fully appreciated that many of the key figures
> in the history of the postwar Cowles Commission cut their
> eyeteeth on this [calculation] controversy. Jacob Marschak's

first published article (1923) was a response to the Mises broadside. Leonard Hurwicz, who joined Cowles in 1942, subsequently constructed a separate interpretation of the controversy. (p. 233)

For some of the Cowles group, the issue between capitalism and socialism became entirely practical: which could come closer to realizing the requirements of equilibrium, a state of perfect efficiency? The distinguished Dutch economist Tjalling Koopmans, later a Nobel laureate,

> helped innovate Cowles's explicit novel response to Hayek, that the Walrasian model actually illustrated the "economy of information" that existed in a perfect market or in decentralized market socialism. (p. 259)

According to Mirowski, an even more famous economist found himself gripped by the need to respond to Mises and Hayek. Kenneth Arrow's impossibility theorem "was also a direct product of Cowles's participation in the socialist calculation controversy, although few have seen fit to situate it within that context" (p. 302).

Mises and Hayek said that a socialist economy could not function. Arrow turned the tables on them by claiming that a democratic system of majority rule could not generate a consistent set of social preferences. Only "dictatorial or imposed regimes" could achieve complete logical consistency.

> For anyone steeped in the socialist calculation controversies of the 1930s, it is hard to see it [Arrow's theorem] as anything other than a reprise of the Cowles theme that the Walrasian market is a computer sans commitment to any computational architecture or algorithmic specification; the novel departure came with the assertion that democratic voting is an inferior type of computer for calculating the welfare optima already putatively identified by the Walrasian computer. (pp. 303–304)

I am not sure this account of Arrow will stand up: does a problem with democratic voting show a weakness in the free market? But Mirowski has established his main point: much of the elaboration of general equilibrium by the Cowles economists aimed to reply to Mises. Why, though, should this lead to a crisis in economic theory?

The answer lies ready to hand. These models have no relevance to the real world: they give us an economics "that never was, on sea or land." Our author might have noted that Mises knew this perfectly well. He found it

> a serious mistake to believe that the state of equilibrium could be computed, by means of mathematical operations, on the basis of the knowledge of conditions in a nonequilibrium state. It was no less erroneous to believe that such a knowledge of the conditions under a hypothetical state of equilibrium could be of any use to acting man in the search for the best possible solution of the problems with which he is faced in his daily choices and activities. (*Human Action*, pp. 710–711)

Of course the Cowles economists did not admit that they had failed to answer Mises's challenge to socialism. But, even from their own point of view, their models proved unsatisfactory. They were not praxeologists in the style of Mises, who could claim that their results are known a priori to apply to the real world. Rather, they sought empirical validation for their models, but this was not in the offing. Mirowski stresses in this regard the failed attempts of Harold Hotelling and Henry Schultz to derive demand curves on Walrasian principles.

> Schultz wrote up the results of his decade-long search . . . in his 1938 book *Theory and Measurement of Demand*. . . . Schultz bravely reported the empirical debacle in detail, and then produced a litany of excuses why things had not worked out as hoped. (p. 195)

Here then lay the problem for general equilibrium economics as it stood at the onset of World War II. In a vain attempt to refute Mises, the Cowles economists attempted to elaborate detailed equilibrium models. But these proved useless for understanding the world. What, then, was to be done?

Once more, Mises offered a way out. The proper method of economics neither admits of, nor requires, empirical validation:

> [Schultz's results] are, at best, rather questionable and unsatisfactory contributions to various chapters of economic history. They are certainly not steps toward the realization of the confused and contradictory program of quantitative economics. . . . There is in

the field of human action no means of dealing with future events other than that provided by understanding. (*Human Action*, p. 349)

The Cowles group, along with their RAND confreres, chose a different way to respond to the crisis. Perhaps economics, as they practiced it, had been too narrowly conceived; the key to progress was to embed economics within a general science of information.

Our question recurs: How was this to be done? Once more, there was an Austrian answer, this time provided by Hayek.

> The need to refute "market socialists" such as Lange thus led directly to the initial landmark revision of the image of market functioning away from static allocation and toward information processing. The clearest statement of this momentous shift can be found in Hayek's "Use of Knowledge in Society." (p. 238)

Once more Mirowski's economists spurned the Austrian approach: it was not "scientific" enough to suit them. Hayek presumed to write about economics without using high-powered mathematics.

> By his own admission, Hayek was incapable of appreciating von Neumann's mathematical enthusiasms. He may also have been oblivious of the withering skepticism trained in his direction by his former colleague [Oskar] Morgenstern. . . . The Morgenstern diaries are replete with disparaging remarks about Hayek. (p. 238)

The Cowles economists wanted a general science of information; and, fortunately for them, a mathematical genius offered the tools to proceed. John von Neumann first devised game theory as a new approach to the study of rational action. Not content with this, he shifted his attention to an even more sweeping study:

> I [Mirowski] believe the best way of making sense of the evidence from von Neumann's last decade is to regard game theory as being progressively displaced as a general theory of rationality by the theory of automata. (p. 146)

Such economists as Arrow, Debreu, and Koopmans did not make full use of the opportunity von Neumann's innovations provided them. Instead,

blinded by their unwillingness to cast general equilibrium aside, they incon-
sistently attempted to combine cyborg science with their old models.

Here the book's archfiend, John Nash, enters to exert his malign influence. His famous Nash Equilibrium took game theory away from the cooperative solutions that interested von Neumann toward "terminal paranoia"
(p. 340). In Nash equilibrium, no player can benefit from a change in strategy, so long as everyone else's strategy remains unchanged. By a process of
reasoning I am unable to fathom, Mirowski considers this idea an expression of Nash's well-known mental illness (or weirdness, if you take the Sza-
szian view that mental illness is a myth). Again in a way difficult to understand, our author regards Nash equilibrium as somehow inconsistent with
"cyborg science."

In the midst of his crude psychologistic reductionism directed at this veri-
table Lucifer, Mirowski makes a valuable historical point. "John von Neumann
himself explicitly rejected the Nash equilibrium as a 'reasonable' solution concept" (p. 334, emphasis removed). Nevertheless, because Nash's views fit the
strategic war-gaming practiced at RAND, they prevailed. Later exponents of
game theory, including Robert Aumann and Kenneth Binmore, have papered
over the breach between von Neumann and Nash, in the process virtually
expunging von Neumann from the history of game theory.

However gifted such figures as Arrow and Debreu, these economists proved
too tied to old ways of thinking. Though they saw the Promised Land of a true
machine science, they turned back. If they had been willing to follow von Neumann, they would have demoted game theory to a minor place and devoted
full attention to cyborgs.

I cannot think that Mirowski's bold thesis succeeds. Von Neumann, as
our author rightly claims, endeavored to investigate the general properties
of automata. But it does not follow from this undoubted fact that he wished
to replace economics with this study. Mirowski offers no evidence that von
Neumann favored such a replacement, much less that he counseled economists to abandon their discipline for "cyborg science."

I have delayed long enough; I must here confess abject failure. Despite
Mirowski's best efforts, I have been unable to grasp why the study of cyborgs
is supposed to revolutionize economics. The idea does not seem altogether
useless; but the relevance of the new discipline is hard to grasp. When we
learn, for example, that Alain Lewis has proved that under certain conditions, a Walrasian general equilibrium cannot be programmable on a Turing

Machine, how much does this damage the Walrasian system? Is it essential to the Walrasian view that it be thus programmable?

Toward the end of the book, one sees better Mirowski's aim.

> [T]he logical apotheosis of all the various cyborg incursions into economics recounted in this book resides in a formal in-stitutional economics that portrays markets as evolving com-putational entities. (p. 539)

If you think this, then the conditions of equilibrium, and everything else for that matter, had better be programmable. But as to the reasons for adopting the cyborg view, we are left in darkness. Mirowski sees cyborgs as the wave of the future. In his view, economists must ape the progressive science of the day. Would it not be better for them to study human action? And how bet-ter to do so than to study *Human Action*?

The Market System: What It Is, How It Works, and What to Make of It*

CHARLES E. LINDBLOM

Still Trashing the Market

July 1, 2002, *Mises Review*

CHARLES LINDBLOM IS AT IT AGAIN. In *God and Man at Yale*, William Buckley, Jr.'s indictment of leftist teaching at Yale University written half a century ago, a young teacher at the college was mentioned as a source of anticapitalist sentiment. How can one justify the large incomes obtained by the fortunate few, this instructor wanted to know, when these lucky ones owe their opportunities to society? Professor Lindblom, long since retired, still finds persuasive this sophism of his youth.

In *The Market System*, he challenges those who defend the justice of market allocation. Given an initial assignment of resources, a capitalist system leaves everything else to the voluntary transactions of individuals. If you earn a great deal of money, you do so because other people voluntarily pay you for the goods and services you provide them. Concerning this line of argument, Lindblom asks us to consider a case where someone increases his price while making the "same" contribution.

He remarks:

---

* Yale University Press, 2001.

> Perhaps all that has changed is the distribution of wealth and
> income, with the result that some people who earlier valued
> your services no less than they do now are now able to spend
> more on them, thus raising the price you can charge. General-
> ized, that conclusion means that because what the market pays
> anyone depends on the existing distribution of wealth and in-
> come, we cannot measure a person's market contribution . . .
> by looking at what one is paid. . . . What any individual can ac-
> complish in market cooperation depends on the skills, capaci-
> ties, and placements of the others and thus on the degree and
> quality of organization of the whole system. (p. 119)

Professor Lindblom's argument manifests a fundamental misunderstanding of the case for capitalism. Unless some people with money to spend
wanted to read books critical of capitalism written by leftist intellectuals, our
author would be unable to sell his book. But this does not weaken his claim
to the money he is paid for the book: quite the contrary, that very fact just is
his claim to the money. Lindblom assumes without argument a principle of
the form, "Someone in the market system is justly entitled only to the value
which he bears exclusive responsibility for creating." Triumphantly discov-
ering that nothing meets this requirement, he concludes that market allocation lacks an ethical basis. But his conclusion follows only if one adopts his
odd and ungrounded premise.

Lindblom's abuse of logic in his argument goes further. Suppose one grants
him that because the value of his book in large part depends on the preferences and actions of people besides him, he is not entitled to what people
choose to pay him. It hardly follows that it is up to "society" to decide the
issue. Lindblom has argued in this way: The value of what someone produces
depends on the actions of everyone else, that is, on "the whole system." But
this is to reify "the whole system" as if it were a separate entity with rights and
entitlements of its own.

I fear that Professor Lindblom has a bee in his bonnet about laissez-faire
capitalism. He simply will not let up in directing bad arguments against this
most productive of all social systems. He complains:

> The market quid pro quo rule acknowledges no ethical value—no
> human merit or contribution to society worth rewarding—other
> than the capacity to offer the kinds of objects and performances

that can be sold in markets. . . . I [Lindblom] know of no ethical principle that defends distributing the benefits of social life
only in response to market contributions, in disregard of all
other contributions. (p. 118)

One is reminded of the opening line of one of Kipling's last articles: "what
nonsense!" Of course a free-market society does not confine its rewards to what
can be bought and sold in markets. Only what is offered for sale in a market
receives a market reward, but this is not a controversial ethical principle. Rather,
it is a mere tautology. Objects and performances not sold in markets receive non-
market rewards. Why does Lindblom assume that people in a capitalist society
value nothing but what the market produces? His confusion is all the more surprising as he himself elsewhere reminds us that the market is only part of society:

the idea of a society in which the market system alone is society's
coordinator is obviously nonsense and is fortunately only rarely es-
poused. Most of us well understand the need for state, family, enterprise, and the various arrangements of civil society. (pp. 106–107)

Some of us would demur about the need for a state, but Lindblom's point is
in substance right. Why then does he forget it when he indicts capitalism for
recognizing only market values?

Professor Lindblom next tugs at our heartstrings. Does not the market
system with its quid pro quo rule allow those who have no productive contribution to make to starve? He imagines a visitor from another planet who,
encountering a free-enterprise system, shrinks back in horror when he dis-
covers that people have no rights to welfare. The interplanetary visitor says,
in Lindblom's rendition,

Do you mean to tell me that in your society, other than a claim
to liberty to work for wages and to hold and use assets if you can
get any, no one has any claim on anyone else, on government,
or on society other than what one can claim by offering something in return. . . . You call yourselves human beings? (p. 114)

Clearly, the spaceman speaks for our author, who elsewhere bemoans the
millions of people who would starve, were the market rule strictly applied.
Would not all infants fail to reach adulthood, since they make no market
contribution? "[T]he world would lie depopulated in a generation" (p. 120).

I venture to suggest that Lindblom has totally misapprehended the issue. The question is not whether people without assets or marketable skills should starve; of course they should not. But does it help these unfortunates to give them enforceable rights to sustenance? A legal enactment of this kind will not conjure into existence any resources, and these can be obtained only from the productive. Why will the poor fare better if they depend on the state to seize wealth from others, rather than rely on charity? Again Lindblom falls into the fallacy of thinking that a market society contains nothing but market transactions.*

One must give Lindblom credit. He tosses out arguments against the free market in almost endless profusion. One of these is ingenious, though mistaken. When defenders of the market laud it as efficient, they mean by this that it tends to produce goods and services at the least cost in resources, given an initial distribution of assets. I will exchange my apples for your oranges, so long as trade benefits us both. The distribution of apples and oranges that results from our trades will thus be efficient, relative to our starting point.

With entire correctness, Lindblom emphasizes that market efficiency is relative to a starting point. But then, incredibly, he claims that because of this fact, the market is not really efficient.

> Market systems . . . largely give up the possibility of an efficient resource allocation and pattern of production. They settle instead on inefficient allocations improved to the degree that voluntary transactions make improvement possible. (p. 174)

I gather that what he means is this: A market system always begins from an initial distribution, and we cannot ask whether this is efficient. A planner, however, is not bound by an initial allocation of resources. He can ask what is efficient in a wider, common-sense use of the term.

> But for our purposes it is regrettable that economists wish to appropriate the word "efficiency" for only the mutually advantageous interactions. The more common definition of efficiency—and the one used throughout our analysis—says that

---

* A fuller treatment would also need to consider whether the notion of welfare rights is coherent. I touch on this in my review of *The Ideal of Equality* found in Volume 2, "Political Theory."

> a choice is efficient if the gains warrant the losses, no matter on
> whom the gains or losses fall. (p. 285)

The planners, then, will assess gains and losses; and society will end up more "efficient." How the gains and losses are to be assessed we are not told. To be informed, "Judgments of that kind are inescapable" (p. 285) does not help very much. In practice, Lindblom's "efficiency" merely substitutes the judgment of the planners for the free choices of market participants.

I have so far been very critical of *The Market System*, much against my easy-going nature; so I am happy to acknowledge that the book contains some good things. Professor Lindblom has no use for the anticapitalist argument that the free market degrades work, "because its ennobling purposes are either lost or subordinated to gaining income" (p. 203). He aptly points out that the

> most conclusive refutation of the degradation-of-work thesis ...
> simply points to attitudes toward work in premarket societies,
> To Aristotle, labor was degrading, a judgment dominant into
> the nineteenth century, as illustrated in English upper-class con-
> tempt for both work and trade. It is only with the rise of the
> market system that the contempt begins to die away. (p. 204)

The book contains several other insightful points, but I shall mention just one more. Lindblom notes that

> monopoly is a lesser source of inefficiency than commonly thought
> because, in the extreme form in which it is often imagined, it
> does not exist. All sellers compete with all other sellers, and
> each limits the power of the others to manipulate prices (p. 155)

Unfortunately, insights like this appear but rarely. Lindblom is for the most part content to repeat his arguments of fifty years ago. Perhaps in another half-century he will grasp what is wrong with them.*

---

* I hope he will also acquire a more accurate knowledge of Newton's *Principia*. It is not true that Newton attributes "nothing to God except responsibility for setting celestial mutual adjustment in motion" (p. 29).

Marx's Revenge: The Resurgence of Capitalism and the Death of Statist Socialism*

MEGHNAD DESAI

Marx the Capitalist

October 1, 2002, *Mises Review*

P ROFESSOR DESAI has given us two books in one: a new interpretation of Marxism, and a history of twentieth-century capitalism. I propose to concentrate, with one exception, on the first of these, owing to its revolutionary thesis: Desai presents Marx as a supporter of capitalism.

How can this be? Has Desai never read the closing lines of the *Manifesto*: "Working men of all countries, unite"? Of course our author, a distinguished Marxist economist, has done so; and he needs no instruction from me on Marx's revolutionary activities. But this just deepens our paradox: how can he possibly say that Marx defended capitalism?

Just in this sense. Marx, like Adam Smith before him, believed in what Desai calls a "stadial" theory. History proceeds in stages: in Marx's account, these are primitive communism, slavery, feudalism, capitalism, and socialism. Each stage best develops the forces of production—roughly speaking, the technology—available at the time.

Now we can resolve our difficulty. Marx indeed hoped for the onset of a socialist order. But socialism cannot arrive except in its proper sequence in the

---

* Verso, 2002.

progression of stages: capitalism must precede the New Jerusalem. At once, then, a new question arises: how can capitalism be brought to an end as soon as possible, so that we can reach the glorious consummation of history?

If this question must be addressed, though, does this not deepen our paradox? Marx wished to get through the capitalist stage by the most rapid means; he can hardly then be called a supporter of capitalism.

But we have so far left out a key part of Marxism that entirely changes the picture. Marx believed that no stage of history ever ends before the productive possibilities of which it is capable develop fully. Desai quotes a famous passage from the preface to the *Contribution to the Critique of Political Economy*:

> No social order ever disappears before all the productive forces for which there is room in it have been developed; and new higher relations of production never appear before the material conditions of their existence have matured in the womb of the old society itself. Therefore, mankind only sets itself such tasks as it can solve. (p. 44, quoting Marx)

Given this doctrine, we can at last understand Desai's argument. In order to bring capitalism to an end, it must be developed as much as possible. Hence a socialist must be, for the indefinite future, a supporter of capitalism. Our author claims, "Practically all the commentary on Marx, particularly since 1917, has been an attempt to deny this" (p. 44).

Desai's argument as so far presented seems incomplete. Suppose Desai is correct in what he has so far claimed. A socialist will want capitalism developed to the maximum extent possible. But this is quite consistent with thinking that capitalism will soon come to an end. Perhaps the productive potential of capitalism has been fully realized, and the task remaining for socialists is simply to topple the system over. Indeed, did not Marx claim in *Capital* that ever more severe crises doom capitalism to destruction? The considerations advanced by Desai do not suffice to turn Marx into a precursor of Mises.

Our author has anticipated this response. He contends that in the second volume of *Capital*, Marx devised a model in which capitalism results in stable growth, possibly for hundreds of years. In essence, there need be no problem of general underconsumption. Capital goods can be shifted to the production of other capital goods, should demand for consumption goods decline. In this model, "[t]here are no cycles, no crises, no problems. Capitalism grows forever, without any cycles but in steady-state growth" (p. 73).

But does this not prove too much? If Marx believed that capitalism would last "'til the sun grows cold, and stars are old,'" then he was not a socialist at all. And this is absurd. Once more, our author has an escape.

Desai does not contend that Marx fully committed himself to the indefinite expansion model. Elsewhere, Marx suggests that a long-term tendency for the rate of profit to fall may eventually bring capitalism to an end. Even here, though, this tendency takes effect only after a very long time. Capitalists have several resources to delay the fall.

One of these is to seek out foreign markets, where the rate of profit may at least temporarily be high. Readers will of course see here the germ of Lenin's theory of imperialism. But what is less well known is Marx's attitude toward this phenomenon. According to Desai, Marx not only supported capitalism: he was an imperialist as well.

Desai sets forward the evidence for his surprising thesis:

> Marx had welcomed the British East India Company's role in destroying the old precapitalist institutions in India; his only complaint was that they had not finished the job properly in 1857. . . . He and Engels had approved of France's takeover of Algeria. In Marx's view, capitalism was a progressive force which had to destroy older modes even if this destruction was effected by a colonial power. (pp. 154–155)

Desai draws attention in this connection to a book I have long admired, Bill Warren's *Imperialism, the Pioneer of Development* (p. 330, n.12).

In further support for his unusual interpretation of Marx, Desai notes that the founder of scientific socialism said almost nothing about the sort of society that would eventually replace capitalism. For Marx, socialism stood for little more than a cipher representing a better world to come. But our author does Marx one better. He thinks that Hayek won the socialist calculation argument.

Desai believes—wrongly, in my view—that Oskar Lange and Fred Taylor successfully solved the calculation problem as Mises originally posed it. (He also speaks favorably of linear programming as a way to compute prices.) But he maintains that the Lange-Taylor solution is in practice useless because of a problem posed by Hayek. Of what use are the equations of Walrasian equilibrium when the economy is never in this state of affairs? The real problems of the economy are of an entirely different order.

Desai, then, is a socialist of an unusual type:

> Hayek was undermining the entire basis of equilibrium theorizing as it was—and still is—taught in economics, yet his ideas were ignored at the time. An entire generation came to believe that capitalism and socialism were symmetrical; markets and planning were the same thing. . . . The idea that an economy is a self-organizing process . . . was forgotten. The point was not that a socialist planner could not compute all those equations. The point was that even making the most extreme assumptions, it is impossible to centralize knowledge. (p. 198)

Our author's strategy is ingenious, but I cannot think it altogether succeeds. Faced with the brutal tyranny and utter economic failure of twentieth-century communism, how can any rational person remain a Marxist? Simple, Desai answers. One merely says that Marx was not a socialist and in fact anticipated the major criticisms of that doctrine advanced by critics such as Hayek. Thus, the idea that market participants act on the basis of local knowledge was one "that Marx shared with Hayek" (p. 198).

Desai's strategy suffers from a basic flaw. Suppose that he is right: at least for the indefinite future, Marx favored the full development of capitalism. All well and good; but why is Marx an important economist, worth studying today?

True enough, Marx's model of stable growth under capitalism ranks as an important contribution. (Desai might also have noted that, to an extent, it anticipates the Austrian view of the structure of production.) But not even Desai's earnest advocacy suffices to rescue the linchpin of Marx's economics, the labor theory of value. He is constrained to admit that Marx failed to establish the central claim of that theory. "One can accept that prices are proportional to [labor] values, but still refuse to say that all profits come from the exploitation of labour" (p. 65). Piero Sraffa and his student Ian Steedman were "able to show up anomalies in Marx's argument. One could have negative surplus-value, yet positive profits" (p. 264). Paul Samuelson once famously dismissed Marx as a "minor post-Ricardian." Does Desai's tour de force, if successful, do anything but reinforce Samelson's verdict?

At the outset, I mentioned one exception to my plan of concentration on Desai's account of Marxism. Our author makes an important historical observation that cannot be ignored. He notes that much of "development economics" copies the ideas of Nazi Germany.

> The subsequent history of the war and the Holocaust has so totally destroyed the National Socialists' reputation that few today would admit that much of the planning in developing countries after 1945—in India, for example—drew on ideas from this experiment. The Soviet Union was claimed as a model more often, but wherever capitalism and planning have coexisted, the original model has been the German one. (p. 165)

Readers of Mises's *Omnipotent Government* will not be surprised. We will make an Austrian of Desai yet! On page 163, the name of the Nazi finance minister, Count Schwerin von Krosigk, is misspelled.

A History of Money and Banking in the United States: From the Colonial Era to World War II*

MURRAY N. ROTHBARD

Edited by JOSEPH T. SALERNO

Banking, Flesh, and Blood

December 1, 2002, *Mises Review*

MURRAY ROTHBARD had a remarkable ability to throw unexpected light on historical controversies. Again and again in his work, he pointed out factors that earlier authors had overlooked. After Rothbard has finished with a topic, we can never see it in the same way again. This talent is much in evidence in the present book, a collection of several long articles by Rothbard that together constitute a comprehensive history of American monetary history for the period indicated in the book's title.

An example will illustrate Rothbard's technique. Everyone knows Lenin's theory of imperialism. Developed capitalist economies, Lenin maintained, characteristically produce more than they can sell domestically. To find an outlet for their surplus goods, capitalists seek markets abroad. Their endeavors bring about a struggle for colonies; the "highest stage" of capitalism is imperialism.

So much is well known; but how did Lenin arrive at this account? Rothbard has unearthed a surprising source. The theory stems ultimately from capitalist supporters of imperialism:

---

* Mises Institute, 2002.

By the late 1890s, groups of theoreticians in the United States were working on what would later be called the "Leninist" theory of capitalist imperialism. The theory was originated, not by Lenin but by advocates of imperialism, centering around such Morgan-oriented friends and brain trusters of Theodore Roosevelt as Henry Adams, Brooks Adams, Admiral Alfred T. Mahan, and Massachusetts Senator Henry Cabot Lodge.... The ever lower rate of profit from the "surplus capital" was in danger of crippling capitalism, except that salvation loomed in the form of foreign markets and especially foreign investments.... Hence, to save advanced capitalism, it was necessary for Western governments to engage in outright imperialist or neo-imperialist ventures, which would force other countries to open their markets for American products and would force open investment opportunities abroad. (pp. 209–210)

I have concentrated on this detail, not only for its own sake, but because from it, we can see in operation several themes in Rothbard's conception of American financial history. Most obviously, he agrees with Michelet that history is a resurrection of the flesh. Not for him are impersonal trends and forces: History always involves the motives and actions of particular persons. (Professor Salerno, in his excellent introduction, explains the theoretical basis for Rothbard's stress on the particular.)

To illustrate, Rothbard does not confine himself to a general statement of the monopoly capitalist origins of the Leninist theory. He describes in great detail the activities of Charles Conant, a leading advocate of imperialism. Conant, it transpires, did much more than theorize. He actively worked to install the gold-exchange standard, a key tool of American monetary imperialism, in Latin America and elsewhere. Rothbard describes Conant's activities in his unique style: "Conant, as usual, was the major theoretician and finagler" (p. 226).

Neither as theorist nor practitioner did Conant act on his own, and to see why not enables us to grasp a central plank of Rothbard's edifice.

Nor should it be thought that Charles A. Conant was the purely disinterested scientist he claimed to be. His currency reforms directly benefited his investment banker employers. Thus, Conant was treasurer, from 1902 to 1906, of the Morgan-run Morton Trust Company of New York, and it was surely no coincidence that Morton Trust was the bank that held the reserve funds for the governments of the Philippines, Panama, and the Dominican Republic, after their respective currency reforms. (pp. 232–233)

Rothbard maintains that the House of Morgan held effective control of the American government for much of the late nineteenth and early twentieth centuries, down to the onset of Roosevelt's New Deal in 1933. He traces in detail Morgan backing for a central bank, culminating in the creation of the Federal Reserve System in 1913.

Through an overwhelming mass of detail, Rothbard makes his case; but a question here arises. Why did the Morgan interests (or anyone else, for that matter) wish to establish a central banking system?

Our author explains the main reason in great detail. A central banking system vastly increases the ability of bankers to lend more money than they possess in reserves. Absent central control, monetary expansion in a fractional reserve system faces limits. If a bank, desiring to increase its profits, expands too much, rival banks will call in its notes. If it cannot meet its obligations, it will collapse. A central banking system removes this obstacle.

The House of Morgan by no means was the first group in American history to seek the ill-gotten gains of centralized banking; Rothbard discusses in great detail, e.g., the struggles over the First and Second Banks of the United States. Throughout his narrative, Rothbard stresses a point vital to the understanding of monetary history. A popular belief holds that poor people, likely to be in debt, favor easy money, while their rich creditors oppose it.

Often, this turns out to be the reverse of the truth.

> Debtors benefit from inflation and creditors lose; realizing this fact, older historians assumed that debtors were largely poor agrarians and creditors were wealthy merchants and that therefore the former were the main sponsors of inflationary nostrums. But of course, there are no rigid "classes" of creditors and debtors; indeed, wealthy merchants and land speculators are often the heaviest debtors. (p. 58)

Bankers, then, favor monetary expansion; but why should the rest of us oppose it? Do we not require an "elastic" currency to deal with the failure of prices quickly to adjust to changing business conditions? Not at all, answers Rothbard. "As 'Austrian' business cycle theory has pointed out, any bank credit inflation creates conditions of boom-and-bust" (p. 94).

"Suppose all this is true," we can imagine an expansionist protesting. "Do we not still need monetary expansion to rescue us from recession?" Rothbard demurs; in his view, the business liquidations that accompany recessions are precisely the cure for the preceding boom. Efforts to interfere with these liquidations through inflation will induce another cycle.

Although Austrian theory provides the framework for Rothbard's history, its intricacies are not at the heart of the book. Let us then return to what I found the book's most valuable historical contribution, the discussion of the Morgan bank and its influence.

Rothbard makes clear that the Morgan interests aimed at much more than profits. To this very powerful group, the interests of Great Britain and her empire were paramount; and the Morgan bank constantly aimed to subordinate the interests of the United States to this superior power. After the onset of World War I, "the Morgans played a substantial role in bringing the United States into the war on Britain's side, and, as head of the Fed, Benjamin Strong obligingly doubled the money supply to finance America's role in the war effort" (p. 270).

Rothbard's point serves to introduce a story within the larger story of Morgan influence. Benjamin Strong, the Governor of the New York Federal Reserve Bank, was by far the most influential figure in the entire Federal Reserve system from its inception until his death in 1928. He entered into close association with Montagu Norman, Governor of the Bank of England. Both men had enlisted in the Morgan camp:

> While the close personal relations between Strong and Norman were of course highly important for the collaboration that formed the international monetary world of the 1920s, it should not be overlooked that both were intimately bound to the House of Morgan. (p. 374)

At Norman's behest, Strong inflated the US monetary supply, in order to enable Britain to maintain in operation the gold-exchange standard. By doing so, Rothbard claims, Strong bears heavy responsibility for the onset of the 1929 stock market crash and the ensuing depression.

> The United States inflated its money and credit in order to prevent inflationary Britain from losing gold to the United States, a loss which would endanger the new, jerry-built "gold standard"

structure. The result, however, was eventual collapse of money and credit in the US and abroad, and a worldwide depression. Benjamin Strong was the Morgans's architect of a disastrous policy of inflationary boom that led inevitably to bust. (p. 271)

Rothbard goes even further in his assault on Federal Reserve inflationism. Contrary to Milton Friedman, the Federal Reserve did not follow a contractionist policy once the depression began. Rothbard assails

> the spuriousness of the monetarist legend that the Federal Reserve was responsible for the great contraction of money from 1929 to 1933. On the contrary, the Fed and the administration tried their best to inflate, efforts foiled by the good sense, and by the increasing mistrust of the banking system, of the American people. (p. 275)

The book's narrative is a complex one, and by no means reduces to an account of the vicissitudes of the House of Morgan. A rival banking group, consisting most importantly of Rockefeller interests, challenged it for supremacy. For Rothbard, the New Deal can best be viewed as the victory of the Rockefeller group. Although the Morgans recovered some of their influence after the mid-1930s, they henceforward occupied a subordinate position.

Throughout the book, Rothbard pursues with tenacity a biographical method of analysis that stresses the ties of influential figures to central financial groups, such as the Morgans. In his intricate tracing of patrons and clients, Rothbard brings to mind the great works of Ronald Syme and Lewis Namier. But Rothbard has the advantage over these renowned historians in that he does not restrict himself to the amassing of biographical detail. He has in addition a carefully worked out theory, Austrian economics, to guide him. I have endeavored in this review to mirror Rothbard's constant movement between detail and general theory, but I have at best been able to provide a small taste of this outstanding book.

Epistemological Problems of Economics[*]

LUDWIG VON MISES

Third Edition

Translated by GEORGE REISMAN
Introduction by JÖRG GUIDO HÜLSMANN

The Formalism of Mises

July 1, 2003, *Mises Review*

S EVERY READER of *Human Action* knows, Ludwig von Mises devoted much attention to methodology. Many people interested in Austrian economics turn from his discussions of the a priori and *verstehen* in bafflement and boredom. "Enough of these philosophical abstractions," they say; "what we want is economics." No greater mistake can be imagined if one wishes to understand Mises's work.

Mises's methodological views are vital to the grasp of his concrete teaching on economic issues. This we are in a position to understand better than ever before, thanks to Guido Hülsmann's brilliant introduction to this welcome reissue of Mises's most extended discussion of the nature of our knowledge of economics.

The vital core of Mises's conception of economics can be seen in his confrontation with the great sociologist Max Weber. According to Weber, only some human actions count as rational. Weber contrasted "purposive-rational"

---

[*] Ludwig von Mises Institute, 2003.

action, in which an actor uses means to achieve ends, with other sorts of action, which, he claimed, do not display a means-ends structure.

Among these other sorts was what Weber termed valuational action. This is "guided by conscious belief in the unqualified *intrinsic* value of a definite mode of conduct—ethical, aesthetic, religious, or any other—purely for its own sake and independently of its consequences." (p. 88, quoting Weber)

Mises quickly identified the fallacy in Weber's claim that valuational action lacks a means-ends structure.

> [I]t is quite clear that what Weber calls "valuational" behavior cannot be fundamentally distinguished from "rational" behavior. The results that rational conduct aims at are also values, and, as such, they are beyond rationality." (p. 90)

For economics, the ends of action are neither rational nor irrational: rationality refers only to means.

Both "rational" and "valuational" behavior, in Weber's sense, display exactly the same means-ends structure. Contrary to Weber's view,

> [I]t would be more accurate to say that there are men who place the value of duty, honor, beauty and the like so high that they set aside other goals for their sake ... an action directed at their realization must likewise be termed rational. (p. 91)

Mises argues in parallel fashion that Weber's other cases of alleged nonrational action fall into the means-end pattern.

But why does this matter? Is not Mises's long analysis of whether all action displays his favored structure precisely a case of the useless, abstract discussions his critics dismiss as inconsequential?

Quite the contrary, Mises's discussion is essential to his entire project of economic science. Once he has shown that all action involves the use of means to achieve ends, he is in a position to develop, in a detailed way, various theorems about action, e.g., that an actor always seeks his most highly valued end.

Critics of Mises dismiss his results as formalistic. Is it not the merest tautology to say that an actor chooses what he values most highly? As Guido Hülsmann enables us to see, Mises's formalism is the key to his entire conception of economics.

To Mises, action always involves a choice among ends. One expected out-come is preferred to another; and the actor selects the means he deems best suited to achieve this goal. In a purely formal sense, the actor has maximized his expected utility; he has chosen what, at the time of his action, he most wants. But, as Hülsmann rightly stresses, there is for Mises no calculation in terms of units of utility.

Here, Hülsmann notes, Mises stood in stark opposition to many of his colleagues:

> Now contrast this [view of Mises] with the perspective of those economists who think that economic calculation can be made in terms of utils [i.e., units of utility]. They too cannot get around the fact that the calculus does not in any sense determine hu-man action. What is the significance then of marginal-utility theory, understood as a theory of calculated action? It means that this theory does not apply to just any human behavior, but only to those actions that would be observed if the acting per-son strictly followed the results of the utility calculus. From this point of view, therefore, economics does not deal with hu-man action *per se*, but only with *one aspect* of human action— "rational" or "logical" action. (p. xxvi)

Hülsmann points out that both Wieser and Pareto adopted this position.

Hülsmann seems to me exactly on target here. I should like in this connec-tion to call attention to a crucial, but little noticed, passage in *Human Action*:

> The attempt has been made to attain the notion of a nonra-tional action by this reasoning: If *a* is preferred to *b* and *b* to *c*, logically *a* should be preferred to *c*. But if actually *c* is preferred to *a*, we are faced with a mode of acting to which we cannot as-cribe consistency and rationality. This reasoning disregards the fact that two acts of an individual can never be synchronous. (*Human Action, Scholar's Edition*, p. 103)

Just as Hülsmann has indicated, Mises repudiates a basic assumption used by economists who endeavor to construct a value calculus.

But have we met the objection raised earlier? Once again, is not the ques-tion of whether economic theory governs all human action, or only a more narrowly delimited class of rational action, exactly the sort of desiccated abstraction that repels many potential readers of Mises?

Not at all. Suppose that, contrary to Mises, value calculation was possible. Then, one might attempt to determine an "efficient" scheme of production and distribution in entire independence of the market. In like fashion, the results obtained on the free market could be tested against the standards derived by value calculations. The market might be "weighed, and found wanting in the balance."

For Mises, all this is impossible. Economic calculation arises only with monetary prices, and these can exist only in a market economy.

> Money... thus becomes an indispensable mental prerequisite of any action that undertakes to conduct relatively long-range processes of production. Without the aid of monetary calculation, bookkeeping, and the computation of profit and loss in terms of money, technology would have had to confine itself to the simplest, and therefore the least productive, methods. (p. 166)

Mises goes so far as to call this emphasis on monetary calculation

> the most important discovery made by economic theory. Its practical significance can scarcely be overestimated. It alone gives us the basis for pronouncing a final judgment on all kinds of socialism, communism, and planned economies. (p. 166)

Thus a seemingly abstract point lies at the heart of an issue of the utmost practical importance. Can socialists escape the force Mises's contention that calculation in values is impossible? Their only hope is to acknowledge that economic calculation requires prices but go on to claim that a socialist system can generate them. Elsewhere in his work, Mises readily showed the futility of these claims.*

He steers carefully between Scylla and Charybdis, in order to maintain his view that economics is a science that applies to all human action. . . . Against the classical economists of the nineteenth century, who largely confined economics to actions motivated by monetary gain, Mises contended that all action, whether or not motivated by the hope of maximizing monetary

---

* See especially *Human Action*, (Ludwig von Mises Institute, 1998), pp.701-711.

income, shares a common structure. But against some of his fellow supporters of the subjective theory of value, he denied that economics studies only a delimited class of rational actions, governed by a value calculus.

Mises treats with scorn those who presumed to reject the teachings of his general science of action. Alfred Vierkandt, a once-prominent German sociologist, denied that human beings always aim to maximize their welfare, as they understand it. This view was nothing more than an individualistic fallacy. Instead, people frequently acted instinctively, in ways that subordinated their selfish concerns to the good of society.

One such "innate social propensity," Vierkandt tells us, is the instinct of subordination. Animals already manifest this tendency, as in the loyalty and obedience a dog displays for his master. Mises remarks:

> we do not doubt that he [Vierkandt] has really experienced all this. Indeed, we shall go still further and not deny his qualifications to speak from direct personal experience about the "truly human inner devotion of the dog to his master." (p. 58)

Mises did not frequently display his talent as a satirist; and I shall end with another aspect of his work that he usually kept below the surface. Mises was a scholar of great learning, but he did not put his erudition on display. In one passing remark, though, he shows his level of knowledge:

> Gresham's law—which, incidentally, was referred to by Aristophanes in the *Frogs*, and clearly enunciated by Nicolaus Oresmius (1364), and not until 1858 named after Sir Thomas Gresham by Macleod—is a special application of the general theory of price controls to monetary relations. (p. 93)

A Poverty of Reason: Sustainable Development and Economic Growth*†

WILFRED BECKERMAN

Do Future Generations Have Rights?

October 1, 2003, *Mises Review*

WILFRED BECKERMAN IS an outstanding economist of a type probably more common in Britain than America. Like Anthony de Jasay, Amartya Sen, and I. M. D. Little, Beckerman is thoroughly at home in philosophy; and in *A Poverty of Reason*, he makes insightful remarks about the rights of future generations, equality, and the so-called "precautionary principle."

Some environmentalists are outright enemies of humanity, who favor a drastic reduction in human population, if not the elimination altogether of our species. Once at a conference, I was seated at dinner next to that eminent Luddite, Kirkpatrick Sale. I mentioned that a critic had accused him of wishing to return to the Stone Age. To my surprise, he said that this was just what he wanted.

More moderate environmentalists do not propose to crawl on all fours, and Beckerman here analyzes the views of those who seek the seemingly

---

* The Independent Institute, 2002.

† I cite the title as it is given on the cover. The title page omits "and Economic Growth."

reasonable goal of "sustainable development." They do not propose to do away with economic growth altogether; but must not the rights of future generations be guaranteed? We must leave to them an environment at least as good as that which we have enjoyed. In particular, we must make sure that vital resources remain available, act to contain global warming, and endeavor to prevent "biodiversity" from unacceptable reduction.

But will not the free market take care of all such issues? Owners of private property have every incentive to conserve their resources rather than squander them for immediate gain. Further, most people wish to provide for their children; insuring the welfare of future generations requires no collective action beyond this.

For proponents of sustainable development, the free market is not enough. People will indeed endeavor to conserve what they own; but they will do so guided by an economic principle. For actors on the market, maximizing expected utility is the be-all and end-all.

Is this not unfair to future generations? People will make provision for their children and grandchildren but will rarely seek to conserve their resources beyond what is needed to do this. So long as people can leave something to their heirs, the pursuit of profit will impel them to wasteful use of scarce resources. Must not the government protect the rights of future generations, in order to prevent this catastrophe?

Beckerman identifies a fundamental failing in this line of thought. Let us grant that the present generation ought not to squander all its resources and leave nothing for distant future generations. It does not follow that these future generations have an enforceable right that resources be conserved at a certain rate. To introduce here the language of rights, our author maintains, is to assume without basis that whatever moral claims future generations have on the present bind us absolutely, or close to it. Why not instead view obligations to the future as one item to be weighed against other things?

Our author goes further. He maintains that ascribing rights to those who do not yet exist makes no sense.

> More generally it is difficult to see how future generations can be said to have any rights because properties, such as being green or wealthy or having rights, can be predicated only of some subject that exists. . . . If I were to say "X has a fantastic collection of CDs," and you were to ask me who is X, and I were to reply,

"Well actually, there isn't any X," you would think I had taken leave of my senses. And you would be right . . . unborn people cannot have anything. They cannot have two legs or long hair or a taste for Mozart. (pp. 67–68)*

One might object,

Is not Beckerman simply playing with words? Let us grant him his point: might we still not have a binding moral obligation to preserve a sustainable environment for future generations? Where has his semantic wordplay gotten him?

We can, as the objection supposes, speak of binding moral obligations without reference to rights, but Beckerman's point nevertheless helps us grasp an essential issue. The language of rights at once takes us into the realm of absolute claims; and if we grasp that we need not—or cannot, if Beckerman is right—ascribe rights to future generations, we can begin to think clearly about our obligations to them. Beckerman has freed us from the prison of a false assumption.

Beckerman's point about rights can be used, in a way that he does not consider, to strengthen his case against sustainability advocates. Future persons may not have rights, but presently existing people do have them. If so, then efforts by even moderate environmentalists to restrict property rights may be illegitimate on their face. Beckerman very effectively demonstrates that environmentalist arguments fail on their own terms. But even if these arguments were cogent, this would not suffice to justify compelling property owners to restrict their consumption. The issue of rights would first have to be addressed.

Beckerman has exposed a hidden assumption that lies behind the environmentalist case, but this is not his greatest contribution. He challenges head-on a key premise of much contemporary moral philosophy. The sustainability advocates maintain that each future generation should be provided with an equally good environment to the one we now have. With great daring, Beckerman asks, what is so good about equality?

---

* But past people do not now exist, but you can violate the rights of someone now dead. Suppose, e.g., that you dispose of someone's estate contrary to the directions of his will: have you not violated his rights? Beckerman seems to me on the correct lines, but his argument needs more careful statement than he gives it here.

Arguments for equality often hide behind feelings of sympathy many people have for the impoverished. Environmentalists paint a bleak picture of a future in which essential fuels are exhausted and people confront catastrophically high temperatures. Is it not unfair, they inquire, to subject people to such conditions?

If it is unfair, what is wrong is that people should not be subjected to bad conditions: equality has nothing to do with the case. Harry Frankfurt has brilliantly elucidated the essential point:

> The egalitarian condemnation of inequality as inherently bad loses much of its force ... when we recognize that those who are doing worse than others may nevertheless be doing rather well ... what is of genuine moral concern is whether people have good lives, and not how their lives compare with the lives of others. (pp. 72–73)

Beckerman applies this fundamental insight to sustainability, with devastating results. So long as those in future generations are expected to prosper, why does it matter morally if their environment is not in all respects equally good with our own?

If we nevertheless insist on equality, matters take a surprising turn. Those who will live in the future are likely to benefit from continued economic growth. If they turn out to be more prosperous than we, do they not, by the criterion of equality, owe us recompense for their superior good fortune? Of course, they cannot pay us, since they do not now exist. But we can do our best to achieve equality by refusing to conserve our resources. The poorer environment that results for our successors balances their superior prosperity and thus helps to achieve equality.

Beckerman states the reductio in this way:

> But suppose future generations were expected to be richer than we are for reasons that are outside our control. ... But if we regard natural inequalities as unjust, we would be morally obliged to take some action ... to reduce our poverty compared with future generations by, say, slowing down future growth (e.g., by investing less or using up more of the earth's supposedly scarce resources). (p. 71)

Beckerman's argument reduces to ruins the case for sustainable development, since this is based precisely on the claim that future generations are entitled to an equally good environment to our own. But what if environmentalists, chastened by Beckerman's attack, withdraw to less demanding claims? Even if future generations are not entitled to an equal environment, is it not common sense to conserve scarce fuels and counteract global warming?

Our author addresses these issues in detail, but I should like instead to look at another fundamental point he raises that applies more generally. Many environmentalists show themselves well aware of the fact that their predictions of disaster are controversial. But they claim to have an argument that their pessimistic views should prevail. If the optimists are in the right, and we follow their advice, we shall have somewhat higher growth rates than otherwise. But if the environmentalists are right, and we ignore them, disaster threatens. Should we not then err on their side?

This is the so-called precautionary principle: "Where there are threats of serious or irreversible damage, lack of full scientific certainty should not be used as a reason for postponing measures to prevent environmental degradation" (p. 41, quoting a Ministerial Declaration of the UN Economic Conference for Europe).

To pose the issue this way, Beckerman shows, rests on a false assumption. Why must the decision be made immediately? If "scientific certainty" is not available, why not wait until we have a clearer idea of what will happen? Why now install costly measures designed to curb global warming, if in a few years we may find out that our efforts are futile or that global warming is not so bad?

> To think that possible environmental disaster requires immediate response is falsely to assume that we risk disaster by waiting for a short time before acting. But this does not follow, even if the environmentalists turn out to be right in their predictions. So far as climate change is concerned, "delaying action by several years makes a negligible difference" (p. 47).

But what happens if we allow for this point? Suppose, e.g., that after several further years of research, we still face conflicting views about global warming. Should we then follow the pessimists, lest catastrophe follow?

Not necessarily. Beckerman points out that the principle of avoiding disaster can be carried too far. We should indeed be cautious, but the benefits of economic development should never be ignored. The precautionary principle

> is just a pompous way of saying that one should consider the case for making some investments now in order to minimize

the danger of some unpleasant event taking place later. But no-body in their senses would make investments to avoid every re-mote possibility since that would leave precious little time for the enjoyment of life. (pp. 44–45)

I have stressed in this review general principles rather than the particular details of Beckerman's analysis of fuels, climate change, and biodiversity. I am happy to assure readers that he finds little cause for alarm in any of these areas.

In Defense of Globalization[*]
&
Free Trade Today[†]

Jagdish Bhagwati

A Reluctant Purist

July 1, 2004, *Mises Review*

NEOCLASSICAL ECONOMISTS often make matters more complicated than necessary; but, fortunately, the best of them manage to stumble close to the truth. Jagdish Bhagwati is by no means a committed supporter of the free market. For him, restrictions on the right of labor unions to strike are little better than slavery. Further, he began his career as an international trade theorist by devising models in which free trade was not the best policy. Nonetheless, he has worked his way to becoming a committed supporter of free trade; and, in the two books we have here to consider, he refutes a large number of fallacious arguments in favor of trade restrictions.

The *prima facie* case for free trade is straightforward: is it not vastly more productive to specialize in one's best products, and then exchange with the specialties of others, than to try to produce everything for oneself? The argument does not differ whether we take individuals or countries as the trading partners.

---

[*] Oxford University Press, 2004.

[†] Princeton University Press, 2002.

Further, both partners can benefit from trade even if one of them is better than the other in producing every good exchanged. As David Ricardo argued, it is to the advantage of the nation more efficient in producing all goods to concentrate in the area its edge is greatest. The poorer producer will then specialize in the product at which it is least bad, i.e., where it has a comparative advantage.

As our author notes, many people find this elementary truth hard to grasp.

> When asked by the mathematician Stanislaw Ulam . . . which proposition in the social sciences was the most counterintuitive yet compelling, Paul Samuelson chose the law of comparative advantage. . . . Most people think it intuitively sound that you should do most things that you do better than others, not specialize. (*Free Trade*, p. 5)

Austrians find this truth very easy to grasp, and Mises extended Ricardo's principle into a general law of association. But neoclassicals are not so easily satisfied. Although Bhagwati accepts the general purport of Ricardo's results, he tells us that "the analytically satisfactory proofs of free trade that we modern economists demand are the handiwork of theorists working in the twentieth century" (*Free Trade*, p. 4).*

Why are Bhagwati and his fellow neoclassicals so demanding? For Austrians, the market as actually created by producers and consumers suffices: not so for neoclassicals. Let the slightest hint of "monopoly," by their definitions, arise, and they are overcome with anguish. The conditions for efficiency set forward in their models are not perfectly fulfilled; we have, then, a case of "market failure" and the benign state must step in to secure an optimal outcome.

Such reasoning did not await the twentieth century. Thus, Robert Torrens opposed Sir Robert Peel's call to end the Corn Laws. Because of British monopoly power in trade of the goods concerned, an optimal tariff would

---

* Bhagwati is a trade theorist of international standing; but he never mentions the argument, claimed by Paul Craig Roberts to be at the heart of international trade theory, that Ricardo's law shows that free trade is advantageous only if capital goods are immobile. Small wonder, as Roberts's claim is false. The law is indeed dependent on the restriction Roberts mentions, but it hardly follows that free trade is advantageous only if one trading partner has an absolute advantage in all goods traded, the condition in which Ricardo's law applies. If factors of production move to where they have an absolute advantage, will not mutually advantageous trade take place in accord with the new conditions?

excel in efficiency, the results of full free trade. Again, John Stuart Mill used another instance of "market failure" to justify tariffs. Do not infant industries constitute an exception to the generally desirable rule of free trade? (To my surprise, Bhagwati accepts Mill's argument as theoretically sound. I should have thought the analysis by Mises in *Human Action* [*Scholar's Edition*, pp. 505–507] tells decisively the contrary.)

Austrians, who reject the neoclassical view of market failure, find it easy to dismiss arguments that presuppose what they reject; but Bhagwati's work has great value for those who prefer to take matters the hard way.* He shows that even if one accepts the neoclassical view, free trade is usually the order of the day.

He raises three principal points that radically reduce the cases in which deviations from free trade count as efficient, on the neoclassical view. First, various models may show that free trade is not perfectly efficient; but the question then arises, how much do these deviations matter? Such questions arouse our high-powered neoclassicals to furious calculations; and it transpires that often the efforts to "correct" the market cost more than they are worth.

> As it happens, the younger free trade theorists of imperfect competition in product markets ... came back to free trade precisely on the ground that the gains to be had from pursuing a policy of optimal departures from free trade in industries characterized by imperfect competition were not large enough to justify intervention. (*Free Trade*, p. 30)

The next point I shall pass over briefly, since readers of this journal will I suspect find it of little interest. Cases in which domestic problems allegedly dictate a departure from free trade are often better handled by a different measure of government interference that preserves free trade. Keynes once suggested that tariffs are desirable in cases of mass unemployment; why not instead leave trade free and increase aggregate demand directly? Concerning this, I can only echo Lincoln: "If you like this sort of thing, this is the sort of thing you'll like."

Bhagwati's last point seems to me much more significant. If tariffs and other trade restrictions are imposed, people trying to divert these gains to

---

* In addition to the standard Austrian literature, Joseph Schumpeter, *Capitalism, Socialism, and Democracy* (Harper, 1942) gives an immensely valuable criticism of the standard analysis of monopoly and competition.

themselves may spend immense resources. Such resources make no apparent contribution to production. Bhagwati anxiously forestalls readers inclined to see this as a case of rent seeking: what we have here, he assures us, is directly unproductive profit seeking, a concept of his own devising that is entirely different. Bhagwati is not afflicted by the vice of false modesty; and, I regret to say, he is always alert to stress his own importance, though in an amiable way. Those who do not share our author's investment in his own reputation may find the two ideas hard to distinguish.

Be that as it may, the important issue is this. Such rent seeking, or unproductive profit seeking, may be so extensive as to rule out tariffs as a measure of efficient economic policy. Anne Krueger estimated that these expenditures for Turkey were "of the order of 40 percent of GNP" (*Free Trade*, p. 40).

If Bhagwati is right, neoclassicals can in good conscience embrace free trade. Well and good, but what about the rest of us? Why should those not beguiled by neoclassical siren songs be interested in Bhagwati's books? Our author has a ready answer. He analyzes a large number of objections to free trade, and his responses to these, and his various illuminating remarks on related subjects, usually do not depend on controversial neoclassical assumptions.

A common objection to free trade rests on an undeniable fact. In the free market, every exchange takes place because all the parties involved expect to benefit; but it by no means follows that everything that happens in the market benefits everybody. If lower prices by the restaurant across the street put your establishment out of business, you have certainly not gained.

If so, are not proofs of the market's efficiency of limited value? Will it help American workers sent into unemployment or reduced to penury by low wage competition from abroad to be told that the overall efficiency of the world's economy has risen? The Stolper-Samuelson theorem offers a proof that under certain conditions, the low wages of foreign workers can indeed drive down domestic wages.

Bhagwati maintains that this line of thought fails to fit reality, so far as America is concerned. The effect in question requires that the goods that undercut high American wages be labor intensive. Foreign competition that drives American firms out of business for other reasons, such as technological superiority, is not here in point. But imported labor-intensive goods will lower domestic wages only if their relative prices fall; otherwise, there is no increased pressure on the wages of those who produce competing American goods.

Thus the key issue is whether the prices of such goods have actually been falling, triggering the declining real wages. Here the evidence does not support the assertion. During the 1980s, when the real wages of American workers were stagnant, the prices of the labor-intensive goods as a group actually rose relative to the prices of the set of all goods in world trade. (*Globalization*, p. 124)

Sometimes opponents of free trade raise a different sort of objection. Here what concerns them is not the plight of workers in rich countries. Quite the contrary, it is alleged that free trade is part of a strategy by predatory multinational corporations to exploit the Third World. Do not these companies make enormous profits by paying a pittance to the impoverished denizens of the Third World?

Bhagwati replies with a point that is no less effective because it is obvious. If workers accept what we regard as extremely low wages, they must regard these wages as improvements.

[S]everal empirical studies do find that multinationals pay what economists now call a "wage premium"; they pay an average wage that exceeds the going rate, mostly up to 10 percent and exceeding it in some cases, with affiliates of US multinationals sometimes paying a premium that ranges from 40 to 100 percent. (*Globalization*, p. 172)

Those who find convincing the case for free trade must avoid a pitfall that our alert author, like Lew Rockwell in *Speaking of Liberty*, is careful to emphasize. The advantages of free trade stem from the genuine article, not counterfeits that claim the name of freedom. In particular, so-called free-trade areas are not at all what supporters of free enterprise should want. As

the great economist Jacob Viner pointed out ... free trade areas (FTAs) are not free trade. While they remove tariffs for member countries, they also increase the handicap (for any given external tariff) that nonmembers suffer vis-à-vis member-country producers in the markets of the member countries, implying therefore protection against them. (*Free Trade*, p. 107)

Does not this consideration vindicate free trade opponents of NAFTA?

In Praise of Empires: Globalization and Order*

Deepak Lal

Trade and the Iron Hand

December 1, 2004, *Mises Review*

Deepak Lal writes as a convinced advocate of American Empire. But in the course of the book, he undermines his own reasons for defending imperialism and offers a devastating criticism of democratic imperialism and of Woodrow Wilson's Utopianism.

Lal's basic argument for empire is straightforward: International trade is essential to prosperity. But given a high degree of disorder, large scale trade cannot occur, or at least will be greatly impeded. Throughout history, empires have been the main means by which order has been preserved and trade promoted: "By creating order over a large economic space, empires have inevitably generated [Adam] Smithian intensive growth" (p. 43).

Applied to the present, Lal's argument becomes this: International trade requires an imperial power. Only the United States has the resources to maintain hegemonic control. Therefore, the United States ought to exercise imperial power.

Lal attempts to refute in advance an obvious counterargument. What about the evils of empire? Have not many empires tyrannized and exploited those whom they have conquered? Even if Lal is right about the benefits of empire, must not its costs be set against these?

---

* Palgrave, 2004.

Lal responds by distinguishing two kinds of empire. Good empires are what Michael Oakeshott calls civil associations. They are content to preserve order. The bad empires are, in Oakeshott's terms, enterprise associations. Here,

> the state is seen as the manager of an enterprise seeking to use the law for its own substantive purposes and, in particular, for the legislation of morality. . . . Most of the empires which have been regarded as evil fall into the latter [enterprise] category. (pp. 41, 43)

An empire, then, can be a force for good, so long as it avoids moralizing. Should we, as Lal wishes, support non-moralizing American imperialism?

His arguments strike me as entirely unconvincing. First, though he touts the benefits of empire for trade and economic growth, he is constrained to admit that the greatest period of economic growth in world history did not occur under the aegis of an empire. "Promethean intensive growth remains a European miracle of the anarchical systems of nation-states established after the breakdown of the Roman empire" (p. 43). Does this not give us some reason to question Lal's claim that empire is needed to promote world trade?

Lal has ready his response. He says: "But as I have argued in detail elsewhere, it is incorrect to infer that it was this anarchy which caused the miracle" (p. 43). Suppose that Lal is right: so what? It is still not the case that empire is needed for trade and growth.

Our author's case for American empire fares no better when we turn for this general claim to his specific assessment of present dangers that call for American action. He fears two sources of world disorder: failed states in Africa and Islamic aggression and terrorism.

The first of these may be readily set aside. The African nations are weak and do not account for a significant part of either world or American trade. Lal, incredibly, acknowledges this but finds it a cause for regret: if only Africa posed a threat to us so that we could give it the "basic order" it needs. "But (sadly)[!] with the ending of the Cold War, Africa does not represent a strategic challenge to the United States or any of the potential great powers" (p. 84).

Professor Lal possesses an enviable knowledge of his adopted American society, but evidently he has not come across the adage that warns us not to buy trouble. Even he admits, though, that

> the best policy toward Africa, if direct imperialism is ruled out as being too costly, is to keep markets for African goods and

capital flows to Africa open, and leave it to the Africans to sort
out their own problems. (p. 85)

Lal's real concerns lie elsewhere. Must we not act as an imperial power in
order to contain Islamic terrorism? Must we not realize "the obsolescence
of the view still being peddled by isolationists such as Pat Buchanan and
expressed in the title of his recent book, *A Republic, Not an Empire?*" (p. 55).

Lal may choose to mock Jeffersonians who hope that the American empire
will go away, but his own comments on the Islamic danger show, contrary to
his intent, that nonintervention is far better for us and the rest of the world
than empire. He finds the major threat from Islam to come from a particular
variety of that religion, Wahabism:

> The Saudis have directly and indirectly funded the mosques and
> madrasas which preach hatred against the infidels—Jews, Chris-
> tians, and above all Hindus—to young minds. . . . But for the
> Saudis to eschew or put a stop to this funding would undoubt-
> edly create a Wahabi backlash in Saudi Arabia and end the dy-
> nasty. . . . For the rest of the world, the poison being spread by
> this Wahabi evangelism is becoming intolerable. . . . If there is
> to be an end to the "war on terror," this poisoning of the Mus-
> lim mind clearly has to stop. (p. 97)

Has not Lal here given us an excellent argument to cease our aid to Saudi
Arabia? Why support a regime that sponsors a religious ideology of this
kind? Further, as Lal himself recognizes, "one of Osama bin Laden's osten-
sible reasons for his jihad was the presence of Americans in the kingdom
[Saudi Arabia] housing Islam's holiest shrines" (p. 200). Does this not give
us an even stronger reason to leave the area forthwith?

Lal himself feels the force of these considerations, but his imperialist ideology prevents him from urging the course of reason—immediate and total
withdrawal. In his view, we should reduce our ties to the Saudi monarchy,
but only after conquering Iraq. In that way, we can secure a source of oil independent of Saudi Arabia. Did it ever occur to Lal that the Iraqis might have
been happy to sell us oil, were we to have ended the inhumane and ineffective blockade against them?

Lal inadvertently provides another reason we should reject the imperialist
program he favors. He warns us against trying to impose our own system of

values and beliefs on foreign countries. In his view, terrorists are apt to be educated young men with some exposure to Western education. They cannot cope with the Western challenges to their accustomed Islamic way of life. In particular, Western sexual freedom puts them under intolerable pressure, and they lash out in fury against us. In our imperialist endeavors, Lal warns, we must keep intact the prevailing morality lest the terrorists rise against us more than they have already done. He condemns those who urge that we impose democracy and Western values on this region. To do so will lead to disaster; Lal's favored imperialism resolutely avoids such meddling. Would it not be simpler to stay out of their way altogether? Lal promotes imperialism as a means to counter terror; but it seems that without an interventionist policy, we would not have to confront a terrorist threat.

In economic matters, Lal is a firm supporter of the free market; and he develops a model of the state as predator that could be taken from Franz Oppenheimer and Albert Jay Nock. Yet this state skeptic wishes the American state to assume a gigantic burden. We must, as an example, solve the Arab-Israeli conflict and impose a peace settlement on the Middle East.

> The primary task of a Pax Americana must be to find ways to create a new order in the Middle East. . . . Far from being objectionable, imperialism is precisely what is needed to restore order in the Middle East. . . . The purpose of the American imperium would be to maintain the threat or actual use of force to prevent any international disorder arising from the region. Additionally, some way has to be found for maintaining domestic order in the states in the region. (pp. 99–100)

Lal devotes some attention to arguing that the United States has the material resources to carry out the program he suggests.* He never asks why we should trust the state to limit itself to the benevolent program he envisions.

How can someone of Lal's undoubted intelligence fail to see these obvious problems? I should like to offer a suggestion that can be no more than highly speculative. Lal, though he teaches in America and has strong ties to England, remains at heart a committed Indian nationalist. Hence his surprising remark, earlier quoted, that Wahabi Islam is a threat "above all" to Hindus. The United States need not be seriously menaced by Islamic terrorism unless,

---

* For a very different view, see Michael Mann, *Incoherent Empire* (Verso, 2003).

by intervention in the Middle East we embroil ourselves in matters that do not really concern us. India is not so fortunate. Many Muslims in Pakistan and India itself wish to reconstitute India as a Muslim theocracy and are not averse to using violence to achieve their goals. Hence Lal's alarm over Saudi financing of Wahabi Islamic schools in Pakistan. Further, if America follows an imperial course, Lal looks forward to a commanding role for cosmopolitans such as himself:

> Moreover, the United States and many other countries are recognizing dual citizenship.... With the growth of a cosmopolitan class ... of primarily US trained technicians and executives at work in many different countries, the core of a global "Roman" political and economic elite—open to the talents of all—already exists. It could run this new US imperium. (pp. 74–75)

A book by Deepak Lal cannot be wholly bad. While defending his own version of imperialism, Lal is anxious to refute competing programs of American world meddling. His criticism of Wilsonianism rewards close study. Wilson sought to achieve a Utopia, in which all nations would adhere strictly to moral principles. National interest as a guide to policy was outdated; instead, "the instrument for achieving this Utopia was to be the League of Nations, which would ensure collective security by bringing transgressors of the new order into line through sanctions" (p. 56). Lal raises a simple but decisive objection to this program: economic sanctions do not work. "These sanctions, as the 1990 detailed study by Gary Hufbauer and his associates shows, have been ineffective and inefficient in serving foreign policy goals" (p. 58, citing G. Hufbauer et al., *Economic Sanctions Revisited*, 1990).

Lal cites a little-known comment by Wilson, written in 1886, that tells us all we need to know about the aims of that pretentious busybody: "For it is very clear that in fundamental theory socialism and democracy are almost if not quite one and the same" (p. 226). We can now better understand what Wilson meant when he said, "The world must be made safe for democracy."

Lal is an excellent economist, and when he confines himself to issues that affect economic development, he has a great deal to offer. In a brief but brilliant account of global warming, he notes that scientists, such as Stephen Schneider, who advance alarmist models to justify government interference with the free market "openly admitted they were creating alarm about a phenomenon which they themselves recognized was highly speculative" (p. 149).

But do not the alarmists have a point? If we follow their advice and restrict economic development, what is the worst that can happen? We will not be as prosperous as we otherwise might have been, and we will have taken precautions against an imaginary danger. If they are right, we have averted disaster. Is it not better to be safe than sorry? Lal, here following Julian Simon, uncovers a fatal flaw in this reasoning. Economic growth tends to increase population; a restrictive environmentalist policy means that population will be less. Must not the interests of those people prevented from coming into existence be taken into account, when the costs of restricting the market are assessed? "[Paul] Ehrlich [an extreme environmentalist] bets what he thinks will be the economic gains that we and our descendants might enjoy against the unborn's very lives" (p. 151, quoting Simon).

The Abolition of Antitrust[*]

Edited by

GARY HULL

Competition Can't Be Planned

October 1, 2005, *Mises Review*

THE AUTHORS OF THIS IMPORTANT BOOK have undertaken a two-fold task. They continue the free-market criticism of antitrust legislation by Dominick Armentano and other economists who defend laissez-faire. Armentano himself has an excellent article here; and Thomas Bowden and Eric Daniels contribute outstanding discussions of the legal and historical background of antitrust.

But the authors have in mind a more ambitious and original goal. Economic and legal arguments against antitrust, they contend, do not suffice: we must penetrate to the philosophically flawed essence of antitrust in order fully to uproot this misbegotten product of modern interventionism. To accomplish this ambitious goal, we must of course think from the standpoint of a sound philosophy; and this, in the opinion of our authors, is Objectivism.[†]

Proponents of antitrust maintain that monopoly prices impose a welfare loss on the economy. Murray Rothbard, the most far-reaching of all critics of the economic theory of monopoly, explains the standard view in this way:

> A certain quantity of a good, when produced and sold, yields
> a *competitive price* on the market. A monopolist or a cartel of

---

[*] Transaction Publishers, 2005.

[†] I do not know the philosophical views of Professor Armentano, but all of the other contributors are Objectivists.

> firms can, *if the demand curve is inelastic at the competitive-price point*, restrict sales and raise the price, to arrive at the point of maximum returns. (*Man, Economy, and State, Scholar's Edition*, [Mises Institute, 2004], p. 672)

Unfortunately, none of the contributors cite Rothbard's work.

Suppose the standard view were correct; and suppose further that the higher price imposes a welfare loss on society. Harry Binswanger raises a fundamental point:

> The owners [of a firm] have the inalienable right to decide how they will use and dispose of the firm's product. They may charge nothing for the product, a billion dollars for it, or anything in between. . . . It is *their* product, just as the customer's money is his. (p. 132)

As Binswanger rightly notes, antitrust advocates act with particular ill grace when they assail the prices charged by monopolists who introduce altogether new products. Rather than praise innovators for their efforts to satisfy consumers in radically new ways, these carping critics indict them for deviations from what they deem the socially correct price.

But Binswanger's argument, as it stands, is not complete. If the monopolist holds legitimate title to his property, then Binswanger's point hits home: why should he not be free to seek whatever price he can get? But under what conditions does one acquire property? Binswanger does not tell us; and I do not think that Objectivists of his school have given a satisfactory account of this issue. Absent such an account, a defender of antitrust can say to Binswanger: "I grant you that an owner of property can ask whatever prices he wishes for what he owns. But, in my view, capitalists are not 'owners' in the sense you suggest."

Unclarity about property rights also weakens the force of the claim that antitrust theory rests on the false philosophical doctrine of altruism. If capitalists are required to price their products according to the dictates of a certain welfare ideal, has not altruism supplanted individualism? Why must the businessman sacrifice his own interests for those of others?

> Thus, on the premise of altruism, businessmen are extortionists: businessmen charge money for relinquishing possession of goods, but these goods, altruism holds, rightfully belong to those who hold or need them. . . . The moral theory of altruism

results in an inverted version of property rights: ownership by means of non-production. (p. 139)

This argument strikes me as confused. An altruist would contend that the businessman must sacrifice his own property to others. But do not advocates of antitrust contend rather that individuals can acquire property only subject to certain limitations? They do not then say that businessmen should altruistically give up what they own. Binswanger might respond that only an altruist could hold such a view of property rights, but this is not so. Those who contend that "society" owns all resources are to my mind profoundly mistaken. But to adopt the views of, e.g., Henry George or Hillel Steiner on property acquisition does not make one an altruist.*

John Ridpath endeavors to show the philosophical mistakes involved in Frank Knight's view of economics. Knight in *Risk, Uncertainty, and Profit* developed the model of perfect competition that, Ridpath holds, underlies modern antitrust policy; if so, a convincing attack on Knight strikes a decisive blow to antitrust. Ridpath's efforts are not altogether a success. Under perfect competition, all firms in an industry have the same costs, and everyone has full knowledge of all relevant information. Ridpath objects:

> The basic fact of reality is that everything that exists has an identity—everything, including human knowledge, is specific and finite. A world of undifferentiated products, traded by infinitely numerous and infinitely knowledgeable beings, is metaphysically impossible. (p. 19)

But surely the postulate of the perfect competition model is that firms have very specific knowledge, i.e., whatever they need to know to make judgments about price and cost. Their knowledge is hardly infinite in any questionable sense. Ridpath, though, may also have in mind another objection. How can two different firms be identical in all their attributes? Does not Leibniz's Law tell us that entities with the same attributes are identical? Here once more the argument relies on a false assumption. Only in certain relevant respects are the firms under perfect competition the same: so long as, e.g., a different person owns each firm, the appeal to Leibniz's Law is unavailing.

---

* See my discussion of the "left libertarianism" of Michael Otsuka, *Libertarianism Without Inequality*, found in Volume 2, "Political Theory."

Knight famously argued that profit depends on uncertainty: the entrepreneur cannot calculate in advance the chances his investment will be successful. By "profit" he of course meant a return that exceeds the rate of return on capital, i.e., the rate of interest. Knight here is making a very similar point to that stressed by these Objectivist authors themselves. Businessmen are creative, and it is this that accounts for their ability to earn profits.

> As was the case with earlier market leaders—Ford, Alcoa, Kodak, Xerox, and IBM—Microsoft *earned* its position of leadership. All of these companies were not just market leaders: they were *market creators*. . . . The market creator provides a practical demonstration of the value and salability of a new product. (p. 134)

Ridpath ascribes this perfectly true claim to Knight's irrationalism. Knight was a philosophical disciple of Heraclitus and Henri Bergson; as such, he held that change could not be explained.

> In the world of perfect competition, the "pure" profits earned by entrepreneurs would not exist. Knight concluded that these profits must have their source in Heraclitean uncertainty. Profits, which in fact are the earned reward for intelligently and courageously producing material values, are to Knight nothing more than manna randomly sprinkled by the unknowable flux and human irrationality. (p. 23)

The fact that entrepreneurial gain cannot be calculated in advance is a perfectly ordinary truth of experience; it does not depend on controversial philosophical views. Ridpath is right that, on Knight's view, there is a type of change, which Knight calls "Bergsonian," that cannot be rationally explained (p. 21). It hardly follows from this, though, that Knight thought that no change whatever can be explained. It also does not follow from Knight's reference to Bergsonian change that he was a disciple of Bergson, who was, by the way, as much a twentieth-century philosopher as a "nineteenth-century Heraclitean" (p. 21).

Much more successful are the essays in Part II, "The Legal History of Antitrust." Thomas A. Bowden maintains that the progress of civilization depends on the extension of contract.

> Contract law, then, aims not at benefiting a privileged economic class but at supplying an objective requirement of life in civilized

society. Because the ability to make contracts serves man's basic
economic needs, the wider the scope of contract, the greater will
be the potential for individuals to grow and prosper. (p. 103)

During the nineteenth century, the development of contract took giant
steps forward.

The great, largely unrecognized achievement of nineteenth century lawmakers was to take the broad, general structure of government handed down to them by the Founding Fathers and
translate it into a capitalist legal system, with freedom of contract as its keystone. (p. 107)

This happy tale came to an "abrupt end" once antitrust legislation began
to be enacted in the 1890s. No longer could firms make contracts as they
wished. If, e.g., a company wanted to guarantee price discounts to regular
customers, it might find that antitrust laws barred the way. Its discounts
might constitute unacceptable "price discrimination."

Bowden's argument must face an objection, but to this he has an insightful response. All contracts take place within a certain legal framework
that defines property rights. If I steal your copy of *Atlas Shrugged* and
trade it for a copy of Lou Thesz's autobiography, I cannot complain that
when the law refuses to recognize my exchange, it has restricted my freedom of contract. In like fashion, why cannot defenders of antitrust claim
that they are specifying property rights, rather than destroying freedom
of contract?

But in a legal framework that allows freedom of contract, people must
have a clear idea of what actions fall within their legal powers. Here precisely lies the failing of antitrust legislation. Virtually any action of a business
stands subject to condemnation as "restraint of trade"; any contract may be
without notice overturned by a court or administrative tribunal. "Because
antitrust laws can be employed arbitrarily to outlaw any type of contract,
parties to an agreement cannot know *in advance* whether their actions will
be deemed legal or illegal" (p. 111).

Bowden emphasizes the role of freedom of contract in American legal history; and Eric Daniels in his excellent "Reversing Course: American Attitudes
about Monopolies, 1607–1890" discusses a closely related theme. Following
English legal precedent, Americans in the eighteenth and early nineteenth

centuries saw monopoly as a government grant of privilege, and a movement against such grants found considerable support in the courts.

But

> [b]eginning in the 1790s, pro-monopoly politicians exhibited a deep-seated belief that certain businesses—banking, canals, roads, harbors, schools, even manufacturing and industrial concerns—were inherently different from others because of their public character. (p. 75)

Unfortunately, the courts also took up this doctrine, and the distinction between coercive monopolies and voluntary business activities was attenuated. With *Munn v. Illinois* (1876), disaster struck. Here the Supreme Court held that states could regulate any business where the public claims an interest.

> On this standard, no business could possibly escape state regulation—when the "public" dictates what private individuals may do with their property, all pretense of rights vanishes. (p. 86)

No review of this book could be complete that ignored a remarkable discovery made by one of the contributors. Richard M. Salsman has identified a hitherto unsuspected enemy of the free market—none other than Ludwig von Mises. Incredibly, he holds that Mises

> improperly attributed profit to entrepreneurs and never refuted the myth that capitalists, in his own words, "are merely parasites who pocket the dividends." For Mises, even entrepreneurs merely buy low and sell high as a passive service to consumers who, he claims, are the real drivers of the economy and profit. (p. 45)

A more complete misunderstanding of Mises can hardly be imagined. In Mises's view, the most significant entrepreneurs are capitalists, who use their judgment to decide how to invest their money in order to satisfy customers. Their activity is not at all passive: capitalists creatively anticipate the wants of consumers.

How has Salsman fallen into an error of such "numbing grossness," in Peter Strawson's phrase? The causes of mental aberration far exceed my competence, but our learned author has apparently misread Mises's comment that entrepreneurs "earn profit not because they are clever in performing their tasks, but because they are more clever or less clumsy than other people are" (p. 45, quoting Mises). Incredibly, he takes Mises to be saying that entrepreneurs are passive. Can he not grasp that Mises means that to be successful, the entrepreneur must be better than the competition, rather than "better" in some absolute sense? Salsman is also horrified by Mises's claim that profits do not exist in his "imaginary friend," the evenly rotating economy (p. 45). Profits, says Mises, are never normal; is this not definitive proof that Mises is anticapitalist? If Salsman finds Mises's use of the ERE beyond him, this is no concern of mine; but it is puzzling why the editor allowed his book to be disfigured by such obvious nonsense.

Falling Behind:
How Rising Inequality
Harms the Middle Class*

Robert H. Frank

A Race to the Top?

December 1, 2007, *Mises Review*

F*ALLING BEHIND* belongs to an unfortunate genre: books by well-known economists that endeavor to justify crude soak-the-rich policies.[†] Paul Krugman and, from an earlier day, John Kenneth Galbraith are perhaps the best-known authors of such works; but Frank fully equals these eminent figures in his railings against the well-off. Tax relief for the rich fills him with dismay:

> Facing enormous federal budget deficits at a time when we are not paying teachers enough, not repairing our roads, bridges, and municipal water supply systems, and not inspecting the meat we eat, can multi-trillion-dollar tax cuts really be a sensible policy? At a time when top earners have been reaping virtually all the fruits of the nation's economic growth, can targeting more than 50 percent of the benefits of these tax cuts to the top 5 percent of earners really be a sensible step? (pp. 111–112)

---

[*] University of California Press, 2007.

[†] Frank, not content to leave ill enough alone, continues the argument of his earlier *Luxury Fever*. See my review found in Volume 1, "Economics."

Frank proposes instead a steeply progressive consumption tax that, at its upper reaches, is confiscatory. His plan exempts savings from tax altogether: the tax burden falls entirely on consumption.

> Because high-income families save a substantially higher proportion of their incomes than low-income families, maintaining the current tax burden across income levels would require top marginal tax rates on consumption that are much higher than the current top marginal tax rates on income. (p. 106)

Frank is not kidding: he offers an example in which the marginal tax rate on consumption spending of $1,000,000 per year is 100 percent. This rises to 200 percent for $4,000,000.

Frank's principal argument for his draconian policy is this: for many important consumption goods, such as housing, the choices of other people strongly influence our own preferences. Most people, e.g., do not wish to live in a house significantly smaller than other houses in their neighborhood. If other people build larger houses, they will endeavor to keep up, even though they were entirely at ease before in their less spacious accommodations. Following Fred Hirsch, Frank calls consumption goods of this type positional goods: how much we value them depends on how our holdings compare with those of others.

Why do positional goods create a problem? People want to have larger houses than their neighbors'; but, if the neighbors keep up, they will not succeed in their endeavors. They will instead have spent resources to arrive at a situation in which they are no better off competitively than they were before. Nonpositional goods, such as leisure, the preferences for which are less dependent on comparison with others, suffer in consequence. In a key passage, Frank states his central thesis:

1. People care about relative consumption more in some domains than others. . . .

2. Concerns about relative consumption lead to "positional arms races," or expenditure arms races focused on positional goods. . . .

3. Positional arms races divert resources from nonpositional goods, causing large welfare losses. (p. 3, emphasis removed)

Frank uses a familiar example to help explain his point. Suppose a spectator at a football game stands up in order to get a better view. If other spectators have the same thought and also rise, no one will succeed in improving his view. Moreover, all the spectators will be worse off, if one reasonably assumes that, holding their view constant, they prefer sitting to standing.

Frank's model can be challenged on several grounds. First, he fails to distinguish two different senses in which a good can be positional. In one sense, the term "positional" is equivalent to "contextual"; as Frank says, "if you are not somebody for whom context matters, you are not a normal person" (p. 39).

Whether I think I am living in a good house depends, it seems reasonable to say, on how my house compares with the houses of others in my reference group. But it does not follow from this plausible view that people wish to surpass the possessions of those in their reference group. I may think my cheap apartment not very good because others around me live in expensive condominiums, but this is not to say that I shall feel impelled to try to keep up with my more fortunate neighbors. A good can be positional or contextual in this first sense without being positional in the stronger sense that implies a competitive struggle to surpass, or at least not to fall behind, one's reference group.

Frank's failure to distinguish these two senses of positional vitiates one of his key arguments. Tax policies such as his, that strike at the consumption of the rich, seem motivated by envy. Because people have more than I do, they should be penalized to assuage my ill feeling at finding myself inferior in this way. What is that but envy?

Not so, Frank responds. If people judge their houses and other goods by comparing them with their neighbors', they do not stand convicted of envy. Context is not envy. Indeed not: but if people go on from their comparative judgments to demands to level the superiorities of others, the specter of envy has hardly been exorcised. And envy seems a poor basis for policy.

Frank has overlooked another vital distinction, this one within the second of the senses of "positional" I have distinguished. Let us once more turn to housing, the chief, though far from only, good that concerns our author. Does it not make a considerable difference whether people do not wish to fall significantly behind their neighbors, or whether they wish to surpass them? Only the latter case has the potential to generate the positional arms race that so arouses Frank's leveling passions. Suppose that people are satisfied to keep up with their neighbors. If the less well housed improve themselves to equal their better-housed neighbors, no further action by anyone is mandated. By failing to separate these two different motivations, Frank exaggerates the potential for positional arms races.

What happens, though, if people do have the stronger motivation? What if I cannot resist the temptation to build a bigger house than those around me? If those in my reference group are likewise motivated, will not a positional arms race of just the sort Frank fears ensue? People will waste resources, in a futile effort to come out ahead of everyone else.

Once more, Frank has moved too fast. Suppose someone tries to top his neighbors, and they respond in kind. It does not follow that an arms race, i.e., repeated efforts by everyone to continue the battle, will occur. People may stop at a certain level, believing it too costly to continue. Even if people wish to surpass others, the costs of fulfilling this wish must be weighed against other goods. Here is one example: Frank calls attention to the fact that, because of the importance of the initial impression in a job interview, people spend money on expensive "interview suits." By purchasing an expensive suit, an applicant hopes to gain a step on his rivals; but if his rivals do so as well,* he has not gained anything. So far, we have exactly the sort of positional battle that Frank has in mind. But job applicants have not extended the struggle, so that an applicant for assistant janitor will be wasting his time if he appears for his interview in anything less than a handmade suit from a Savile Row tailor.

Frank might here respond that, so far as housing is concerned, people are indeed engaged in an extended positional arms race. Have not the prices of houses drastically risen in the last twenty-five years? Do not people in the middle class find themselves constantly squeezed by the pressure to keep up with their neighbors? The rise in prices is an undoubted fact, but Frank does not consider alternative explanations to the one he favors. Thomas Sowell has suggested another hypothesis: government restrictions on building, not ever-increasing demand for larger houses, explain the high cost of housing.

> Where builders are allowed to construct homes and apartments without severe government restrictions, even growing populations and rising incomes do not cause housing prices to shoot up, because the supply of newly constructed housing keeps up with the growing demand, as in Las Vegas or Houston. (Thomas Sowell, *Economic Facts and Fallacies*, Basic Books, 2007, p. 30)

---

* I resist the temptation to say, "if his rivals follow suit."

Sowell's argument seems to me plausible, but its cogency is not here my point. Rather, it is Frank's tunnel vision to which I wish to draw attention. He sees only his own account.

Frank's model suffers from other problems. He assumes that the struggle to attain positional goods will result in an undersupply of nonpositional goods like leisure. This view does not take account of the fact that consumers weigh all goods against one another in arriving at their spending decisions. Perhaps a positional war will take resources from struggles for other positional goods. If so, total "waste," in Frank's terms, will face a limit.

Frank makes still another unwarranted assumption. The sum and substance of his reform proposal is that, because the struggle to surpass others in positional goods does not result in anyone's gaining an advantage, everyone would be better off if the struggle were curtailed. I want a bigger house than yours, but if adding space to my house fails to achieve this goal, because you add to your house as well, a limit on house construction helps us both. The limit prevents us from wasting resources in a futile battle.

This contention wrongly takes for granted that people will be in the same relative positions after the struggle as before. Suppose I add to my house; you match me; and then I add yet more. Perhaps you will drop out of the battle. Not all arms races end in a draw.

Let us put aside all these problems of Frank's positional goods model. The model, by itself, will not give him the progressive consumption tax he wants. Even if we eliminate social "waste" through a consumption tax, why target the extremely rich? Frank needs another questionable assumption for his tax policy. He contends that high spending by those at the top leads to high spending by those just below them. *Their* increased spending generates more spending by the next lower group, and so on. "Even the gifts that middle-income families feel compelled to give have been affected by the greater affluence of top earners" (p. 48). High taxes on the wealthiest aim at the "cascade effects" of their increased spending.

Frank does not offer evidence in support of this view. Instead, he describes several examples of lavish spending by the super-rich and then sets forward his cascades hypothesis. He does not offer us any reason, though, for thinking that each group has in fact acted in response to a change by the group immediately above it in the wealth chain. For all that he has shown, positional arms races, such as they are, may be in large part locally caused. Further, what if there are large gaps in the wealth chain? Perhaps Bill Gates and his few peers are so far above anyone else that *no one* counts as "just below" them. In that case, increased spending by Gates will not generate cascade effects.

Once more, though, let us assume this difficulty away. Frank still has not provided an adequate justification for his progressive tax. He imagines an objector, who says,

> So what? If top earners want to spend the wealth they have generated on bigger houses and cars, why should Congress second-guess them? And if middle-class families can't afford to keep up, why can't they summon the will to live within their means? (p. 114)

In response, he says, "the problem confronting a family is like one confronting a participant in a military arms race. It can choose how much of its money to spend, but it cannot choose how much others spend" (p. 115). Because of the collective effects he has been at pains to describe, people would be better off if a restrictive consumption tax were imposed.

This response takes for granted a consequentialist rationale for policy. We, or at least those of us who are of interest to Frank, would be better off if the government restricted consumption: it follows that the government should do so. But what happened to the view that people have rights that restrict what government may do, even to promote overall "happiness"? Frank does not so much as mention it.

Mises: The Last Knight of Liberalism[*]

Jörg Guido Hülsmann

A Monumental Contribution to Scholarship

December 1, 2007, *Mises Review*

G UIDO HÜLSMANN SHOWS US in this monumental biography that a common view of Mises is mistaken. As even Macaulay's schoolboy knows, the American economics profession, dominated by Keynesianism, shunted Mises aside when he came to America. He was viewed as a relic, preaching an extremist view of free enterprise; and, as the mainstream had it, his famous calculation argument that showed the impossibility of socialism had been refuted both in theory, by Lange, Taylor *et hoc genus omne*, and in practice by the immense achievements of Soviet Russia. Private funds paid Mises's salary at the business school of New York University: no major university economics department could find space for this world-renowned scholar.

The situation had been better for Mises in his native Vienna. His famous seminar attracted visitors from all over the world. He was recognized not only as a famous teacher but also as a theorist of striking originality. But even here, the common picture has it, Mises remained a figure on the margins. He never held the rank of full professor at the University of Vienna.

---

[*] Ludwig von Mises Institute, 2007.

Hülsmann overturns this picture. Despite his situation at the University of Vienna, Mises was, during the late 1920s and early '30s, a major presence in European economic thought. Even members of the German Historical School, his chief adversaries, were forced to make concessions to him.

> But the real knockout for academic socialism in Germany came at the hands of its own vicar. Heinrich Herkner had succeeded Schmoller in his position at the University of Berlin and as the president of the *Verein für Socialpolitik*. For practical purposes, this meant he had become Schmoller's heir as head of the Historical School... Herkner singled out Mises's *Socialism* as the single most important work of this liberal resurgence, endorsing virtually all criticisms that Mises had leveled against socialism. (pp. 398–399)

Herkner was not a lone voice.

> The year 1928 marked the highpoint of his [Mises's] influence on German monetary thought. The majority of the contributions to the meeting of the *Verein für Socialpolitik* in Zurich elaborated on his writings.... A few months later, [in 1929] Mises was one of six new members elected to the board of the *Verein* ... it symbolized better than anything else his professional standing in those days. Starting as an eccentric in 1912, Mises had become a respected academic leader. (pp. 585, 588–589)

This happy development was rudely interrupted and frustrated by the advent of National Socialism in Germany in 1933.

If Mises for a time won wide acclaim, it did not follow that his views were always correctly understood. Often, Hülsmann suggests, Mises's views were wrongly conflated with those of Wieser. The two Austrian economists differed on a fundamental point. For Mises, economic calculation can only take place by using money. There is no way in which one can bypass money and calculate directly in terms of value. Mises held this point clearly in mind in his first great book, *The Theory of Money and Credit*:

> Mises refuted the idea that money prices are a measure of value. Here he relied on the work of the Czech economist Franz Cuhel.... It follows that there is no such thing as value calculation or even value measurement. Even money does not have a constant value,

and is therefore unable to provide the basis for a value calculus.... Contrary to what Walras's system of equations suggests, there are no constant relationships between money prices of different times and places. (pp. 218–220)

Wieser took a diametrically opposed position.

[He] insisted that while money does enable the "transfer" of commodities from one owner to another, it more importantly *measures* the value of the commodities it helps to transfer. In short, money is essentially a standard of value, a measuring rod or *numéraire*, and it is used in market exchanges to measure the value of the commodities against which it is exchanged. (pp. 227–228)

Unfortunately for clarity of thought, Mises's leading spokesman during the 1930s in the English-speaking world, Friedrich Hayek, had been trained by Wieser and inclined to his views. "Hayek was and would remain throughout his life a disciple of Wieser's" (p. 639). Like his mentor, Hayek emphasized the importance of general equilibrium. From this perspective, money prices on the market express economic values. By contrast, Mises's pathbreaking contention was that there is no measurement of economic value at all. Calculation, to repeat, is entirely a monetary affair. (In his presentation of the differences between Hayek and Wieser, Hülsmann has been influenced by the pioneering research of Joseph Salerno.)

The issue, Hülsmann contends, led to a difference in the way Mises and Hayek understood the calculation argument against socialism. Hayek thought that it was in practice impossible for economic planners to express correct valuations without market prices: they could not, absent the market, gather the requisite information to do so. For Mises, the problem with socialism was deeper:

For Mises, the "pricing process" was not just the solution to an economic puzzle—it did not merely "express" the knowable reality of value in terms of some other knowable reality of money prices. Rather, the pricing process *created* a reality that could not possibly be known otherwise. Hayek would contend—following Wieser—that *if* the fundamental knowledge problems could be solved, one could calculate the correct prices for factors of production. Mises denied this even as a theoretical possibility. Socialist calculation was for him a conceptual impossibility. (p. 704)

Hayek's great influence at the London School of Economics thus had both good and bad consequences for those interested in a Misesian brand of theory. On the one hand, Hayek, together with his close friend and ally Lionel Robbins, acquainted the rising generation of English theorists with Mises's work. On the other hand, his unstable combination of Wieser with Mises elided Mises's break with standard equilibrium views.

If socialism, according to Mises, was impossible, this was not a circumstance that we should regret. The alternative to socialism, the free market, enables social cooperation and economic production to develop to the highest possible level. David Ricardo long ago showed the benefits of free trade; but Hülsmann insightfully points out that Mises extended Ricardo's law of comparative costs into a general law of human association:

> So why do people cooperate at all? Generalizing a discovery that David Ricardo had famously made in the special case of foreign trade, Mises gave a simple answer: human beings associate with each other because the division of labor is more physically productive than the atomistic production of isolated individuals.... This law applies under virtually all circumstances, because it presupposes only that the susceptible associates be *different* in talents or location.... This led to a surprising conclusion. The very differences in which the theory of class struggle could see only the causes of violent conflict now appeared in a far more benign light. For these differences between individuals and groups *also* harbored great potentials for mutually advantageous cooperation ... it was clear that government should regulate the economy as little as possible, in order not to prevent mutually beneficial associations. (pp. 427–429)*

With his characteristic erudition, Hülsmann points out that St. Thomas Aquinas was well aware of the economic benefits of the division of labor.

---

* The common communitarian complaint that classical liberalism is an "atomistic" philosophy is thus the precise reverse of the truth.

The state, by interfering in the economy, can only make matters worse. One particular sort of intervention especially troubled Mises. In his great volume of 1919, *Nation, State, and Economy*, Mises showed how aggressive economic nationalism leads to imperialism and war. (Mises at first planned to call the book *Imperialism*.) During the late nineteenth century, many Germans sought for a better life through emigration. In an effort to keep them at home, the German government resorted to a policy of high tariffs.

> Many Germans had moved to colonies that were predominantly populated by English settlers. Surrounded by an English majority, the German émigrés quickly assimilated and thus were lost to the German nation. In a desperate attempt to counter this development, the German government established a system of protective tariffs, to reduce the incentives of German workers to emigrate. . . . When the failure of this policy became apparent, the government changed its strategy and decided instead to conquer British colonies. It began to build a mighty fleet to combat the Royal Navy. . . . This in turn prompted the British entry into World War I. (p. 302)

In like fashion, Mises argued in *Omnipotent Government* that economic nationalism, brought on by fears of overpopulation, lay behind the Nazi drive to expand eastwards. Intervention in the economy not only has counterproductive economic consequences, but can lead to the most deleterious political consequences as well.

Mises was particularly sensitive to the interplay of economic interventionism and conflict among national groups because he was born and raised in that checkerboard of nationalities, the Austro-Hungarian Empire. One of the great strengths of Hülsmann's biography is that it thoroughly describes the national conflicts in the empire. In particular, Hülsmann gives a full account of the Jewish community of Lemberg, where Mises was born, and of Vienna, where Mises attended school and attained fame as an economist.*

---

* As Hülsmann points out, Mises's great-grandfather was a leader of the secular, progressive wing of Lemberg Jewry. Conflict in Lemberg between the traditionalists and progressives in Lemberg was bitter. In one famous case, a liberal rabbi was poisoned. See on this incident, Michael Stanislawski, *A Murder in Lemberg* (Princeton University Press, 2007).

Interventionism, then, cannot solve the conflicts of ethnic and national groups: it only makes these conflicts worse. What, then, is to be done? Mises forcefully maintained that no group of people should be compelled to remain as an ethnic minority within a state. Not only groups but even individuals should be free to make whatever political arrangements they wished:

> Mises advocated a complete liberalization of society. There should be no political limits to this process.... Mises welcomed the unhampered competition among national territories, which in a free "inter-national" society would be a peaceful competition between language-based cultures, in which each individual, through his assimilation choices, would determine the fate of the various language communities.... Mises argued not only that political rule is unnecessary to improve the condition of a nation, but that it is incapable of doing so. In a free society people constantly migrate to those locations offering the most favorable conditions for production. (p. 323)

Mises's radical views meant that he could never be a conventional conservative, though he was quite capable of alliance with rightwing governments to advance the cause of economic liberty. (He was an economic adviser to the conservative chancellor Monsignor Seipel and, under the Dollfuss regime, joined the Patriotic Front.) He retained his early radicalism throughout his long life. In a letter of 1960 to Hayek, he remarked:

> I [Mises] completely agree with your rejection of conservatism. In his book *Up from Liberalism*, [William F.] Buckley ... has clearly defined his standpoint: "Conservatism is the tacit acknowledgment that all that is finally important in human experience is behind us.... Whatever is to come cannot outweigh the importance to man of what has gone before." ... It is a sad truth that this program is more attractive than everything that has been said about liberty and about the idealistic and materialistic benefits of the free economy. (pp. 994–995)

I have been able to discuss only a few topics in this book; so vast is its scope that it would have been easy to write several different reviews, each covering entirely different themes. Hülsmann combines to an extraordinary degree the skills of a penetrating analytical economist with those of an assiduous researcher. He is in this regard a worthy successor to Murray Rothbard. *Mises: The Last Knight of Liberalism* is an outstanding scholarly achievement and, by the way, a beautifully produced book. Everyone interested in Austrian economics must read it.

Nudge: Improving Decisions About Health, Wealth, and Happiness*

Richard H. Thaler & Cass Sunstein

When Nudge Comes to Shove

July 1, 2008, *Mises Review*

THALER AND SUNSTEIN have set themselves a seemingly impossible task. Paternalists maintain that it is sometimes justifiable to interfere with someone's freedom, if doing so will promote his own good. Smokers, putting aside the issue of secondary smoke, do not violate others' rights: they harm only themselves. Nevertheless, a paternalist about smoking would think it justifiable forcibly to prevent people from smoking. Libertarians deny that such interference is acceptable. Force may be used only in response to aggression.

Given these uncontroversial characterizations of the two positions, is it not obvious that they cannot be combined with each other? To devise a libertarian paternalism seems no more promising an endeavor than to construct a square circle. Our eminent authors, though, are not convinced: libertarian paternalism is exactly the position they wish to defend.

Their escape from apparent contradiction is ingenious. It is indeed unlibertarian, they say, to use force to compel someone to act for his own good.

---

* Yale University Press, 2008.

They do not favor doing so; but this leaves them free to support a less exigent variety of paternalism. It is all right to render it difficult for people to make certain choices, as long as doing so does not impose substantial costs on them. People, as their title suggests, may be subject to paternalistic "nudges," so long as these nudges do not coerce them.

> Libertarian paternalism is a relatively weak, soft, and nonin-
> trusive type of paternalism because choices are not blocked,
> fenced off, or significantly burdened. If people want to smoke
> cigarettes, to eat a lot of candy, to choose an unsuitable health
> care plan, or to fail to save for retirement, libertarian paternal-
> ists will not force them to do otherwise—or even make things
> hard for them. . . . A nudge, as we will use the term, is any as-
> pect of the choice architecture that alters people's behavior in a
> predictable way without forbidding any options or significantly
> changing their economic incentives. (pp. 5–6)

There is a problem here that Thaler and Sunstein fail to note. Not all cases of using force on people impose substantial costs on them. Suppose that you are about to reach for a cigarette, and I hold your wrist to prevent you from doing so. You were aware that I might do this and could easily have avoided my company. Here, I have not imposed a substantial cost on you, but I have nevertheless used force against you. Given cases of this kind, their alternative ways of stating their proposal, i.e., not imposing substantial costs and nudg-ing but not using force, are not always consistent.

They extend their view further. It is also justifiable to nudge people to act in a "good" way, even when doing so is not for their own good. In current American law, people are free to direct that their organs be made available for transplants after they die. Unless, though, they have filled out a donor card, doctors who wish to transplant organs must secure the consent of whoever has legal custody of the body. Thaler and Sunstein suggest that we change the default position. Why not allow transplants, unless someone has signed a declaration forbidding that his body be used in this way? They think it likely that many more trans-plants would be obtained under this system. But libertarians can support it, because it forces no one to donate. If you do not want to do so, all you need to do is sign a statement to that effect. (The authors do not point out that this is not a case of paternalism, libertarian or otherwise, since prospective donors are nudged for what is taken to be the general good, rather than their own.)

An obvious objection to their proposals arises, and their efforts to respond to this objection form the theoretical substance of the book. Let us return to those who, despite the health risks, continue to smoke. Is it not, in a free society, up to them to assess the costs of doing so, weighing them against what they gain from smoking? What right have other people to a say in the matter? Are not paternalists, even of the soft variety who confine their ministrations to nudges, substituting their preferences for the freely chosen decisions of others?

The authors respond that this objection rests on an unrealistic view of choice. Economics textbooks assume that people act on their preferences rationally, based on full information.

> Whether or not they have ever studied economics, many people seem at least implicitly committed to the idea of *homo economicus*, or economic man—the notion that each of us thinks and chooses unfailingly well, and thus fits within the textbook picture of human beings offered by economists. (p. 6)

But a great deal of research, by both economists and psychologists, shows that the assumptions of the standard view cannot be retained in unmodified form. People often make mistakes in logic. Further, they are often divided against themselves: an impulsive self struggles against another self that takes greater account of the long run. (Thaler and Sunstein do not suggest that rationality always requires suppressing the impulsive self, but often it does.) As if this were not enough, people often lack the information required for an informed choice.

Thaler and Sunstein are right to think that the standard model is flawed, but they themselves remain too much its prisoner. What they in effect are saying is that unless someone meets the textbook criteria for rationality and information, he is not really choosing in the full sense. If, e.g., someone commits a "logical" error, in the extended sense they give to logical error, he is not giving expression to his freely chosen preferences. What he "really" wants is that his preferences be fulfilled in the way best fitted to do so. His faulty reasoning does not count as part of his free choice.

Further, people's ultimate goals are often not the concrete objects that they seek to obtain: these are only means to their ends. A smoker does not want a pack of cigarettes as an end in itself. Rather, he wants certain feelings, e.g., pleasant sensations or relief from unpleasant cravings, which he thinks the cigarettes will provide him. Thaler and Sunstein thus have yet another way to question people's choices: perhaps people have selected a poor way to achieve what they "really" want.

To reiterate, in their view, only actions that meet rigid requirements count as full choices. Smokers, research indicates, haven't fully taken into account the health risks of smoking. Thus, they cannot be said "really" to choose to smoke. Further, people are often subject to so-called "framing" effects: they will "choose" differently when confronted with identical options, depending on how the options are presented. Choices in these circumstances, Thaler and Sunstein aver, are problematic: how can we say that people in the grip of conceptual illusions are freely choosing?

What is left? Given the authors' wide net, few actions count as rational choices. There is thus practically unlimited scope for the state to suppress liberty: in doing so, it is not interfering with what the self "really" wants. True enough, the authors preach a mild doctrine. Nudges, not force, are on their agenda. But they lack a rational basis for this limit. If people do not "really" choose their actions, why not forcibly restrict them? After all, doing so may enable them better to achieve what they "really" want—as experts, suitably instructed by Thaler and Sunstein, determine.

The authors consider a related objection, but they do not fully grasp the key point. They answer worries that libertarian paternalism will lead to more severe restrictions by treating this complaint as an ordinary "slippery-slope" argument. Why, they ask, need one progress down it? Their proposal endeavors to be both libertarian and paternalistic: why assume that the paternalistic aspects must supplant the libertarian?

> [O]ur own libertarian condition, requiring low-cost opt-out rights, reduces the steepness of the ostensibly slippery slope.... Slippery slope arguments are most convincing when it is not possible to distinguish the proposed course of action from abhorrent, unacceptable, or scary courses of action. (p. 237)

But the real issue is not the inevitable progression of the slippery slope but the rational basis for the restriction in the first place.

Those who wish to preserve liberty must take people's actions as they find them, not substitute for them "better" or more "rational" actions, based on an assessment of what people "really" want. To return to the transplant case, if the state says to people that their organs will be taken from them unless they explicitly direct otherwise, it is claiming to set forward the terms under which people can retain control of their own bodies. This is hardly libertarian. Instead, the state needs to step away entirely and allow people to dispose of their organs as they wish. Why not rely on a free market in organs, rather than concoct schemes to restrict liberty in the guise of preserving it?*

Thaler and Sunstein might respond in this way: Even if one grants (as of course they would not) that their scheme threatens liberty, it has not been shown that their view of choice is wrong. Is it not obviously true that people often act impulsively or illogically, in ways that they later come to regret? Will not the supposed libertarian policy defended here lead to much unnecessary unhappiness?

Libertarians need not deny obvious facts. People often do regret their choices. Those who find convincing the explanations of bad choices put forward by Thaler and Sunstein are free to make arrangements with others that will alleviate these problems. If you think that sudden impulses when confronted with tempting food will lead you to fall off your diet, you may contract with a friend to forfeit money should you fail to meet certain weight requirements. But, in a free society, doing so is up to you; the state may not nudge you into this sort of contract. The authors might answer that decisions on whether to restrict one's future choices are themselves less than fully rational and informed; but to say this is merely to reiterate their original argument, and the libertarian rejoinder to it is unchanged. Also, they do not present any evidence that choices of this kind are flawed by their criteria.

Thaler and Sunstein offer a further argument for the nudges they favor. They suggest that influencing choice is unavoidable: if we do not nudge people to make good choices, we will influence them to make bad ones. Sometimes their contention has merit. Suppose an employer has a voluntary plan that allows workers to save for retirement. He has a choice: either he allows his employees to sign for the plan or he selects the plan as the default option, allowing workers to remove themselves. He cannot avoid the choice altogether, so long as he wishes to offer the plan. But not all cases are like this, as the transplants example illustrates. Here, once more, the state does not have to choose a default option. It can avoid doing anything at all.

---

* For an excellent study of how a free market in organs might work, see David Kaserman and A. H. Barnett, *The US Organ Procurement System: A Prescription for Reform* (American Enterprise Institute, 2002).

So far, I have not questioned the evidence Thaler and Sunstein offer that people act irrationally but have instead tried to show that, accepting their evidence, their case for libertarian paternalism has not been established. Sometimes, though, the evidence for irrationality, taken in their economic textbook sense, is weak.

They offer as a case of irrationality purchasing an extended warranty for household appliances. In many instances, the cost of the warranty, combined with the small chance that the appliance will break down, suggests that buying the warranty is a poor option. But what if the purchaser has a strong aversion to paying for repairs when an appliance has broken down? He strongly prefers that payments for breakdowns be handled in advance. There seems nothing "irrational" about this preference, but if someone has it, purchasing the extended warranty makes sense. Thaler and Sunstein may not share this preference, but their doing so is not a requirement of rationality in preferences.

The authors make their case in part by rhetoric, not argument: they cite an episode of the Simpsons that makes fun of these warranties. Richard Epstein has written a detailed response to many of the arguments for irrationality that Thaler has advanced on previous occasions: *Skepticism and Freedom* (University of Chicago Press, 2003). Though the authors cite two papers by Epstein, they do not respond to this book or even mention it in their bibliography.

Tocqueville long ago warned against the policies of which libertarian paternalism is an example:

> Above this race of men stands an immense and tutelary power, which takes upon itself alone to secure their gratifications and to watch over their fate. That power is absolute, minute, regular, provident, and mild. ... The will of man is not shattered, but softened, bent, and guided; men are seldom forced by it to act, but they are constantly restrained from acting. Such a power does not destroy, but it prevents existence; it does not tyrannize, but it compresses, enervates, extinguishes, and stupefies a people, till each nation is reduced to nothing better than a flock of timid and industrious animals, of which the government is the shepherd. (Alexis de Tocqueville, *Democracy in America*, Volume II, Section 4, Chapter 6)

Against Intellectual Monopoly[*]

MICHELE BOLDRIN & DAVID K. LEVINE

Do We Need Patents and Copyrights?

April 1, 2009, *Mises Review*

ONE OF THE MOST IMPORTANT recent advances in libertarian theory has come in the field of intellectual property. Several writers, Stephan Kinsella most notably among them, have argued that patents and copyrights should not form part of a proper libertarian law code. These writers modify and extend the work of Murray Rothbard, who allowed copyrights but not patents.

These writers must confront an important objection. However convincing one may find their analysis of the implications of libertarian theory, what if the policy that they recommend leads to economic disaster? Without patents, would not inventions drastically decrease, crippling economic progress? Could writers earn a decent return without being able to copyright their work? If one sets aside these questions, insisting that libertarian theory requires that patents and copyrights be ended and that is that, critics stand ready to pounce. They will say that libertarians dogmatically disregard consequences, insisting on principles at whatever cost.[†]

Against Intellectual Monopoly enables us to meet this challenge on its own ground.[‡] Boldrin and Levine, though quite sympathetic to the free market,

---

[*] Cambridge University Press, 2008.

[†] For an example of this sort of criticism, though not applied to intellectual property, see Leland Yeager, *Ethics as Social Science*. I discuss his criticism in Volume 1, "Philosophy."

[‡] I am grateful to Jeff Tucker for calling my attention to this book.

are neither Austrians nor libertarians, much less natural-rights libertarians of Rothbardian views. They are mainstream neoclassical economists and their ethical views seem, broadly speaking, to be utilitarian. Arguing strictly on consequentialist grounds, they oppose intellectual property. Patents and copyrights do not promote economic progress but impede it.

Their argument for this view consists of two parts. First, even if patents and copyrights encourage innovation, they produce so many bad effects that, on balance, these measures have negative consequences. Second, though benefits from promoting new ideas of patents and copyright cannot on a priori grounds be ruled out, there is strong reason to believe that these effects have been greatly exaggerated.

I can discuss only a small sample of the profusion of arguments the authors deploy in support of these contentions. They begin by posing a sharp challenge to those who think patents essential for innovation. Innovative industries have often flourished without them:

> In few industries has there been such extensive innovation as in the software industry—and few technologies have changed our way of life so much. Will it surprise you to learn that virtually none of the innovations in this industry took place with the protection of intellectual monopoly? . . . The software industry is a leading illustration of one of the subthemes of this book. Intellectual monopoly is not a cause of innovation, but rather an unwelcome consequence of it. In a young, dynamic industry full of ideas and creativity, intellectual monopoly does not play a useful role. (pp. 15–17)

Even if this is true, though, this shows only that patents are unneeded; why are they bad? Boldrin and Levine answer that the struggle to secure patents often involves costly and unproductive activities:

> Part of the enormous increase in the number of patents is because patents beget yet other patents to defend against existing patents. . . . Pundits and lawyers call this navigating the patent thickets, and a whole literature, not to speak of a lucrative new profession, has sprung up around it in the past fifteen years. (p. 73)

But the most obvious cost of patents lies not in the side effects of the struggle to obtain them but in their direct purpose:

> [P]atents and "intellectual property" more generally are, by defini-
> tion, aimed at blocking competition, as their main aim is to prevent
> others from competing with the innovator by producing the same
> thing either a little more cheaply or of a little better quality. (p. 77)

The "submarine patent" is an especially insidious means of impeding competition. Here, someone files for a patent on a general idea without complet-
ing the application process:

> Although the patent term was measured from the date of award, ...
> the validity of the patent [is] ... measured from the day of submis-
> sion. Hence, the submarine patent—the filing of a useless patent
> on a broad idea that might, one day, be useful. The existence of the
> filing is secret ... and the application process is dragged out un-
> til some actual innovator invests the time and effort to make the
> idea useful. At that time, the amendment filing stops, the patent is
> awarded, and the submarine surfaces to demand license fees. (p. 84)

The risk of being undermined by a submarine patent surely tends to dis-
courage innovation.

As this example shows, the authors display a thorough familiarity with the
ins and outs of intellectual property law. But even more important is a less technical point that they emphasize. People learn through imitating others, and to
the extent that patents and copyrights impede this process, they block progress:

> Imitation is a great thing. It is among the most powerful tech-
> nologies humans have ever developed ... imitation is a tech-
> nology that allows us to increase productive capacity. Inno-
> vators increase productive capacity directly, while imitators
> increase productive capacity by purchasing one or more cop-
> ies of the idea and then imitating it. ... The output of the im-
> itation process is additional productive capacity ... imitation
> is also a technology that allows further innovation ... mak-
> ing your copy of the idea a bit better, or cheaper, than the one
> the original innovators are selling is one way to increase your
> [competitive] rents. ... Intellectual monopoly greatly discour-
> ages imitation. ... If an imitator improves upon the product or
> learns how to produce it at a cheaper cost ... your competitor
> now has the upper hand and is a threat to your monopoly. It is

> far more sensible simply to prevent imitation in the first place,
> by aggressive legal enforcement of patents and other forms of
> intellectual monopoly. (pp. 145–146)

Even if the authors are so far correct, they must confront a formidable objection. Suppose, as they wish, that patents and copyrights were abolished. According to their neoclassical model of competition, is there not a strong argument that innovators could derive little profit? Once the innovation is on the market, copiers can quickly expand production until marginal revenue equals marginal cost, driving profits down to nothing.

Boldrin and Levine prove fully equal to the challenge. Within their neoclassical framework, they find ample room for profit for both innovators and imitators:

> Because copies of ideas are always limited . . . they always command a positive price. Nowhere is limited capacity more important than in a nascent industry. The first entrants earn large rents, over and above the opportunity cost of capital, for quite a while, until enough productive capacity is built up to push prices down toward marginal cost. . . . Eventually the competitive process increases capacity and reduces competitive rents, but not to zero . . . to the extent that even the last entrant must build a costly plant, she will have to earn some rents . . . to pay for the cost of the plant. (pp. 132–133)

The authors acknowledge, though, that their argument does not cover all possible cases:

> In contrast to shoe factories, even with minimal installed capacity, the copies of a book that can be made over an extremely short period of time may be so many as to essentially flood the market, dropping the price to near marginal cost almost immediately. . . . The resultant difference between price and marginal cost may be so small that, when multiplied by the number of copies, it yields an insufficient rent. The rent is insufficient because, say, the book is very complicated, and it took a long time to complete. . . . Most ideas are not divisible, and there are cases in which the cost required to come up with the first prototype of an idea is quite large compared to the size of the market for copies of the idea. (p. 135)

But these cases of indivisibility do not amount to much in practice.

> We are not arguing [that] the case of large initial capacity and small market size cannot arise, just that it is far from being the only possible case.... Is indivisibility a relevant practical problem?... [A]vailable evidence suggests that it is not. (p. 136).

For one thing, the "first-mover advantage" of the innovator generally offers ample opportunities for profit.

What if the objector persists? Even if innovators can gain profits without recourse to intellectual monopoly, can they not in at least some cases gain higher profits with legal protection of their discoveries? If so, perhaps the gains from such innovations would outweigh all the considerations the authors have amassed on the other side.

Little evidence supports this conjecture:

> [A] number of scientific studies have attempted to examine whether introducing or strengthening patent protection leads to greater innovation by using data from post-Second World War advanced economies.... The executive summary: these studies find weak or no evidence that strengthening patent regimes increases innovation. (p. 192)

The book is packed with arguments; I shall conclude with one I found especially telling:

> Insofar as innovators have unique ideas, it may make sense to reward them with monopolies to make sure we get advantage of their unusual talents.... As it happens, simultaneous discoveries tend to be the rule rather than the exception. (p. 202).

In addition to the sources our authors cite to back up this claim, Murray Rothbard also notes the importance of simultaneous discovery in *Man, Economy, and State*. The point was also a favorite of my old friend S. Colum Gilfillan, and his books from the 1930s, *The Sociology of Invention* and *Inventing the Ship*, lend strong support to the authors' case. All future work on intellectual property will have to take account of *Against Intellectual Monopoly*.

Free Market Madness: Why Human Nature Is at Odds With Economics— And Why It Matters[*]

PETER A. UBEL

In Defense of Paternalism

April 1, 2009, *Mises Review*

PETER UBEL has written an informative and useful book, but not entirely for the reasons he thinks. He presents a very well-written and easy-to-understand account of behavioral economics; in doing so, he illustrates, contrary to his intention, the dangers that this movement poses to our freedom.

Ubel, a physician trained in economics and psychology, uses behavioral economics to advocate restrictions on the free market. The market, he thinks, has its place: he quotes Adam Smith on the benefits of the division of labor and enthusiastically agrees. But market fanatics have gone too far. They defend the shocking contention that people should be free to choose as they wish, so long as they do not use or threaten force against others. Accordingly, these misguided people defend an unlimited free market: in it, the choice of consumers determines what will be produced.

---

[*] Harvard Business Press, 2009.

Ubel agrees, at least to a large extent, that the market does exactly this. (Like most economists except Austrians, he makes an exception for public goods and externalities, but his attack on the free market in this book lies elsewhere.) But he dissents from the view that this justifies the free market. It would do so only if people chose rationally in their self-interest, and this by no means always holds true.

Science, Ubel tells us, has demonstrated people's irrationality beyond reasonable doubt. Ubel's tale here has three principal heroes: the psychologists Daniel Kahneman and Amos Tversky, who performed pioneering experiments that show how unreasonably people decide, and the economist Richard Thaler, who developed similar ideas and brought the work of these psychologists to the attention of the economics profession. Their research explodes market fundamentalism.

How does it do so? For one thing, our heroes say, people often make mistakes in reasoning. If people reason wrongly, how can they hope to get what they really want? The fact that the market gives them what they choose has little significance if this choice results from logical failings. I do not deny the problem: far be it from me to claim that people reason infallibly. But a number of the examples that they cite to make their case strike me as unconvincing.

One of the most famous of these concerns an imaginary young woman.

> Linda is thirty-one years old, single, outspoken, and very bright. She majored in philosophy. As a student, she was deeply concerned with issues of discrimination and social justice, and also participated in antinuclear demonstrations. (p. 35)

People presented with Linda's story assess the probability of various statements, including "Linda is active in the feminist movement," "Linda is a bank teller," and "Linda is a bank teller and is active in the feminist movement." Many people rate the probability of the third statement higher than the second, but of course it cannot be. The probability of a conjunction must be lower than that of any of its conjuncts, so long as the conjuncts are neither all certain nor all of zero probability.

I do not think this result demonstrates that the people in the survey have reasoned wrongly. Suppose, when asked about the probability of Linda's occupation, people think it very unlikely that she has chosen to be a bank teller. They think, by contrast, that she very likely identifies with feminism. When asked about Linda's being both a feminist and bank teller, they may not recall their earlier estimate of her being a teller. Rather, they may simply lower their estimate that she is a feminist, to reflect the new information that she is also a teller. To convict them of fallacy, they should also be asked: "Given that you estimate the joint probability of Linda's being a feminist and a bank teller as x, what is the probability of her being a bank teller?" Only if they do not give an estimate higher than x should they be convicted of fallacy. Along similar lines, they should be asked, "Given that you estimate the chances of Linda's being a bank teller as y, what is your estimate of the probability that she is both a teller and a feminist?" Only if the new estimate is y or higher have they fallen into error.

Although the example does not convince me, for the reason given, one must at least admit one thing. If people in fact do estimate the probability of a conjunction higher than that of any of its conjuncts, they have made a mistake. Other examples that Kahneman and Tversky give do not suffice to show this. They present a number of cases in which people violate Leonard Savage's axioms of rational decision. For example, people tend to prefer getting an amount of money for certain to a chance of getting a larger amount. Given the strength of this preference, one can in some instances derive judgments of preference for probabilities less than one of getting various amounts of money that contradict each other. (I shall omit numerical examples, as I almost always botch them.) But, contrary to what Ubel says, this does not at all show that "If you chose this way [that generates these judgments], my friend, you are contradicting yourself" (p. 41).

Ubel has missed the boat. The person who values certainty does not judge solely by estimates of probabilities: he has added something, the high value he places on certainty, to the equation. The fact that he *would* make contradictory judgments if he *were* to decide only on probability judgments has no force. What Ubel offers as a contradiction is nothing more than a version of the familiar Allais paradox, a major challenge to the Savage approach. Amazingly, when Ubel claims contradiction, he cites Allais as a reference (p. 229, note 11): has he read his source? In like fashion, people who view the same probability distributions differently when they face a loss from when they face prospective gain do not commit any mistake in reasoning in so doing.

One might imagine Ubel responding in this way:

> Enough of these niggling technical points. Even if my conclusions can be disputed, irrational decisions put human lives at stake.

What about, e.g., smokers who ignore the risks of lung cancer?
Must not the state step in to protect these people from themselves?

Ubel himself admits, though, that smokers do not underestimate the risks of contracting lung cancer.

> By 1985, experts had estimated that lifelong smokers faced a 5–10 percent chance of developing lung cancer. . . . But it paled in comparison with the risk perceptions of the people responding to [economist Kip] Viscusi's survey. On average, Viscusi's respondents, many of whom were adolescents, . . . thought that lifelong smokers faced almost a 50 percent chance of developing lung cancer. (p. 133)

Whatever the failings of smokers, does not Viscusi's research give us reason to think that smokers have not acted irrationally through turning a blind eye to risk? If you want to show smokers irrational, must you not seek some other way to do it? Ubel does not agree. He spurns Viscusi's argument as "hyper-rational." People often decide matters in the grip of emotion rather than through calculation. Thus, even if smokers profess to believe smoking highly risky to health, they have not taken these risks to heart. They do not really picture to themselves in its full intensity what having lung cancer would be like. Further, people's numerical assignments of risk cannot be trusted. Many people lack all facility with how numbers work; they think, e.g., that "fifty percent" is the proper response when they do not know the correct chances.

It is odd that Ubel bemoans the failure of smokers to be sufficiently frightened by the dire peril of cancer, when he elsewhere laments that people often decide matters through emotion and ignore the dictates of reason. Evidently, one either should or should not decide emotionally, depending on whether the conclusion comes out as Ubel wishes.

Further, how does he know that smokers have not adequately imagined the ills that their habit might bring them and that they are innumerate as well? Ubel does no more than describe these problems; he fails to show that smokers fall victim to them. Perhaps the argument is that smokers must exhibit some cognitive or emotional failing, since otherwise they would not decide to smoke; but this blatantly begs the question.

One medical condition worries Ubel even more than lung cancer. In his work as a physician, he often treats morbidly obese patients. Their eating habits shorten their lives. An epidemic of obesity confronts America, and naturally the free market bears the blame.

> Because cooking takes less time and labor than it used to, the cost of eating has dropped. . . . This is what I mean when I say that free markets have created the obesity epidemic. Advances in food technology have reduced the monetary and time costs of eating, and these technological advances are a result of free market enterprises responding to consumer demand. Some market defenders might dispute me on this matter, pointing out that the obesity epidemic has only taken off in the last several decades, whereas capitalist enterprise has only been around for at least two hundred years. But by this reasoning, we'd be forced to conclude that free markets aren't responsible for HDTVs, or iPods, or aluminum siding, none of which existed at the dawn of time. (pp. 27–28)

Ubel's argument, then, is that technological advances, made possible by capitalism, bear primary responsibility for the obesity epidemic. He rightly notes that the fact that capitalism long preceded the epidemic leaves his argument intact. But if the technological advances to which he draws attention arrived substantially before the obesity problem, his argument would indeed be open to question.

In fact, he admits at one point, without noticing how it ruins his argument, that exactly this happened: "In 1991, only four states in the United States had obesity rates of 15 percent or higher; by 2001 some thirty-seven states did" (p. 10). Surely the technology behind easy-to-prepare food was well in place in 1991; modern methods of food preparation did not spring up only in the last twenty years. One must beware the fallacy of thinking that the good old days when people slaved over the stove ended only a few years ago. If so, how can technology, and behind it the free market, be blamed for mass obesity?

Regardless of its causes, though, obesity unquestionably poses health risks to many people, and Ubel wants to bring in the state to rectify matters. If you object to him that people ought to be free to decide how much to eat, or whether to smoke, for themselves, he will answer that their choices, marred by cognitive mistakes, cannot be considered the outcome of rationally self-interested deliberation. This contention, I have endeavored to show, he has failed to prove.

But he also says something else. Why, he asks, should one exalt freedom as the supreme political virtue? Must not freedom be balanced against other components of the good life? Ubel invokes Aristotle, who

> viewed one of the major functions of society as being to create an environment that develops virtuous actions in its citizens. We could do worse than to follow his advice. (p. 224)

Ubel for once is right. In order to decide on correct social policy, one must possess a sound philosophy of ethics and politics, one that will consider how various goods can be achieved. Despite this bow to philosophy, though, Ubel shows no awareness that state paternalism is a controversial issue. For him, once we know that a choice has bad results, we can at once legitimately ask what the state can do to improve matters. To think otherwise makes a fetish of freedom; and he quite readily describes his proposals as paternalist.

Has he ever so much as glanced at Mill's *On Liberty*? In a famous passage in that essay, Mill said,

> The object of this Essay is to assert one very simple principle, as entitled to govern absolutely the dealings of society with the individual in the way of compulsion and control, whether the means used be physical force in the form of legal penalties, or the moral coercion of public opinion. That principle is, that the sole end for which mankind are warranted, individually or collectively, in interfering with the liberty of action of any of their number, is self-protection. That the only purpose for which power can be rightfully exercised over any member of a civilized community, against his will is to prevent harm to others. His own good, either physical or moral, is not sufficient warrant.

Ubel is perfectly free to disagree with Mill's claim and to advance arguments on the other side. But he shows no awareness of the essay or the enormous critical literature it has generated. The whole controversy has passed him by: for him, opposition to paternalism reduces to the blathering of free-market fundamentalists. The fact that he elsewhere gives a very good account of Mill's criticism of Bentham makes his omission even stranger.

Even if one did have a philosophy that justified considerable state action, a further problem would arise—one that Ubel also ignores. Why should we think that existing states would act rationally to carry out the dictates of that philosophy? Would not holders of state power be subject to exactly the errors of rationality that Ubel complains about in participants in the free market?

The matter of course worsens if, like Oppenheimer, Nock, Chodorov, and Rothbard, one views the state as a predatory gang. Then we have no reason at all to think the state would improve on what free individuals can achieve for themselves. Ubel mocks those who speak of a "nanny state"; but the real problem is not that the state officiously looks out for our best interests at the expense of our freedom.* It is that the state exploits us.

---

* In his challenge to those who complain of a nanny state, Ubel says, "One of my favorites is a book titled *A Nation of Sheep*, in which the government isn't portrayed as treating people like children, but, instead, as if they were mindless animals" (p. 206). This grossly misrepresents Judge Napolitano's book, which argues that people have failed to protest assaults on their civil liberties, principally occasioned by the so-called war on terror. Once again, whether Ubel has read his source is questionable.

Marxism Unmasked: From Delusion to Destruction*

LUDWIG VON MISES

Introduction by
RICHARD M. EBELING

Lessons From the Master

April 1, 2009, *Mises Review*

N JUNE AND JULY 1952, Ludwig von Mises delivered nine lectures in San Francisco on Marxism and capitalism. Bettina Greaves transcribed these lectures, and she has done us a great service in making these lectures available to the public. They display Mises's unparalleled insight, and even experienced students of him will learn much from what he says here.

Fashionable Western Marxists such as Erich Fromm have stressed Marx's humanism, principally on display in his early manuscripts, but Mises sees Marx differently. For him, Marx embraced a crude version of materialism:

> According to Marx, everybody is forced—by the material productive forces—to think in a way that the result shows his class interests. You think in the way your "interests" force you to think.... Your "interests" are something independent of your mind and your ideas. Consequently the production of your ideas is not truth. Before the appearance of Karl Marx, the notion of truth had no meaning for the whole historical period.

---

* Foundation for Economic Education, 2006.

What the thinking of the people produced in the past was "ideology," not truth. (p. 6)

Mises locates a contradiction in Marx's theory that, so far as I am aware, has escaped other critics. Marx contended that class interests determine a thinker's ideas. He also maintained, though, that these ideas directly reflect the material productive forces. But these two accounts by no means come to the same thing:

> (1) The interpretation he [Marx] gives to Descartes is that he was living in an age when machines were introduced and, therefore, Descartes explained the animal as a machine; and (2) The interpretation that he gave to John Locke's inspiration—that it came from the fact that he was a representative of bourgeois class interests. Here are two incompatible explanations for the source of ideas. (p. 6)

In his discussion of materialism, Mises makes in passing a brilliant remark:

> No materialist philosopher ever fails to use the word "simply" [as in, "thoughts are simply secretions of the brain"]. That means, "I know, but I can't explain it." (p. 3)

Economics of course lies at the heart of Marxism, and Mises expertly exposes Marx's key errors. Marx claimed that he had discovered the "law of motion" of capitalism, just as Newton had discovered the laws of motion in physics. The value of a commodity under capitalism depends on the socially necessary time required to produce it. This applies to labor as well: the value of labor depends on how much labor is required to keep a laborer alive and able to work. But, in return for paying this amount, the capitalist employer obtains the worker's labor power. He must work for the capitalist a certain number of hours; and, in that time, he expends labor, the source of value. If the amount of labor he expends exceeds what the employer has paid him, the employer makes a profit.

This famous exploitation theory of profit rests, as Mises points out, on the "iron law of wages." If wages rise above subsistence, population increases will drive them back down again. The rising standard of living in England in Marx's own day, as capitalism continued to develop, falsified the iron law, but Marx ignored this.

Mises finds another problem with this part of Marx's theory:

> If you think it is absolutely impossible under the capitalist system for wages to deviate from this rate [of subsistence], then how can you still talk, as Marx did, about the progressive impoverishment of the workers as being inevitable? There is an insoluble contradiction between the iron law of wage rates . . . and his philosophy of history, which maintains that the workers will be more and more impoverished until they are driven to open rebellion, thus bringing about socialism. Of course both doctrines are untenable. . . . What is amazing is that, during the century since Marx's writings, no one has pointed out this contradiction. (p. 13)

Mises resolves a question that has long puzzled me. Marx thinks that when socialism arrives, people will no longer be subjected to the division of labor. How can he believe this? Surely his extensive knowledge of economic history must have taught him that civilization cannot exist without the division of labor.* Mises contends that Marx read the history of technology in a different way:

> Marx didn't take into account the evolution of mankind above the level of very primitive men. He considered unskilled labor to be the normal type of labor and skilled labor to be the exception. He wrote in one of his books that progress in the technological improvement of machines causes the disappearance of specialists because the machine can be operated by anyone; it takes no special skill to operate a machine. Therefore the normal type of man in the future will be the non-specialist. (p. 14)

Again and again Mises draws from his extraordinary knowledge to make illuminating remarks. He says, e.g.,

> In French, the words "organize" and "organizer" were unknown before the end of the eighteenth century or the beginning of the

---

* For an excellent discussion of the division of labor, see Murray Rothbard, "Freedom, Inequality, Primitivism, and the Division of Labor" in *Egalitarianism as a Revolt Against Nature and Other Essays* (Mises Institute, 2000).

nineteenth century. With regard to the term "organize," Balzac observed "This is a new-fangled Napoleonic term. This means you alone are the dictator and you deal with the individual as the builder deals with stones." (p. 45)

I have concentrated in this review on Mises's analysis of Marxism, but four of the lectures deal with capitalism. I shall confine myself to two important remarks Mises makes about Austrian business-cycle theory. First, he does not claim that the theory accounts for all business fluctuations:

> We do not mean economic crises brought about by some obvious event that makes it possible to explain the emergence of this crisis . . . [such as the crisis in Europe when the Civil War prevented cotton exports]. We do not deal with such crises due to a definite identifiable situation. We deal with a genuine crisis in all branches of business—although it is sometimes worse in some branches than in others—a crisis for which people couldn't see any special reason. (p. 69)

Mises's second remark is of vital importance today, when, in our present troubles, cries for bailout and stimulus abound. Mises says, by contrast, that all expansion of bank credit must absolutely cease: *"no more legal tender banknotes and no more credit expansion!"* (p. 75, emphasis in original).

I cannot resist one more of Mises's brilliant remarks:

> Hegel was the man who destroyed German thinking and German philosophy for more than a century, at least. He found a warning in Immanuel Kant . . . who said the philosophy of history can be written only by a man who has the courage to pretend that he sees the world with the eyes of God. Hegel believed he had the "eyes of god," that he knew the end of history, that he knew the plans of God. (pp. 8–9)

I have noted a few mistakes in the text: The reference to those who interpreted history as the history of technology cannot have been to Leopold von Ranke: this was not his view (p. 5). "Albrecht von Heiler" should be "von Haller" (p. 6). Mannheim's sociology of knowledge grew out of Marx's ideas, not Hitler's (p. 7). "Darwin's *Origin of the Species*" should be *"Origin of Species"* (p. 14). The abbreviation for "dialectical materialism" is "diamat," not "diamet" (p. 15). Bergson's *élan vital* does not mean "myths, fairy tales, and legends" (p. 30). "House of Orange" should be "House of Orléans" (p. 30). The famous book of Friedrich Lange was *The History of Materialism*, not *The History of Marxism* (p. 43).

"Friedrich Hayek as a Teacher"

DAVID GORDON

May 8, 2009, *Mises Daily*

IN 1969, FRIEDRICH HAYEK taught at UCLA; he was Flint Professor of Philosophy, a visiting position of great prestige which had in past years been held by Bertrand Russell and Alfred Tarski. I was then a senior and enrolled in his only undergraduate class, Philosophy of the Social Sciences. He also taught a graduate seminar that covered the manuscript of his then forthcoming *Law, Legislation, and Liberty*. I was too shy to ask Hayek whether I could attend this also; but memories of what I was fortunate enough to hear have stayed with me in the forty years since that time.

Most of the students—I think there were about thirty-five in the class—hadn't previously heard of Hayek; but it was at once obvious to everyone that their professor was someone of extraordinary intelligence. (One student who already admired Hayek was David Glasner, who went on to become a well-known economist.)

At the first session, Hayek told us that in order to understand the philosophy of the social sciences, one needed to know something about the philosophy of science in general. Because he would not be lecturing on this subject, he asked everyone to read a book on the topic, such as his friend Karl Popper's *The Logic of Scientific Discovery*. He did not just tell us this but went around the room, asking each person to promise to read a book on the philosophy of science. After a number of people had promised, someone asked Hayek why it was necessary for each person to promise individually. Hayek replied that he wanted to make sure everyone had made a commitment. He did not refer to this requirement again, except once to wonder whether those who had chosen Popper's book had quit when they got to the sections on probability theory.

Mention of Popper's book brings to mind another time he mentioned it. When he called the book *The Logic of Research*, a student raised his hand. "Isn't the title *The Logic of Scientific Discovery*?" he asked. Hayek smiled and responded,

> You are quite right that when the book appeared in English translation in 1959, it was under the title *The Logic of Scientific Discovery*. But you see, when the book was published in Vienna in 1935, it was under the title *Logik der Forschung*, which translates, "The Logic of Research."

It was very hard to catch Hayek out on a factual inaccuracy, although I recall he once erred on the date of Julius Caesar's assassination.

Hayek delivered his lectures seated at a desk. He never used notes, but his lectures could easily be printed verbatim. When a student asked a question, Hayek would pause and then deliver an answer in language as equally exact as his lectures. He would sometimes twist his head in order to hear the question better. He said that he found it an interesting historical coincidence that he was deaf in the left ear, and Karl Marx had been deaf in the right ear.

The main assigned reading was an anthology edited by May Brodbeck, *Readings in the Philosophy of the Social Sciences*. She was a positivist, whose views contrasted sharply with Hayek's. As a counterweight, he also assigned his own *The Counter-Revolution of Science*. (Her positivist views did not prevent her from becoming friends with Murray Rothbard.) Often, his lecture would be a critical reading of a selection from the anthology. As he countered the positivist missteps, he would flick ashes from the cigarettes he smoked on the pages of the offending article.

He was keen to stress methodological individualism, the view that only individuals act. References to collectives such as nations and classes that act must in principle be capable of being reduced to individuals' actions. He thought highly of an article on the topic by J. W. N. Watkins, "The Principle of Methodological Individualism." Like Watkins, Hayek noted that methodological individualism does not require us to identify specific actors: one can explain social phenomena by appeal to the actions of anonymous individuals.

A noted opponent of methodological individualism, Othmar Spann, was one of Hayek's teachers at the University of Vienna. He reversed methodological individualism, holding that the collective was prior to the individual.

Spann used an odd diagram, which showed a larger and smaller circle connected at the top by arcs, to illustrate his theory. Hayek said that when Spann put this diagram on the blackboard and had his back turned to the class, students would put their arms over their heads to make fun of Spann.

Some people explain social institutions by appealing to their function. Marxists, e.g., claim that the function of the relations of production is to advance the development of the forces of production. Methodological individualists do not accept this type of explanation, unless the functions can be cashed out in individuals' actions. On this topic, Hayek recommended a famous article by Robert K. Merton, "Manifest and Latent Functions." He said, "Merton is about the best of the sociologists. Of course, this isn't saying very much."

Methodological individualism, as Hayek taught it, went together with subjectivism. To explain social phenomena, one had to start from the preferences and perceptions of individual actors. He rejected strongly behaviorist pretensions to characterize thought and perception without reference to private impressions. He said, e.g., that perceived colors could not be identified with an objectively measurable place on the light spectrum. He develops this argument, along with many related ones, in more detail in *The Sensory Order.* I managed once to make him laugh with a joke about two behaviorists who meet each other. One of them says, "You're fine; how am I?"

Of course, appeal to the individual actor does not imply that all social institutions are the product of conscious intentions. To the contrary, Hayek emphasized the importance of unintended consequences; the study of these consequences, he held, was the principal task of social science. He emphasized that Kant's notion of "unsocial sociability" influenced him here. Overall, he said, Kant and Hume were the two philosophers from whom he had learned the most.

All readers of Hayek will be familiar with tacit knowledge; and once he gave us a striking example of this. He said that a few years before, he had resumed skiing after a long absence from the slopes. While he was skiing downwards at a fast pace, he suddenly saw a body lying directly in front of him. Without thinking about it, he immediately swerved aside.

Hayek emphasized the a priori character of praxeology much less than Mises did. (Though Hayek differed from Mises on this issue of method, he held Mises in the greatest esteem. He recommended Mises's *Theory and History* very highly.) Usually, people ascribe this shift to Popper's influence; but his comments in class showed that this is not the full story. He was very impressed by W. V. O. Quine, whose famous challenge to the analytic-synthetic distinction, if accepted, is usually taken to rule out synthetic a priori truths. Hayek told me, "I regard Quine as one of our most stimulating philosophers." I do not mean to deny Popper's influence, though: it was clear that Hayek held him in high regard. He told me that Popper's *The Open Society and Its Enemies* gives a convincing account of Plato and Hegel but is probably too hard on Aristotle.

He also, by the way, had a high opinion of Murray Rothbard. When I asked him about *America's Great Depression*, he said it was an excellent book and gave a convincing interpretation of the Depression. He did not like to speak, though, of a business "cycle," because the term implies that there is a return to the original starting point. This normally does not happen when a depression ends. For the economics of Milton Friedman, he had much less sympathy: he once strongly criticized Friedman's proposal of a negative income tax.

As the story about "cycle" shows, Hayek emphasized precise use of words. Once, when a student used "criteria" as a singular noun, Hayek said that when people said "criteria" when they should have said "criterion" and "phenomena" instead of "phenomenon," it hurt his ears.

He gave some talks on social and cultural evolution, and it was evident that Darwinian evolution was a strong influence on his thought. Though he recommended the work of his friend Ludwig von Bertalanffy on general systems theory, he dismissed entirely Bertalanffy's skepticism about standard evolutionary theory.

The required work for the course was a single paper, due near the end of the course. Hayek gave me some advice on my paper that has been of great help to me in later work. I did a critical review of an article by Ernest Nagel on method in economics. "Remember," Hayek said to me, "point-by-point refutation." In his own critical work, Hayek was not satisfied with a challenge to the main thesis of an opponent. He responded to every argument advanced in the adversary's work. Those who wish to see this method in action should see his famous response to Foster and Catchings, "The 'Paradox' of Saving," in *Prices and Production and Other Works* (edited by Joseph T. Salerno). It remains only to say that Hayek, despite his ferocity as a critic, was a very easy grader.

The Economic Naturalist's Field Guide: Commonsense Principles for Troubled Times[*]

ROBERT H. FRANK

A Field Guide to Interventionism

July 1, 2009, *Mises Review*

BEWARE OF ECONOMICS COLUMNISTS for *the New York Times*. The days when Mises and Henry Hazlitt wrote for the paper have long since passed. Nowadays, Paul Krugman in his columns seems determined to disguise the undoubted intelligence that won him a Nobel Prize. Robert Frank, also a distinguished theorist, contributes a column to the *Times* as well and does little better than Krugman. Somehow, in this collection of Frank's columns, the free market nearly always is the object of indictment.

Around fifty years ago, John Kenneth Galbraith in *The Affluent Society* complained about the way Americans spent money. We spent too much, he alleged, on useless luxuries such as cars with high tail-fins. As a result, needed public services were starved of funds.

Frank agrees with Galbraith's conclusions but recognizes that there is a problem—Galbraith's arguments were wrong:

---

[*] Basic Books, 2009.

> [Galbraith's] critics argued . . . that if consumers were paying
> high prices for goods of little intrinsic value, there would be
> "cash on the table," the economist's metaphor for unexploited
> profit opportunities. Rivals could thus earn easy money by of-
> fering slightly cheaper and better products, in the process lur-
> ing exploited customers away. . . . Galbraith's critics had a point.
> Indeed, his explanation for society's spending imbalance suf-
> fered from the same deficiency that has plagued arguments of
> social critics on the left since Karl Marx. Because it implied that
> greedy capitalists were leaving cash on the table, most econo-
> mists couldn't accept it. (p. 78)

Fortunately, says Frank, he can now come up with better arguments for
Galbraith's conclusions: Galbraith was right but for the wrong reasons. So
enamored is Frank of Galbraith's anti-market views, though, that he nevertheless thinks that he deserved the Nobel Prize.

The key to the correct anti-market position is this. Critics of the market
want more government programs and support measures to curb inequality.
But, defenders of the market claim, interference with the market reduces
productivity. We thus face an "equity-efficiency trade-off." Frank's good
news is that the trade-off can be avoided. Some types of intervention entail
no loss in efficiency and may even promote it.

> Traditional economic discourse—as exemplified in the late Ar-
> thur Okun's 1975 book *Equity and Efficiency: The Big Tradeoff*—
> has conditioned us to think of efficiency and equality as com-
> peting goals. Consequently many believe that we must tolerate
> a certain measure of waste in the name of fairness. But I argue
> here for the opposite claim—that efficiency is always and ev-
> erywhere the best way to promote equity. (p. 5)

In brief, Frank's argument is that certain types of consumer spending do
not really advance welfare. By imposing taxes on them, we can provide funds
for needed public services without a corresponding loss in welfare from
those taxed. A net gain to efficiency thus results from these taxes. Frank also
worries about the malign effect on efficiency of "winner-take-all" markets.

Before turning to his claims, though, it is worth examining an argument
that threatens to derail Frank's reformist project before it starts. Are not

people free to spend their money as they wish, regardless of Frank's efficiency schemes? Rush Limbaugh thought so, and told Frank to mind his own business. Frank responds:

> Yet consider the absurdity of the claim that we have a right to spend every nickel of our pretax income. If taxes were purely voluntary, our government would not be able to raise revenue to build roads or schools. It could not field an army ... perhaps those who oppose compulsory taxation should just move to a country where taxes are voluntary. But there is no such country. Given that reality, our best option is to have an intelligent conversation about what services we want government to provide and who should be taxed to pay for them. (p. 10)

Libertarian anarchists, as well as those minarchists who believe in voluntary taxation, will of course not be so ready to dismiss as absurd the view that people "have a right to spend every nickel" of their income. Let us, though, put this aside for the moment; Frank is here relying on the fact that most people do concede the necessity of a government supported by compulsory taxation. Does it then follow, as Frank thinks, that it is then up to "us," i.e., the voting public, to determine what taxes and government services we want?

I do not think that it does. All that follows if one accepts Frank's points that a government is necessary and that it must be supported by compulsory taxation (once more, of course, points I reject) is that there is a justification for the taxes required to support the minimum functions of government. Frank has not at all established that everyone's entire income is "up for grabs."

Unfortunately, Frank is one of many eminent economists who wrongly think that they are competent political philosophers as well. The notion that people have a natural right to their property apparently baffles him. Thus, he points out that in some situations people have a tendency to consider equal distribution as fair:

> Imagine that you and two friends are hiking in the Canadian woods when you spot a sparkling object beneath a bush just off the trail. You pick it up and see that it is a large diamond in the rough. A jeweler you trust offers you $900,000 for it. How should this money be apportioned between you and your friends? Most people say you should share the proceeds equally.... In attempting

274 of Mof this response, psychologists say that most people

> to make sense of this response, psychologists say that most people
> feel a strong commitment to equality as a moral norm. (p. 163)

Despite this commitment, it would be wrong to impose absolute equality
of income because

> that would be a recipe for economic disaster ... the reason most
> people think complete equality is an unrealistic goal is that we
> need to maintain work incentives. Unless individual incomes
> are linked to work in some clear way, we consign ourselves to
> lives of abject poverty. (pp. 163–164)

Frank here ignores the fact that other examples evoke quite contrary moral
intuitions. Suppose that you are prospecting for gold by yourself and discover
some. Several other prospectors approach you. Are you obliged to share your
gold with them? Frank's case, to the extent we find his egalitarian conclusion
from it plausible, depends on the special assumption that the hiking friends
are on a trip together and may be thought to have an implicit agreement to
pool lucky finds. Frank wrongly generalizes from his case to a general principle of egalitarian distribution. In thinking that only efficiency considerations
tell against the full implementation of equality, he shows himself tone deaf to
Lockean claims that individuals justly can acquire title to unowned resources.

However much we disagree with them, the two arguments by Frank just
considered are not outright disasters. The same cannot be said of another
claim he advances. Seeing what is wrong with the next argument will show
us why Frank's proposals would not work, even if his arguments about inefficient consumption were right.

Frank defends an estate tax, and in its support he offers this incredible
argument:

> Another attraction of the estate tax is that it works like a law-
> yer's contingency fee. Injured parties who could not otherwise
> afford access to the legal system can try to collect damages be-
> cause lawyers are willing to work without pay if their client does
> not win. Similarly, the estate tax enables us to enjoy valuable
> public services that we would be happy to pay for if we knew
> we would end up wealthy, but that we might be reluctant to de-
> mand otherwise. With the estate tax, the surcharge kicks in only
> if we are lucky enough to be one of life's biggest winners. (p. 26)

But the lawyer who works on a contingency fee will do so because he thinks he has a good chance to win the case and earn a substantial reward for his efforts. This situation differs altogether from the situation that Frank envisions, in which people vote to provide themselves with services, knowing that there is little chance they will have to pay for them. Because the estate tax falls only on the very rich, and most people realize that they have little chance of attaining great wealth, by voting for public services paid for by the estate tax they compel others to provide them with benefits.

This brings to light a fundamental error in Frank's entire case, even if he is right that there are egalitarian measures that do not lessen efficiency. Even if there are cases where there is no "equity-efficiency tradeoff," these will be swamped by other cases where egalitarian measures *are* inefficient. These cases arise from the circumstance just mentioned, that people can vote from programs that benefit them while shifting the burden of payment to others.

But what of Frank's main contention, i.e., that cases existing where everyone gains through taxes on inefficient consumption? An example will illustrate Frank's point. Suppose that you want to have a house at least as large as those of your neighbors. If one of the neighbors enlarges his house, you will be tempted to do likewise, in order to keep up with him. This may set off a competitive struggle, in which people enlarge their houses only to keep pace with neighbors. All of them would be better off if a consumption tax made it difficult for them to engage in such arms races. They would be better off because the additional space does not "really" increase their utility: everyone is perfectly content if no one expands.

I have offered criticisms of this argument in earlier reviews of Frank's books and will not repeat these points here.* Rather, let us ask a different question. Assuming that Frank has made an acceptable argument that wasteful rivalrous consumption is possible, does he show that it is an important factor in the American economy?

He fails to do so, and we can use his own words against him. In order to have a case of the kind he wants, he needs to show, e.g., that people derive no direct benefit from, e.g., a larger house: any gain in utility exists only because of a competitive arms race. Yet as he admits:

---

* See my reviews of *Luxury Fever* and *Falling Behind* found in Volume 1, "Economics."

> Perceptions of quality influence the demand for virtually every good, including even basic goods like food. . . . There are no obvious limits to the escalation of quality standards. . . . By placing the desire to outdo others at the heart of his description of insatiable demands, Keynes relegated such demands to the periphery. But the desire for higher quality has no natural limits. Keynes and others were wrong to imagine a two-hour work-week enabling us to buy everything we want. That hasn't happened and never will. (p. 57)

Frank does not grasp that he has here refuted his main reason for a consumption tax. By assuming that people want certain goods only because others want them, he ignores the likelihood that people consider the consumption Frank deems wasteful to be genuine quality improvements.

This is not the only instance in which Frank refutes his own arguments. Like most good leftists, Frank dislikes SUVs. People want them because it is an advantage to have a large vehicle, in case of an accident. But is this not a case of rivalrous competition, of just the sort Frank decries? People would not want large vehicles unless they feared that others would obtain them. Will not a tax on SUVs benefit everyone? But Frank himself says:

> Nor can safety concerns explain the success of SUVs . . . their weight confers some advantages in head-on collisions with smaller vehicles . . . but their poor handling, high propensity to roll over, and longer stopping distances make them more dangerous, on balance, than cars. (p. 141)

How can Frank fail to see that he has knocked out his earlier claim that any "family that unilaterally bought a smaller vehicle might thus put itself at risk by unilaterally disarming" (p. 122)? A columnist can no doubt forget what he wrote years before; but is it too much to ask that a collection of columns be edited for consistency?

The Keynes Solution: The Path to Global Economic Prosperity*

PAUL DAVIDSON

Left Wing Keynesianism: An Infantile Disorder

October 1, 2009, *Mises Review*

IT IS NOT often that Paul Samuelson and Paul Krugman are indicted for lack of fidelity to Keynes, but this is exactly Paul Davidson's complaint against them. Davidson is a leading Post Keynesian, who holds that almost all economists, even professed Keynesians, have been untrue to the radical vision of *The General Theory*. The pseudo Keynesians attempt to domesticate Keynes by combining his theories with neoclassical economics; in fact, the two approaches are diametrically opposed.

He remarks that

> Samuelson has called himself a "Keynesian" and even a "post-Keynesian" in several editions of his famous textbook. Nevertheless, it should be obvious that by his own admission Samuelson, who became the premier American Keynesian of his time, had not understood Keynes's *General Theory* book. (p. 171)

---

* Palgrave Macmillan, 2009.

Krugman is also weighed in the balance and found wanting:

> In a December 14, 2007, piece, [on the housing bubble] . . . Paul
> Krugman . . . did not suggest any remedies that government could
> take to relieve the distress caused by the deflating housing bubble.
> He wrote that the market would solve the problem by deflating
> housing prices until they would fall by approximately 30 percent
> to restore a normal ratio relative to people's income. (pp. 24–25)

Davidson's complaint about Krugman suggests the nature of the misunderstanding of Keynes that concerns him. In the view that he opposes, the price system is held to be basically in order. Government needs on occasion to supplement it: in particular, because of labor unions and the "money illusion," government spending in a depression is needed to drive down real wages.

Samuelson adopts exactly this perspective:

> In 1986, 50 years after Keynes's *General Theory* was published,
> Samuelson was still claiming that "we [Keynesians] always as-
> sumed that the Keynesian underemployment equilibrium floated
> on a substructure of administered prices and imperfect compe-
> tition." . . . If sticky wages and prices cause unemployment, how-
> ever, there was nothing revolutionary about Keynes's analysis.
> After all, nineteenth-century economists had already demon-
> strated that if wages were rigid in a Walrasian classical theory
> model, unemployment would result. (p. 171)

Keynes's idea was entirely different. He denied that his analysis depended on inflexible prices and wages:

> In Chapter 19 of his *General Theory*, Keynes specifically stated
> that his theory of unemployment did not rely on the assump-
> tion of wage and/or price rigidities. He claimed that his theory
> provided a different analysis where the cause of unemployment
> was related to the operation of financial markets and the pub-
> lic's desire to hold liquid assets. (p. 163)

To grasp Keynes's theory, one must first consider the contrasting framework, accepted down to our day by most economists, which Keynes rejected. In that view, everything is fine as long as prices and wages are flexible. If prices can adjust to changes in business expectations, why should there ever be a serious problem? Davidson contends that this way of thinking rests on a flawed assumption. Advocates of the standard model imagine that accurate markets exist, not only for present transactions, but for future contracts as well.

The assumption of accurate futures markets in turn rests on a hypothesis, which Davidson deems the crucial principle of neoclassical economics.

> Since drawing a sample from the future is not possible, efficient market theorists presume that probabilities calculated from already existing past and current market data are equivalent to drawing a sample from markets that will exist in the future . . . the presumption that data samples from the past are equivalent to data samples from the future is called *the ergodic axiom*. Those who invoke this ergodic assertion argue that economics can be a "hard science" like physics or astronomy *only* if the ergodic axiom is part of the economist's model. . . . The ergodic presumption is the essential foundation of classical efficient market theory. (p. 37)

Readers will not be surprised to learn that Samuelson, who evidently ranks high on the list of Davidson's villains, fervently endorses the ergodic axiom.

Keynes saw the fallacy in this assumption. The future is in fact radically uncertain.

> The classical ergodic axiom, which assumes that the future is known and can be calculated as the statistical shadow of the past, was one of the most important classical assumptions that Keynes rejected. . . . For decisions that involved potential large spending outflows or possible large income inflows that span a significant length of time, [Keynes argued that] people "know" that they do not know what the future will be. They do know that for these important decisions, making a mistake about the future can be very costly. . . . (pp. 46–47)

Keynes, the author of *A Treatise on Probability*, was well equipped to make this fundamental point.

Davidson is right that Keynes has here scored heavily against neoclassical economics. But the uncertainty of the future hardly suffices to establish the validity of the Keynesian system. For one thing, Austrian economics also emphasizes the uncertainty of the future. It is constantly stressed by Mises, who goes so far as to claim that the uncertainty of the future is a praxeological law, deduced from the action axiom. Davidson never so much as mentions the Austrian School in this book. For him, only the efficient-market economists, with their false ergodic assumption, and their Keynesian rivals count.

In what way is Keynes supposed to be superior to Mises? Perhaps the answer lies in the second main assumption that Keynes made. In his view, at least in Davidson's rendition of it, a capitalist economy rests on people's ability to fulfill their contracts. To do so, they must have ready access to money.

> In Keynes's view, the sanctity of money contracts is the essence of the entrepreneurial system we call capitalism. Since money is that thing that can always discharge a contractual obligation under the civil law of contracts, money is the most liquid of all assets. (p. 51, emphasis omitted)

If, owing to uncertainty about the future, people fear that they will lack liquidity, they will endeavor to increase their cash balances. Private spending and investment will then fall. Faced with falling demand, businessmen will prove even more reluctant to invest and the demand for liquidity will increase further. A spiral downwards can quickly occur.

> Business firms will start reinvesting in plant and equipment only after market demand has risen sufficiently so that firms believe sales will be pressing on existing capacity. Accordingly, in a recession, we cannot expect enterprises to increase their spending on investment. (p. 56)

What is the solution? Government must come to the rescue through an increase in spending. Once businesses respond to the increased demand created by the government's spending, the economy will revive.

> Accordingly, in a recession, it is just the federal government [in the United States] that is able not only to maintain but actually to increase spending on the profits of private enterprise, even if tax receipts are due to declining incomes for business firms and households. Of course, to buy more while revenues are declining, the federal government must finance these purchases

by borrowing money—that is, by increasing the annual deficit and adding to the national debt. . . . (p. 57)

An increase in government spending during a recession is precisely the opposite of what Austrian economists would recommend. But this difference does not count as an advantage for Keynes—quite the contrary. Davidson seems oblivious to the fact that money has a purchasing power. For him, what counts is the existence of a certain number of monetary units, principally so that people can fulfill their contracts. If people want more of these units to increase their liquidity, fewer units are available to purchase goods and services. The result is an economic collapse. Had he taken account of purchasing power, he would have realized that if people increase their demand to hold money, the purchasing power of money will rise. So long as prices are flexible, there need be no fall in demand for goods and services.

Davidson's odd view of money becomes evident from what he says about money neutrality. He denies that an increase in government spending is inflationary. The view to the contrary depends on a false axiom: "This neutral money axiom asserts that any increase in the supply of money into the economy will affect neither the volume of goods produced nor the level of employment in the economy" (p. 65).

Davidson, by claiming that the axiom is false, asserts that a mere increase in the number of monetary units increases productivity and, correspondingly, that a decrease in the number of monetary units curtails the volume of goods produced. Again, he disregards prices: for him, apparently, the purchasing power of money is a useless complication.

Davidson's Post Keynesian account suffers from a related problem. Against his enemies, the proponents of efficient markets, Davidson is anxious to assure us that the future is uncertain. But he nevertheless has a mechanical view of what will happen if government spending in a recession takes place as massively as he wishes. Then, he assures us, the economic doldrums will end and all will be well. How does he know that business and consumer confidence will respond so readily to the injection of government money? Evidently, the future is uncertain, but somehow this state of affairs alters when government enters the scene.

Why should we believe this? Why assume that business confidence is so rigidly determined? Is it not rather the result of many causes that, if indeed the future is uncertain, cannot be readily specified?

Davidson writes very clearly, and his readers will find it easy to grasp his account of Keynes's contributions. But he fails completely to show that these supposed discoveries represent genuine insights, and he seems to have a real gift for focusing on Keynes's worst ideas. One example must here suffice. Following the unfortunate article "National Self-Sufficiency" (1933) that even most of Keynes's followers prefer to forget, Davidson has little use for free trade. Yet he is constrained to admit,

> Suppose the Chinese spent the $10 billion [savings on international earnings] on the products of American industries, instead of using their international savings to buy Treasury bonds. The result would be that (1) more products from American factories would be available in China to enhance the standard of living of Chinese workers, and (2) American businesses and their workers would earn more income and not have to borrow from the Chinese to finance their excessive import purchases of Chinese goods. (p. 124)

Why in that case the imports would be "excessive" he does not tell us; but here the advantages of international exchange do not entirely escape this eminent Post Keynesian.

End This Depression Now!*

PAUL KRUGMAN

Spending Our Way to Prosperity

July 1, 2012, *Mises Review*

S
UPPORTERS OF KEYNESIAN ECONOMICS sometimes claim it to be
a crude caricature of the Master that he thought the government
has only to spend more money to get us out of a depression and that
getting us into debt doesn't matter because we owe it to ourselves. Keynes, it
is alleged, was a vastly more sophisticated thinker than this caricature portrays him to be. These defenders may find *End This Depression Now!* discon-
certing. Krugman, who whatever his faults certainly is not lacking in technical sophistication, defends pretty much the cartoon version of Keynesianism
that we are told is oversimplified.

He makes unmistakably clear the lesson he intends to convey: the government needs to spend a great deal of money to extricate us from our depressed
economic conditions.

> But the essential point is that what we really need to get out of
> this current depression is another burst of government spend-
> ing. Is it really that simple? Would it really be that easy? Basi-
> cally, yes. (p. 39)

To those who worry that spending on the scale he has in mind would add
to the already huge government deficit, he says,

---

* Norton, 2012.

It's true that people like me believe that the depression we're in was in large part caused by the buildup of household debt, which set the stage for a [Hyman] Minsky moment in which highly indebted households were forced to slash their spending. How, then, can even more debt be part of the appropriate policy response? The key point is that this argument against deficit spending assumes, implicitly, that debt is debt—that it doesn't matter who owes the money. Yet that can't be right; if it were, we wouldn't have a problem in the first place. After all, to a first approximation debt is money we owe to ourselves; yes, the United States has debt to China and other countries, but . . . our net debt to foreigners is relatively small and not the heart of the problem. (p. 146)

Why does Krugman favor increased government spending? After the collapse of the housing market and the bank and investment house failures that accompanied this collapse, consumers' spending fell. Faced with the prospect of diminished spending by consumers, investors were reluctant to invest. Unless the government acted, the economy threatened to spiral downward. Government aid programs and actions by the Fed prevented total collapse, but spending has not been sufficient. The government needs to do more. "Why is unemployment so high, and economic output so low? Because we—where by 'we' I mean consumers, businesses, and governments combined—aren't spending enough" (p. 24).

One might at first object to Krugman's argument in this way. If the government spends more but does not increase the supply of money, must it not be the case that someone else has spent less money? In this view, there cannot be an overall failure of demand. More of particular goods can be produced than people want at the price they are offered for sale, but there cannot be general overproduction.

Krugman rejects this counterposition. "This is the fallacy Keynes called 'Say's Law'" (p. 25).

What is wrong with Say's law, in brief, is that money need not be either spent or invested. People can hoard money; and, if they do so, a failure in total demand can indeed result. Surprisingly, he does not offer a detailed account of how hoarding produces this failure in total demand. "You can write down a little mathematical model to illustrate the issues, but this works only with economists, not with normal human beings (and it doesn't even work with some economists)" (p. 26). Instead, he supports his criticism of Say's law with a story that he has already used in his *The Return of Depression Economics*. The story is about a babysitting cooperative, the members of which find themselves at cross-purposes.

I do not propose to rehearse here the details of Krugman's babysitting example and its relevance to the case of economic depression.* Let us instead look at the Keynesian analysis directly. Does it rest on plausible assumptions? What evidence supports it?

It will come as no surprise to readers that the Keynesian account strikes me as unpersuasive. For one thing, as Krugman himself acknowledges, the depression starts with the collapse of particular markets such as housing. If this is so, why are investors supposed to fear a general fall in future consumer demand? Is not the problem rather that there has been malinvestment in specific areas? The solution would then be to shift resources away from these areas into others. So long as this is done, why would businessmen refuse to invest?

Krugman is aware of this response, but he believes it is just what we need to avoid. He cites Joseph Schumpeter, who warned against policies of government stimulus to end depressions. Instead, bad investments should be left to fail:

> For any revival which is merely due to artificial stimulus leaves part of the work of depressions undone and adds, to an undigested remnant of maladjustment, new maladjustment of its own which has to be liquidated in turn, thus threatening business with another crisis ahead. (p. 204, quoting Schumpeter)

Krugman does not tell us what is wrong with Schumpeter's reasoning. Instead, he takes for granted that investors in a depression expect a general collapse in consumers' demand.

But suppose, contrary to fact, that investors did expect a general fall in consumer demand. Would it follow that investment would stop, miring the economy in continuing depression? By no means. As Friedrich Hayek noted long ago, investment in a business can be profitable even if demand for the product of the industry has fallen. What concerns the businessman is not the quantity of his product that buyers demand at a given price, considered

---

* I have elsewhere discussed the babysitting cooperative and Krugman's use of it. See my "Krugman's Nanny State" in the *American Conservative* for January 12, 2009.

in isolation, but rather that amount compared with his costs. If his costs have also fallen, why cannot investment continue?

As Hayek says,

> As it is not the absolute level of the prices of the product, but only their relative level in comparison with factor prices which determines the remunerativeness of production, it is, therefore, never the absolute size of the demand for consumption goods, but the relative size of the demands for the means of production to be used for the various methods of producing consumption goods that determines this relative profitableness.[*]

Krugman might respond to our objections in this way: "You may cavil at various details of Keynes, but the evidence demonstrates that he is right. Government spending does indeed revive prosperity and create jobs."

Does not this response ignore the obvious? The government under Bush and Obama has spent a great deal of money; but, on Krugman's own showing, the economy has failed fully to recover. Does this not give us some reason to think that the Keynesian prescription is inadequate? Krugman does not think so. He says the problem with current American policy is that the government has not spent enough. Further, he says, he does not here speak with the wisdom of hindsight. He warned long ago that the amount of money the government proposed to spend would not suffice to bring about recovery.

> I personally was more or less tearing my hair out in public as the shape of the [Obama] administration's plan began to come clear. . . . I feared that an inadequate stimulus would both fail to produce adequate recovery and undermine the political case for further action. (p. 119)

In cases where a correlation exists between government spending and increases in employment, he awards full marks to Keynes:

> As military spending [in 1940] created jobs and family incomes rose, consumer spending also picked up (it would eventually be restrained by rationing, but that came later). As businesses saw

---

[*] Hayek, "The 'Paradox' of Saving" in *Prices and Production and Other Works* (Mises Institute 2008), p. 177.

their sales growing, they also responded by ramping up spending. And just like that, the Depression was over. (p. 39)*

Krugman does not so much as mention the pioneering work of Robert Higgs, *Depression, War, and Cold War*, which decisively challenges the contention that World War II ended the Great Depression. Higgs convincingly shows that prosperity returned only after the war ended. But let us, very much contrary to fact, suppose that Krugman is correct about the effects of government spending in the years after 1940. His defense of Keynes would still be grossly deficient.

What he is in effect saying is this: "Instances that appear to confirm the claim that government spending ends depressions count in favor of Keynes. But cases that go against Keynes do not count, because we cannot rule out the possibility that greater spending would have worked."

What Keynes's friend Piero Sraffa, who cannot be suspected of bias in favor of the Austrian School, wrote in his copy of Keynes's *General Theory* applies to Krugman as well: "as usual, heads I win, tails you lose."[†]

One passage in the book is unintentionally revealing. Given Krugman's stress on the importance of propping up investment through government stimulus, one might have expected him to favor measures to boost business confidence. Instead, he cites with approval the Polish Marxist Michal Kalecki, who warned that appeals to business confidence were an instrument by which the capitalist class endeavored to control policy. Government should not placate business but instead control the economy directly:

> Every widening of state activity is looked upon by business with suspicion, but the creation of employment by government spending has a special aspect which makes the opposition particularly intense. Under a laissez-faire system the level of employment depends to a great extent on the so-called state of confidence. . . . This gives the capitalists a powerful indirect control over government policy; everything which may shake the state of confidence must be carefully avoided because it would cause an economic crisis. But once the government learns

---

* See also the discussion of military spending, pp. 234 ff.

† Heinz D. Kurz, "Keynes, Sraffa, and the Latter's 'Secret Skepticism'" in Bradley W. Bateman, et al., eds. *The Return to Keynes* (Harvard 2010), p. 199.

288 ⛸ AN AUSTRO-LIBERTARIAN VIEW, VOL. 1: ECONOMICS

> the trick of increasing employment by its own purchases, this
> powerful controlling device loses its effectiveness. (pp. 94–95,
> quoting Kalecki)

Krugman remarks, "This sounded a bit extreme to me the first time I read it, but it now seems all too plausible" (p. 95).

Krugman yearns for the glory that was Roosevelt and the grandeur that was Truman, but he evidently thinks that their revolution against capitalism needs to proceed further.

Krugman has nothing to say about the Austrian theory of the business cycle. Hayek is mentioned once (p. 205) in connection with the passage from Schumpeter previously quoted, but his name does not appear in the book's index. Mises and Rothbard are not mentioned at all. Given his manifest lack of understanding of the Austrian theory in earlier work, this is just as well.*

---

* See Krugman's "The Hangover Theory" in *Slate*, December 3, 1998.

Is the Market a Test of Truth and Beauty?: Essays in Political Economy[*]

LELAND B. YEAGER

The Nature and Limits of the Market

July 1, 2012, *Mises Review*

ALTHOUGH LELAND YEAGER calls himself a fellow traveler of the Austrian School (p. 100), rather than a full-fledged member of it—he is a fellow traveler of the Chicago School as well—no reader of his essays can fail to note one respect in which he resembles two quintessential Austrian economists, Ludwig von Mises and Murray Rothbard. Like them, Yeager is a scholar of enormous learning, a fact in evidence in each of the 28 essays of his collected here. As an example, few of his colleagues, one suspects, would know that "Thomas Hobbes . . . suggested that one might test whether a piece of abstract philosophizing means anything by seeing how readily it could be translated from the original language into another" (p. 267, n. 2).

Often, his own views emerge from the critical comments he makes on other writers. Yeager insists, against Robert Clower and Axel Leijonhufvud, that Keynes was a Keynesian. The writers whom Yeager opposes take Keynes to be an advocate of monetary-disequilibrium theory, stressing especially the difficulties in adjusting prices to changes in the demand to hold money.

---

[*] Ludwig von Mises Institute, 2011.

Yeager mordantly comments,

> Clower and Leijonhufvud admit that Keynes did not explicitly
> state what they suppose he meant. They offer excuses for him. In
> trying to break free from orthodoxy, he was handicapped by un-
> availability of the required concepts. The orthodox doctrine he
> was attacking had not yet been spelled out explicitly enough. Still,
> ample excuses for not having done or said something are not, af-
> ter all, the same as actually having done or said it. (pp. 159–160)

Instead, Keynes supported the crude doctrine from which his sophisticated defenders are anxious to extricate him. "I [Yeager] blame the Keynesians for lingering notions that government budget deficits, apart from how
they are financed, unequivocally 'stimulate' the economy" (p. 165). It is this
false doctrine that has had undeserved influence. The tale is best continued
in Yeager's inimitable way:

> While a visiting professor at George Mason University in the fall
> of 1983, I not only had to clean the blackboard after my classes,
> as a professor should; I also had to clear away what the incon-
> siderate professor before me had left on the board. Through
> the entire semester, more often than not, it seemed to me, what
> was left was the Keynesian cross-diagram illustrating the sim-
> ple-minded Keynesian multiplier. (p. 165. I have reversed the
> order of the two quotations from this page.)

Much more to Yeager's liking are the views of W. H. Hutt, who criticized
Keynes from a standpoint that stressed price discoordination in depressions;
in this he resembled Clower and Leijonhufvud, although he did not work
out the monetary implications to the extent these later theorists did. These
economists argued that sticky prices arise from rational behavior under the
circumstances, but

> Hutt blames government for not suppressing the basic rea-
> son—villainy—why prices and wages do not clear markets
> and assure continuous coordination. He perceives villainy—
> but the word is mine, not his—on the part of labour unions,
> business monopolists, and government itself. Villainy includes
> such things as union control over wages, minimum-wage laws,

overgenerous unemployment compensation, and monopoly and collusion. (p. 178)

I shall not resist the temptation to quote Yeager again. Hutt has not had the influence he deserves, Yeager thinks, owing to his wretched style:

> Hutt's exposition is a collection of discursive and often cryptic remarks . . . in no readily intelligible order, we find bits of positive analysis, jabs at Keynesianism, historical allusions, policy proposals, and autobiographical asides. . . . Strewn through Hutt's writings are echoes of long-standing obsessions, including, of course, his obsession with labour unions. . . . Hutt often covered himself against challenge by qualifying apparently egregious propositions with cryptic phrases that are hardly understandable unless the reader is already familiar with his terminology and allusions. (pp. 184–186)

In "Tautologies in Economics and the Natural Sciences," Yeager makes an outstanding contribution to understanding praxeology, although the essay does not have that as its purpose. The theorems of praxeology are a priori true: how, then can they give us new knowledge about the actual world? Are not such propositions mere tautologies, empty of empirical content? So, at any rate, said Mises's logical-positivist critics.

Yeager's comments on tautologies take exactly the line followed by Mises in *Human Action*, though this has not won favor among many of Mises's followers. Yeager contends that tautologies are more useful than their detractors suppose:

> Tautologies are analytic or logically necessary propositions. . . . Analytic propositions *can* give us new knowledge (or aid us in its pursuit). . . . Logic and mathematics, although apodictically certain, can sometimes yield surprising results. . . . Concepts may legitimately be formulated so that certain propositions about relations among them are not merely true but necessarily true. Many propositions of science are true as a matter of convention, yet conventions are not arbitrary. (pp. 263–264, 277)

Not content with this contribution, Yeager in another essay, directly devoted to Mises, offers another line of defense for praxeology. He says that

Mises took a priori propositions in economics to be common-sense truths: they are empirical, but of a character whose truth is immediately apparent without testing.

> The Austrians' concern for facts of reality is often overlooked because of their supposed insistence on a *purely* a priori method. The term, notably as used by Ludwig von Mises, unfortunately invites misinterpretation. So used, a priori suggests an unintended sharp contrast with *empirical*. Mises did not mean that all important propositions of economic theory can be spun out of factually empty logical truisms. He relied, rather, on axioms for which factual evidence constantly presses itself on us so abundantly that we can hardly imagine a world to which those axioms did not apply. (p. 138)

Readers no doubt have noted that these two defenses are not the same, but I do not think that we have here a genuine inconsistency. Perhaps some theorems of praxeology are better defended in one of these ways, and others in the other way.*

Given Yeager's resolute defense of a priori truth in economics, it is surprising that he also endorses W. W. Bartley's misguided assault on "justificationism." Yeager, following Bartley, says,

> An often unrecognized trait running through the history of philosophy, justificationism is the expectation that all proposition be justified (demonstrated, proved, warranted) by appeal to some authority, whether reason in the style of Descartes, empirical observation, divine revelation, or some other definitive source. But no interesting proposition can be justified in such a way. . . . It is reasonable to accept, tentatively, laws and theories not yet rejected on logical or empirical grounds and not yet displaced by more attractive alternatives. Accepting them in that way is not the same, however, as holding them to be justified or proved, for positive justification is downright impossible. (p. 235)

---

* I am not sure there is even the appearance of inconsistency in Yeager's own presentation. His examples of analytic tautologies in economics, such as Walras's Law and the equation of exchange, do not come from Mises. Perhaps he did not intend his account to apply to praxeology at all. But it manifestly does apply; and, in any case, Yeager cites the law of comparative advantage as a tautology (pp. 273–274) and this is part of Mises's economics.

Is it really open to doubt, e.g., that the law of diminishing marginal utility is true or that an exchange will take place only if the parties to it expect to benefit from it? I cannot see why, against Yeager's own apt remarks in support of the a priori quoted above, we should reject such apodictic truths because of some antijustificationist dogma. Most philosophers seek to avoid skepticism: Popper, Bartley, and their followers embrace it, holding, e.g., that there is no good reason to believe anything. Why join them?

Yeager's wide interests extend to ethics, and here he forcefully defends the utilitarianism of Mises and Henry Hazlitt against other views. To him, ethics rests on the ultimate value judgment that happiness is better than unhappiness. Given this judgment, which nearly everyone shares, we can say further that the best way to achieve happiness is through social cooperation in the free market. Promotion of such social cooperation thus becomes the proximate goal of ethics.

He sharply criticizes Rothbard's defense of natural rights. What is the point of natural rights, if they do not advance human happiness? Rothbard grounds natural rights in natural law. "Each entity, including the species man, has its own distinct nature." After a quotation from Rothbard, Yeager says, "To appeal to what is necessary for man's life and prosperity, given his nature, sounds like a utilitarian argument" (p. 430).

In the broad sense in which Yeager uses the term "utilitarian," no supporter of Rothbard need quarrel with what Yeager says. He is right that utilitarianism as he has characterized it is not vacuous: clearly there are some views of ethics that do not accord primacy to human happiness. Samuel Hopkins, e.g., an 18th-century Congregationalist theologian, said that people should be willing to be damned to hell, if necessary, for the greater glory of God.

Hopkins would not qualify as a utilitarian in Yeager's sense, so his utilitarianism has content; but it is nevertheless not fully specified. Whose happiness counts? Everyone's? Only that of a certain group? These and many other questions remain open. We may I think regard Rothbard's account of rights as a way of specifying Yeager's utilitarianism, rather than as a rejection of it. Yeager is free to disavow it, but if so, he needs to put in the field a competing theory. Merely to announce a preference for happiness and the market does not suffice as an ethical theory: Yeager has as it stands done no more than give us a criterion that such a theory must satisfy.

Yeager is a forceful and effective critic of numerous theories of ethics; his penetrating discussion of Buchanan's contractarianism, e.g., deserves careful study. In a few places, though, his remarks about various writers seem to me mistaken. He surprisingly treats Brand Blanshard's account of the "rational will" with favor. He says of it, "Briefly interpreted, Blanshard's rational-will doctrine says that the obligation to support government is binding because—and to the extent that—it serves social cooperation" (p. 502).

The doctrine does say this, but it also says much more. The rational-will doctrine holds that if support for the government in fact serves social cooperation then people actually do support it, even though they imagine they do not. Their conscious will need not reflect their real or rational will.

This position opens the door to the denial of freedom: the government, in restricting people, has only to say that it is enforcing the people's rational will. Indeed, the view closely resembles one which Yeager in another essay condemns. He notes the claim of Father Bernard Häring that liberty is the power to do what is good, and says of it, "On this interpretation, when the state prevents an individual from acting in a way considered bad, it is *not* infringing his liberty (or his *true* liberty). What equivocation!" (p. 312).*

Yeager remarks about John Harsanyi's defense of utilitarianism,

> If Harsanyi's method resembles Rawls's 1971 notion of choice behind a veil of ignorance, the similarity goes to show that such a conception of impartiality need not be a distinctively contractarian one, as Rawls seems to think. (p. 499)

I do not see why Yeager says this. Harsanyi's project is precisely a contractarian argument for utilitarianism.

Also, his criticism of Nozick's use of the Lockean proviso seems to me wrong. He says, "Nozick misapplies the Lockean proviso anyway, since it concerns original acquisition of property, not its retention in the face of changed circumstances of other persons" (p. 507). But Nozick is endeavoring to construct his own theory, rather than to interpret Locke. If his theory differs from Locke's, it is not by that fact alone shown to be mistaken.

---

* I have translated this, I hope correctly, from the original Interlingua. This is an artificial language Yeager has long championed. Fortunately for me, all of the other essays are written in English. The essay slightly misspells Father Häring's name.

These are minor matters. One leaves Yeager's outstanding book with admiration for the author's learning, incisive arguments, and love of liberty. Yeager mentions more than once Ayn Rand's criticism of "second-hand" thinkers. He is no second-hander but rather a proudly original thinker and scholar.

Living Economics: Yesterday, Today, and Tomorrow[*]

PETER J. BOETTKE

A Teacher of Economics

July 1, 2012, *Mises Review*

T HIS NOTABLE BOOK collects 22 articles by Peter Boettke; 8 of these
have been written in collaboration with others, including Peter
Leeson, Christopher Coyne, Steve Horwitz, David Prychitko, and
Frederic Sautet. (Boettke is a renowned teacher of economics, and Coyne
and Leeson are former students of his.) Boettke is probably best known as
an economist for his studies of Soviet socialism and for his work on development economics; but his interests range much wider than this. He displays
a remarkable ability to portray sympathetically scholars of widely varying
views; the book includes, e.g., valuable discussions of Warren Samuels, Peter
Berger, Gordon Tullock, and Kenneth Boulding.

It is not too much to say, though, that two schools of economic thought
have principally shaped his own outlook. These are the Austrian School and the
Virginia Public Choice School. These two schools of thought provide Boettke
with his main ammunition in a battle he wages through much of the book. As
he sees matters, a great deal of contemporary economic theory is dominated
by a mechanical, scientistic doctrine. This false doctrine ignores the realities of
action, time, and ignorance, in a futile quest for the false god of static perfection.

---

[*] Independent Institute in cooperation with Universidad Francisco Marroquin, 2012.

No one could read this book without being impressed by Boettke's wide knowledge, but I do not always agree with his interpretations. I propose in what follows to examine three important elements of the book: the account of Austrian methodology, especially as found in the work of Mises; the use made of James Buchanan's appeal to the status quo as the starting point for policy proposals; and the criticisms of contemporary neoclassical economics.

Boettke rightly points out that Mises thought the propositions of economic theory were a priori true. "Mises pointed out that the *aprioristic* character of the pure logic of choice implies that economic theory can never be empirically validated or invalidated" (p. 207). So far, so good; but now the question arises, how did Mises regard the character of the a priori?

Boettke again is accurate when he says. "According to Mises, it is true that like the laws of geometry, the pure logic of choice is entirely tautological" (p. 209). But why does he also say, just before this, "Although Mises can be understood as building upon Kant, he ultimately goes beyond Kant by rejecting the traditional analytic/synthetic distinction altogether" (p. 209). Tautologies *are* analytic truths: how can someone who believes that the pure logic of choice consists of tautologies also deny altogether the analytic-synthetic distinction?*

If the principles of praxeology are tautologies, how can Boettke also think that

> there is a [Barry] Smith-like "fallibilistic" element to Mises's conception of a priori knowledge, which though "true" for acting man at the present may ultimately be revealed to be mistaken (i.e., inconsistent with objective reality) with further developments in the evolution of the human mind. (pp. 205–206)

How can a tautology become false at some time in the future?

Boettke's account seems difficult to reconcile with this passage of *Human Action*:

> The problem of whether there are or whether there are not a priori elements of thought—i.e., necessary and ineluctable

---

* Mises did not think that the laws of economics are substitution instances of the laws of logic, so Boettke could not appeal to Quine in order to reconcile accepting tautologies with rejecting the analytic-synthetic distinction. I thank Terrance Tomkow for reminding me of Quine's view on tautologies.

intellectual conditions of thinking, anterior to any actual instance of conception and experience—must not be confused
with the genetic problem of how man acquired his characteristically human mental ability. Man is descended from non-
human ancestors who lacked this ability. . . . Hence the *empiricist concludes* that the foundational principles of reasoning
are an outcome of experience and represent an adaptation of
man to the conditions of his environment. . . . Reason, intellect, and logic are historical phenomena. . . . Nothing suggests
that logic as we know it is the last and final stage of intellectual
evolution. Human logic is a historical phase between prehu-
man nonlogic on the one hand and superhuman logic on the
other. . . . But the problem of the a priori is of a different character. It does not deal with the problem of how consciousness
and reason have emerged. It refers to the essential and necessary character of the logical structure of the human mind.
(*Human Action, Scholar's Edition*, pp.33–34, emphasis added.)

Boettke has ascribed to Mises the exact empiricist position against which
Mises argues.*

Unfortunately, this is not the only instance in which Boettke makes inac-
curate remarks about Mises. He says,

Deployed as an ideal type, equilibrium analysis allowed economics to describe what the world would be like in the absence
of imperfections such as uncertainty and change. . . . Equilibrium was used as an ideal type by such Austrian economists as
Mises and Hayek. (p. 281)

Boettke's central point here is correct: Mises did not intend the *evenly
rotating economy* (ERE) to be either a description of reality or a standard by
which the world should be judged. Rather, it was an imaginary construction
useful to the economist in developing economic theory.

---

* Mises's position does not exclude Darwinian accounts of the origin of the human mind.
To the contrary, in *Ultimate Foundation of Economic Science*, he advances one himself,
as Boettke notes (p. 204). But a genetic account of this kind does not, in Mises's view,
make the validity of a priori knowledge something subject to change. This is the key
issue that I think Boettke misses.

The problem lies rather in Boettke's use of the phrase "ideal type." Mises expressly says that the abstractions of economics are *not* ideal types.

> Ideal types are the specific notions employed in historical research and in the representation of its results. They are concepts of understanding. As such they are entirely different from praxeological categories and concepts and from the concepts of the natural sciences. An ideal type is not a class concept, because its description does not indicate the marks whose presence definitely and unambiguously determines class membership. An ideal type cannot be defined. (*Human Action*, pp. 59–60)

The ERE, of course, *can* be defined. The issue is not a mere matter of terms: by calling the ERE an ideal type, Boettke has elided a key distinction in Mises's epistemology.

Boettke's articles on James Buchanan convey very well his enthusiasm for that eminent economist; but I think that he has too readily agreed with Buchanan's embrace of the status quo as the necessary starting point for proposed changes in policy. In Buchanan's view, proposed changes must command a consensus among the interested parties. Starting with the existing situation, we may be able to arrive at proposals that everyone will accept as improvements.

But is there not an obvious problem with this view? What if we begin from a situation in which rights are being violated? Must slaves negotiate with their masters to secure their freedom? No doubt, it will often be prudentially rational for them to do so. But why are we debarred from saying that they ought not to be enslaved and that the masters deserve no compensation? People do not lose their rights because in the existing situation they are violated.

Boettke is aware of the problem:

> [Warren] Samuels ... correctly points out that while Buchanan's approach does not have any propriety save its existence, the unanimity criterion does privilege the existing situation.... It seems to me [Boettke] that Samuels is right; there is "conservatism" built into the analysis as Buchanan develops the approach. But what is the alternative? ... A mutual-consent-driven model does not

have to deny Samuels's points about either the nonneutrality of
affairs . . . but it does suggest that we can strive to minimize the
impact of nonneutrality. (pp. 119–120)

To see matters in this way, though, makes an undue concession to Buchanan.
He is an ethical skeptic: for him, claims that something is "right" merely
express personal preferences. One can attempt to impose these preferences on
others; but if one wishes to avoid this, one must take people's preferences as
they stand. Buchanan says in a letter to Samuels,

> But my defense of the status quo stems from my unwillingness,
> indeed inability, to discuss changes other than those that are
> contractual in status. I can, of course, lay down my own notions
> and think about how God might listen to me and impose these
> changes on you, me, and everyone else. (p. 119)

The idea of an objectively true ethics is alien to Buchanan. If Boettke wishes
to embrace ethical skepticism of this sort, he ought to have offered some
considerations in its favor.*

As mentioned earlier, there is a central theme that unifies Boettke's book.
Sound economics must take seriously time and change, and to do so the sterile models of the neoclassicals must be replaced. In his famous inaugural lecture at the London School of Economics in 1933, Hayek suggested that the
main danger to economics came from the opposition to theory of the German Historical School and similar groups. Now the situation is entirely different. "Seven decades of disastrous formalization" must be abandoned and
"the realities of economic life . . . [be] re-engaged" (p. 315).

This is an ambitious claim, and sometimes Boettke succeeds in striking
decisive blows against neoclassical formalism. In the chapter that I found most
impressive, "The Forgotten Contribution: Murray Rothbard on Socialism in
Theory and Practice," Boettke aptly shows how the neoclassicals' models of
socialism vastly overrated the ability of planners to cope with the concrete data
of the economy. Here his thesis is exactly right: arid formalism occluded the
need for realistic appraisal.

---

* I do not think it would be a good response to say that Buchanan is speaking strictly as a
descriptive social scientist, who cannot introduce his own value judgments. Clearly, he
is engaged in making normative judgments.

> The equilibrium economics of Taylor-Lange-Lerner was unable
> to grasp the nature of economic calculation because it solves the
> problem by assumption, which in fact is no solution at all. . . .
> It is this real world of heterogeneous capital goods with multi-
> ple specificity where the ability to engage in rational economic
> calculation is vital to the success or failure of the economic sys-
> tem. Without the guideposts of market prices and profit and
> loss accounting, economic planners would be set adrift on the
> sea of possibilities. (p. 83)

That is well said indeed. But one wonders why, in the course of an insightful tribute to Rothbard's contributions to the socialist-calculation debate,
he omits an important fact. He rightly says that "Rothbard's presentation
in 1962 already implied the failure of equilibrium economics to adequately
address the issues in the socialist calculation debate that was stressed in later
contributions" (p. 82). He fails to note that Mises in 1949 already fully recognized the irrelevance of general-equilibrium solutions to the debate. The
section "The Differential Equations of Mathematical Economics" in *Human
Action* is here of decisive significance.

Although Boettke seems to me to be right in his protests against the excesses
of formalism, at times his assault rests on assertion unsupported by argument.
He says that Chicago School economists held that "real markets come breath-
takingly close to approximating the efficiency properties of general competitive
equilibrium" (p. 280), but he fails to show that all of these economists had been
beguiled by their mathematical models into ignoring reality. Was this true, e.g.,
of Milton Freidman and Yale Brozen? These economists seemed rather to argue
that many important markets consisted of large numbers of small firms and that
claims that monopolies engage in predatory pricing are exaggerated. His case
seems stronger for Robert Lucas; but even here, Boettke does not show exactly
where Lucas's models fail. He acts rather as if it were enough to state Lucas's
view to show its absurdity: the New Classical view is "obviously contrary to
reality" (p. 301). Perhaps it is, but Boettke needs to prove it and not just say it.

Despite these criticisms, Boettke's book merits the attention of all students of Austrian economics. Boettke's enthusiasm and devotion to a free
economy are everywhere apparent. He says that he often tells students

> that humankind has demonstrated two natural propensities—
> to truck, barter, and exchange (as Adam Smith taught); and

to rape, pillage, and plunder (as Thomas Hobbes taught us)—
and which propensity is pursued is a function of the institutional framework within which individuals find themselves
living and interacting. (p. 385)

There can be no doubt which of these propensities Boettke wishes to
encourage.*

---

* It would be churlish to point out that the quotation gives a misleading account of Hobbes.

Money: How the Destruction of the Dollar Threatens the Global Economy—and What We Can Do about It*

STEVE FORBES & ELIZABETH AMES

The Problem with Steve Forbes's New Gold Standard

October 9, 2014, *Mises Daily*

MONEY IS AN ODD BOOK. Its odd character can be brought out through an analogy. Imagine that someone wrote an eloquent book about price and wage controls. The book showed how attempts to control prices led to economic disaster. Faced with an abundance of incontrovertible evidence that demonstrated the bad effects of these measures, an informed policymaker would find only one rational choice available to him. He should not impose comprehensive price controls but rather should use controls in moderation.

Would it not be obvious what had gone wrong with our imagined book? If price controls do not work, they should be done away with altogether. "Moderation" in the use of a bad measure is no virtue. If cyanide is poison, "drink in small doses" is not the appropriate response.

---

* McGraw Hill, 2014

Money falls exactly into the bad pattern just described. Forbes and Ames write with insight about the dangers of inflation and easy money. In response, they propose that the monetary system should be based on gold. What could be better? Unfortunately, they do not favor a genuine gold standard: instead, their plan calls for limiting monetary expansion by tying the dollar to gold at a fixed rate. In sum, monetary expansion is bad, so we ought to reduce the extent to which the Fed may engage in it.

Forbes and Ames aptly quote Ron Paul on the fundamental fallacy of inflationism: "If governments or central banks really can create wealth simply by creating money, why does poverty exist anywhere on earth?"[*] Money is valuable because we can use it to purchase goods and services: increasing the number of monetary units does not add new goods or services to those already produced. (An exception must be made for non-monetary uses of a monetary commodity, such as jewelry.)

The point seems obvious once stated; why do so many ignore it? As Forbes and Ames point out, many nations favor inflation because it will increase exports and reduce imports. Foreign buyers, so long as the money of their own nation has not also expanded as quickly, will find that they can purchase more goods for the same nominal amount of their money; and importers will find that, with their inflated money, they can purchase less.

In this view, exports are good and imports are bad; but why should we accept this?

> Trade deficits and surpluses have historically reflected little about the health of an economy. Neo-mercantilists overlook the fact that the United States has had a merchandise trade deficit for roughly 350 out of the last 400 years. . . . The fact that the United States buys products and services from other nations doesn't mean it is weak; it means that the US economy is strong and has the wealth and resources to buy what others are selling.

The authors strike forcefully at the Keynesian claim that inflation is needed to combat unemployment.

---

[*] P. 81, quoting Ron Paul. The same page mentions "noted economic historian" Murray Rothbard but Rothbard's name does not appear in the book's index.

According to [William] Phillips and his fellow Keynesians, vigorous growth corresponded to price increases, while lower inflation correlated with higher jobless levels. In other words, there was a trade-off between inflation and employment.

As the "stagflation" of the 1970s showed, the Keynesian claim is false. Inflation and unemployment

don't move the way Keynesians would have you believe. In the inflationary boom/bust era of the 1970s and early 1980s, unemployment reached higher levels than during the financial crisis.

Broadening their critical assault, Forbes and Ames show the deleterious moral effects of inflation.

Weak, unstable money inflames perceptions of unfairness. People with fixed incomes struggling with rising prices in an uncertain economy become enraged when they see others appear to get rich through speculation or crony capitalism, not honest effort. (For more on this, see Wilhelm Röpke's, *Welfare, Freedom, and Inflation*).

The natural conclusion from all this criticism of inflation is that the government ought to refrain entirely from monetary expansion; but a theoretical error blocks the authors from seeing this. The error is that money is a measure of value that must be kept constant.

Money is a standard of measurement, like a ruler or a clock, but instead of measuring inches or time, it measures what something is worth. . . . Just as we need to be sure of the number of inches in a foot or the minutes in an hour, people in the economy must be certain that their money is an accurate measure of worth.

What is wrong with this? When you pay $25,000 for a car, you are not measuring the value of the car. Rather, you are showing that you prefer the car to the money: the person who sells you the car has the reverse valuation. Without this difference in preferences, no exchange would take place. If, as Forbes and Ames imagine, money measures value, both you and the car seller would arrive at the same "measure" of the car's value. We would have no account at all of why an exchange takes place.

We can trace further the source of the authors' mistake. They rightly note that money "originated in the marketplace as a solution to a problem. It arose spontaneously, like the spoon or the personal computer, in response to a need." With money, it is much easier to achieve the "double coincidence of wants" required for an exchange than without it. But they miss why this is so. The reason is that practically everyone is willing to accept money in an exchange; it is a commodity that everyone wants. Instead, Forbes and Ames identify the need as "for a stable unit of value to facilitate trade."

This fundamental error leads them to recommend inadequate policies. Their plan leaves plenty of room for monetary expansion. Their

> gold standard allows the money supply to expand naturally in a vibrant economy. Remember that gold, a measuring rod, is stable in value. It does not restrict the supply of dollars any more than a foot with twelve inches restricts the number of rulers being used in the economy.

Money needs to expand if the economy is growing, because without the expansion, prices would fall; and then, *horribile dictu*, money would cease to be a constant measuring rod. Further, if a "major financial panic" demanded "an emergency injection of liquidity," the Fed would be able to act as a lender of last resort.

How is the goal of stable money to be achieved?

> The twenty-first century gold standard would fix the dollar to gold at a particular price.... The Federal Reserve would use its tools, primarily open market operations, to keep the value of the dollar tied at that rate of gold.

In this etiolated gold standard, only the United States would need to fix its money to gold in the fashion just mentioned.

> If the United States went to gold, other countries would likely fix their money to the dollar, if only for convenience.... Of course, if a country wanted to attach its currency directly to gold instead of the gold-backed dollar, it could do so.

An obvious objection to this proposal is that "setting a fixed dollar/gold ratio is price fixing and therefore anti-free market." To this, the authors incredibly answer:

> Having fixed weights and measures is essential for fair and free markets. We don't let markets each day determine how many ounces there are in a pound or how many inches there are in a foot.... Money, similarly, is a measure of value.

They fail to grasp that economic value is subjective: there are no fixed units of value that correspond to units of measurement of physical objects.

Their proposal, as they readily acknowledge, revives the interwar gold exchange standard and the post-World War II Bretton Woods arrangement. For them, this is no objection: those were excellent monetary systems. True enough, there are a few "gold standard purists" who argue that the policy of credit expansion pursued by the Fed in the 1920s under the gold exchange standard "produced the disaster of 1929." These purists are wrong. "The cause of the Depression was the US enactment of the Smoot-Hawley Tariff." So much for Mises, Hayek, and Rothbard! Readers in search of a deeper analysis of monetary policy should put aside this superficial book and turn instead to the works of these great Austrian theorists. A good beginning would be *America's Great Depression* by "noted economic historian" Murray Rothbard.

Philosophy

Austrian Philosophy: The Legacy of Franz Brentano[*]

BARRY SMITH

Why the Austrian School Is Austrian

December 1, 1995, *Mises Review*

A S ANY READER in the tradition will know, Austrian economics has deep links to philosophy. To understand the philosophical background out of which the Austrian School emerged is essential to a grasp of the School's doctrine. Barry Smith, in his exhaustively researched and carefully argued book, has done more than any other scholar to elucidate that background.

Lenin once observed that one cannot understand Marx without studying Hegel's *Logic*. After reading Smith, we can say: one cannot fully understand Mises without knowing something about Franz Brentano.

In Smith's view, Brentano inaugurated an approach to philosophy that became influential in the Austro-Hungarian Empire. Brentano's style of philosophy broke sharply with that prevailing in Germany, where the idealist philosophy of Kant and his successors held sway.

The

> strength of idealist metaphysics had derived in no small part
> from the fact that it was closely associated with the develop-
> ment both of German national consciousness and of the Ger-
> man nation itself, so that Kant, Hegel, Fichte, and Schelling have

---

[*] Open Court, 1994.

> come to occupy an entrenched position in German thought and
> feeling of a sort that is unparalleled in any other culture. (p. 13)

Philosophers in Kant's tradition tended to concentrate heavily on the theory of knowledge. Human beings have no direct knowledge of the world as it exists in itself. Instead, the mind (also unknowable in itself) imposes categories on reality. Given this view, Smith argues, it is hardly surprising that German philosophy developed independently of the work of scientists. Stress on the "ultimate unintelligibility of the world is often inimical to scientific theory" (p. 4).

Defenders of Kant might contend that he in fact did allow knowledge of the real world. J. N. Findlay has made a case for this view in *Kant and the Transcendental Object*. And if Kant exalted epistemology, Hegel argued strongly against its primacy. But Smith is certainly right that many in Germany read Kant in exactly the way he describes.

Even more important, in my view, is Smith's remark that the "main currents of German philosophy . . . have tended to strive for philosophical *depth*, often at the expense of clarity, which they have associated with shallowness of thinking" (p. 4).

Franz Brentano, who taught at the University of Vienna for twenty years, conceived of philosophy in an entirely different way. In his view, philosophy should be carried out in a rigorously scientific manner. Against the neo-Kantians, those in the tradition of Brentano think that

> we can know what the world is like both in its individual and
> in its general aspect, and our knowledge will likely manifest a
> progressive improvement, both in depth of penetration and in
> adequacy to the structures penetrated. (p. 323)

We can, if this view is right, know reality as it is in itself. But how do Brentano and his successors prove that we have such knowledge? This question, however natural to ask, is in the Austrian view radically misconceived. We do not have to prove that we know the world: for Brentano, the problem of skepticism is not of prime importance.

Instead, the nature of the world is "read off" directly, using both external observation and introspection. Not only is it held that we know the actual world: sometimes, just by operating in a commonsense way, we can see how the world must be.

Here there is a precise parallel with the views of Carl Menger about economics; and this parallel is, as the Trotskyists would say, "no accident."

> There are, he [Menger] holds, certain simple economic categories which are *universal* . . . and which are capable of being grasped as such by the economic theorist. Propositions expressing the relations among such categories are called by Menger exact laws. (p. 301)

Ludwig von Mises also maintained that economics grasps a priori truths; but, under neo-Kantian influence, he took these truths to be purely logical implications of the concept of action, rather than perceived necessities in the world. Smith boldly contends that Mises misdescribed his own practice. The laws of praxeology are *not*, as Mises sometimes described them, tautologies. Mises operated in a fashion that the Brentanist tradition enables us to understand better than he himself did.

Smith seems to me on firm ground here; and I venture one point as a supplement, though I fear it so obvious as hardly to be worth stating. Mises often described the propositions of economics as "synthetic a priori"; but a proposition can hardly be both a tautology and synthetic. I suspect that Mises did not write on these issues from a fixed philosophical standpoint. Smith's analysis, further, is entirely in accord with the views and practices of Murray Rothbard.

Smith again and again makes illuminating remarks about Austrian methodology. He rejects the attempt by several recent writers to connect Austrian economics with the problem of interpretation studied by hermeneutics. Claims of this sort are "quite astonishing" and reflect a "muddled confounding of the distinct intellectual traditions of Austria and Germany" (p. 320 n. 21).

Smith's treatment of the a priori is a model of clarity. At only one point in it am I inclined to dissent. Against Kantians and positivists who take a priori truths to be entirely imposed by the mind, Smith directs this argument:

> Imagine that the totality of all laws or propositions is laid out before us. Is it to be completely arbitrary which of these laws or propositions are to enjoy the imposed quality of aprioricity? A positive answer . . . is belied by the extent to which there is wide agreement across times and cultures as to which the candidate a priori laws or propositions might be. A negative answer, on the

other hand, implies that there is some non-arbitrary quality on the side of certain laws or propositions themselves, in virtue of which precisely those laws or propositions do indeed serve as the targets of imposition. (p. 310)

I think that the positivist has an escape. He can grant that there is a real quality possessed by the propositions that people take to be a priori. This quality, he may concede, is not imposed by the mind. But why need it make these propositions a priori true in a stronger sense than the conventional? What if, for example, evolutionary pressures lead people to regard some truths as a priori?

At this point I fear I must be grossly unfair to Smith. The bulk of his book is devoted to a painstaking elaboration of the views of Brentano and several of his followers. He presents, for example, a brilliantly illuminating discussion of the correspondence theory of truth, as developed by Anton Marty (pp. 113–119. He calls this section "The Martian Theory of Truth"). And he carefully expounds Brentano's often misunderstood view of intentionality (pp. 42–45).

Unfortunately, a detailed discussion of these and other points far exceeds the scope of the *Mises Review*, and my abilities as well. But I think that if, say, you are seriously interested in learning the differences between Brentano's and Kotarbinski's doctrines of reism, you need no help from me and can consult the book directly.

Everyone interested in the Austrian School needs to study thoroughly this outstanding book, at the very least the Introduction and the Chapters "Austrian Philosophy and the Brentano School" and "Carl Menger: On Austrian Philosophy and Austrian Economics."

Against the Idols of the Age[*]

DAVID STOVE

Edited by ROGER KIMBALL

Sweet Rationality

July 1, 2000, *Mises Review*

T HE PRESENT ANTHOLOGY of David Stove articles is an excellent
book throughout, but I should like first to concentrate on a few
pages that make a decisive contribution to contemporary thought.

Current irrationalist modes of thought, e.g., Marxism, feminist epistemology, and deconstruction, share a common pattern. Each contends that
because our thinking about the world is conditioned in a certain way, it does
not grasp the world as it really exists.

Marxists contend that class position determines thought. Those of us so
unfortunate enough as to be classed as "bourgeois" cannot be expected to
grasp the intricacies of the dialectic. (Of course, the thought of proletarians
and their self-proclaimed leaders is also class-determined, by this theory, but
somehow the Marxists sweep this aside.) Feminists argue in a similar way,
substituting "gender" for "class." And deconstructionalists go Marxists and
feminists one better. They claim that language by its nature dooms everyone
to paradox and contradiction.

Many readers, I am sure, already know how to refute these sophistical
doctrines. Are they not all self-refuting? This we have already suggested for
Marxism: if all thought is class-determined, and this fact makes thought

---

[*] Transaction, 1999.

unfit to grasp reality, is not Marxism also class-determined and unfit to give us truth? The appropriate refutations of feminism and deconstruction should present readers no problem.

The self-refutation argument suffices to clear these intellectual monstrosities from the field, but many will be left uneasy. Don't the fashionable leftist doctrines have a point? Is not our thought in large part conditioned by our background? One would not expect someone raised as a Dutch Calvinist to think the life of a Samurai warrior the supreme good.

It is Mr. Stove's inestimable merit to have discovered a simple logical fallacy at the heart of the pattern of false argument we have begun studying. Once exposed, the intellectual temptation of the pattern dissolves.

The story is best told in Mr. Stove's own words:

> The members of this family [of arguments] are so very various, that it is not easy to distill a schema of which they are all instances. But it is not necessary, either, because their family resemblance is so pronounced that, once you have met one member, you will easily recognize any other. The following [is a] specimen . . . We can think of things only under the forms of our thought, so, we cannot think of things as they are in themselves. (p. 171)

Once the matter has been stated in Stove's pellucidly clear way, we can at once see the fallacy. The conclusion does not follow from the premise. Of course, we can think of things only under the forms of our own thought: this is only a pretentious way of saying that we think as we think. But from this nothing follows about whether our thought can attain truth. Stove sums up: "Only three things are essential: idealism in the conclusion, tautology in the premise, and pomposity throughout" (p. 172).

How does Stove's devastating point apply to the three examples we have looked at? The Marxist claim is, "Our thought is conditioned by our class position." Either this statement is a mere tautology, as Stove alleges in his pattern, in which case it is to be read, "The thought of members of our class is the thought of members of our class." In this case, nothing whatsoever follows about whether our thoughts are true. Alternatively, it is an empirical hypothesis of some unspecified kind, and once more how it proves that class-determined thought masks reality is not obvious. Readers may apply for themselves Stove's analysis to feminism and deconstruction.

To expose as fallacious key patterns in modern thought is no small matter, but Stove's achievement does not stop here. I can best illustrate Stove's virtues by cheating a little bit. Let us consider Stove's "The Columbus Argument," which Mr. Kimball here speaks of favorably (pp. xiv, xxxi) but is available in another Stove anthology rather than the present book. Here Stove skewers the central argument of John Stuart Mill's *On Liberty*.

Mill supported freedom for "innovators" on the grounds that no improvements in society can arise without them. Against this, Stove maintains that new ideas are far more likely to cause harm than good:

> Now human societies, at least ones as large and rich as ours, are incomparably more complex than TV sets, and in fact no one understands them well enough to repair or improve them. Whatever some people may claim, there are no society repairmen, as there are TV repairmen. So if anyone gets to try out in practice his new idea for repairing or improving our society, it is something like billions-to-one that he will actually make things worse if he changes them at all. (D. Stove, *Cricket Versus Republicanism,* Sydney, 1995, p. 60)

I suspect that many readers will have interjected, "Aren't we libertarians? Do we not favor freedom? How can Stove be praised for an argument that backs suppression?" This query misconceives what Stove has accomplished. He has poked a hole in Mill's utilitarian case for freedom to innovate. He leaves entirely untouched natural rights arguments for liberty in the style of Murray Rothbard. Like Rothbard, Stove regarded Mill as a confused thinker, often governed by emotion.

Rothbard, I suspect, would have delighted in this less than favorable passage:

> Mill pleaded in *On Liberty* for the widest variety of what he chose to call "experiments in living." The phrase was a sickeningly dishonest attempt to capture some of the deserved prestige of science for things which had not the remotest connection with science; principally—need I say—certain sexual and domestic arrangements of a then "novel kind." (ibid., p. 61)

I wish that I could write invective of this quality.

Mr. Stove has fatally wounded both contemporary relativism and John Stuart Mill. Not one to rest on his laurels, he takes on another of the supposed greats of modernity—the philosopher of science Thomas Kuhn.

Who has not heard of Kuhn's catch phrase "paradigm shift"? According to Kuhn, science proceeds not by means of universally rational standards. Instead, a group of scientists who favor a new paradigm replace those entangled in the problems of the previously dominant model. Stove quickly locates the central fallacy:

> Now you could . . . take all this just as an account of the history of science, and find more or less of value in it . . . but that is not at all how . . . Kuhn himself takes it. He will not talk himself, or let you talk if he can help it of *truth* in science, or . . . of falsity: he claims he cannot understand that class of talk. (p. 13)

Kuhn has thus wrongly eviscerated the normative dimension of science. From the fact, or alleged fact, that scientists have acted in a certain way, Kuhn wrongly concludes that what they do cannot be evaluated by principles of reason. Once more, our author stands firm as a champion of reason, in a way that Misesians can only applaud.

A final example of Stove's defense of rationality must here suffice. According to sociobiologists such as E. O. Wilson, morality stems not from reason or direct perception of the good but rather from Darwinian imperatives. We help our children, e.g., because doing so helps us perpetuate our genes. Animals that practice "kin selection" win out in the struggle for survival, other things being equal, against those who do not. What we call moral behavior is what helped our prehistoric ancestors to survive and has as a result been built into us.

I venture to think that classical liberals have here a vital interest at stake. If we wish to claim that a free-market order is required by justice, surely we cannot look with favor on a theory that collapses morality into ancestral instincts.

We must once more, then, acknowledge a debt to David Stove, who subjects the sociobiological view to withering assault. As he notes, it simply does not fit the facts. By the doctrine of kin selection, people should be as ready to sacrifice for their brothers and sisters as for their children: both your brother and your child share half your genes. But of course people do not usually act as the theory predicts. In like manner, the theory predicts that an animal "will always sacrifice its life to save the lives of three or more conspecifics with each of whom it shares half its genes [such as its offspring or siblings]" (p. 314). This prediction fails in even more spectacular fashion than the previous example.

Surprisingly, Mr. Stove does not mention the most obvious defect of kin selection. People often prefer their wife or husband to a close relative, yet your spouse will share many fewer genes with you than relatives.

This example, though, merely serves to supplement Stove's powerful indictment. His unfailing defense of reason and his polemical skills of surpassing excellence command our respect.

Philosophy and Social Hope*

RICHARD RORTY

A Man Possessed

July 1, 2000, *Mises Review*

RICHARD RORTY IS A MAN POSSESSED. Like his grandfather, the Social Gospel theologian Walter Rauschenbusch, he knows what ails the world and how we may ascend to the secular equivalent of paradise. Unfortunately, a slight obstacle confronts our would-be savior: his fantasies fly in the face of reality. But, he might answer, what is that to us? If the world is not as we wish, let us simply abolish the appearance-reality distinction. We have only to change our vocabulary, and all will be well.

The plot of what the *Communist Manifesto* calls "all hitherto existing history" is a simple one, and Mr. Rorty stands ready to let us in on the secret. A few people control the world's wealth and keep everyone else in subjection.

> To say that history is "the history of class struggle" is still true, if it is interpreted to mean that in every culture, under every form of government, and in every imaginable situation . . . the people who have got their hands on money and power will lie, cheat, and steal in order to make sure that they and their descendants monopolize both forever. (p. 206)

Is there no hope for those of us not in the power elite? Fortunately, Karl Marx, if not the Messiah himself, is at least John the Baptist. "The use of Marxist doctrine to raise the consciousness of workers—to make it clear to them how they are being cheated—shows Marxism at its best" (p. 206). If

---

* Penguin Books, 1999.

a nonsupernatural version of Christianity can be blended with Marxism, so much the better.

Let us, for the moment, leave aside a principal objection to Mr. Rorty's epic: his notion of history is utterly distorted. Does not civilization depend, as Mises has better than anyone else taught, on social cooperation through the free market? If Rorty dissents, must he not confront Mises's arguments? Let us, I repeat, put aside for the moment those questions: we shall see later how our author deals with truth. Very well, then. We take as given Rorty's fantasies about history. Would he still not confront a difficulty? Why should we think that Rorty's "democratic socialism" offers any improvement over present conditions? Surely, one hopes, not even Rorty can be unaware of socialism's dismal record during the twentieth century. Perhaps it is asking too much to expect Rorty to know Mises, but can he have escaped hearing of the collapse of communism? For once, our author's historical naïveté has some limits. He readily acknowledges that socialism has failed. "Just about the only constructive suggestion Marx made, the abolition of private property, has been tried. It did not work" (p. 214). Here, I am afraid, readers may underestimate Mr. Rorty's ingenuity. He favors arousing the working class through Marxist propaganda, while at the same time he abandons Marxism. Has he not painted himself into a corner?

Not at all! So trivial a matter as an apparent contradiction is child's play to Rorty's mighty mind. He escapes his predicament by redefining socialism: in his view, it need not involve a centrally-planned economy at all. Instead, it consists of efforts to achieve "humanistic values." Even Marx's analysis of capitalism can be jettisoned: Keynes will do just as well, if not better, to analyze the antagonistic class relations of modern society.

But, you might object, far from dissolving the apparent contradiction, Rorty has only worsened his trouble. If he abandons both Marx's analysis of capitalism and his prescription for its evils, does it not become all the more strange that Rorty wants the proletariat to rally round Marx?

Here at last the solution comes to light. What interests Rorty is not the truth or falsity of Marxism. Instead, Marxism is valuable because it arouses workers' hatred of the rich. "So now it is hard to find what Derrida calls a 'political imperative' in Marx—an imperative more specific or more novel than the old, old injunction to prevent the rich from continuing to steal from the poor" (p. 214). Marx, Keynes, liberation theology, it does not matter: whatever it takes to bring down the world will win Rorty's approval.

Rorty pictures history as a struggle between the rich and the poor. On this basis, he finds useful any doctrine—true or false—which arouses the workers to fury at their chains. But must he not now respond to the query: is this account of society true?

Indeed he must: but I propose one last time to postpone consideration of his response, as it is best approached indirectly. Suppose one gives Rorty not only his picture of history, but also turns a blind eye to his admission that Marxism has no remedy for the alleged ills of capitalism. Would Rorty still not find himself in a quandary?

The difficulty he faces is this: if history were a struggle between the rich and the poor, why would Rorty join the impoverished many? Is he not one of the rich and privileged himself? If it is replied that morality requires this, we face yet more questions: What is the basis of morality? Given an adequate foundation for morality, can Rorty's call for class war be supported?

Now at last we are in a good position to grasp Rorty's nihilism. Morality is not a matter of rational principles. Quite the contrary, it simply expresses what "we" want. The fact that a group of leftist intellectuals take capitalism to be unjust is all the "justification" we need. In morality there is no distinction between appearance and reality: nothing beyond what particular groups hold to be right exists as a standard.

Mr. Rorty's conception of morality may at first strike readers as strange: an example of Rorty in action in a particular case will help to clarify what he means. In the notorious *Roe v. Wade* (1973) abortion decision, the Supreme Court rightly decided that "the political waters badly needed roiling" (p. 99). Women who wanted to have abortions could not be expected to wait until a consensus developed to support them. The Court stepped into the breach and acted.

But you may object, what can Rorty say against those whose preferences differ from his own? Suppose that a group of religious opponents of abortion overturned *Roe v. Wade*. What could Rorty say against them, other than to reiterate his disagreement? Ah, but you see, where religion is concerned, matters are entirely different. In a democracy, "the only test of a political proposal is its ability to gain assent from people who retain radically diverse ideas about the point and meaning of human life, about the path of private perfection" (p. 173).

Since some people, our author not least among them, are atheistic, one cannot appeal to religion "as a source of moral knowledge." Religion is a private matter: this is the "Jeffersonian compromise." Nor is this unfair to believers. They are free to derive their premises from a religious source: they are precluded only from appeal to that source in argument, at least so long as skeptics like Rorty are around.

Foolishly, I thought Rorty here open to decisive refutation. If opponents of abortion cannot appeal to religious premises that secularists will reject, then how can Rorty use premises, e.g., the "right to reproductive freedom," that religious believers will reject? If consensus is our goal, are not controversial premises of this type excluded from the dialogue? But I had temporarily forgotten: Rorty sets the rules. From these there is no appeal.

I can at last postpone no longer what to my mind is the key issue for understanding Rorty. Suppose that one accepts his view of morality. What is right is what our Rortyean group deems appropriate. What about the world of fact? Surely this is not determined by consensus of a suitably selected elite.

So far as I can make out, this is exactly what Rorty *does* contend. We should not "think of truth as something towards which we are moving, something we get closer to the more justification we have" (p. 38). Truth is not "out there." It concerns rather the goals we aim to achieve: "the only point in contrasting the true with the merely justified is to contrast a possible future with the actual present" (p. 39, emphasis removed).

On the surface, Rorty's doctrine seems a simple-minded relativism and, as such, open to standard objections. Of this Rorty shows himself well aware:

> If we take the distinction between making and finding at face value, our opponents will be able to ask us an awkward question, viz., have we discovered the surprising fact that was thought to be objective is actually subjective, or have we invented it? (pp. xxvii-xxviii)

Rorty's response to these excellent questions is characteristic. We must "repudiate the vocabulary our opponents use" (p. 39). By refusing to recognize the objective-subjective and absolute-relative polarities, we prevent our Platonist enemies from raising the awkward questions just canvassed. Throughout Rorty's philosophy, a sheer willfulness constantly manifests itself. I should have thought that "triumph of the will" has a resonance that Rorty would not find altogether congenial.

Sovereign Virtue: The Theory and Practice of Equality*

RONALD DWORKIN

Dworkin: Inadvertent Libertarian?

December 1, 2000, *Mises Review*

ONALD DWORKIN gets off to a poor start, but things are not so bad as they first appear. He tells us that equality is the sovereign political virtue. What could be more anti-libertarian? But we must not move too quickly: his "sovereign virtue" need not be taken in a conventionally egalitarian way. Dworkin's basic principle states: "[n]o government is legitimate that does not show equal concern for the fate of all those citizens over whom it claims dominion and from whom it claims allegiance" (p. 1).

Oddly enough, this principle can be read in a way that makes it entirely consistent with strict adherence to the free market. A libertarian should respond to Dworkin that in a free market, the government (or, as Rothbardians prefer, the private protection agencies) does treat everyone under its jurisdiction with equal concern. It does so by respecting everyone's rights to life, liberty, and property. This, not the elaborately detailed schemes for redistribution our author sets forward, is the correct understanding of equal concern.

Dworkin, who rarely misses a philosophical trick, anticipates this objection. "Those who embrace it [laissez-faire] can also accept the abstract

---

* Harvard University Press, 2000.

egalitarian principle and claim their theory as the best interpretation of that principle" (p. 481).

Unfortunately, Dworkin has little directly to say about this theory: perhaps to him it is obviously wrong. But it is not too difficult to see why he opposes the free market. In his view, the poor in a market society could claim that they have been subject to harmful discrimination.

But how can this be? However limited their resources, do not the poor in a free-market order have exactly the same rights as anyone else? No, responds Dworkin. The fact that individuals do poorly on the market in part arises from the legal system in place.

> [W]hen a nation's wealth is very unequally distributed... then its equal concern is suspect. For the distribution of wealth is the product of a legal order... when government enacts or sustains one set of such laws rather than another, it is not only predictable that some citizens' lives will be worsened by its choice but also, to a considerable degree, which citizens these will be. ....
> We must be prepared to explain, to those who suffer in that way, why they have nevertheless been treated with the equal concern that is their right. (pp. 1–2)

Dworkin's response just pushes back the issue one step. Granted that how people fare in the market depends on how the legal system defines their property rights, what then follows? What criteria govern a proper legal system? Here our author arrives at surprising answer. Although he dismisses laissez-faire capitalism with barely a mention, his own principle of distribution grasps a key truth about the market. In a free market, goods pass to those who are willing to pay the most to get them.

An example will clarify the point. What determines who gets to own a copy of that most valuable commodity, the *Mises Review*? Obviously, the magazine goes to that select group willing to pay the subscription price. If more people clamored for the journal than there were copies in print, demanders would bid up the price until the quantity demanded equaled the available supply. No, I have not by mistake inserted notes for an economics lecture into my review of Dworkin. The example has the utmost relevance to Dworkin's principle of equal concern. A legal system that allows people to bid against one another for the goods they want displays equal concern for its citizens.

Dworkin states the central point precisely:

> The [market] auction proposes . . . that the true measure of the
> social resources devoted to the life of one person is fixed by ask-
> ing how important, in fact, that resource is for others. It insists
> that the cost, measured in that way, figures in each person's sense
> of what is rightly his and in each person's judgment of what life
> he should lead, given that command of justice. (p. 70)

What has happened? Has Dworkin, an arch-leftist, suddenly converted to
free-market orthodoxy? Not at all; I have omitted to mention a vital piece in
the puzzle. Dworkin insists that a market, to be fair, must start from a position of equality of resources: "Of course it is sovereign in this . . . connection
between the market and equality of resources, that people enter the market
on equal terms" (p. 70).

Here we reach the decisive difference between Dworkin's conception of
equal concern and that of the free-market advocate. As Mises long ago noted,
some people indeed have more dollar votes than others. But, as market advocates look at matters, the government has no business attempting to "correct"
for the differing talents and resources with which people start out. We show
equal concern by taking people as we find them: to do otherwise is drastically
to interfere with individual freedom.

But, Dworkin would reply, what about luck? Is it not unfair that, e.g. I
was not gifted with the golfing ability that has earned Tiger Woods millions? Should he not be required to give me a large chunk of his money
before we can acknowledge the justice of the market?

We could, I suppose, at this point simply throw up our hands and say:
"Here we have an irreconcilable clash of moral judgments. It is because of his
aberrant judgments that Dworkin must be cast into utter darkness."

I venture to suggest that this is to quit too soon: we can narrow the area of
conflict. Dworkin thinks that some matters of luck may be insured against:
these he terms "option luck" and permits within his system. If, in the market, you could have insured against accident but failed to do so, you cannot demand that others pay your medical bills in case you suffer accidental
injury. Dworkin is here at one with Mises and Rothbard.

What he objects to is the effect of "brute luck." Some instances of bad
luck cannot be anticipated through insurance. "Some people are born with
handicaps, or develop them before they have either sufficient knowledge or

funds to insure on their own behalf. They cannot buy insurance after the event" (p. 77). In Dworkin's view, the government should counteract, by an elaborate "insurance" scheme that he sets forward, the effects of brute luck, both good and bad. Suffice it to say that the "insurance" is compulsory and redistributive in intent.

Now, to my mind, the basic issue that separates Dworkin from defenders of the market emerges clearly. Does the government manifest respect for people by attempting to correct for "brute" luck that cannot be dealt with by ordinary insurance?

Even here, I suggest, we need not depend on controversial moral intuitions to answer. Even those inclined to accept Dworkin's insurance plan should think twice before attempting to put the scheme into practice.

Surely no government can be trusted with the immense powers needed to "correct" the market. Would not the holders of power intervene in order to promote their own interests, rather than to enact Dworkin's convoluted plan?

Rather than stress Dworkin's deficient understanding of politics, I prefer to reiterate a fact that greatly surprised me. If we eliminate Dworkin's controversial premise about "brute luck," he offers a powerful defense of the market, along Misesian lines.

This is not the only instance in which Dworkin, no doubt against his intentions, provides ammunition for classical liberals. He sharply criticizes a pet aversion of mine, Rawls's difference principle. He asks a simple but devastating question: why should a theory of economic justice be concerned only with the worst-off class? "[I]t seems callous to say that the only people for whom a theory of justice has concern are those whose lives are the most damaged, even though others, who work as hard as they can, are seriously injured" (p. 331).

More generally, Rawls does not show why people in "his original position, ignorant of their own future status, would choose the difference principle out of their own self-interest" (p. 331). Even more generally, why is what people would choose in the original position of any relevance for moral theory? Dworkin is not the only writer to raise these issues, but he does so in a particularly effective way.

At many other points, Dworkin's book proves a valuable quarry for those aiming to defend the market. Space limitations prevent further discussion, but I commend to readers the withering analysis Dworkin offers of equality of welfare.

To readers tempted to think that I have gone soft, I offer one argument to the contrary. Dworkin will probably dislike being mined for pro-market arguments more than he would recoil from any invective of which I am capable.

Ethics as Social Science: The Moral Philosophy of Social Cooperation[*]

LELAND B. YEAGER

In Defense of Misesian Ethics

July 1, 2001, *Mises Review*

T O THOSE WHO KNOW Leland Yeager's work, it will come as no surprise that he has given us an illuminating book, informed by careful
thought and wide-ranging scholarship. Professor Yeager finds much
of contemporary moral philosophy unsatisfactory, and he offers as an alternative view a variety of utilitarianism. In my opinion, his ambitious project
does not entirely succeed; but we can learn much from his valiant attempt.

To philosophers tempted to dismiss him as an outsider, he has a ready
response. Precisely his expertise as an economist fits him for the immense
task he has undertaken. Yeager puts the point in this way:

> Economists are professionally equipped to deal with ethics not
> only because they recognize what scarcity implies for interper-
> sonal conflict and cooperation but also because they are alert
> to regularities and patterns in human affairs that may not have
> resulted from anyone's deliberate intentions. (p. 9)

---

[*] Edward Elgar, 2001.

To understand our author's case, one must first grasp his indictment of non-utilitarian ethics. As he sees matters, statements about what one ought to do cannot be derived from factual premises alone, as David Hume demonstrated long ago. Somewhere in one's ethics, one must introduce one or more value judgments, and these do not admit of complete objectivity. Faced with this situation, many have been tempted to follow a barren path. They maintain that their value judgments rest on moral intuitions that convey an insight into reality. Such assertions arbitrarily claim authority for one's own preferences.

Other philosophers seek to escape the threat of the subjective in another way. They allege that reason establishes certain ethical truths; one must acknowledge these, or be branded irrational. Professor Yeager finds all such claims unacceptable. Readers of the *Mises Review* will be interested to find that Murray Rothbard does not escape his far-flung condemnation; he too, Yeager avers, dogmatically insists on the truth of his own arbitrary judgments.

But has not our author painted himself into a corner? Ethics, he says, cannot do without value judgments, yet these cannot be demonstrated. You must either take them or leave them. If so, how can Yeager escape his own indictment? Will he not give us an ethic that rests on his subjective judgments? Why are his preferences less arbitrary than, say, Rothbard's?

To this he has an ingenious answer. Value judgments cannot be avoided, but their use can be minimized. In particular, Yeager proposes what he deems a noncontroversial assertion as his fundamental value judgment: happiness is better than misery.

> If pressed to explain why happiness and misery are intrinsically good and bad, most people (or I anyway) would merely say something to the effect that they just are; one cannot explain anything so obvious; one either sees it or does not. (p. 30)

Given this patently evident judgment, Professor Yeager is in business. All else in ethics stands before the bar of reason and fact. If Yeager has not been able totally to excise unsupported value judgments, his sweeping use of Occam's razor has rendered his problem manageable.

Let us grant the author his fundamental value judgment; what ethical guidance does he derive from it? He maintains:

> one means to satisfying it [the happiness of individuals] is so pervasively requisite that it becomes almost a substitute criterion. It is

> social cooperation, which means a well-functioning society—the whole complex of institutions, practices, and precepts whereby people can interact peacefully and to mutual advantage. (p. 13)

Our author has here been much influenced by Henry Hazlitt's *The Foundations of Morality*, which is "the best single book on ethics that I know of" (p. vii).

Here indeed is ethics in the style of Hazlitt and also of Mises, for whom the vital importance of social cooperation is a constant theme. Since social cooperation, as Mises has abundantly shown, can best take place in an unhampered market economy, we arrive at a result that I find appealing. Much of ethics consists in promoting the virtues and institutions that best fit the free market.

When I read Yeager's paean to social cooperation, I thought of an objection; but our author has forestalled me. He writes:

> critics sometimes object . . . [that utilitarianism] fails to settle the controversy over abortion, or, one might add, over capital punishment. . . . Pondering such issues may require looking beyond the proxy moral criterion of social cooperation to more nearly direct effects on individual happiness and to particular facts of specific cases. (p. 293)

I read this passage with the shock of recognition. Several years ago in these pages, I raised this objection:

> Yeager clearly has identified a central element in ethics, but I doubt that the sum and substance of ethics can be derived from social cooperation alone. How, as an instance, does social cooperation bear on the rightness or wrongness of abortion? (the *Mises Review*, 1995, p. 21)

Professor Yeager has replied to my objection with characteristic directness. He need not appeal to social cooperation to decide the morality of abortion. That, after all, is only the proximate criterion of morality. The ultimate criterion is happiness, and that must be our resort, should the proximate criterion leave us in doubt.

As it seems to me, Professor Yeager has escaped my problem only to land himself in a more severe difficulty, one that strikes at the root of his ethical system. A great advantage of using social cooperation as a criterion is that one can often readily tell what measures will advance it. We can safely say, e.g., that, judged from the point of view of social cooperation, tariffs and minimum wage laws must be rejected.

The situation changes completely if one directly brings to bear the ultimate criterion, happiness. By itself, the judgment "happiness is better than misery" tells us little. Whose happiness is to be considered? All human beings? All sentient creatures, as Bentham thought? Only the members of a certain race, nation, or class? Are we to take account only of individuals who now exist, or do future generations also matter? And what, by the way, is meant by happiness?

But, it may be said, I am here being grossly unfair. The issues I have raised are well known to Professor Yeager. Several of them he discusses in the book. Why should I suppose that the mere fact that these and other questions must be answered in some way or other poses a major difficulty for his approach?

The problem, I suggest, is this: Yeager wishes to cope with value judgments by minimizing their ungrounded use. Accordingly, he claims to assume only one fundamental value judgment—fundamental in the sense that it rests on no argument. Further, the fundamental principle he advances is one it seems impossible to reject: happiness is better than misery. Who but a misanthrope could cavil at this?

But Yeager's bold tactic fails, because in order to answer the questions posed above, he must resort to additional value judgments, ungrounded in the fundamental judgment. Should one, in thinking about the morality of abortion, take account of the interests of both the mother and the fetus? It is no good to repeat, "Happiness is better than misery"; the question we need to answer is, whose happiness? Our answer as regards abortion may turn out to depend on whether fetuses are to be included among those whose happiness is to be taken into account. Nor will it do to allege that social science can tell us that society will be happier if our question is answered in a particular way. Once again, the question arises, who is to be included within society?

If, then, one fills out the fundamental value judgment in a way sufficient to answer controversial moral issues, one will find oneself saddled with a large number of other value judgments. Whether these are fundamental judgments, in the sense that they are not derived from more basic premises, I do not know. But Professor Yeager's fundamental value judgment does not suffice to ground them, and he then has not shown his approach to ethics less arbitrary than the intuitionist rivals he so readily condemns.

Professor Yeager, ever resourceful, has anticipated a criticism related to, but not identical with, my own. He considers the charge that utilitarianism is vacuous.

> Many critics . . . see the defensive maneuvers available to util-
> itarians as evidence of how feeble their position is in the first
> place. Utilitarianism is called plastic or vacuous or tautologi-
> cal, evading any challenge by transforming itself or wriggling
> away. (p. 227)

In response, Yeager lists a large number of ethical systems at variance with utilitarianism; his favored doctrine is not at all empty. Clearly, he is right: the fundamental value judgment, e.g., rules out the principle "maximize mis-ery." But this rejoinder does not suffice to turn my difficulty aside. I claim not that Yeager's variety of utilitarianism is empty, but that it requires more value judgments than he bargains for.

"But," Yeager may reply, "my system has at least this to be said for it, against its many rivals. They claim that certain ethical truths, e.g., our duty to keep promises, have a basis independent of utility. Is this not senseless? If something does not promote happiness, what can be the point of accepting it? Would we not have here an instance of blind rule worship?"

The argument that I have just suggested Yeager might make rests on a fallacy. Let us imagine an ethical rule that had consequences disastrous for happiness, e.g., never permit food to pass your lips. Would we not at once laugh out of court anyone so foolish as to claim this practice to be ethically required? No doubt; but here danger threatens.

It does not follow from the fact that we would abandon a rule, if it led to enough unhappiness, that happiness is our real criterion of ethics. A fur-ther example will I think make evident the fallacy. I would do a great deal to avoid losing all my money; but it hardly follows that my supreme goal is to make as much money as possible.

Professor Yeager, I regret to say, falls into this mistaken pattern of infer-ence. He states:

> Suppose two situations: (1) rights are fully respected but peo-
> ple are miserable; (2) rights are taken casually but people are
> happy. Which situation is preferable? . . . If, faced with the need
> to choose, one is unwilling to prefer rights over happiness, isn't

one giving up any claim that a rights approach is distinctive and takes precedence? (p. 225)

By no means. Someone can hold, with entire consistency, both that a rights claim should be abandoned if it leads to enough unhappiness, and also that the claim has a moral basis independent of happiness.

Even if successful, my arguments do not show that Professor Yeager's system is wrong, but only that he has failed to prove its superiority to rival approaches. I propose, in conclusion, to compare Yeager's indirect utilitarianism with Murray Rothbard's different conception of political ethics.

As one might anticipate, Yeager criticizes Rothbard for dogmatic reliance on a few favored moral intuitions.

> Rothbard... tries to deduce all sorts of specific judgments from a few axioms about rights. These include the right of self-ownership, the right to property acquired through the Lockean process of mixing one's labor with hitherto unowned resources, and the right to property acquired through voluntary transactions. (p. 277)

Rothbardians who ask what Yeager wishes to put in place of these axioms are in for a pleasant surprise. Our author himself accepts them, on utilitarian grounds. Rothbard might have written his defense of self-ownership:

> If each person does not own his own body, who does? Other particular persons?... Or is each person to be owned collectively, by everybody? How workable would each of these alternatives be? Would its consequences be coherent with a society of effective and happy men and women? Almost certainly not. (p. 272)

I commend to the reader the entire page as a brilliant exercise in Rothbardian thought.

If Yeager accepts principles quite similar to those of Rothbard, why does he condemn him as dogmatic? Yeager's complaint is that Rothbard deduces from the axioms various consequences that he considers implausible; the example he stresses is that Rothbard considers libel and slander legally permissible.

But what exactly is Professor Yeager's complaint? Does he admit that the consequences follow from the axioms? If they do, how does Yeager avoid accepting these conclusions, since he too accepts the axioms? And if they do not, then Rothbardians will gladly expunge them from their ethics. But Yeager may have something else in mind. He may mean that even if the conclusions about libel and slander proceed properly from the axioms, they should still be rejected on utilitarian grounds. We should not accept what follows from our axioms, come what may. Should we not be willing to modify our axioms, to avoid conclusions sufficiently unpalatable?

I do not see why a Rothbardian should reject this. Yeager himself notes that Rothbard offers utilitarian arguments in defense of his views about libel and slander. But, our author claims, "[r]esort to them almost concedes that the program of deriving all policy stances from a very few axioms about rights does not work after all" (p. 279). I should prefer to say that resort to them shows that Rothbard's program is less dogmatic than Yeager thinks. Once more Yeager wrongly supposes that any use of utilitarian considerations entails total surrender to that system.

Professor Yeager sheds light on an enormous number of issues in the course of his wide-ranging book. I especially recommend his incisive discussion of democracy (pp. 245–247); the analysis of John Harsanyi's treatment of utility (pp. 123 ff.); and the spirited reply to Bernard Williams's criticisms of utilitarianism (pp. 149–151).

Invariances: The Structure of the Objective World*

ROBERT NOZICK

A Substitute for Knowing

December 1, 2001, *Mises Review*

R EADERS OF THIS JOURNAL will probably be most interested in
Nozick's views on ethics, especially as they relate to libertarianism, and it is on these that I propose to concentrate. In doing so,
I run the risk of distortion. *Invariances* is full of new ideas, and no review
that stresses a small part of the book can do it justice.

Nozick's remarks on libertarianism, though brief, are full of interest. He
distinguishes several layers of ethics:

> The first layer is the ethics of respect, which corresponds to an
> (extended) ethics mandating cooperation to mutual benefit.
> Here there are rules and principles mandating respecting an-
> other (adult) person's life and autonomy, forbidding murder
> and enslavement, restricting interference with a person's do-
> main of choice, and issuing in a set of (what have been termed
> negative) rights (p. 280, emphasis removed).

Other layers, such as the ethics of caring, go beyond the duty of noninterfer-
ence with others and call for positive aid to them.

---

* Harvard University Press, 2001.

Given these various levels, the question at once arises: which of them, if any, may be enforced by coercion? In his response, Nozick weighs in as a libertarian:

> The ethics of respect ... is the part, the one part (I think) that is (that should be) mandatory across all societies.... [S]ome particular society may attempt to make one or another of these further levels mandatory within it ... I also believe ... that no society should take this further step. All that any society should (coercively) demand is adherence to the ethics of respect. (pp. 281–282)

Can one defend libertarianism adequately on this basis? At first sight, one might think so: has Nozick not stated succinctly and accurately the essence of a free-market order? But his profession of belief raises a problem. What is the status of his contention that coercion should not pass beyond the ethics of respect? Can it itself be coercively enforced, or does it merely reflect a "personal ideal" that Nozick holds? Where does this principle fit within the doctrine of moral levels?

Unless Nozick holds that the principle limiting coercion to the morality of respect itself forms part of the morality of respect, he has failed to reach an adequate libertarian standpoint. To tell us that he himself prefers that society limit enforcement in this way has no more than biographical interest: the question is whether morality demands it.

There is, I think, a more fundamental problem with Nozick's view of morality. He questions whether ethical truths exist at all.

> How can ethical statements be true, if truth consists in correspondence to the facts? Are there special kinds of facts, ethical ones, and if so, by what route do we discover them? ... The history of philosophy is abundant with unsuccessful attempts to establish a firm basis for ethical truths. Inductively, we infer that the task is unpromising. (p. 236)

But do not our considered moral judgments put us in touch with real values "out there" in the world? Nozick finds no basis in evolutionary theory to account for this claimed grasp of values. He then endeavors, with great ingenuity, to piece together an ersatz objectivity that makes no dubious claims about real values.

But why is Nozick's project necessary? Suppose he is right that we cannot explain by use of Darwinian evolution how we can grasp ethical truth. Why should we take this as a decisive reason to abandon the claim that we know such truths? Perhaps we have instead grounds to doubt that Darwinian processes account for all our knowledge.

We might press the point further. It is hard to explain through evolution how we know necessary truths. Does this give us reason to abandon necessary truth? If not, why should we toss moral truths overboard on Darwinian grounds?

Nozick of course fully anticipates this response. Indeed, it is virtually impossible to think of a point that this most brilliant and imaginative of contemporary philosophers has not already considered. But his answer I find astonishing. He does propose to abandon necessity, in large part because he cannot account by evolution for how we might attain such knowledge. Why he accords evolutionary considerations such enormous weight escapes me.

But my skepticism is not an argument, and Nozick's intricately elaborated alternative to ethical truth merits attention. Once again, Darwinian evolution exerts decisive weight. Nozick endeavors to determine the evolutionary function of ethics. Why has natural selection endowed us with the capacity to make moral judgments? He plausibly suggests that cooperative behavior in some circumstances increases that be-all and end-all of those enamored of evolutionary theory, "inclusive fitness."

Suppose Nozick is right. Why does this matter for ethics? As always, our author has considered the objection:

> Derek Parfit . . . asks the pertinent question of what difference is made by something's being the function of ethics. Many things have bad functions (war, slavery, etc.). And even when the function is a good one, as evaluated by the standards instilled to go with cooperation, is normative force added by saying that this good effect of ethical principles (namely, enhancing mutual cooperation) also is the function of ethics? (p. 390, n. 15)

Nozick's response brings out a key feature of the book. Ethical rules not only have a function but also exhibit certain properties that enable them to carry out this function effectively. One of these has to our author decisive importance. "Objective ethical truths . . . are held to involve a certain symmetry or invariance. . . . The Golden Rule mandates doing unto others as you would have others do unto you" (p. 289). As Nozick sees matters, invariance under transformation is the mark of truth. Once we combine function with invariance, in a vastly more complicated way than I can here explain, we arrive at objective truth—or at least a close substitute for it.

Surely Nozick is right that cooperative behavior of various sorts might have benefited our ancestors. On evolutionary grounds, though, would not a tightly knit group able to prey on others also have enjoyed a selective advantage? So, at any rate, Sir Arthur Keith long ago maintained in *A New Theory of Human Evolution.* Why do not rules that mandate aggression against strangers also qualify as part of an objective ethics? Nozick might counter with the claim that such rules do not admit of generalization in the way that he holds is required for objectivity. But this remains to be shown. Generalization need not bring us to "love to all people, perhaps all living creatures," much less to "being a vessel and vehicle of Light," the two highest levels of Nozick's ethics (p. 280); it can equally well eventuate in a far more Nietzschean outcome. It all depends where one starts.

Faced with Nozick's convoluted analysis, which he himself worries has too many epicycles, one wants to say: can't he just see that values are really present in the world? Why need one abandon what is self-evident in favor of a speculative and endlessly imbricated substitute for genuinely objective values?

Here we reach bedrock. Fundamental to *Invariances* is Nozick's distrust of claims of direct knowledge of the nonempirical. We do not "just know" that people have rights, anymore than we directly see that both sides of a contradiction cannot at the same time be true. Once again, evolution forbids it.

> Such debates [about necessary truth] would be avoided if we possessed a faculty of reason that could directly assess the possibility of general statements and of their denials. . . . However, we do not appear to have such a faculty, and it is implausible that evolutionary processes would instill that within us. (p. 122)

But does this not create a problem for Nozick's libertarianism? He famously began *Anarchy, State, and Utopia* by telling us, "Individuals have rights." Are not such absolute claims ruled by Nozick's newly installed divinity, Evolution? He can at most say that an evolutionary fable makes somewhat plausible that one can hold, as a personal ideal, that people cannot be coerced beyond what the level of respect mandates. This hardly seems worth writing home about.

Nozick's rejoinder is obvious. No doubt it would be convenient for libertarians if we could claim our doctrine to be true a priori; but fairness to the facts requires that we abandon this claim. And to support his denial that we directly grasp necessary truth, he deploys an intriguing argument. To claim something is necessarily true is to say that it is true in all possible worlds: it cannot be otherwise. Is this not an extraordinary claim to make? To claim, by contrast, that something is possible is a much more modest assertion. "It is easier to think of possibilities than of necessities, easier to know that something is possible than that it is necessary" (p. 121). Do not exponents of necessary knowledge seek mistakenly to limit the imagination? Who are we to say that something must be so?

Many things, no doubt, are easy to imagine; but our ability to think of something hardly shows that it is really possible. If something is possible, then nothing in any possible world renders it impossible. Is this not as radical a claim as the one Nozick would deny to us? Oddly, Nozick elsewhere makes an analogous claim: "[A] theory can appear consistent and transparent . . . yet still harbor contradictions. . . . Not everything that looks consistent really is possible" (p. 162). But he does not note the bearing of this on his earlier contention. Nozick's argument leaves claims to necessary truth undamaged, unless he also wishes to throw into question our knowledge of possibility.

Further, why do those who claim direct access to real values have to say that propositions about value are necessary? Why is it not enough to assert that the value propositions are true? Nozick goes to great lengths to imagine "an admittedly extremely gruesome" case in which it is not wrong to torture babies to death for fun (p. 349, n. 35). Even if one seriously entertains his case, does this throw into doubt our knowledge that, in the actual world, such torture is wrong?

Nozick has studied carefully a wide range of difficult subjects, quantum mechanics and string theory not least among them; and I cannot pretend to grasp more than a few regions, on earth or near it, of his vast philosophical cosmos. I shall close with a few points of detail. One of his arguments that the law of noncontradiction may fail to hold depends upon a questionable appeal to a principle of sufficient reason (p. 303, n.1). He seeks to disarm C. I. Lewis's claim "that each relative statement corresponds to an absolute one, viz., the one that makes the relativity explicit" by adducing Einstein's theory of relativity.

But the claim that Einstein's invariant statement is "not simply the explicit statement (à la C. I. Lewis) of this relativity" leaves Lewis's assertion intact (p. 319, n. 76). He takes "nothing can be red and green all over at the same time" to be about whether these particular two colors can be combined. The fact that we cannot see reddish green he takes to depend on contingent scientific facts; hence the much-debated statement is not necessary. But the proposition is not about mixed colors at all (pp. 136–138). His statement about wave-packet collapse, "that failure of derivability comes precisely at the point where physical systems that are identical with conscious beings interact with physical systems in a superposition" (p. 230), begs the question against dualism about the mind.

Though I find myself in strong disagreement with many of the views in *Invariances*, I closed the book with admiration. The old master has not lost his power to fascinate. What an extraordinary mind, and what an unusual way of looking at the world!

John Stuart Mill and the Religion of Humanity*

Linda C. Raeder

The Dark Side of Mill

October 1, 2002, *Mises Review*

MOST PEOPLE REGARD JOHN STUART MILL as one of the great classical liberals of the nineteenth century. Though Mill made unnecessary concessions to socialism, did he not in *On Liberty* defend without compromise personal liberty, following his great German predecessor Wilhelm von Humboldt? Linda Raeder offers a powerful challenge to this conventional view. Like Maurice Cowling and Joseph Hamburger, by whom she has been much influenced, she sees Mill as mainly a propagandist anxious to replace Christianity with a Religion of Humanity, guided by intellectuals such as himself.

Raeder finds opposition to Christianity at the heart of Mill's ethics. As everyone knows, Mill was a utilitarian; but our author raises a penetrating question. What exactly made Mill's utilitarianism distinct from earlier versions of the theory? Views that analyzed morality according to what makes human beings happy, she notes, are hardly unique to Bentham and Mill. Quite the contrary, theologians such as William Paley held exactly this position.

> Until well into the 1830s, the principal representative of the utilitarian outlook in England was not Bentham but William Paley, the conservative Anglican divine and Bentham's

---

* University of Missouri Press, 2002.

acknowledged rival. . . . Both thinkers postulated the "greatest happiness of the greatest number" as the ultimate end of
moral action. Both identified the good with the pleasant or
beneficial, the "beneficial" meaning that which is productive
of happiness, and "happiness" meaning the excess of pleasure
over pain. (p. 25)

Paley's theological morality solved a problem that baffled the secular utilitarians. Why should a person be concerned with the general happiness,
rather than exclusively with his own? Paley had a ready response. God has
arranged matters so that an individual will always find it in his own interest
to promote the greatest happiness of the greatest number.

But is not Paley's contention obviously false? Suppose you had a chance
to steal $1 million, without danger of detection. Surely here your moral
duty not to steal conflicts with what benefits you, given some plausible
assumptions.

Paley dissents: he maintains that to argue in this way is to take a short-
sighted position. God's system of rewards and punishments ensures that the
thief acts against his own interests, as he will discover to his cost after he dies.
Here precisely is the point where Mill broke with the theological moralists.
As he saw matters, hopes and fears concerning the afterlife should not enter
into our calculation of consequences.*

Raeder makes an excellent case that Mill's ethics is resolutely secular; but
what has this to do with classical liberalism? She may believe Mill's opposition to Christianity mistaken, but why should this lead her to question his
devotion to liberty?

The answer to this query brings us to the center of Raeder's case. Mill did
not merely hold as a private opinion that the dominant religious doctrines
of his time were false. Quite the contrary, he wanted his own views to prevail
among the public.

But once more our question recurs: why does this wish conflict with classical liberalism? Open discussions of essential issues such as religion seem at
the essence of a libertarian outlook. Raeder does not claim otherwise, but
again she stands ready with a counter.

---

* The greatest of all nineteenth-century utilitarians after Mill, Henry Sidgwick, agreed with
  Paley that only a system of divine rewards and punishments could reconcile morality with
  self-interest.

Mill did not merely want open debate about religion.

> The lesson [Auguste] Comte and then Mill drew from the con-
> temporary authority of science was the necessity of establishing a
> *method* by which philosophers can reach unanimity regarding moral
> and political truths. Once such a method has been devised and
> accepted, the results obtained by means of it must gain unanimous
> acceptance among the experts. Their unanimity, in turn, will
> ensure that the masses . . . will place as unfailing a trust in the
> new spiritual power as they do in the scientific authorities. The
> spiritual power to which all defer as the ultimate authority on
> matters moral and political is thus triumphant. (p. 79)

In her effort to prove that Mill favored intellectual dictatorship by an elite, Raeder deploys an ingenious stratagem. She attempts to tie Mill as closely as possible to Comte, universally recognized as an enemy of freedom. If Mill followed Comte, does this not suffice to render dubious his classical liberal credentials?

Here our author confronts an obstacle. No one doubts Mill's early enthusiasm for Comte, but did he not in later life repudiate Comte's authoritarian politics? Indeed, he went so far as to describe Comte's minutely detailed plans for a hierarchical society as "liberticide."

To Raeder, Mill's criticism of Comte did not alter the fundamental agreement between the two thinkers. In *Auguste Comte and Positivism*, Mill claimed that Comte first stated "the true moral and social ideal of Labour." The ideal in question hardly sounds libertarian: "Until labourers and employers perform the work of industry in the spirit in which soldiers perform that of an army, industry will never be moralised and military life will remain . . . the chief school of moral cooperation" (p. 334, emphasis removed, quoting Mill). Comte thought that workers should regard themselves as "public functionaries"; Mill found in this idea "great beauty and grandeur" (p. 334).

Has Raeder adequately met the obstacle to her thesis? One might object that her quotations do not suffice. Certainly Mill, here and elsewhere shows himself well-disposed to socialism; but this we knew from the start. The question at issue is whether, despite his collectivist sympathies in economics, Mill counts as a classical liberal in political matters. Of course, if Mill thought that civil liberties could be consistently joined with socialism, he erred grievously; but perhaps he held just this mistaken belief.

Raeder's response, once more, is to stress Mill's sympathy with the entire scope of Comte's philosophy. The fervent passages defending freedom in *On Liberty* had a pragmatic purpose.

> We have suggested that *On Liberty* should be understood as one of the instruments by which Mill sought to realize his long-standing religious purpose: to undermine Christianity and institute the Religion of Humanity. . . . Mill did not wish to de-claw coercive public opinion in general but only such opinions and sanctions that embodied traditional religious belief. (p. 261)

To evaluate Raeder's daring suggestion that the true meaning of *On Liberty* lies hidden beneath its surface, I should like to pose two questions: Is Raeder right that Mill remained throughout his life a committed supporter of Comte? And should Mill's desire to promote a Religion of Humanity lead us to see his defense of liberty as insincere?

Raeder supports her Comtist reading of Mill with a detailed analysis of his main essays on religion; but Mill's "Theism," published only after his death, does not fully support her interpretation. She of course acknowledges that Mill in that work defended a version of the design argument for the existence of God, but she fails to note the anti-Comtist implications of this. According to Comte, to explain nature by personal powers reflects a primitive stage of human thought. The final, positivist stage of thought renounces altogether the search for ultimate causes. Mill's use of the design argument in "Theism" utterly opposes this rejection of metaphysics.

Our resourceful author has not yet been defeated. She claims that Mill's theism is half-hearted:

> [W]hat Mill gives he immediately takes away. For he immediately points out that the evidences of design in nature, while they may point to a God . . . may, on the other hand, be the product of naturalistic evolutionary forces. (p. 191)

Raeder here ignores a crucial point. Mill considers Darwin's theory of evolution no more than an interesting hypothesis; he does not think it has been established. Once more, Mill declines an opportunity to adopt an anti-religious standpoint.

But suppose Raeder is right: what follows if Mill remained a Comtist to the end? Does this render the arguments of *On Liberty* merely tactical maneuvers? I do not think so. Our author notes that Mill hoped for an antireligious consensus; but it does not follow from this that he wished to suppress dissent. He explicitly states in *On Liberty* that to debate accepted truths is a great good; even to debate the truths of mathematics is valuable. Why should we decline to take Mill at his word?

Although Raeder has not persuaded me of her principal thesis, her book contains a great deal of value. Her discussion of Mill's attitude toward nature, in particular, displays sensitive insight. She finds in Mill hostility to the world: "For Mill, nature as given is not good. Indeed, nature is not good at all but a realm of 'perfect and absolute recklessness' . . . Mill, like the Grand Inquisitor, will 'correct' God's work" (pp. 99, 101).

Raeder's study is impressively erudite, but her discussion of the alleged fallacy in Mill's proof of utilitarianism (pp. 302 ff.) makes no reference to the important discussions by Fred Berger and others in the recent philosophical literature. The remarks on page 149 wrongly conflate theological utilitarianism with moral views altogether nonconsequentialist.

The Collapse of the Fact/Value Dichotomy and Other Essays*

Hilary Putnam

The Facts of Economic Life

December 1, 2002, *Mises Review*

HILARY PUTNAM RANKS as one of the outstanding American philosophers of the twentieth century, but never before now has he shown any interest in economics. It transpires that he has been a friend for 50 years of Vivian Walsh, a philosophically-inclined economist; and owing to Walsh's influence, Putnam has decided to bring to bear his formidable philosophical talent on welfare economics. Putnam hardly inclines to classical liberalism. For him, the economist of the age is Amartya Sen— very much a social democrat of the usual boring sort. Nevertheless, Putnam's book has much to offer Austrians.

As Putnam rightly notes, Lionel Robbins, writing in the 1930s, established the conceptual framework of modern welfare economics:

> it was during the depths of the Depression that Lionel Robbins, certainly one of the most influential economists in the world, persuaded the entire economics profession that interpersonal comparisons of utility are "meaningless." (p. 53, emphasis removed)

The old welfare economics of A. C. Pigou was cast aside.

---

* Harvard University Press, 2002.

Pigou famously argued that, owing to the law of diminishing marginal utility, transfers of money from the rich to the poor would increase social welfare, other things being equal. Is it not plausible "that the marginal utility of, say, a thousand dollars to someone at the point of going hungry . . . is greater than the marginal utility of a thousand dollars to, say, Bill Gates?" (p. 53). But if Robbins was right, such judgments lack a scientific basis.

What then could stand in their place? Given Robbins's skepticism about ethics, one would expect him to answer, "nothing." Rational argument could not settle questions of ethics. Putnam, here following Walsh, maintains that the logical positivists crucially influenced Robbins. Judgments of ethics reflect no more than subjective preferences. As Robbins phrased the matter with characteristic flair, "If we disagree about ends, it is a case of thy blood or mine—or live and let live, according to the importance of the difference, or the relative strength of our opponents" (p. 54, quoting Robbins).

Given this view of ethics, must not welfare economics be totally cast out? Since value judgments are of their essence subjective, any discipline purporting to determine objectively how to advance social welfare seems doomed.

Robbins and his colleagues found an ingenious escape: if valid, it would secure the scientific status of welfare economics and, not coincidentally, their own continued employment as expositors of the new wisdom. Suppose that a course of action increases someone's welfare without hurting anyone else's. Can we not say, then, that the action is objectively desirable? We have not claimed to measure interpersonal utility; and in what way does the appeal to the principle suggested, the Pareto criterion, involve us in any subjective value judgments?

In just this way, Putnam responds. An increase in anyone's utility that harms no one else, it is contended, is desirable; but is not this very claim a judgment of value? If so, on the subjectivist reading of ethics that underlies Robbins's analysis, the principle itself is groundless. If, in response, one detaches the principle from ethical subjectivism, declaring it objectively true, an obvious inquiry rises up to threaten the sufficiency of the new welfare economics. If the Pareto criterion is more than an arbitrary preference, then at least one objective ethical judgment is possible. But then what rules out appeal to other principles alleged to be objectively true?

Putnam explains the vital point at issue:

> if the reason for favoring Pareto optimality as a criterion is that
> one approves the underlying value judgment that every agent's

right to maximize his or her utility is as important as every other's, then it would seem that Pareto optimality isn't a value neutral
criterion of "optimality" at all. How could there be a value neutral criterion of optimality, anyway? (p. 56, emphasis removed)

The Pareto criterion *et hoc genus omne* do not then rescue us from ethical
subjectivism. But our author does not write to berate Robbins for insufficient
faith in the logical positivist creed. Rather, he contends, contrary to the logical positivists, that ethical judgments are not mere subjective preferences. Like
ordinary factual judgments, they are objectively true or false. In pressing his
case, Putnam's skill as an outstanding philosopher emerges in full force.

To refute the positivist argument is no easy task. Is it not obvious that
factual judgments, e.g., "this table is brown," differ entirely from such value
judgments as "I like professional wrestling"? Further, who can deny that factual judgments are objective in a sense that value judgments are not? We
can look at a table and see what color it is: we cannot test whether wrestling
"really" is good. Logical positivism may be outdated, but is not the fact-value
gap as wide as it ever has been?

Putnam deftly turns these points aside. There are indeed statements that
consist purely of factual terms; others are entirely valuational. But many
statements fall into neither class. Consider the judgment: "A free market is
the only workable social system." (This example is mine: I doubt that Putnam himself would accept it.) Its truth can be established by rational argument, as readers of Mises and Rothbard will know. Yet surely "workable" is a
value term. In sum, values are not always a matter of choice. Values are inextricably bound up with our ordinary factual concepts.

As Putnam knows full well, defenders of the gap will not at once retire
from the field of battle. True enough, defenders of the gap like R. M. Hare
will concede, some terms have both factual and valuational aspects, but
must philosophical analysis stop here? Rather, can one not always separate
a "mixed" judgment into descriptive and valuational parts? If so, the fact-
value gap returns.

Putnam finds this response unconvincing. "The attempt of noncognitiv-
ists to split thick ethical concepts into a 'descriptive meaning component' and
a 'prescriptive meaning component' founders on the impossibility of saying
what the 'descriptive meaning' of, say, 'cruel' is without using the word 'cruel'
or a synonym" (p. 38).

If Putnam is right, economists cannot dismiss ethics as subjective. What, then, is the next step for economists who accept Putnam's arguments? How exactly can an objectively true welfare economics be achieved? I cannot think that Putnam's suggestions are of much help.

He maintains that, contrary to Robbins, interpersonal utility comparisons can validly be made. How can Putnam say this? He himself recognizes that "the idea that the amount of satisfaction different people get from various goods and services (and from such intangibles as opportunities) can be linearly ordered . . . seems absurd" (p. 55). Is this not the essence of the case against interpersonal comparisons?

To Putnam, this consideration does not suffice to dispatch all such comparisons. We cannot place in a single order all rankings of goods, but can we not arrive at some valid rankings? To return to an example previously mentioned, is it not obvious that a starving man values one thousand dollars more than Bill Gates does?

Putnam is entirely right that people in ordinary life frequently make such comparisons. It hardly follows from this, though, that in doing so people judge that the starving man obtains more fixed units of utility from the money than does Gates. Quite the contrary, such comparative judgments are rough and ready: how then can they form part of a scientific welfare economics?

To his credit, Putnam does not attempt to elevate his interpersonal comparisons into full-fledged scientific assessments. Rather, he contends that such commonsense judgments are all we need. He cites with approval Amartya Sen:

> In arriving at an "agreed" range for social evaluation . . . there has to be some kind of a reasoned "consensus" on weights, or at least on a range of weights. This is a "social choice" exercise, and it requires public discussion and a democratic understanding and acceptance. (p. 55, emphasis removed, quoting Sen)

Here Putnam falls into just the arbitrary subjectivism against which he has so effectively argued. Let us grant him the "commonsense" comparisons of utility he wants. Putnam has done nothing to show that these comparisons have any relevance for welfare economics. If a starving man values one thousand dollars "more" than Bill Gates does, how is it supposed to follow that money should be taken from Gates? Surely some set of ethical principles needs to be offered to support redistribution, but Putnam fails to provide any.

Our author would, I suspect, reply in two ways. First, have I not begged the question against him? His contention is that issues of social evaluation need to be settled through democratic discussion, leading to consensus. In asking for principles to justify despoiling Gates, do I not implicitly assume that democracy is not enough?

By no means. If there are objectively true principles that mandate democratic consensus, I have done nothing to exclude them without a hearing. Rather, I simply want to have a look at them. It surely does not suffice for Putnam to postulate democratic consensus without argument, as he appears to do.

Putnam might reply in a different way. Perhaps Sen's "equal capabilities" view is supposed to provide just the grounding in principles for consensus that I have demanded. But neither Putnam nor Sen shows that the equal capabilities approach leads to decision by consensus.

Putnam's analysis of welfare economics thus begins well but ends on an unpromising note. Putnam makes excellent points against the ethical subjectivism that underlies much of standard welfare economics. But he provides us with no adequate replacement.*

---

* I confine to a note this more technical point. Putnam, following Walsh and Sen, claims that the standard assumption of transitivity of preferences is controversial (pp. 163 ff., n.3). Misesian praxeology does not assume transitivity (*Human Action*, p. 103), and thus seems to have an advantage over standard neoclassical models.

Explaining Postmodernism: Skepticism and Socialism from Rousseau to Foucault[*]

Stephen R. C. Hicks

Finding Meaning

October 1, 2005, *Mises Review*

S TEPHEN HICKS has written a trenchant and provocative book on a vital topic, but I undertake this review with reluctance. I may unleash against myself that direst of all fates for a reviewer—a profusion of critical letters. The reason for my fear will emerge later, but to preserve suspense I shall address some themes in the book out of the order in which the author has placed them.

As befits a good philosopher, Hicks tells us exactly what he means by postmodernism:

> *Metaphysically*, post-modernism is anti-realist, holding that it is impossible to speak meaningfully about an independently existing reality. Postmodernism substitutes instead a social-linguistic, constructionist account of reality. *Epistemologically*, having rejected the notion of an independently existing reality, postmodernism denies that reason or any other method is

---

[*] Scholargy Publishing, 2004.

> a means of acquiring direct knowledge of that reality.... Post-
> modern accounts of *human nature* are consistently collectiv-
> ist, holding that individuals' identities are constructed largely
> by the social-linguistic groups they are a part of... postmod-
> ern themes in *ethics* and *politics* are characterized by an iden-
> tification with and sympathy for the groups perceived to be
> oppressed in the conflicts, and a willingness to enter the fray
> on their behalf. (pp. 6–7, emphasis in original)

Who advocates this assortment of strange views? Hicks tells us that the "names of the postmodern vanguard are now familiar: Michel Foucault, Jacques Derrida, Jean-François Lyotard, and Richard Rorty. They are its leading strategists" (p. 1). Hicks also mentions another group of "familiar and often infamous names" that aids the vanguard. He rightly includes on his list the feminist philosopher Luce Irigaray; but, contrary to our author, her specialty is not "the criticism of science" (p. 2).

Hicks does not devote much space to a detailed account of the various postmodernists he mentions; he devotes his principal attention to a general portrayal of the movement and an account of its philosophical genealogy. He does give an excellent brief discussion of Derrida, for whom there is nothing beyond language. "Language connects only with more language, never with a non-linguistic reality. In Jacques Derrida's words, '[t]he fact of language is probably the only fact to resist all parenthization.' That is to say, we cannot get outside of language" (p. 175). Elsewhere he calls attention to "Derrida's 'crossing-out' device of using a word but then the crossing it out to indicate that its use is ironical" (p. 73).

Behind Derrida lies Martin Heidegger, and Hicks offers a superb analysis of this vastly influential thinker.

> [L]ike all good German philosophers, Heidegger agreed that
> when we get to the core of Being we will find conflict and
> contradiction at the heart of things.... Heidegger's distinc-
> tiveness was his use of phenomenology... simply and clearly
> describing the phenomena of experience and change. On Hei-
> degger's account, what one finds when starting so is a sense of
> projection into a field of experience and change. Do not think
> *objects*, Heidegger counsels, think *fields*. Do not think *subject*,
> think *experience*. (pp. 59–60)

This new sort of thinking challenged standard logic and reasoning "as merely one superficial way of thinking—one that the Greeks had established fatefully for all subsequent Western thought" (pp. 62–63). Instead, we must seek Being through "an exploratory letting go into the revelatory emotions of boredom, fear, guilt, and dread" (p. 63).

As will be already apparent, Hicks does not believe in understatement; and at one point in his discussion of Foucault, he goes too far. He claims that

> Foucault extends his desire for effacement to the entire human species. At the end of *The Order of Things*, he speaks almost long-ingly about the coming erasure of mankind. Man is "an inven-tion of recent date" that will soon "be erased, like a face drawn in sand at the edge of the sea." (p. 195)

Hicks has here read Foucault uncharitably. When Foucault foresees "the end of man," he does not mean that all human beings will soon face extermination. Rather, he predicts the end of a certain conception of man—roughly, a conception based on a universal human nature. The conception in question had, in Foucault's view, a definite origin in time; and, just as human beings long predated this conception, so they may be expected to continue afterwards.

Even if one quarrels with an occasional detail in Hicks's account of the post-moderns, in broad outlines he is clearly right. He proceeds to ask an insightful question: what is the appeal of these irrational views to contemporary intellectuals? In response, he calls attention to a key aspect of contemporary history.

Leftist intellectuals during most of the twentieth century looked to social-ism as a secular equivalent of salvation. To many, the Soviet Union was no brutal tyranny but rather a Worker's Paradise. Such views can no longer ratio-nally be maintained. Readers of *The Gulag Archipelago* learned that the Stalin-ist regime rested on mass murder; and Mao, long a favorite among radicals, was even more bloodthirsty. Nor can socialists comfort themselves by responding that Stalin and Mao were historical aberrations whose failings leave the social-ist project unscathed. Mises and Hayek demonstrated incontrovertibly that a socialist economy cannot work; to make matters worse, the attempt to estab-lish such an economy makes likely the onset of a totalitarian order.

The socialist intellectuals were in a quandary. They ought rationally to have abandoned their views, since their doctrine was fallacious in theory and disas-trous in practice; but rationality is not a trait much in evidence among the socialistically inclined. If reason speaks against socialism, is not the solution obvious: out with reason! If reason provides no access to reality, but is rather a mask for power, the critique of socialism is disabled.

How, though, can socialists claim that reason is relative and at the same time aver an absolute belief in socialist politics? Are they not here caught in a contradiction that even they cannot dismiss? Hicks finds plausible two explanations of the contradiction. On one account, "absolutist politics are primary, while the relativism is a rhetorical strategy that is used to advance that politics"; on the other, "both the relativism and the absolutism coexist in postmodernism, but the contradictions between them simply do not matter psychologically to those who hold them" (p. 185). Hicks rejects the view that relativism is primary and the politics secondary. If it were true, "then postmodernists would be adopting political positions across the spectrum, and that is simply not happening" (p. 186).

Hicks devotes considerable attention to the intellectual origins of the contemporary trends he finds so deplorable. He draws attention to the malign influence of Rousseau, whom he terms a proponent of the Counter-Enlightenment that opposed untrammeled reason, individualism, and capitalism. "Name a dominant feature of the Enlightenment, and Rousseau was against it" (p. 92).

He did not celebrate civilization, but deplored its onset. "There is an inverse relationship between cultural and moral development: Culture does generate much learning, luxury, and sophistication—but learning, luxury, and sophistication all cause moral degradation" (p. 92). The unfortunate rise of reason drove humans from their simple, primitive life.

Reason, once awakened, cannot be expunged; and, we cannot, Rousseau held, return from civilization to primitivism. But society must be tightly controlled. "A society properly founded on natural passion and religion will override the self-centered individualism that reason leads to, making it possible for individuals to form a new, collectivized social organism" (p. 99).

Hicks rightly calls attention to the influence of Rousseau on the Jacobins during the French Revolution, with all of its appalling destruction and massacres. But his discussion contains one minor slip, though I perhaps read him unfairly. He says that "in an enormously symbolic act, Louis XVI and Marie Antoinette were executed in 1793" (p. 102). The king was executed some ten months before the queen, not in the same act.

Now comes trouble. Rousseau is not the principal villain in Hicks's rogue's gallery. The main source of intellectual corruption, in his view, lies in the skepticism and subjectivism of Immanuel Kant. I have to confess that he has not persuaded me, and here is where I fear for the worst. Many years ago, I reviewed Leonard Peikoff's *Ominous Parallels*, a book that also located in Kant the chief source of modern irrationalism. (Hicks, like Peikoff, is an Objectivist, but he is an associate of David Kelley, once Peikoff's colleague and now his bitter antagonist. Perhaps as a result, Hicks never cites *Ominous Parallels*, though he lists it in his bibliography [p. 211]. But this is by the way.)

I did not review Peikoff's volume with much favor; in those days, I regret to say, I was sometimes prone to rather strong condemnations. This did not serve me well with Objectivists; Peikoff's book, one was given to understand, not only had Ayn Rand's approval but had in part been written by her. I did not hear the end of it for years afterwards; an *ex cathedra* dismissal of my objections from a writer for whom the letter to the editor is an art form remains vivid in my mind.

Though Hicks's account is far more convincing than Peikoff's, his presentation of Kant is open to challenge. The vital core of his interpretation is that Kant denied that we know reality.

> The fundamental question of reason is its relationship to reality.
> Is reason capable of knowing reality—or is it not? . . . Kant is
> crystal clear about his answer. Reality—real, noumenal reality—
> is forever closed off to reason, and reason is limited to aware-
> ness and understanding of its own subjective products. (p. 28)

Hicks's claim rests on a disputable premise. He rightly says that Kant denies that human beings grasp the noumenal world. It does not follow from this, though, that Kant denies that reason is capable of knowing reality, unless "reality" is equated with the "noumenal world." Why assume this? The world of ordinary reality seems very much closer to Kant's phenomenal world than to the noumenal. It is the former, not the latter, after all, to which the category of causality applies; and the precise point of Kant's massive efforts in the first *Critique* is to establish that reason *does* grasp the phenomenal world. Concerning the noumenal almost nothing can be said: why then is it the "real" world?

In brief, Hicks has very controversially assumed that Kant's phenomenal world is a private realm of sense data, to be distinguished from the "real," noumenal world of ordinary objects. I do not contend that Hicks's view of Kant is absurd on its face; distinguished commentators on Kant have adopted just this view. But the view needs much more defense than Hicks gives it. He ought at least to confront the account of Kant offered in Henry Allison's magisterial *Kant's Transcendental Idealism*.

On one point, Hicks seems to me not only disputable but altogether mistaken. He states: "While Kant was willing to give up the noumenal object, he held onto the belief in an underlying, noumenal self with a specific nature available to us for our investigation" (p. 59). Quite the contrary, Kant denies reason access to the noumenal self: our knowledge is confined to the phenomenal self.

One might counter my main objection in this way. Despite what Kant may "really" have meant, his successors among the German Idealists took him as just the sort of subjectivist that Hicks portrays and, accordingly, followed him in succumbing to skepticism. But this defense also fails. As Hicks himself rightly notes, Hegel "was dissatisfied with the principled separation of subject and object. This strain [represented by Hegel] granted Kant's claim that the separation cannot be bridged *epistemologically* by reason, and so proposed to bridge it *metaphysically* by identifying the subject with the object" (p. 44).

How can Hicks claim that Kant inaugurated a fatal skeptical trend, when he admits that a central strand of Kant's successors disclaimed skepticism? If he responds that "Kant's closest followers decided to accept the gulf [between subject and object] and live with it" (p. 43), a new objection arises. He offers no evidence that these neo-Kantian followers took the position he attributes to them. Putting this aside, in order to show that Kant lies at the source of modern skepticism about reason, he would need to establish a line of continuity between these "closest followers" and modern developments. His endeavor to do so rests on the very non-standard view, offered without support, that structuralism and phenomenology are varieties of neo-Kantianism.

Another theme in Hicks's gallop through the history of philosophy seems to me eminently questionable. He displays an extreme hostility to religion, and this often biases his historical claims. Thus, he portrays the Middle Ages as dominated by Augustinian "mysticism" and faith. (He acknowledges that in "the later medieval era," matters changed somewhat. "Thomism was an attempt to marry Christianity with a naturalistic Aristotelian philosophy" [p. 8].) What is one to make of Anselm on this view? Did not this "Augustinian" claim that God's existence can be rationally established? For that matter, did not Augustine himself argue to the same conclusion? Hicks operates with a simpleminded dichotomy between faith and reason that does not do justice to medieval thought.

At one point, Hicks's repugnance for Kant and religion leads to an ironical outcome. He condemns Kierkegaard for his

> panegyric to Abraham, a hero of the Hebrew Scriptures who in
> defiance of all reason and morality was willing to turn off his
> mind and kill his son Isaac. Why? Because God ordered him
> to. How could that be—would a good God make such a de-
> mand of a man? That makes God incomprehensibly cruel. . . .
> Does Abraham rebel? No. Does he even question? No. He shuts
> down his mind and obeys. (p. 54)

Hicks's eloquent remarks echo the views of Kant, the thinker he is most anxious to condemn. Kant held that Abraham should have realized that since God is good, no instructions to kill his innocent son could have come from God. He should thus have ignored the alleged divine command.

I do not suggest that only a Kantian view of ethics makes plausible the position Hicks adopts. But it is difficult to see how he would justify his stance on the ethical egoist view that I assume that he, as an Objectivist, adopts. He of course can deny, on metaphysical grounds, that an all-powerful divine being exists. My question involves a different issue. If such a being did exist, and issued a command of the type Hicks challenges, on what ethical grounds could he refuse obedience? Surely it would best promote his own survival or flourishing to obey rather than rebel.

Also questionable is Hicks's surprising assertion that Quine was a conventionalist about logic and mathematics.

> It was the neo-Humean option . . . emphasized by pragma-
> tists such as Quine, Nelson Goodman, and Ernest Nagel that
> prevailed. On this account, logical and mathematical prop-
> ositions are merely a function of how we have *decided* to use
> words and which combinations of words we have *decided* to
> privilege. (p. 76)

Did not Quine write a famous essay, "Truth by Convention," challenging the view here attributed to him?

On another matter, Hicks deserves great praise. Breaking with much contemporary scholarship, he reaffirms the older view that Hegel completely subordinated the individual to the state.

> The State, to the extent that it participates in the Absolute, is
> God's instrument for achieving his purposes.... The consequence
> of this, morally, is that the individual is of less significance than
> the state ... it is also true, Hegel granted, that in many cases the
> individual's freedoms and interests will genuinely be set aside,
> overridden, and even smashed. (pp. 121–122)

Though I have at times disagreed with Hicks, he has an excellent eye for
essential issues and his views always repay careful consideration.

Actual Ethics[*]

JAMES R. OTTESON

A Successor to Bastiat

July 1, 2006, *Mises Review*

T HE TITLE OF JAMES OTTESON'S BOOK IS, I am sure unintentionally, misleading. Readers might expect a dry and abstract philosophical treatment of ethics. In fact, what Otteson offers is a full-scale
defense of classical liberalism. He has written his book for a popular audience, and he intends it for use in college courses in ethical problems. But he
does not confine himself to repeating the lessons of others, though he has
certainly learned from his great predecessors.[†] He addresses several issues
in an insightful and original way, and it is on his treatment of a few of these
issues that I propose to concentrate.

Ethics, in Otteson's view, must take account of the realities of human
nature. Persons, e.g., care more about their families and close friends than
they do about strangers; and proposals that ignore this are doomed to fail.
A "proposed system of moral or political order that is premised on universal benevolence or an absence, even in the long run, of self-interest is a non-
starter" (p. 20). It is attention to the empirical realities of human nature that
Otteson has in mind by his title. Following Max Hocutt's *Grounded Ethics*
(Transaction, 2000), he makes no use of a priori deductions of rights.

---

[*] Cambridge University Press, 2006.

[†] Otteson has been especially influenced by Adam Smith, about whom he has written
an important book. See his *Adam Smith's Marketplace of Life* (Cambridge University
Press, 2002) and my review found in Volume 2, "Political Theory."

Ethics, then, must be empirical; but a descriptive account of human nature is not enough. We need also a "bedrock moral principle" (p. 7). For Otteson, this is Kantian directive to treat every person with respect: no one is to be used merely as a means.

Few, if any contemporary philosophers would differ with Otteson; I cannot think of anyone who argues that persons *shouldn't* be treated with respect or that we should disregard the realities of human nature. But unfortunately, the way Otteson develops these principles puts him in a decided minority. He maintains that persons need to develop their powers of judgment. To fulfill this demanding goal, an individual needs to take responsibility for his life. In particular, persons must not be protected from the "natural necessities" of human life. Individuals can learn to judge properly only by coping with the consequences of their mistakes. Rights to welfare subvert this conception of human development; enforceable claims to rights must be confined to the classical trio of life, liberty, and property.

Those inclined to dismiss Otteson will find his detailed discussions of particular issues hard to refute. He maintains, e.g., that simple facts about human nature rule out socialism. Under socialism, the state decides what is best for us. But

> each of us has a far greater stake in the outcome of our actions than anyone else does. If you make a mistake that leads to bad consequences, it is likely to be *you* who suffers the consequences ... but no one else has similar incentives in your case, and the farther away the decision maker is, the more likely he is to be unconcerned with the consequences of his decisions as they materialize in your life. (p. 53)

Otteson has a striking illustration of the lack of concern for individuals that one can expect from the state. Everyone is familiar with the Exxon *Valdez* case, in which an oil tanker that ran aground dumped 11 million gallons of oil into the ocean. But how many know about an incident involving the Minnesota Metropolitan Sewerage District? (I certainly did not.) In this incident, the MMSD

> "dumped an unprecedented 4.6 billion gallons of raw sewage" into Lake Michigan. The dumping was not a mistake or error, but was rather the MMSD's policy: when their sewage system

receives a lot of rainwater . . . then it is programmed simply to
dump the untreated sewage into Lake Michigan. (p. 54)

Otteson notes that this "disaster released some *four hundred times* as much
pollution as did the *Valdez*, and into a lake a fraction of the size of the north
Pacific Ocean" (p. 55). Why did this happen?

Is it not likely, Otteson suggests, that a "large part of the answer . . . is that
politicians *knew* they could not be held responsible" (p. 55). By long tradition, government officials are immune from prosecution for their official
acts. Besides this, government officials are not personally involved with the
victims of their callousness or inattention. And can we not go further, Otteson asks? Do not the atrocities of communism stem in part from the fact
that Lenin and his successors "did not *themselves* endure any of the suffering caused by their decisions and actions, and neither did their loved ones or
friends" (p. 56; this is not completely true for Stalin).

One might object to Otteson that the principle of government immunity
is not intrinsic to socialism; but his claim about the indifference of government officials cannot be denied. On one minor point about the history of
socialism, though, our author has fallen into error. He says that in the *Communist Manifesto*, Marx and Engels say "that there is some single good for
everyone which only the most 'advanced intellectuals' . . . are qualified to
apprehend and interpret"(p. 47). Marx and Engels do not say this, and the
words placed in quotation marks are not in the *Manifesto*. They do speak of a
section of the "bourgeois ideologists" who join the proletariat, because they
understand the movement of history, but they do not say that only these
intellectuals possess this knowledge.

Otteson's argument against socialism is convincing, but does it suffice to
show that a regime of laissez-faire capitalism should be established? What
about the poor? Are there not people so impoverished that they require
immediate aid, regardless of what they are able to earn on the free market?
And if private charity does not meet their needs, is not a program of forcible
intervention on their behalf justifiable?

Peter Singer has influentially pressed this case, and Otteson subjects his
arguments to careful analysis. Singer places great store on an example called
the Pond Case: A person passes by a child who is drowning in a small pond.
He could easily rescue the child and has no good reason not to do so. "Singer
would have us judge the passerby to be immoral if he does not help the child"

(p. 29). From this case, Singer draws the general principle that if one can avert death or suffering at an insignificant cost, one ought to do so.

The principle at first seems difficult to controvert, but does it not have radical consequences? Are we not required drastically to increase our donations to the poor? Surely my desire to dine at an expensive restaurant is morally insignificant, as compared to the need for food of someone in Bangladesh who is starving. Am I not obligated to send him or others like him all that I do not require for my own subsistence? And what I do not do myself the state can compel me to do.

Against this, Otteson presses a number of considerations. One of these will be familiar to all students of Austrian economics. Singer's principle requires us to transfer wealth if nothing of comparable moral significance is at stake. (A weaker version of the principle allows us to retain wealth if anything of moral significance would be lost by the transfer; but this is too vague for use.) But how can one assess moral significance? Must we not compare the utility of one person with that of another? Suppose that a wealthy person has the choice of spending money on a trinket or giving the money to a hungry Bengali. The question the follower of Singer's principle must ask "is whether the trinket is worth more to the wealthy person than the meal is to the Bengali" (p. 145, emphasis removed).

But does not Austrian economics show that no such comparisons of utility can be made? It is incoherent to ask whether the trinket or the meal is "objectively" more valuable. Judgments of value reduce without remainder to subjective preferences, and these cannot be ranked between individuals.

Otteson is of course correct that Austrian economics does not use objective values. To explain someone's actions, one must consider the preferences that he actually has. But in like fashion, to explain his actions, one must consider his beliefs, not what is really true. To explain, e.g., why someone campaigns for socialism, one might invoke his belief that socialism will vastly increase wealth. The belief is false, but it still explains his actions.

This hardly shows, though, that there are no objectively true beliefs. Similarly, the fact that explaining action requires the use of subjective preferences does not show that there are no objective values. Otteson has failed to show that any notion of objective value is incoherent; but he can certainly urge against Singer that it is for him to justify such a notion if he wishes to appeal to it.

Otteson advances a number of other considerations against Singer's principle, and one of these seems to me especially compelling. Singer supports his view by appeal to certain moral intuitions. We are supposed to grasp immediately that the trinket has less moral significance than the meal to the Bengali. But if one appeals to intuitions, is not obvious that someone who buys a gift for his wife, rather than give the money it cost to a poor person, is not acting immorally?

> Indeed, a moral position that makes a father immoral for buying his daughter a ribbon for her hair so stretches the limits of common moral communication as to suggest a refutation by reductio ad absurdum. (p. 154)

I should like to suggest an additional objection to Singer's principle. Singer supports his principle by appeal to the Pond Case. But that case—the man who refuses to rescue a drowning child—involves someone who does not help, even though there is only a trivial cost in doing so. The example then cannot properly be used to support a principle that mandates substantial sacrifice.*

Otteson maintains that there should be no government schools, a contention that few of his non-libertarian readers can be expected to view with sympathy. But, with a brilliant argument, he puts his conventionally liberal opponents on this issue in a tight corner. Most people strongly oppose the government's involvement in religion. Does it not violate freedom of conscience if someone is compelled to support financially a church whose doctrines he rejects? And would it not be even worse if were compelled to attend the church?

But does not government schooling entail equally severe violations of freedom of conscience?

> Finally, government support for education also commits whatever rights violations that government support for religion does. It infringes on a person's right to free speech to make him support an educational system with which he disagrees . . . And if a person has beliefs about religion, morality, or politics that

---

* The best attempt to extend the Pond Case to justify substantial sacrifice is that of Peter Unger in *Living High and Letting Die* (Oxford, 1996). He presents several cases, each slightly different, that start with little or no sacrifice and end with substantial sacrifice. He suggests that if one accepts the initial case, one will be rationally unable to get off before the end. But his argument is merely an application of the sorites problem and has no weight in this context. See my review found in Volume 2, "Political Theory."

differ from what is taught in the government schools, forcing
him nevertheless to support that school system involves the
same rights violation as does forcing him to support a religion
in which he does not believe. Educational policies and curri-
cula are ultimately dependent on our views about deep matters
of conscience—such as conceptions of the good life or religious
commitments—and hence are protected by the same freedom
of conscience that would protect our beliefs about matters of
religion. You simply cannot have it both ways. (p. 225)

Otteson cites in support of his view the classic essay by H. George Resch,
"Human Variation and Individuality" (In William F. Rickenbacker, ed., *The
Twelve Year Sentence*, Open Court, 1974).

Otteson, it is apparent, is a committed classical liberal of the old school;
and those inclined to the views of Murray Rothbard will applaud his efforts.
In one area, though, he does not go all the way with us. He rejects anarcho-
capitalism. A limited state that confines itself to protecting life, liberty, and
property, is in his opinion justifiable; moreover, it can tax people to pay for
its services.

How can Otteson hold this view? Has he not argued himself that taxation is akin to forced labor? He responds with a distinction:

I [Otteson] believe the classical liberal state can indeed be justified on the following grounds: its purpose is to secure the conditions for the exercise of personhood, and it may do nothing
else ... the minimal protections of life, liberty, and property can
be supported and endorsed by all persons, regardless of whatever their ends and purposes are, because these protections are
necessary to pursue *any* ends or purposes. Anything else a state
would do, however, will *conflict* with at least the ends or purposes of at least *some* persons. Hence the classical liberal state
is justified, but nothing beyond it is. (p. 109)

I do not think that this argument succeeds. If rights protection is a necessary condition to pursue any (legitimate) purpose, then everyone has reason
to support the protection of rights. But how does it follow from this that
a monopoly agency has the right coercively to extract resources to protect
rights? Should one not at least consider the possibility that protection can

be provided through voluntary agencies? Otteson is well aware that a number of writers have defended anarcho-capitalism, and remarks of this position: "Just because it is new to you does not mean it is absurd or without plausible foundation" (p. 103). Unfortunately, he does not consider any of the arguments raised by the writers he cites.

Perhaps, though, I have been too hard on our author. He raises the question: what happens if someone rejects the state and wants to protect himself? What if he wishes to employ his own private protection agency? Otteson responds that the objector must be allowed to leave.

> Respect for personhood entails that we must respect people's decision to take even this extreme step. If he does not want to pay taxes to the state to provide justice for him, he may opt out; but of course he thereby also gives up the right to ask the state to save him if things go south. (p. 110)

If Otteson says this, though, has he not fully embraced anarchism? Why should one speak of taxation if one does not have to pay?

I do not want to end on a negative note, however muted. To me the highlight of the book occurs in a discussion about the distinction between rights and other parts of morality. Classical liberals sharply distinguish between offenses against justice and unvirtuous conduct that does not violate rights. If I steal from you, I may justifiably be compelled to return your property; but if I wish to drink myself to death, the state cannot stop me. People are free to persuade me to modify my conduct, or shun me if I will not; but they cannot use force against me.

Many people find this sharp separation implausible, but Otteson suggests that most people implicitly accept it.

> You may have been taken aback by my suggestion that, on the one hand, people should be allowed to engage in activity we all know is wrong or foolish, and, on the other hand, that people should be left to face the consequences of their decisions, even if they are bad or degrading or cause suffering. But even if that offends your sensibilities, I would bet the farm that that is precisely what *you* do and believe, though perhaps implicitly, in your own life ... if your co-worker is wasting her income on bad movies and gambling ... you do not forcibly take over management of

her finances . . . why not? Because it is none of my business, you say. Precisely. Other people should enjoy the same freedom as you do, even if they use that freedom unwisely. (p. 121)

Otteson has restated in exemplary fashion a key argument made by Frédéric Bastiat in *The Law*: the state does not acquire new rights not possessed by individuals. He lists Bastiat as one of his "central sources" (p. vii), and his book establishes him as one of Bastiat's major successors.

Secular Philosophy and the Religious Temperament: Essays 2002–2008[*]

Thomas Nagel

Against Cosmopolitan Justice

October 1, 2009, *Mises Review*

Thomas Nagel has a remarkable ability to penetrate to the essence of important issues; and this collection of his recent essays and reviews displays his characteristic depth. I should like to concentrate first on "The Problem of Global Justice," which addresses issues of crucial importance for libertarians.[†]

Nagel is decidedly not a libertarian, but he poses the issues in a way that even those who differ with his conclusions will find illuminating. Much influenced by his teacher John Rawls's *Political Liberalism*, Nagel rejects the conception of justice common among libertarians. It is not just that he has different views from those of libertarians; he sees justice in an entirely different way. As libertarians see matters, persons have property rights, which do not depend on the state for their existence. Everyone possesses the same moral rights, regardless of the political community of which he is a member.

---

[*] Oxford University Press, 2010

[†] I have discussed this essay on an earlier occasion but I now think that I understand it better.

The libertarian position is an example of what Nagel calls a cosmopolitan view of justice:

> According to the first conception, which is usually called *cosmopolitanism*, the demands of justice derive from an equal concern or a duty of fairness that we owe in principle to all our fellow human beings, and the institutions to which standards of justice can be applied are instruments for the fulfillment of that duty. (p. 66)

He holds, by contrast, a political conception: the requirements of justice are relative to a political community. By no means does he maintain that all rights are relative in this way. Freedom of speech and religion are liberties to which everyone is entitled, and societies that do not recognize these rights are acting badly.

> The protection, under sovereign power, of negative rights like bodily inviolability, freedom of expression, and freedom of religion is morally unmysterious. Those rights, if they exist, set universal and prepolitical limits to the legitimate use of power, independent of special forms of association. (p. 73)

But property is another matter. People in a society may establish the property rights that seem reasonable to them.* "Reasonable" here should by no means be equated with "rationally self-interested"; unlike, e.g., John Harsanyi, Jan Narveson, and David Gauthier, Nagel does not derive the requirements of justice by asking what would command agreement among self-interested contractors. Rather, he thinks that people in society are morally bound to each other in ways that generate egalitarian obligations. He does not endeavor to fix exactly the strength of these obligations: that is a matter left to the citizens of each particular society.

Nagel's view puts him at odds with many followers of Rawls. Because he takes justice to be relative to political communities, Nagel denies that the obligations of justice extend worldwide. Rich nations, like the United States, stand under no obligation of justice to redistribute wealth to residents of less prosperous societies. There are, Nagel holds, humanitarian duties to relieve distress; but

---

* The parallel with T. M. Scanlon's conditions it would not be reasonable to reject is apparent. See Scanlon, *What We Owe to Each Other*.

these obligations do not fall under justice and do not require any approximation to equality. Nagel declines to support a global Rawlsian difference principle.

In taking this stance, Nagel finds himself at odds with many followers of Rawls, though not with Rawls himself. In *The Law of Peoples,* Rawls likewise drastically limited the scope of international redistribution.* Nagel and Rawls, to reiterate, stress the political context of justice. In the absence of international institutions that can subject nations to their control, the bonds that establish obligations of justice do not cross national borders.[†]

Oddly, libertarians are here allied with Rawlsians who favor international redistribution. Both support cosmopolitan justice, rejecting the political conception. Libertarians maintain that one's natural right to property holds against everyone: it is not limited to the confines of a particular political society. In like fashion, the cosmopolitan Rawlsians also apply their notions of justice universally. (I do not mean to suggest that no cosmopolitan could hold that there are special obligations regarding justice that are confined within a particular society. Rather, what defines this position is that justice at least in part extends beyond such confines.)

Nagel, who characterizes his position as Hobbesian, begins from an initial possession of territory by a political society. Justice, to reiterate, applies once such an initial appropriation has taken place: it does not extend "all the way down." (Incidentally, readers should not miss Nagel's brilliant early essay on Howard Warrender's interpretation of Hobbes, "Hobbes's Concept of Obligation," *Philosophical Review*, 1959.) Nagel here adopts the same view as a more extreme Hobbesian thinker, one whose thought is in most respects antipodal to his own—Carl Schmitt. Schmitt also held that a society's initial possession of territory was primary, requiring no justification.[‡]

Libertarians might at first imagine that it is easy to escape from the egalitarian demands of Nagel's conception of justice. If people have special obligations that stem from the bonds between them in a political society, can they not refuse to enter a society that imposes demands that they reject? Libertarians, after all, have nothing against voluntarily assumed egalitarianism.

---

* See my review of *Law of Peoples* found in Volume 2, "Political Theory."

† In response to criticism by Joshua Cohen and Charles Sabel, Nagel allows that there may be a "continuous function" theory of international institutions that does lead to obligations of justice, on a sliding scale.

‡ See Carl Schmitt, *The Nomos of the Earth* and my review found in Volume 2, "Political Theory."

378 ⚷ AN AUSTRO-LIBERTARIAN VIEW, VOL. 1: PHILOSOPHY

But Nagel cannot be shunted aside this easily. Because Nagel does not accept natural rights to acquire property, he would not acknowledge that those who prefer not to belong to an overly egalitarian polity can decamp with "their" property. Precisely what he denies is that people do have property rights independent of society.

But why does Nagel reject libertarian property rights? In his famous review of *Anarchy, State, and Utopia* ("Libertarianism without Foundations" in *Other Minds: Critical Essays 1969–1994*), Nagel contended that Nozick had arbitrarily postulated such individual property rights. It is not intuitively obvious that such rights exist, and in the absence of strong moral intuitions that support them, argument on their behalf is required.

Nagel goes further. In a later work, written with Liam Murphy, *The Myth of Ownership*, he contends that it is a conceptual error to deny that property rights rest on convention. If a libertarian were to say to Nagel, "Disagree with Nozick all you like. But surely his Lockean view counts as a theory; he and other libertarians haven't simply misused the concept of property," I imagine that Nagel would reply in this way: Even if one were to concede that individuals in a society must be afforded the opportunity to acquire property individually, surely it is undeniable that the overwhelming bulk of property is purely conventional. What items may be owned and exactly what ownership rights entail depend nearly entirely on the laws and customs of particular societies.

I do not think that this consideration suffices to rule out libertarian accounts of property rights. One may concede that the specific details of property rights in a particular society must be settled through convention. But a supporter of natural rights may consistently hold that in settling such matters, the conventions must conform to prior claims that individuals acquire through natural rights. In particular, the state, or other agency that establishes the legal limits of property, is not free to take over income or wealth as it sees fit. Its function is purely that of filling in an arrangement of property that it did not create.

An analogy may clarify this contention. Free speech in a society cannot exist without a body of regulations that set forward the content of free-speech rights. But it does not follow that the right to free speech exists entirely by convention; it is entirely coherent to think that whoever sets these regulations is strictly bound to respect preexisting rights and cannot overturn them. Libertarians think exactly the same about property.

To claim that the libertarian view of property rights is coherent does not suffice to establish its truth. Rather than pursue the matter further, though, I should like to raise a problem for Nagel's position. If justice is a political matter, confined in scope to particular societies, why are citizens of less prosperous societies obligated to respect the property arrangements of those situated in more fortunate circumstances? If justice rests on an "arbitrary" distinction, why cannot an equally arbitrary effort endeavor to replace an existing arrangement with something else? The members of the dissatisfied society, by hypothesis, are not bound by the special relationships that create obligations of justice. There may well be prudential reasons that counsel against interference by one society with the property arrangements of another, or moral reasons besides considerations of justice; but on Nagel's view, justice seems not to apply here.

Nagel addresses another issue that libertarians will find of interest. Much controversy has arisen in recent years over teaching alternatives to Darwinian evolution in public schools. The Intelligent Design movement defends "teaching the controversy": its vociferous opponents claim that this movement is religion disguised as science. From a libertarian standpoint, intractable controversies of this kind are the near-inevitable results of public education. In a system where the great majority of children attend public schools, how can disputes over controversial areas of study be avoided? With private education, by contrast, these problems do not arise, since parents can select schools in accord with their preferences.

Nagel's remarks on Intelligent Design are of great philosophical significance. He is an atheist and does not accept the view that a designing mind directed the evolutionary process. But he opposes what he deems a contemporary prejudice in favor of reductionist naturalism. He doubts that Darwinism can adequately explain the existence of objective value and looks instead to an immanent teleology in the world.

Although he does not accept Intelligent Design, Nagel refuses to dismiss the movement as merely religious. Critics claim that design cannot be a legitimate scientific hypothesis; but at the same time, they maintain that the theory can be shown to be false. Nagel pertinently asks, how can both of these assertions be true together? Further, Nagel sees no constitutional obstacle to teaching Intelligent Design.

Nagel's opinions on this issue have led to a remarkable episode. Brian Leiter runs a blog, *Leiter Reports*, which is read by philosophers, owing to detailed accounts of promotions, jobs, and other news about philosophy departments. Leiter's comparative rankings of philosophy departments also attract much attention. Leiter obtrudes his own political and social views on his audience; were he to present these in a separate venue, it is a safe bet that his audience would vastly diminish. Among Leiter's many aversions, the Intelligent Design movement ranks among the foremost: he often attacks what he calls the "Texas Taliban."

When Nagel's article on Intelligent Design appeared, Leiter could not contain his rage. We were presented with the unedifying spectacle of Leiter's speaking in abusive and condescending terms about one of the foremost philosophers of the past half-century. Nagel's *The Possibility of Altruism, The View From Nowhere,* and the essays collected in *Mortal Questions* are classics of contemporary philosophy.

Matters worsened when Nagel recommended in *The Times Literary Supplement* Stephen Meyer's *Signature in the Cell* as one of his "Best Books of the Year." Meyer is a leading proponent of Intelligent Design, and his book argues that naturalistic accounts of the origin of life on earth confront severe difficulties. Only a designing intelligence, Meyer contends, can account for the intricately specified information contained in DNA. Nagel did not endorse Meyer's conclusion but praised the book for its account of the "fiendishly difficult" problem of life's origin.

This recommendation aroused Leiter to new heights of contumely. It seems quite likely that Leiter never bothered to look at Meyer's book. He quoted from an English professor of chemistry protesting Nagel's claim that natural selection cannot account for DNA because it presupposes its existence. The chemistry professor, echoed by Leiter, said that natural selection exists in the preorganic world: was not Nagel ignorant to deny this? Both Leiter and the chemist ignored the fact, much emphasized by Meyer, that such resorts to natural selection are controversial. To appeal to the fact of their existence against Nagel is to assume what is much in dispute. Leiter extended his attack to accuse Nagel of ignorance of the relevant fields of study. Nagel has never claimed authority in biology; but had Leiter bothered to read Nagel's well-known essay, "Brain Bisection and the Unity of Consciousness," he would discover that Nagel has more than a passing acquaintance with neurobiology.

I have gone on at some length about this, because the attempt by Leiter and others to block inquiry that challenges naturalism seems to me altogether deplorable. To some people, evidently, the first line of the False Priestess in

In Memoriam is Holy Writ, not to be questioned: "The stars, she whispers, blindly run." But even if these avid naturalists are correct in their metaphysics, debate needs to be encouraged rather than suppressed. Perhaps Leiter should reread *On Liberty*. Pending that happy event, one can only say of his abuse that the barking of Bill Sikes's dog just tells us that Bill Sikes is in the neighborhood.

The book contains much else of great value, e.g., Nagel's appreciative essays on Bernard Williams, a major thinker with a much more skeptical view of moral objectivity than his own; and a penetrating discussion of Sartre on other minds.

In his range and speculative daring, Nagel reminds me of his friend Robert Nozick. Nozick's *Philosophical Explanations* and Nagel's *The View from Nowhere* are contemporary philosophy at its best. Those who have not previously read Nagel will find *Secular Philosophy and the Religious Temperament* an ideal introduction to his thought.

You and the State: A Short Introduction to Political Philosophy*

JAN NARVESON

Do We Need the State?

October 1, 2009, *Mises Review*

J AN NARVESON is one of the best contemporary moral and political philosophers, and it is not surprising that his introduction to political philosophy raises a vital issue that most people miss. Standard political philosophy asks, what theory best justifies the state? Is it consent? The security benefits that the state is alleged to bring? Something else, such as the "epistemic benefits" of democracy?[†] Narveson contends that this way of looking at the subject rests on an unexamined assumption. Why is it taken for granted that we need a state at all?

> Many strange and curious ideas have been associated with "anarchism," ... but we discuss it under the aegis of [classical] liberalism, which provides considerable impetus toward asking why we do

---

* Rowman & Littlefield, 2008.

† See the recent book by David Estlund, *Democratic Authority: A Philosophical Framework* and my discussion "An Epistemic Justification for Democracy?" in Jörg Guido Hülsmann and Stephan Kinsella, eds., *Property, Freedom, and Society: Essays in Honor of Hans-Hermann Hoppe.*.

> not, instead of relying on government, form our society entirely on
> *voluntary associations.* This possibility is not summarily dismissed
> as it is in almost all introductory books on this subject. (p. x)

Narveson's question cannot be answered without raising a further issue.
Within what moral framework should we endeavor to determine whether
we need the state? Naturally enough, Narveson prefers his own well-devel-
oped view, which he explains succinctly but carefully here.

As Narveson sees matters, the key to finding the correct moral standpoint
lies in abandoning a common assumption. We cannot rely on appeals to
moral intuitions. If, say, one person thinks viewing pornography is wrong
while another does not, how can their dispute be settled? What we have here
is simply two conflicting preferences.

> Sometimes it will be claimed that a premise is "self-evident," and
> occasionally that claim will look very plausible. But you always
> have to be careful: What seems self-evident to Jones can seem
> quite nonevident to Smith—and then what? (p. 4)

We cannot, Narveson thinks, locate objectivity in God's will. (Since Narveson is an atheist, he is hardly likely to find divine-command theories of morality compelling.) He deploys against such accounts the familiar *Euthyphro*
dilemma: should we not say that God commands something because it is
good, rather than that his commands create goodness?

> [T]he claim that we ought to do what god [sic] tells us makes
> no sense unless we assume that god will tell us the right things.
> But what will make those the right things? It cannot be the fact
> that "god" tells us this . . . in order to have a picture of a "supreme
> being" we must have a prior understanding of what sort of prop-
> erties make for the sort of moral supremacy that is claimed for
> him. Thus the claims[s] that these qualities are supreme just be-
> cause god has them and that we are right to do what he tells us
> just because he tells us to are strictly incoherent. (p. 64)

I venture to suggest that more sophisticated versions of divine-command
ethics, e.g., the theory advanced by Robert M. Adams in *Finite and Infinite
Goods,* cannot be so readily dispatched; but Narveson would no doubt reject
this view as well.

But if moral intuitions are cast aside, does this mean that morality is nothing but subjective preference? Narveson denies that this consequence follows. He suggests that we look at the situation in this way: Each of us wishes to advance his interests, including whatever values he considers to be the correct ones. These values are mere preferences and not objective. But we can ask, what rules would it be rational for such self-interested choosers to accept, so that each would have the greatest chance to achieve his goals?

> In short, the social contract is the set of reasonable terms for dealing with others, given what we are generally like. These terms, known as moral principles, are generally pretty clear. People can help you, and they can harm you, and we them. What we want from others is help, not harm. Harm from them is a cost to me, harm from me is a cost to them. The obvious settlement point is, simply, mutual nonharm. It's easy to live up to, usually: All we have to do is nothing, or more generally, to refrain from fairly specific, well-known kinds of harmful activities, notably those that impose physical damage on others or their property. (pp. 82–83)

David Gauthier adopts a similar approach in *Morals by Agreement*, a book that has influenced Narveson.

Narveson thinks that it would be rational for us to agree to respect each other's rights to life and liberty. By doing so, people greatly lessen the chances that their pursuit of their individual goals will be violently disrupted. But, contrary to the dominant beliefs in contemporary political philosophy, rights do not extend beyond this: there are, e.g., no welfare rights or rights to equal distribution of wealth. Why not? Narveson answers that to press such claims inevitably involves an appeal to controversial values that are not universally shared. To command universal assent, or as close to it as it is possible to attain, the hypothetical agreement must be pared to a minimum.

Defenders of the welfare state will no doubt interpose an objection. Even if it is true, they will say, that people would find it rational to agree to respect each other's life and liberty, this does not suffice to rule out the interventionist state of modern liberalism. True enough, if you have a right to liberty, other people cannot commandeer your labor on behalf of the poor. But property is another matter. Nothing has been said in Narveson's tale of a moral social contract to rule out restrictions on private property. Why may we not install a system in which people can acquire property only under rules that allow aid to the disadvantaged?

Narveson proves equal to this challenge. He contends that the unencumbered right to private property follows from the right of self-ownership:

> So what does this [self-ownership] have to do with owning bits of the external world? There is a natural answer. Ownership is authority over, which is authority to use. In the special case where no previous ownership exists, a person, A, coming upon useful things that A begins to use and intends to keep on using are to be reckoned their owners because now, any further person, B, undertaking to use those same objects, will be invading A.... This is wrong because of A's general right to do whatever nonharmful thing he wishes. (p. 93)

One cannot then sneak in welfare statism through the back door, once self-ownership has been accepted.

Narveson offers an interesting perspective on an issue much debated among libertarians: does the right of self-ownership entail the right to sell yourself into slavery? Murray Rothbard denies that it does, but Robert Nozick and Walter Block disagree. Narveson says, "What we probably should say is that people may enslave themselves to others for as long as they want to, but beyond that, we should not uphold the contract" (p. 92).

I am not sure that Narveson's social-contract approach to morality succeeds. He seems entirely right that it is prudentially rational for people to agree on rights to life and liberty. But does this suffice to generate a moral obligation to respect such rights? Is there not a distinct moral "must" that this account of morality misses? But these are very troubled waters, and I shall not pursue the issue here.* Agree with him or not on the foundations of morality, Narveson has come to conclusions about what rights we have that his fellow libertarians cannot but welcome.

Narveson's streamlined view of the rights we possess permits us to look at competing doctrines in an illuminating way. Unlike Narveson's contractarianism, most political theories think it justifiable to impose particular values on people. The use of force is not, in these views, confined to enforcing rights

---

* For an excellent criticism of views that reduce morality to advice, see H. P. Grice, *The Conception of Value.*

to life and liberty. Looked at in this way, political views usually placed in opposition wind up as variants of the same doctrine.

Thus, in

> the analysis here adopted, conservatism is the imposition, by compulsion (if necessary, which it is often presumed to be) of values against the desires of those upon whom they are politically imposed, and on the ground that the imposed values are the right ones, those recalcitrants who resist the imposition being held to be perverse or wrong. (p. 54)

Now for the surprise. Marxists also wish to impose values; so conservatism and Marxism are not opposites but in this crucial respect varieties of the same species. Under socialism a

> small number of people will emerge who claim . . . to represent the rest. The decision-making power will fall upon these few, and what people want, for their own part, becomes immaterial and inaccessible. The Central Committee will decide what people "want," what they "need," what is good for them. . . . This is why I place socialism as a conservative theory. (p. 76)

One can safely predict that most "modern" liberals will reject Narveson's moral theory, even if they cannot refute it. They will ask, can we really get along without government provision of welfare services? Narveson has a convincing answer:

> A claim is made that some important service can be provided only by the government, and this is used as an excuse for trying to prevent anyone else from trying to provide it. As a result, of course, the claim becomes self-confirming. (p. 143)

Narveson, a Canadian, is especially keen to criticize the use of this argument to defend that country's government-controlled medical system.

Narveson extends this brilliant point to bring the entire existence of the State into question.

> This peculiar institution known as "the State" is, despite its fervent and often eloquent press releases, overrated, overpriced, and hugely misused. It is overrated in that its necessity, which has

been trumpeted by almost all writers on the subject and most especially by the State itself, succumbs to analysis with very little remaining. . . . The State is misused in that it continually arrogates to itself the right to rule over our very lives as well as our fortunes and our liberties and has all too often (indeed, nearly always, in historical retrospect) ruled to the extent of murdering, torturing, and incarcerating or exiling, as well as robbing. (p. 195)

You and the State is an essential work for anyone interested in political philosophy.

Understanding Liberal Democracy: Essays in Political Philosophy*

NICHOLAS WOLTERSTORFF

The Problems of Public Reason

October 1, 2012, *Mises Review*

OST CONTEMPORARY political philosophers, unfortunately, are not libertarians. Nicholas Wolterstorff, best known as a founder of "reformed epistemology" but a philosopher of extraordinary range, is no libertarian either—far from it. In the present collection of essays, though, he assails a vastly influential school of thought in a way that libertarians will find useful.

Ever since John Rawls published *Political Liberalism* in 1993, political philosophers have focused on "public reason." This notion responds to a feature of contemporary politics difficult to deny: we have already drawn attention to it. In contemporary democracies, people disagree radically about what should be done politically. They operate from different philosophies, from what Rawls calls "comprehensive doctrines"; they have different "conceptions of the good." Some people are religious and look to what they take to be God's guidance on, e.g., abortion and same-sex marriage; others are atheists and want no part of alleged divine revelations. Some people think the state should mold people's characters to promote virtue; others say this is none of the state's business.

---

* Oxford University Press, 2012.

Faced with conflicts like this, what should be done? One alternative is that the supporters of a particular comprehensive doctrine should attempt to secure a majority for its views. Once they do that, they can ram through their program, regardless of the objections that come from those with other comprehensive doctrines. If you can convince most people that abortion is wrong, then you are free to pass laws that ban it.

Rawls and other supporters of public reason like Robert Audi disagree. They say that to act in the way just described is coercive and fails to show respect for those who hold different conceptions of the good.

> Most if not all exclusivists [advocates of public reason] . . . say something to the effect that *respect* for one's fellow citizens as free and equal requires that, before supporting a piece of proposed legislation, one offer or make available, to those one believes do not already have them, reasons for the legislation that they will or would regard as good ones . . . [an] alternative focuses on *coercion*. It is the coerciveness of legislation that makes reasons of the sort indicated required. A condition of a citizen's properly supporting a piece of coercive legislation is . . . [that] one must offer or make available, to those one believes do not already have them, reasons that they do or would regard as justifying the coercive legislation. (pp. 12–13, emphasis in original)

In brief, you should put aside your own opinions about the good when you are dealing—as you inevitably must in a contemporary democracy like that of the United States—with those with conflicting opinions. Instead, you should confine yourself to arguments that others can accept as reasons. For example, if you oppose easy divorce because you think this practice contravenes what the Bible teaches about marriage, you should not rely on this view in debates about public legislation. People who reject belief in God will not regard the Bible's claims as a reason for action at all. If you appeal exclusively to the Bible, you will be manifesting lack of respect for them and endeavoring to coerce them.*

---

* There is a difference of opinion among supporters of public reason. Some contend that you must confine all of your public arguments to those that meet the test of public reason. Others think that you can refer to your comprehensive doctrine, as long as you bring in arguments from public reason as well.

It is easy to see why Wolterstorff would not like public reason. As already suggested, religious views have no place in public reason, though they are not the only sort of excluded views. This cannot sit well with Wolterstorff, who is a devout Christian and thinks that his religion is very much relevant to politics. He accordingly launches a counterattack: public reason shows much less respect for people than its advocates claim for it; and the view has consequences that are themselves coercive. His powerful arguments should interest libertarians because they weaken the appeal of one of libertarianism's main rivals in political philosophy.

Wolterstorff notes that defenders of public reason do not in fact show respect for everyone's comprehensive doctrine. It is only those deemed "reasonable" who have to be taken into account. If you hold a comprehensive doctrine that is not "reasonable," then you are excluded: it is not necessary, in public argument, to offer you a reason that you would find acceptable.

Of course, the question arises, just what is a reasonable comprehensive doctrine, on this conception? It transpires that in essence it is one that accepts public reason. If you want to impose your comprehensive doctrine regardless of the opinions of those who reject it, you aren't reasonable. Public reason is thus respectful and non-coercive—to those who accept its tenets. Those outside the "legitimation pool" of these accepters do not count.

> All public reason liberals first declare that citizens of certain sorts are irrelevant to determining the permissibility of advocating in public and voting for some piece of legislation. . . . Rawls famously sets off to the side those who are not "reasonable," these being those who do not endorse "the underlying ideas of citizens as free and equal persons and of society as a fair system of cooperation over time." For those whose comprehensive doctrine leads them to be unreasonable in this way, Rawls declares that that doctrine is itself unreasonable. About such doctrines and those who hold them Rawls says that "Within political liberalism, nothing more need be said." (p. 81, quoting Rawls)

Even for the favored few who make it into the legitimation pool, it is by no means always the case that they must be given reasons for laws that they *in fact* accept.

> No public reason liberal holds that, having excluded certain
> sorts of citizens from the legitimation pool, we can now say
> that a condition of its being acceptable to advocate and vote for
> some proposed piece of legislation is that one judges that every-
> one who remains in the pool has a good and decisive reason . . .
> for believing that the legislation would be a good thing. There
> never is that degree of agreement; we can say in confidence that
> there never will be. It's for this reason that public reason liber-
> als all resort to speaking of what those in the legitimation pool
> *would* believe. (pp. 83–84)

In other words, if some people reject a law you propose, you assume that they
would accept it, or at least think it reasonable, if they were better informed or
thought about the issues more clearly. Is this not, Wolterstorff asks, a remarkably condescending view to take of one's fellow citizens?*

If Wolterstorff rejects public reason, what has he to put in its place? He
proposes "the equal right of citizens to full political voice" (p. 113). In this
conception of liberal democracy, people may advocate[†] laws for whatever
reasons seem to them suitable; they are not bound by the restraints of public
reason. If you have had a fair chance to state your case to the public, but the
vote goes against you, then you have not been treated unfairly.

But what about the problems to which public reason theorists have
pointed? What if the majority passes laws that seem to you to lack reason
altogether? Must you accept these laws, simply because the majority backs
them? Has Wolterstorff rejected public reason as not genuinely respectful
of others, only to subject everyone to dominance by the majority of voters?

Wolterstorff is fully aware of this problem. He responds that majority
rule, in his conception of equal political voice, is not untrammeled. Laws
cannot violate people's rights.

> I [Wolterstorff] hold that it is not public reason and the Rawlsian
> duty of civility that lie at the heart of liberal democracy but the

---

* It would not be a good response to say that anyone who favors a position must by
that fact think that he is correct and those who dissent mistaken. If you believe something, then you believe it to be true; but you need not hold that any rational and well-
informed person would agree.

† To my regret, Wolterstorff often uses the barbarism "advocate for" instead of "advocate."

equal right to full political voice, this voice to be exercised within constitutional limits on the powers of government and within legal limits on the infringement by citizens on the rights of their fellow citizens to freely exercise their full political voice. (p. 125)

What are these rights that limit the majority? Wolterstorff does not offer a list of them, though it is safe to say that they include the "standard" list of civil liberties, such as freedom of the press and of religion. But what if, as libertarians think, these rights extend further—to include natural rights to property? What if they leave no scope at all for further public deliberation, except perhaps on details? Wolterstorff assumes without considering alternative arrangements that the key task of political philosophy today is to arrive at an acceptable account of liberal democracy. Libertarians will not be satisfied; but we can be grateful to Wolterstorff for his careful analysis of public reason.*

---

* Wolterstorff in one essay offers an argument that people ought to accept the authority of the state. People have rights, this argument goes, and the state has an obligation to protect these rights. If the state has this obligation, then people have an obligation not to hinder the state in carrying out its proper task. This argument fails, for one reason, because of the gap between "not hindering" and "obeying" or "accepting the authority of." If Wolterstorff has an obligation to deliver a lecture that he has promised to give, I may have an obligation not to disrupt his talk. But it does not follow that I am obligated to do what he asks to assist him. Wolterstorff says that to the best of my knowledge no one has previously explored this way of accounting for the binding political authority of the state" (p. 6); but Randy Barnett offered a similar argument in *Restoring the Lost Constitution* (Princeton University Press, 2004). See my discussion and criticism in Volume 1, "Law."

Radicalizing Rawls: Global Justice and the Foundations of International Law*

Gary Chartier[†]

John Rawls and Market Anarchy

March 13, 2014, *Mises Daily*

Gary Chartier in this impressive book has put readers doubly in his debt. Chartier strikes at the heart of the vastly influential political philosophy of John Rawls. Libertarians can only applaud him for this, but we have even more reason to be grateful to Chartier. Having neatly dispatched Rawls, Chartier goes on to offer a strong defense of market anarchy.

There is, I fear, a problem with what I have just said. Chartier would not agree with my description of what he has accomplished. Although, as he tells us, "I am not a Rawlsian" (p. x), he does not aim to refute Rawls. To the contrary, he aims to show that Rawls's system, suitably modified, leads to market anarchy. I do not think that he succeeds in showing this; but it is in his attempt to do so that he in fact refutes Rawls.

What is the essence of Rawls's distinctive approach? Rawls leaves his readers in little doubt. Near the beginning of *A Theory of Justice*, he says:

* Palgrave Macmillan, 2014.

† I ought to say that I sent Professor Chartier comments on the manuscript of this book, as he kindly acknowledges.

Let us assume, to fix ideas, that a society is a more or less self-sufficient association of persons who in their conduct recognize certain rules of conduct as binding. . . . Suppose further these rules specify a system of cooperation designed to advance the good of those taking part of it. Then, although a society is a co-operative venture for mutual advantage, it is typically marked by a conflict as well as an identity of interests. . . . A set of principles is required for choosing among the various social arrangements which determine this division of advantages and for underwriting an agreement on the division of the proper distributive shares.*

Rawls has set his problem. What is his solution? Again, he offers a clear answer:

The principles are those that free and rational persons concerned to further their own interests would accept in an initial position of equality as defining the fundamental terms of their association. . . . Once we decide to look for a conception of justice that nullifies the accidents of natural endowment and the contingencies of social circumstance as counters in quest for political and economic advantage, we are led to these principles.†

In sum, those in Rawls's social contract view themselves as bound together equally in a common enterprise. Readers will not fail to note here echoes of Rousseau; and the great sociologist Robert Nisbet was among the first critics to stress this influence, as Chartier rightly says (p. 172, note 110).

Chartier resolutely rejects this view of society, and it is in doing so that he undermines Rawls's system. In a brilliant passage, he says:

On the standard Rawlsian view, individual deliberators at the domestic level would treat the goods and services generated in their society as shared products of their efforts and so as theirs to distribute. . . . The characterization of a society as a cooperative venture for mutual advantage seems to imply that the society has some sort of collective identity. Instead, a society may be seen

---

* John Rawls, *A Theory of Justice* (Cambridge, Mass.: Harvard University Press, 1971), p. 4.
† *Ibid., pp. 11, 15.*

as the sum total of a vast number of cooperative interactions, including a variety of interlinked ventures. We can speak of a general pattern in accordance with which social cooperation leads to mutual advantage; but that's quite different from a social contract in which people agree to engage in a shared enterprise and determine how best to divide the proceeds of the enterprise. A society is not an enterprise. (pp. 144–145)

When Chartier says "a society is not an enterprise," I take him to be making an ethical claim rather than a purely factual judgment. We should not conceive society as an enterprise. To talk of people as a collective that "distributes" liberty and property among its members is inimical to what Chartier in a fine phrase calls the "architectonic liberties," the fundamental freedoms most essential to each person's life.

A fairly straightforward way of doing this [making possible people's pursuit of their projects] would be to preclude non-remedial interference with the architectonic basic liberties—protections for bodily integrity and property (both personal and productive). (p. 95)

But now a problem demands our attention. If Chartier has rejected the key assumption in Rawls's theory, why does he present himself as "radicalizing" Rawls instead of abandoning him? Why does he think that it is possible to remain within Rawls's framework, in a way that does not accept the notion of society as a collective enterprise?*

Chartier's answer is simple. He replaces Rawls's collectivism with his own individualist views. People who imagined themselves to be deliberating in the original position, he suggests, would choose market anarchy, given the strength of the arguments for that view.

Chartier has excellent arguments for market anarchy, but without the assumption of an equal division of the gains from social cooperation, no distinct Rawlsian theory of justice is left. One can speak, if one likes, of an "original position," which involves choice behind a "veil of ignorance"; but these phrases do not by themselves suffice to constitute a moral theory. As

---

* To reiterate, I do not mean that Chartier himself is a radicalized Rawlsian, in his sense. He is not but thinks that Rawlsians should modify their views in the way he suggests and that they can do so and yet remain Rawlsians.

Chartier uses these expressions, they mean little more than "choice as a result of careful consideration, after trying to eliminate personal bias." It is surely desirable to think about moral issues in this way, but doing so does not make one a follower of Rawls.

An example will illustrate what is at issue. After he presents a penetrating criticism of the state, which we shall soon examine, Chartier says that Rawlsian deliberators in the original position "would have excellent reason to take account" of the points about the state which he makes (p. 141). Here to invoke the original position adds nothing: all that Chartier is really saying is that Rawlsians, like other people thinking clearly, ought to be critical of the state.*

About this he is clearly right. He points out that

> states are inherently very dangerous. The war making in which they have persistently engaged and to which their taxing power and their leaders' desire for glory and public acclaim render them exceptionally prone, is a particularly good example. But the tendency of the state to constitute and serve the interests of an exploitative ruling class provides a further reason to avoid creating, supporting, or maintaining it. (p. 140)

Chartier offers an exceptionally insightful discussion of why military intervention by states, even intervention that ostensibly aims to defend human rights, is likely to have untoward consequences:

> It frequently and predictably involves the violation of just war constraints on harm to both noncombatants and combatants.... There are also systemic reasons to favor general prohibitions on

---

* With much injustice to Chartier, I shall confine to a note comment on one of the book's principal themes. Chartier argues that Rawls in *The Law of Peoples* wrongly confines the scope of justice to particular societies. Instead, justice should be "cosmopolitan," applying throughout the world. Chartier inquires: do not all human beings possess the two moral powers, the basis for equality as Rawls conceives of it, not just those in particular societies? Indeed they do, and Rawls says so (see, e.g., *Theory of Justice*, pp. 504 ff.); but people are not morally required to enlist in a collective enterprise with everyone who qualifies as a human being. One could imagine everyone in the world engaging in such an enterprise, but no moral imperative in Rawls's view requires this. Again, Chartier underestimates the key place of engagement by a particular group in a common enterprise: without this, there is no distinct Rawlsian theory.

states' engagement in military conflicts not involving the defense of their own territories. Such conflicts are predictably associated with human rights violations ... they breed resentment that can lead to further violence. They are profoundly, uncontrollably, wastefully expensive.... Wars also lead frequently to the implementation of repressive measures, including censorship, propaganda, torture, surveillance, and due process violations of various kinds—which are all too likely to persist after war's official end. (p. 107)

Chartier has written a book of outstanding merit. *Radicalizing Rawls* confirms his place as one of the best political philosophers of our time.

Law

War and Responsibility: Constitutional Lessons of Vietnam and Its Aftermath[*]

John Hart Ely

Hail to the Congress

April 1, 1996, *Mises Review*

AS I WRITE THESE LINES, an American soldier, no doubt the first of many to come, has been killed while taking part in the American "peacekeeping" mission in Bosnia. Many in Congress, as well as most of the Republican candidates for President, oppose sending our troops to "a far away country of which we know nothing." Opinion polls unanimously declare that the American people do not want to go to war in Bosnia.

But in foreign affairs, the rule nowadays seems to be, "Congress (and the American people) propose; the President decides." President Clinton has committed our troops to Bosnia; and patriotic duty, it is alleged, demands that we support the Commander-in-Chief.

War and Responsibility appeared long before President Clintons costly effort to make Bosnia safe for democracy, but it has never been more relevant. John Hart Ely's brilliant book establishes incontrovertibly that it is Congress, not the President, who has under the Constitution the sole power to involve US forces in war.

---

[*] Princeton University Press, 1995.

Many areas of constitutional law generate issues of Byzantine complexity, but this one does not.

> The power to declare war was constitutionally vested in Congress. The debates, and early practice, establish that this meant that all wars, big or small, "declared" in so many words or not—most weren't, even then—had to be legislatively authorized. Indeed, only one delegate to either the Philadelphia [Constitutional] convention or any of the state ratifying conventions, Pierce Butler, is recorded as suggesting that authority to start a war be vested in the president. (p. 3, notes omitted)

Butler's view was at once repudiated.

For most of our history, presidents scrupulously obeyed the command of the Constitution.

> And when certain presidents did play a little fast and loose with congressional prerogatives—Polk at the start of the Mexican War; Wilson and Roosevelt, respectively, in the events leading up to the First and Second World Wars—they obscured or covered up the actual facts, pledging public fealty to the constitutional need for congressional authorization of military action. (p. 10, note omitted)

Ely does not include Lincoln's actions at the start of the Civil War in his list of exceptions, since "for constitutional purposes a domestic rebellion is quite different from a foreign war" (p. 150). Though I think this a mistaken view, this is not the place to argue the point; and even if Lincoln is added to the list of violators, Ely's main contention stands.

But if most presidents on this issue obeyed the constitution, how did we get where we are today? The key figure in the transition is that much-overrated haberdasher, Harry Truman. During the Korean "police action," Truman went out of his way not to seek Congressional approval for his actions. His supporters claimed that as Commander-in-Chief it was within his power to start wars without congressional approval. Ely, not one to mince words, calls this an "outrageous rationale" (p. 152).

Since Truman, the presidential record has been a sorry one. With the exception of Dwight Eisenhower, presidents have continued the path of usurpation pioneered by the man who gave us Hiroshima. But the blame for the violation of the Constitution does not lie solely with our recent presidents. Congress has colluded with them: as Ely sees matters, Congress prefers that the president assume the burden of committing our troops to battle. If a war turns out badly, he, not Congress, will be blamed; if it turns out well, Congress can bask in the president's reflected glory. In addition, individual members of Congress aim primarily to serve the interests of their constituents: they have little to gain by voting to send troops into combat. Presidential usurpation of the war power suits many Congressmen quite well.

Should we go along with the new order of things? Ely thinks not. The original understanding of the war powers clause makes eminent good sense. The framers of the Constitution wished to make wars difficult to start. It is easier for a single person to plunge the country into war, should the decision rest with him alone, than for a group continually sensitive to popular approval to do so.

At one juncture Ely could strengthen his case. He states:

> Of course, if he asked, the president would usually receive rather readily the support of both Congress and the American people when he decided to have a war. . . . [But] the constitutional strategy was to require more than one set of keys to open the Pandora's box of war. (p. 9)

Ely's argument, then, is that having Congress declare war will slightly reduce the probability of war. The chances of war will be reduced, since both Congress and the president must agree, if a war is to occur; but they will be reduced only slightly, since Congress will probably grant the president's request for a declaration.

The last step of the argument does not follow from Ely's premises. Ely I think has reasoned as follows: the president wants a certain number of wars. If the decision is solely up to him, we will have just that number. But Congress, though it will usually go along with him, will on occasion not do so. Therefore, the number of wars with Congressional approval will be slightly less than without it. This argument wrongly assumes that the requests submitted to Congress will consist of the wars the president would have started on his own, had he the power to do so. But this might be false. Perhaps the president, knowing a request will not be approved, will decline to submit it. More simply put, if the president realizes his requests may be turned down, he will be apt to ask for fewer wars than he would have started on his own.

I hope that readers will forgive me for going on too long about this point. Ely is a dialectician of immense subtlety, and the temptation to try to catch him out proved too difficult to resist. Besides, the point materially strengthens his case.

Defenders of the present order will no doubt dismiss the appeal to Congress as an anachronism. Do not the imperatives of modern war demand swift and sudden action? How can one insist on a leisurely appeal to Congress, when the fate of the world may require instant response?

As usual, Ely has anticipated the objection:

> Occasionally—though nowhere near as often as enthusiasts would have us believe—military emergencies can develop faster than Congress can convene and react. This was also true in the late eighteenth century—it was probably truer than it is today. . . . The founders understood this, though, and consequently reserved to the president authority to respond on his own to "sudden attacks" until there was time for Congress to convene and confer. In such situations the president could respond militarily and seek authorization simultaneously. (p. 6, note omitted)

If Ely is right, a difficult problem confronts us. The war powers clause should be obeyed as originally meant; but Congress prefers the present situation. What is to be done?

Ely rests his hopes on the federal judiciary. If the president has committed us to war without the approval of Congress, the courts should declare the executive action unconstitutional and remand the matter to Congress for its decision. I am inclined to think that Ely vastly overestimates the interest of the federal courts in constitutional government; but here readers must judge for themselves.

In one instance, Ely's zeal to bring in the courts leads him to a rare misstep. Supporting the plaintiffs in *Dellums v. Bush*, a suit brought by several members of Congress to enjoin President Bush from sending troops to Kuwait without the consent of Congress, Ely writes:

> it was a suit that said "The president's unilateral actions . . . [are] depriving the fifty-four of us of a right the Constitution guarantees us, that of voting on wars before the president starts them." (p. 60)

If Congress alone has the right to declare war, then should the president begin a war without consent of Congress, he has violated *its* right. But it does not follow that groups of members within Congress have separate rights that have been violated. At any rate, this is an independent step for which argument is needed. But this is a minor matter.

I fear that I have given a skewed account of Ely's book. Much of it is concerned to analyze, in painstaking detail, whether the American involvement in Indochina was constitutional. I have emphasized the underlying thesis, rather than Ely's historical application, since the issue he raises is of vital current interest. He suggests during his historical account that presidents who violated the war powers clause should have been impeached. I hope that readers will not fail to apply the point to the current occupant of the White House.

Overcoming Law[*]

Richard A. Posner

Judges Shall Be As Gods

April 1, 1997, *Mises Review*

T O MOST CONSERVATIVES, constitutional interpretation is straightforward. The judge's task is to understand the Constitution as
intended by its authors. A judge must not anachronistically impose
his own social philosophy on the document; and the principal complaint
against "liberal" judges is that they commit this sin. Notoriously, for example, the Warren Court preferred its understanding of Gunnar Myrdal and
Kenneth Clark over the legislative history of the Fourteenth Amendment.

Much of Richard Posner's long and learned volume is devoted to an
assault on "originalism." More exactly, the book's principal target is a general
category, "formalism" of which originalism is alleged to be a species. Formalism resists exact definition; but, roughly, it holds that law is a fixed body of
principles that may be analyzed without the use of other disciplines, especially the social sciences.

Our author, who is Chief Judge of the United States Court of Appeals,
Seventh Circuit, was in an earlier incarnation the leading academic advocate of law-and-economics, a doctrine in which he still devoutly believes.
To paraphrase Hume, law-and-economics maintains that "law is, and ought
only to be, the slave of wealth maximization." Holders of this position, as
can well be imagined, do not look on originalism with entire favor. Were one
restricted to the text, the pursuit of wealth might be hindered.

---

[*] Harvard University Press, 1995.

What has Posner to say against interpreting the Constitution as written? His key argument is this:

> Many provisions of the Constitution ... are drafted in general terms. This creates flexibility in the face of unforeseen change, but it also creates the possibility of alternative interpretations, and this possibility is an embarrassment for a theory of judicial legitimacy that denies that judges have any right to exercise discretion. (p. 233)

Given an indeterminate text, a judge must choose; and to choose properly he must weigh consequences.

Judge Posner of course is right that much of the Constitution is in form general: "The freedom of speech," "the equal protection of the laws," etc. But it does not follow from this that these provisions are indeterminate in meaning. Posner's argument, when pressed, seems to be that unless we do take the general provisions as indeterminate, we shall be unable to cope with new conditions. The poor, benighted framers could not possibly anticipate what we know today especially if we have thoroughly studied Posner's opera omnia.

To make good his argument, Posner needs to give examples of general constitutional provisions that, if "inflexibly" interpreted, eventuate in disaster; but he fails to do so. In fact, Posner himself in another context notes an instance that goes strongly against his view, though he fails to draw the connection.

During the early years of the New Deal, the Supreme Court used an "inflexible" interpretation of parts of the Constitution, e.g., the commerce clause, to strike down key legislation of the Rooseveltian New Order. Many legal "progressives" maintained that strict construction placed needed social reform in a straitjacket.

Did the Court do this? In fact, the situation is entirely the reverse: had the Court invalidated more New Deal nostrums, we would nearly all have been better off. Let Posner tell the story:

> Many New Deal programs were aimed at raising prices and wages, and by thus reducing economic growth and employment programs delayed the recovery from the Depression as did (in all likelihood) the spirit of restless experimentation and of hostility to business that was characteristic of Roosevelt's pre-World War II Presidency. (p. 221)

Hardly a point for flexible interpretation, is it?

But has Posner nothing at all to cite as an example of the disasters of originalism? It transpires that he does indeed have a case in mind: that old warhorse, *Brown v. Board of Education*. Had Earl Warren paid attention to the historical context of the Fourteenth Amendment, "a history which indicates that the amendment had not been understood by its framers or supporters to require blacks to attend school with whites," he might never have been able to rule segregation unconstitutional (p. 225, Posner in a footnote cites an unpublished work by Michael McConnell which challenges this view of the legislative history. But I venture to suggest that Raoul Berger, whom Posner does not cite, has conclusively shown that the quoted view is correct).

There we have it. Originalism leads to the rejection of Brown; Brown is sacred; therefore, originalism has been "weighed, and found wanting in the balance." This, I suggest, is the essence of Posner's case against strict construction.

He berates the legal theorist Herbert Wechsler for criticizing Brown; although a devout liberal, Wechsler found himself unable to arrive at "neutral principles" on which Brown could be defended.

> One might have supposed that the central question in *Brown v. Board of Education* was not the scope of some abstract principle of freedom of association but whether racial segregation of public facilities in the South was intended or likely to keep the blacks in their traditionally subordinate position. (p. 72)

Perhaps it was; but why is the Supreme Court a roving body to solve social problems? And why must we choose between the preservation of enforced segregation and a "results-oriented" jurisprudence? Did these exhaust the alternatives in the 1950s and '60s? Posner gives us no reason to think so.

Posner does however make one effective point about the controversy over Brown. Many professed originalists defend Brown; and this they cannot with consistency do (unless they read the legislative history aberrantly). Thus, Robert Bork builds up "an unanswerable case on his own [originalist] terms" against Brown, but "flinches" from accepting the implication of his own analysis (p. 247). He too wishes to retain Brown.

Of course, Posner does not, as he should, condemn Bork for flinching. His point, to reiterate, is that given Brown as a "sacred cow" (p. 249), we must embrace a judicial philosophy that entails that the case was rightly decided.

Our author is alert to an objection. Is it not undemocratic for a small group of judges, who hold office for life, to impose their conception of the good on the rest of us? Unlike Bork, Posner does not flinch. He responds, what is so good about unlimited democracy?

> Liberalism is in tension with democracy. Democracy is a means not only of dispersing political power and thus of protecting the private sphere against invasion by the public sphere, but also of enabling people to enforce their dislike of other people's self-regarding behavior. (p. 25)

Further, democracy often fails adequately to reflect the preferences of the majority. A "large and amorphous majority" may be at the mercy of a cohesive special-interest group, which can often "use the political process to transfer wealth to itself" (p. 203). And representatives often do not carry out the wishes of the electors: "They have their own interests, selfish and otherwise" (p. 203).

Posner's challenge to unlimited democracy is effective; but his style of jurisprudence remains vulnerable to a variant of the objection from democracy. We may simply ask: why should an elite coterie of judges rule over us? This objection does not assume anything at all about democracy; but it requires an answer. Preoccupied with his view that judges should decide cases by their consequences, he fails to ask what consequences justify the existence of a Supreme Court at all.

I have so far been unjust to Judge Posner; and this, in a review of a work of legal theory, will never do. His criticism of originalism is not freestanding but is embedded in a larger philosophy, pragmatism, which supports his emphasis on consequences.

On second thought, I withdraw my admission of injustice. Pragmatism as professed by our oracle is monumentally silly. The "support" it offers his jurisprudence is, in Lenin's phrase, "the support which a rope gives a hanging man."

Posner's variety of pragmatist is "skeptical about claims that we can have justified confidence in having arrived at the final truth about anything. Most of our certitudes are simply the beliefs current in whatever community we happen to belong to" (p. 5). We accept such facts as the existence of the external world because it would be disorienting for us to dislodge them.

But even the most unshakable facts are not certain. "One can only pretend" to doubt that the world exists independently of oneself and similar bedrock beliefs. "Yet while unable to doubt them in the sense of being willing to act on our doubts, we can accept intellectually the possibility that they will someday be supplanted by fundamental beliefs equally unshakable and transient" (p. 5).

I freely confess that I am entirely unable to grasp how belief in the external world might be "supplanted." To put words together in meaningless strings, as Posner does here, hardly qualifies as philosophy. Let us pass by Posner's effusions "in silent contempt," as Dante says.

Posner reads remarkably widely; but his reading is not always accurate. Cardinal Bellarmine did not refuse to look through Galileo's telescope; or if he did, history does not record it (p. 344). Pascal did not maintain that belief is "entirely voluntary" (p. 502); his discussion of the wager explicitly takes account of the involuntary aspect of belief. The radio commentator Dennis Prager is not a rabbi (p. 573). None of the construals Posner offers for "bounded rationality" captures what Oliver Williamson means by the term (pp. 435–436). Nelson Goodman's concept "grue" is not a metaphor (p. 524). But the problems of Posner's book go beyond details. The whole structure is rotten.

Presidential War Power[*]

LOUIS FISHER

Who's In Charge?

April 1, 1997, *Mises Review*

T HE CONDUCT OF contemporary American foreign policy flies in the
face of the Constitution and much of our history. Of this unfortunate circumstance, readers of Louis Fisher's definitive book will have
no doubt. Today, President Clinton claims, on his authority as Commander-
in-Chief, the power to commit American troops to Bosnia and elsewhere,
without the consent of Congress. Like his predecessor George Bush in the
Gulf War, he avers that he may act in entire independence of Congress: the
president is supreme in foreign policy. Though the cooperation of Congress
in foreign adventures may be sought, this is a matter of political convenience
rather than legal necessity.

Louis Fisher, probably the foremost expert on the legal questions involved,
rejects entirely the self-serving view of our beloved chief magistrate. The Constitution states without ambiguity that Congress, not the President, has the
power to declare war. As Fisher makes abundantly clear, the framers had good
reason for their language.

Under the British system of government, the power to declare war rested
solely with the king; likewise, it was his prerogative to make treaties that
could irrevocably bind his subjects.

> These models of executive power were well known to the fram-
> ers. They knew that their forebears in England had committed

---

[*] University Press of Kansas, 1995.

to the executive the power to go to war. However, when they declared their independence from England, they rested all executive process in the Continental Congress. (p. 2)

In so doing, the American revolutionaries broke with John Locke. As Fisher notes, Locke in the *Second Treatise* associated the power of war and peace, which he termed the federative power, with the executive. To the framers, this assignment of power threatened tyranny; in so concluding, they were, I suggest, better Lockeans than Locke himself.

The delegates to the Philadelphia convention continued to adhere to the revolutionaries' view of the question. "On numerous occasions the delegates to the constitutional convention emphasized that the power of peace and war associated with monarchy would not be given to the President" (p. 4). Even so ardent a supporter of a strong executive as Alexander Hamilton concurred in the common view.

An objection at once arises to Fisher's contention. No doubt, as he says, the Constitution gives to Congress alone the power to declare war. But is this not a mere formality? The President remains free to send troops into combat as he wishes, through his power as Commander-in-Chief. The clause in question merely restrains him from calling his expeditions "wars" on his own volition. So what?

Our author easily turns this objection aside. Like the Continental Congress, the US Congress's authority extended both "to 'perfect' and 'imperfect' wars to wars that were formally declared by Congress and those that were merely authorized" (p. 2). Fisher emphasizes especially that Congress, not the president, had the constitutional power to authorize private citizens to use armed force against foreign nations, through letters of marque and reprisal.

If thwarted by the text of the Constitution, supporters of presidential power are apt to turn to the Republic's early history. Did not Washington and Jefferson both commit forces to combat without a congressional declaration of war? What of the Indian Wars, the Whiskey Rebellion, and the campaigns against the Barbary pirates?

One of the book's great strengths is its forthright exposure of the myth that the executive in these instances acted independently. In each case, Fisher shows, the president acted with the full consent of Congress.

Recent studies by the Justice Department and statements made during congressional debate imply that Jefferson took military measures against the Barbary powers without seeking the approval or authority of Congress. In fact, in at least ten statutes, Congress explicitly authorized military action by presidents Jefferson and Madison. (p. 26, footnote number omitted)

Those seeking full details of each example must of course consult the book; after Fisher's painstaking survey, the matter admits of no doubt.

In one particular, I venture to suggest that Fisher might have strengthened even further his already overwhelming presentation. He notes Raoul Berger's citation of the Continental Congress's detailed instructions to George Washington as evidence of the narrow scope accorded the commander-in-chief. But he finds fault with Berger's analysis. The Congress often made "extensive delegations" of authority to Washington (p. 11). Further, the limits on an officer subordinate to Congress need not apply to the president, who heads a coequal branch of the government.

Fisher's objections do not speak directly to Berger's argument. True, the Congress delegated power to Washington: but it was theirs to delegate, as Berger's citation of the instructions to Washington shows. And the issue in dispute is not whether the president has more power than a general of the revolutionary army; rather, the question is what power derives from his designation as commander-in-chief. Here, Berger's resort to contemporary usage of the phrase is entirely on point.

If, though, the case for Congressional authority over war is as strong as Fisher alleges, how did we get where we are today? During the first half of the nineteenth century, presidents usually adhered to constitutional requirements, although James Polk behaved in highly dubious fashion during the Mexican War. Of course matters were different with Abraham Lincoln, that fount of all things unconstitutional. "In April 1861, with Congress in recess, he [Lincoln] issued proclamations calling forth the state militia, suspending the writ of habeas corpus, and placing a blockade on the rebellious states" (p. 38). Yet even Lincoln acknowledged that he had acted ultra vires and sought subsequent Congressional approval to make good his illegalities.

If, much against our instincts, Lincoln cannot be saddled with the full blame for presidential usurpation of the war power, who can? Fisher tells a long and involved story, but two presidents especially merit a place in the rogue's gallery.

As Fisher notes, Woodrow Wilson's violation of the Constitution proceeded from long meditated plans. Although the Constitution provides for treaties to be made by the president with the "advice and consent of the Senate," Wilson in two books openly expressed his contempt for this limit to executive power. By his power to take unilateral initiatives, the president could create a situation in which Congress would have no alternative but to back the president. "The initiative in foreign affairs, which the President possesses without any restriction whatever, is virtually the power to control them absolutely" (p. 72, quoting Wilson, *Constitutional Government in the United States*).

When elected president, Wilson adhered faithfully to his designs; but as the battle over the Treaty of Versailles showed all too well, he could not bludgeon Congress into acknowledging the dominance in foreign affairs he claimed. With Harry Truman, who shared Wilson's bloated conception of executive power, matters proved far different.

During the Korean War, Congress was more than willing to give Truman full support for his military moves in Asia. But he disdained the legislative branch's approval. In his view, he did not require its consent to send American troops into battle. Congress might accede if it wished; the question was really of no moment. "President Truman did not seek the approval of members of Congress for his military actions in Korea. As [Secretary of State] Acheson suggested, Truman might only wish to 'tell them what had been decided'" (p. 86).

I need not fear spoiling the reader's surprise if I reveal that the modern Supreme Court has not stood foremost as a champion of the original understanding of the Constitution. Oddly enough, though, a key decision upholding executive supremacy in foreign affairs came from George Sutherland, normally a highly conservative justice. Sutherland, one of the Supreme Court's "Four Horsemen of Reaction," did not hesitate to strike down New Deal domestic legislation as unconstitutional. Yet in foreign affairs he saw matters in an entirely different light.

In the Curtiss-Wright case (1936), Sutherland held that the president's power in foreign affairs existed in entire independence from the Constitution. The power to conduct foreign relations is an "inherent attribute of sovereignty." As such, it passed upon independence directly from the British Crown to the colonies collectively. Somehow, though Sutherland did not make clear in exactly what fashion, the power migrated to the Chief Executive.

Fisher crisply and clearly dissects Sutherland's opinion, and fortunately in recent years the Court has retreated from its extreme language. Our author sees in this a sign of hope. Indeed, he is generally an optimist, believing that if Congress resolutely asserts its constitutional prerogative, the president will be forced to comply with its wishes. He supports his opinion through a detailed account of the War Powers Resolution of 1973.

One may hope that he is right; but even if Congress does assert its authority, the battle is liable to be difficult. Recent presidents, not least among them Bush and Clinton, have done their best to thwart Congressional attempts to rein in the plenary powers they claim for themselves.

Fisher's carefully presented book requires us to answer an underlying question. Granted that the author's constitutional argument is correct, why does this matter for us now? Fisher does not address the issue in elaborate detail, but the response is sufficiently obvious. Congressional authority over war provides an indispensable means to curb a president intent on foreign adventures.

Though Fisher well states the essentials of the case, his book can here usefully be supplemented with the excellent work of John Hart Ely, *War and Responsibility.** More generally, the two books are near perfect complements: Ely is a master of argumentative subtlety, while Fisher excels in historical research.

But what if, against all expectation, the president proves less bellicose than Congress? Here a non-interventionist need fear nothing, since matters are likely to work out as he desires. As commander-in-chief, the president does possess some real powers, and one of them may be used to block an overly aggressive Congress.

Fisher makes this clear through an amusing anecdote about Grover Cleveland. When members of Congress pressed for war with Spain,

> Cleveland responded bluntly. "There will be no war with Spain over Cuba while I am President." A member of Congress protested that the Constitution gave Congress the right to declare war, but Cleveland countered by saying that the Constitution also made him Commander-in-Chief and "I will not mobilize the army." (p. 42)

This kind of presidential defiance we can tolerate.

---

* See page 403 of this volume.

A Matter of Interpretation: Federal Courts and the Law[*]

ANTONIN SCALIA

Inside Scalia's Mind

July 1, 1997, *Mises Review*

T HIS IS MUCH MORE THAN A BOOK: it is a confrontation. It consists of a lecture on constitutional interpretation delivered at Princeton University by Justice Scalia of the Supreme Court; comments on the lecture by Gordon Wood, Lawrence Tribe, Mary Ann Glendon, and Ronald Dworkin; and replies by Scalia to his critics. The exchange between Scalia, on the one hand, and Dworkin, on the other, exposes to view two sharply contrasting ways of looking at the Constitution.

Justice Scalia's principal contention will surprise few conservatives: the Supreme Court has since World War II interpreted the Constitution to promote the social ends its members think desirable. In doing so, the Court pays scant attention to the meaning of the Constitution's text.

> The ascendant school of constitutional interpretation affirms the existence of what is called The Living Constitution, a body of law that (unlike normal statutes) grows and changes from age to age, in order to meet the needs of a changing society. And it is the judges who determine those needs and "find" that changing law. (p. 38)

---

[*] Princeton University Press, 1997.

The basic objection to this method of interpretation is straightforward. Why should it be up to the Supreme Court (or the entire judicial branch) to delimit the basic goals of American society? Is this not a task for the people themselves? To think otherwise substitutes judicial dictatorship for democratic decision. Neither is it the case, as proponents of the conventional wisdom claim, that the Supreme Court's forays in creative jurisprudence are needed to preserve civil liberties from the depredations of an unchecked legislature.

The "record of history refutes the proposition that the evolving Constitution will invariably enlarge individual rights. The most obvious refutation is the modern Court's limitations of the constitutional protections afforded to property. The provision prohibiting impairment of the obligation of contracts," writes Scalia "has been gutted" (p. 43).

Scalia's case remains largely intact even if one does not share his enthusiasm for democracy. Suppose one believes that fixed moral rules (to pick an example not at random, the self-ownership principle) rigidly limit the competence of democratic legislatures, Scalia's question has all the more pertinence: why should a small body of judges rule over us as it thinks best?

At this point, I fear, many readers will nod, not in agreement, but in sleep. Haven't we heard this all before? What can those with an "Impeach Earl Warren" sticker in their attics learn from this book?

Actually, quite a lot. Scalia, far from being a conventional modern-Supreme-Court hater, introduces several new twists in his analysis of the Court. For one thing, he ascribes freewheeling Constitutional interpretation to a surprising source: the use of common-law methods of reasoning.

Scalia adopts a view of the common law made famous by Oliver Wendell Holmes. The common-law judge, faced with a new case, does not decide according to fixed principles that strictly determine his results. Quite the contrary, he weighs conflicting considerations as his sense of equity dictates. The judge does not apply existing law: he creates new law.

But does not this picture ignore a crucial fact? Judges are bound by precedent; they cannot create new law as they please. Has Scalia even heard of *stare decisis*?

Of course he knows the role of precedent full well, and he has ready a response to this objection. Judges are experts in "distinguishing cases": they know how to use analogies and disanalogies between cases so that only the precedents they want to apply to the issue at hand will do so.

Scalia does not reject common-law reasoning. To the contrary, he regards its methods as providing some of the main intellectual excitement of the law. But it must be kept in its proper place. When a judge interprets a statute, matters are entirely different. Here, the judge is bound by fixed canons of construction. He must endeavor to interpret the law as written, not apply his own standards of appropriateness.

Precisely the problem of modern Constitutional interpretation, Scalia thinks, is that judges use common-law methods, not those of statutory construction, when they address constitutional issues. As he sees it, a common-law court is a miniature Warren Court.

Scalia's view of the common law will strike readers of Friedrich Hayek and Bruno Leoni as surprising. These writers hold that common law is discovered, not made; to them, the common law is a source of stability. But, in an odd way, whether Scalia is right about common law really does not matter, so far as his criticism of the modern Supreme Court is concerned. Whether he has located correctly the source of the aberrant methods of interpretation, his assault on those methods remains effective.

Another of Scalia's contentions will strike conventional conservatives as even more surprising. Usually, opponents of the Court call for a return to original intent. Not the wishes of the modern Court, but rather the intent of the framers of the Constitution, ought to prevail. Conservative analysts of the law, e.g. Raoul Berger and M. E. Bradford, have devoted considerable attention to the questions: exactly whose intentions are relevant to interpretation? Bradford argues powerfully that it is the intentions of those who ratified the Constitution, not the authors of the document, which have primacy of place. To a Bradfordian, the debates at the state conventions that adopted the Constitution are of key importance.

Scalia finds this approach entirely without merit.

> The evidence suggests that [in statutory interpretation] we do not really look for subjective legislative intent. We look for a sort of "objectified" intent the intent that a reasonable person would gather from the text of the law, placed alongside the remainder of the *corpus juris*. . . . It is the *law* that governs, not the intent of the lawgiver. (p. 17)

Readers might again be tempted to doze off. Just what most proponents of original intent mean is that judges should interpret the law as written.

Whether one calls this "intent" is a semantic issue of relevance to legal philosophers, but no one else. Who cares?

This reaction ought to be resisted; Scalia's view has drastic practical implications. Scalia refuses to consider the views of the Constitution's framers, except to the extent they indicate common usage.

> I will consult the writings of some men who happened to be delegates to the Constitutional Convention, Hamilton's and Madison's writings in *The Federalist*, for example. I do so, however, not because they were Framers and therefore their intent is authoritative and must be the law; but rather because their writings, like those of other intelligent and informed people of the time, display how the text of the Constitution was originally understood. (p. 38)

Scalia seems to me to go overboard here. If by "intent" he means what the legislator hoped to accomplish by enacting a law, he is entirely correct that intent does not govern law. If the authors of the Second Amendment guaranteed the right to keep and bear arms in order to promote state militias, it does not follow that people have that right only as far as the need of the militia require. What the amendment enacts is the right in question, not its purpose. But because text and intent are different concepts, it does not follow that they should be viewed in nearly complete independence. Often intent provides indispensable guidance to understanding the text. Those who think otherwise might peruse with profit Raoul Berger on the Fourteenth Amendment.

Ronald Dworkin, a leftist legal philosopher of formidable intellect and even more formidable ego, agrees with Scalia that judges should interpret the Constitution as written. But his agreement does not imply that he has switched sides and become a judicial conservative. Far from it.

Just what the Constitution enacts in many of its provisions, according to Dworkin, are broad abstract principles to be filled in by later generations. His response to those who charge leftists with judicial usurpation is, in effect "what you call usurpations really are not. True, judges interpret the Constitution according to moral principles they hold correct. But this is what the Framers intended them to do." Dworkin thus contends, in Orwellian fashion, that judicial "creativity" is really a variety of originalism. However much it goes against the grain, one must concede that Dworkin's position is not self-contradictory. It is only false.

Lawrence Tribe, like Dworkin, is a leading judicial liberal, but at least he avows more honestly what he is about. Refusing to hide behind the mask of "true originalism," he maintains that the court should treat key parts of the Constitution as "aspirational." They state goals that judges of later eras must spell out explicitly.

Tribe opposes original intent with two arguments, both without merit. First, the Constitution does not explicitly state that it is to be interpreted according to the original meaning of the text; and if it did, an infinite regress would result. Further, the appeal to original meaning fails because of "transtemporality." What the Framers meant may differ greatly from what those who proposed later amendments had in mind. Whose intentions are to prevail?

Tribe thinks himself a legal philosopher; and the first argument is just the sort of pseudo-profundity in which he specializes. To resort to original intent is simple common sense: it does not need to be explicitly stated in the document. And if it were, an infinite regress would ensue only if one persisted in applying irrational ways of reading. "Transtemporality" may pose a problem, or it may not; you have to look at particular cases. Tribe's "argument" establishes no general difficulty for original intent.

So much for our two great liberal legal thinkers, and Scalia disposes of them without difficulty in his response. Mary Ann Glendon maintains that European constitutional courts use more reasonable methods of interpretation than our own Supreme Court, a view Scalia does not dispute. Gordon Wood finds activist judges more entrenched in our history than Scalia imagines. But his historical points largely leave current disputes untouched.

The real battle in this book, then, takes place between Scalia, on the one hand, and Dworkin and Tribe on the other. Though Scalia draws what to my mind is an overly sharp distinction between textual meaning and original intent, he remains always on the right side of reason. I cannot say as much for his opponents.

Antidiscrimination Law and Social Equality*

Andrew Koppelman

Central Planning for Self-Esteem

December 1, 1997, *Mises Review*

ANDREW KOPPELMAN is clearly a writer of considerable intelligence, and exceptionally well-read in political philosophy, ethics, and law. But he puts his talent in the service of a bizarre idea.

As our author sees matters, "many, and perhaps most Americans" endorse two contradictory propositions:

> (1) Part of what defines a free society is that it is none of the government's business what citizens believe and that the shaping of citizens' beliefs is not a legitimate task of a liberal state, (2) Racism, sexism, and similar ideologies are so evil and destructive of the proper workings of society that the state should do whatever it can to eradicate them. (p. 1)

Koppelman proposes to resolve the contradiction by weakening the first proposition. Because everyone has a right to equal concern and respect, preferences of people that violate these rights have no moral standing. Hence in pursuit of the "antidiscrimination project" the state may proceed quite radically to attempt to transform its citizens into Good Little Liberals.

---

* Yale University Press, 1996.

Unfortunately for his project, but fortunately for liberty, Koppelman offers no justification for the alleged right of equal concern and respect on which his whole edifice rests. The closest he comes to an argument is found in his discussion of Ronald Dworkin, but his (and Dworkin's) remarks evince numerous fallacies.

Dworkin begins from a utilitarian view in which policy is determined by people's preferences. But, he (and Koppelman following him) suggests, we cannot take account of external preferences; i.e., preferences people have about the welfare of others. To do so is to fail to count everyone's preferences equally. Suppose someone hates androgynous dwarfs and wishes them ill. If the hater's preference that the dwarf be frustrated is allowed into our calculus, then the dwarf's preferences are diluted.

I entirely fail to see the force of this. In the imagined circumstance, everyone's preference is being counted equally. If the dwarf wants a door three feet high and the hater wants him not to get the door, why is it unequal counting to include both preferences?

Well, you might say, the dwarf has less chance to have his preferences realized, other things being equal, than someone whose preferences are not opposed by others. True enough, but so what? Someone with idiosyncratic preferences has, other things being equal, less chance of having his preferences realized than someone with tastes closer to the standard.

If I am the only member of a large club who wishes to buy a bull to sacrifice to Jupiter, I am unlikely to get what I want, even if no one else in the club wishes my preference frustrated. The others simply wish to spend the club's money on less exotic projects. Am I being treated unequally? It hardly seems plausible.

Further, if external preferences cannot be counted, then preferences that certain people receive what they want must also be cast out. And this blocks Koppelman's project from the start: one cannot count his preference that his favored groups have their preferences realized.

And suppose the Dworkin Koppelman argument is correct. How does a right to equal concern and respect follow? All the argument claims to prove is that certain preferences must not be counted. Nothing has been shown about how each person ought to treat others. (I owe this point to Michael Levin.)

But what if everyone should be treated with equal concern and respect? Koppelman needs a further premise to get his antidiscrimination project going, and he fares even worse here than in his attempt to justify equal concern and respect. Not only does he fail to justify the new premise, he does not even see that his argument requires it.

Imagine that I have a moral obligation to treat politely any book that I review. (Let us hope and pray that I do not lie under this obligation otherwise I am finished.) If I fail to be polite in a review, it does not follow that the book's author has a right of redress against me. Perhaps I have just failed to do what I ought, and that ends the matter. If, *per impossible*, it transpires that I have been grossly unfair to Koppelman, it does not follow that he has the right to reply to me in the *Mises Review*.

Note that I do not claim that he lacks such a right; rather, the claim is that my bad treatment of him does not by itself entail that he does have it. (Just let him try. . . .) The application to Koppelman's argument is obvious. Suppose that the groups about which he is concerned—blacks, women, and homosexuals—have been treated without equal consideration and respect. It does not follow that they are entitled to remedial action. Once more, perhaps all that we are justified in asserting is that those who treat them in this malign way should not do so.

Koppelman takes it as obvious that failure to be treated with equal consideration is an injury that calls for remedy. Put crudely, his view is that we all have the right to a certain level of self-esteem. We must not be stigmatized; otherwise, we might not feel good about ourselves. And, especially if you are a member of at least one of Koppelman's Big Three groups, you may enlist the state to mold your detractors so that they behave more suitably.

The antidiscrimination project appears vulnerable on yet another ground. Even if you accept Koppelman's view of rights, you do not yet have enough to set the state going on its reconditioning program. It must first be shown that the relevant groups have in fact been stigmatized in the morally forbidden way.

Koppelman frequently is quite lax about showing this. Too often, he accepts without question statements by radical propagandists. He takes at face value the following gems from Catharine MacKinnon: "Men's . . . perspectives and concern define quality in scholarship, their experiences and obsessions define merit, their objectification of life defines art . . . their genitals define sex" (pp. 122–123, quoting MacKinnon, *Feminism Unmodified*). What the radical feminist said is not evidence.

Furthermore, he regards blacks as one of the main stigmatized groups in American society. But

> [w]hile it is evident that some blacks do suffer this kind of damage, the most thorough aggregate studies of self-concept among blacks have found that "personal self-esteem among black population [is] either equal to or greater than that among whites." (p. 61; the internal quotation is from a paper by Judith R. Porter and Robert E. Washington)

Koppelman responds that even if blacks have satisfactory self-esteem, they may be made angry and resentful by unequal treatment. This seems to me entirely plausible; but how did we get from a right to self-esteem to a right not to be made angry and resentful? If we are supposed to have only "good," non-angry thoughts, we have entered Never Never Land.

The extreme nature of Koppelman's project emerges most clearly in the chapter "Lesbians and Gay Men." As he himself acknowledges, we are not obligated to treat immoral conduct with equal concern and respect. We should not accord equal respect to Jeffrey Dahmer and his less omnivorous fellow citizens. But many people think homosexual conduct immoral: must their position not be shown false before gays and lesbians are welcomed into Koppelman's project?

Koppelman addresses this concern in exactly two sentences: "This is not the place to refute the various justifications for the stigmatization of homosexuality that are on offer. That has been done elsewhere" (p. 151). Well, so much for that.

By "justification" Koppelman means secular arguments. Religious arguments in his view merit no consideration whatsoever:

> The only arguments for the stigma that seem unanswerable are the religious ones, and by their terms they are not open to philosophical critique. [Why not?] For example, many Americans are Christians or Jews who interpret the Bible as forbidding homosexual conduct, and that settles the issues for them. (p. 151)

Our supposed champion of equal respect feels entitled to dismiss the main religions of the West without a moment's concern.

I fear that the Christians and Jews in question would not fare very well in a state run as Koppelman would like. "Inevitably, state efforts to reduce any kind of discrimination will implicitly tell those whose religious beliefs sanction such discrimination that their religious beliefs are false and that they ought to change them" (p. 152). Koppelman's project is a recipe for totalitarianism a fact he regards as a weighty but not conclusive objection to it.

New Birth of Freedom: Human Rights Named and Unnamed*

CHARLES L. BLACK, JR.

In Praise of Centralism

December 1, 1999, *Mises Review*

A S SOON AS YOU GLANCE at this book's dedication, you know that
you are in for it: "To the sacred memory of Abraham Lincoln." Mr.
Black long held court at the Yale Law School: according to Philip
Bobbitt's fawning introduction, Mr. Black was regarded as "the only certified genius" at that institution (p. xii). Well, our author certainly has a genius
for promoting judicial dictatorship.

Like his hero Lincoln, Mr. Black wishes to destroy the power of the states.
All must be subordinated to our masters in Washington. Oddly, Mr. Black
specialized in the structure of American government: evidently, "study" and
"subversion" are for him synonymous terms. The states, it seems, are the chief
obstacles to liberty:

> Attempts at book-banning, de jure or de facto racial segrega-
> tion, the prohibition of the teaching of evolution ... are things
> mostly undertaken by state and local governments. . . . If the

---

* Yale University Press, [1997] 1999.

national "privileges and immunities" are not good against the
states and their subdivisions . . . then we have set up nothing
but a beeswax simulacrum of a free nation. . . . It was just that
kind of result that the Civil War was in the deepest sense fought
and won to prevent. Such a concept is death to Abraham Lincoln's sacred prophecy, at Gettysburg, that this nation as a nation, might have a "new birth of freedom." (p. 33)

The states, then, are the enemy. It seems not to have occurred to our Certified Genius that the Civil War perhaps restricted civil liberties just a little
more than school boards chary of Darwin. But is there not a slight obstacle
in Mr. Black's path? Does not the very constitution he purports to expound
set up a regime in which the states are, at least for some purposes, sovereign?
What happened to the Tenth Amendment?

Our author is not to be gainsaid: we have a national government, not one
that consists of independent states. The Tenth Amendment, which reserves
all powers not delegated by the Constitution to the states, is not a part
of Mr. Black's Constitution: he never mentions it in the book. Instead, he
deploys some bad arguments designed to undercut state sovereignty. For
one thing, he tells us, "[T]he myth of state sovereignty ought to have been
seen to be obsolete when the first state was admitted to the Union out of
territory already belonging to the nation (Kentucky, I make it, in 1792)"
(pp. 127–128). Here is an argument breathtaking in its inconsequence. The
states constituted out of federal territory are now, by hypothesis, states.
How does anything at all follow about what powers the states have from
the fact that some were once territories? By similar "reasoning," one could
show that since the original thirteen states were once colonies, they are not
sovereign either.

Mr. Black does have a slightly better argument, which he next trots out.

Indeed, from 1788 on, state "sovereignty" was a paradoxical puzzle, for the states were subjected to the supremacy of national
law by the Constitution. . . . They were from the beginning
denied powers pertaining to "sovereignty"—coining money,
making treaties, engaging in war. . . . The core power of "sovereignty"—stating what shall be the "supreme law of the land"—
was denied by Article VI of the Constitution of 1788. It's been
downhill for state "sovereignty" ever since. (p. 128)

What is at issue between defenders of states' rights and their nationalist opponents? Not even the most stalwart advocate of the states, not John C. Calhoun himself, denied that the United States is a nation. The key question rather is exactly what this fact entails.

Has all power been surrendered to the central government? The texts cited by Mr. Black do not suggest an affirmative answer. They cede certain defined powers to the federal authorities: others, according to the Tenth Amendment are retained. It is precisely this division of functions that proponents of states' rights have in mind by their talk of sovereignty.

Perhaps Mr. Black's contention is that sovereignty cannot be divided. If so, he begs the question: why must we accept the European notion of absolute and undivided sovereignty? I should have thought the peculiar genius of the American system was to do away with European absolutism.

Nor is our author's citation of the Supremacy Clause to the point. The contention of the anti-centralists is not that the states are supreme over the Constitution; it is rather that this very document divides sovereignty between the states and the federal government.

Mr. Black, it is clear, does not like the states. But what is it that he wishes the expansive national government he favors to do? He thinks that only the federal government can adequately define, develop, and enforce individual rights: to him, national power is a way to ensure liberty. How is the federal government to accomplish this wonderful mission? Our author relies on three principal provisions of the law to found his regime of rights. In first place stands the Declaration of Independence. It famously says that "all men are endowed with certain unalienable rights, that among these are life, liberty, and the pursuit of happiness."

What more do we need? Do not the words "pursuit of happiness" give the federal government, especially the Supreme Court, the power to interfere with the states, to whatever extent it deems necessary, in order to block censorship and make sure the kiddies learn about Darwin? What could be clearer?

Perhaps you think I exaggerate, in a childish attempt to make Mr. Black's thesis look silly. Quite the contrary, he conjures up a right to a decent standard of living out of "pursuit of happiness": to this brainstorm he devotes an entire chapter (Chapter 5, "The Constitutional Justice of Livelihood").

There is, I am afraid, one small problem with Mr. Black's theory. The Declaration of Independence has no force as a grant of power independent of the

Constitution. The question was explicitly raised by Justice Story, who took the view of the Declaration I have suggested; and constitutional case law has never relied on the Declaration to grant the federal government power.

Justice Story be hanged! Mr. Black never mentions the Justice's view: if the Tenth Amendment can be expunged, the Justice is but a minor matter. As one would by now anticipate, Mr. Black has another story: "It is my own view that the doctrine of the Declaration should be taken to have the force of law—the force of law in general commitments from which particular law can be derived" (p. 8).

If you don't like this, do not despair: Mr. Black's ever fertile mind has something else ready at hand. The Ninth Amendment provides, "The enumeration in the Constitution of certain rights, shall not be construed to deny or disparage others retained by the people" (p. 10).

Can you guess our author's argument? Among the rights retained by the people, he holds, is the right to the pursuit of happiness. This right is to be defined and enforced by the federal government against the states. One begins to suspect that Mr. Black has a bee in his bonnet about a certain phrase in the Declaration.

Mr. Black deserves praise for rejecting the "inkblot" theory of the Ninth Amendment. In this view, advocated by Robert Bork (whom our author does not deign to mention), no one knows what rights the Ninth Amendment was supposed to protect. It is as if an ineradicable inkblot had been spattered over the text; hence judges must in their decisions ignore the Amendment.

Mr. Black goes wrong, as it seems to me, in thinking that the Amendment gives the Federal government power to act against the states. Would this not fly in the face of the Tenth Amendment? No doubt an inkblot in his copy of the Constitution has hidden this amendment from our author's perusal.

Aside from the Tenth Amendment, was not the whole purpose of the Bill of Rights to limit the central government as against the states? Even Mr. Black knows full well that the First Amendment restricts Congress, not the states; but this renowned structuralist cannot read the first ten amendments in their context. Hence, he misses their anti-nationalist point.

There is something more than a little strange in Mr. Black's procedure. For his view of the Declaration and Ninth Amendments as sources for federal power, he supplies no case law. In effect, he says, "I, certified genius of Yale that I am, have discovered provisions in the Constitution that have never been interpreted properly before. By a happy coincidence, these provisions support my leftist predilections." The image of a constitutional lawyer as a magician, extracting hitherto unnoticed rabbits from a well-worn hat, strikes one as bizarre.

Our author, admittedly, is not without further resources. He also appeals to the "privileges and immunities" clause of the Fourteenth Amendment. He cites a dictum of Justice Bushrod Washington (George Washington's nephew) to hold that "privileges and immunities" means—surprise—the rights mentioned in the Declaration.

Once more, our author faces a problem. He wants the phrase "privileges and immunities" to support strong claims for the federal government to act against the states. But, as usual, the law is against him. In the famous Slaughterhouse Cases (1871), the Supreme Court narrowly limited the scope of the contested phrase; and subsequent decisions of the Court have left this precedent intact.

Mr. Black cannot contain himself when he discusses the majority verdict in the Slaughterhouse Cases. If you think that I make unkind remarks in my reviews, you should read what he says: "This is probably the worst holding, in its effect on human rights, ever uttered by the Supreme Court" (p. 55).

Readers must judge for themselves Mr. Black's convoluted account of the privileges and immunities clause. His whole argument depends on the premise that the Fourteenth Amendment aimed to abolish the rights of the states altogether. If you do not think so, but on the contrary believe the powers of the central government should be strictly construed, then you are a Calhounite. And of course Calhoun's views are self-evidently immoral. "Until I placed the quoted words from Calhoun's 1833 Senate speech alongside the result in the Slaughterhouse Cases, I had thought Calhoun to be simply a rather unappealing antiquity. He believed human slavery was a positive good" (p. 81).

Mr. Black reasons thusly: Calhoun supported states' rights. Thus, if you support states' rights, you are a Calhounite. As everyone knows, Calhoun favored slavery. But since you are a Calhounite, you too favor slavery. See what happens if you want to limit federal power! I shall leave this logic for our certified genius from Yale. It is too much for me.

Taking the Constitution Away from the Courts[*]

MARK TUSHNET

Quelling Jurists' Imprudence

April 1, 2000, *Mises Review*

L IKE MOST READERS OF THE *MISES REVIEW*, Professor Tushnet is fed up with the Supreme Court. I doubt, though, that his complaint against the Court will have much resonance with most of my readers.

Mr. Tushnet thinks the Court is insufficiently leftist. The Court has, in recent years, limited affirmative action programs and declined to consider welfare benefits as rights. What is to be done?

Our author responds by throwing into question the supremacy of the Court as an interpreter of our basic law. Why need those who differ with the Court's interpretations accede to them? Indeed, why grant the Court at all the power to declare laws unconstitutional?

It is here that the main value of the book resides. In general, his arguments do not depend on his leftist political views. Those of us who think of the Court as a major tool of the left can take over much of what he says:

> My argument takes as its audience liberal supporters of judicial review, largely because they have been the most prominent defenders of judicial review in recent decades. The conclusion I offer . . . is equally applicable to conservative defenders-or critics-of judicial review. (p. 215)

---

[*] Princeton University Press, 1999.

Suppose that you are an official in California faced with enforcing Proposition 187. This, in part, denied free public education to children of illegal immigrants. "A federal court promptly held this part of Proposition 187 to be unconstitutional and barred state officials from enforcing it" (p. 6). (The federal court applied a Supreme Court precedent.)

Suppose further that you disagree with the court's ruling: you think that Proposition 187 is constitutional. (Mr. Tushnet does not add, as he should, that you are right.) Should you obey the court?

To some, the answer is obvious: the Supreme Court (and lesser courts beneath it) say what the law is, and that is that. *Roma locuta, causa finita est.* But why accept this view? Your oath is to obey the Constitution, not the Supreme Court's interpretation of that document. The Court, admittedly, has since *Cooper v. Aaron* (1957) said that its interpretation is final; but so what?

We cannot say that the Court's pronouncement by itself settles the matter without begging the question. Only if the Court is final does its statement that it is preclude further discussion.

But does not rejection of the Court as final quickly lead to anarchy? A well-ordered society needs to have fixed basic rules. Without them, collapse into chaos impends. Thus, our imagined official should swallow his doubts and conform to the dictates of our judicial masters. Professor Larry Alexander and Frederick Schauer have given the best recent defense of this position, but our author has found a key flaw in their argument.

As he points out in his brilliant critique of them, from the claim that a stable system of basic law is needed, it does not follow that the Supreme Court is the fit agency to provide this.

> Alexander and Schauer appear to argue that the rule of law entails their version of judicial supremacy. . . . But their argument actually supports a rather different conclusion. What they establish is that the rule of law entails that a legal system have a set of institutional arrangements sufficient to ensure the [necessary] degree of stability. (p. 27)

The next question is apparent. What institutional arrangement is best fitted to bring about the needed degree of order? Mr. Tushnet maintains, reasonably enough, that this question admits of no a priori answer. Only an empirical investigation can help us. Our author finds little reason to think that the Supreme Court, rather than Congress, is best suited for the job.

We must, Mr. Tushnet thinks, have a reasonably stable way of arriving at constitutional interpretations. But he next takes a more questionable step. He denies that there is an objectively correct way to understand what the constitution says. He is, I fear, a zealous member of the Critical Legal Studies movement.

According to these legal deconstructionists, laws have no fixed meanings. All enactments are subject to conflicting interpretations, these interpretations to yet further controversies, and so on forever.

Our author's radical conclusion does not give what to my mind is the correct view a run for its money. The Constitution, I should have thought, means what its drafters and ratifiers intended it to mean; and, fortunately, the main constitutional disputes on this theory admit of ready settlement. The original intent that this theory mandates usually can be discovered. Professor Tushnet himself provides an excellent example to make my case. He refers to "something close to a consensus" among legal academies that the Second Amendment "really does create an individual right" to own guns (p. 30). If original intent can be fixed here, why not elsewhere?

Tushnet raises a problem for originalism, but his difficulty is not insurmountable. He rightly claims that true originalists could not accept the court's decision in *Brown v. Board of Education.*

> One difficulty for adherents of original understanding is that the very Congress that submitted the Fourteenth Amendment to the states for ratification also supported segregated schools in the District of Columbia. Another is that the Amendment's opponents routinely said that it would lead to integrated schools, and its supporters routinely replied that it would not. (p. 156)

Our author, sensing victory, hurries to administer the *coup de grâce*. How can originalists accept *Bolling v. Sharpe*, which outlawed segregation in the District of Columbia?

> The only relevant constitutional provision the Court could invoke was the due process clause of the Fifth Amendment, adopted in 1791. And, whatever we can say about Congress in 1868, it is surely impossible to believe that the framers of the Fifth Amendment, many of whom owned slaves, thought that

they were somehow making segregation by the national government impossible. (p. 157)

But what, other than political correctness, is the problem? Why should
the originalist want to accept these two decisions? To reject them hardly
commits one to approval of racial segregation. Tushnet himself notes elsewhere, with apparent agreement, the view that the effects of the Court's
decision in Brown should not be overestimated.

To return to our author's successes, he has, I think, successfully shown
that we do not need an authoritative Supreme Court to obtain stability. But
what role, if any, should the Court have in constitutional interpretation? Mr.
Tushnet's answer is surprising, given one of his contentions.

He maintains that, in the long run, the Court's decisions make little difference; as one might expect, he trots out Mr. Dooley's "The Supreme Court follows the election returns" (p. 134). One would have thought he would argue
that it does not matter what role in interpretation the Court is assigned.

He sees matters otherwise. Even if the Court does not in practice have
much effect, nevertheless eliminating judicial review holds much promise.
It will promote a "populist jurisprudence" in which the people interpret the
constitution for themselves.

Mr. Tushnet's populism strikes me as more than a little odd. He cleaves
the Constitution in two. The "thin constitution" carries out the ideals of the
Declaration of Independence; the First Amendment is a paradigm instance
of what this part of the document includes. The "thick constitution" includes
procedural matters, e.g., the rule that senators serve six-year terms. Only the
thin constitution binds us, on the strange ground that people would probably
not risk their lives for the details of the thick constitution. Probably not; but
why does this fact cancel the legal force of these provisions? Also, why does
Tushnet think that the equality clause of the Declaration of Independence, in
Jefferson's interpretation, refers "only to men and owned slaves" (p. 11)?

This book contains many useful and provocative ideas, but I suppose that
in a work written by a Marxist and Critical Legal Studies partisan, one must
expect at least some wackiness.

Legalize This! The Case For Decriminalizing Drugs[*]

Douglas N. Husak

Ruins of the Drug War

December 1, 2002, *Mises Review*

DOUGLAS HUSAK, a distinguished legal philosopher, presents in excellent fashion a key point about drug prohibition.[†] He claims not to be a libertarian; he speaks disparagingly of the libertarian position "that each of us has the right to put anything we like into our bodies" (p. 22). I do not think that Husak has rightly characterized the libertarian view; what libertarian would hold that we have the right to use a drug "that turns us into homicidal maniacs" just "because these effects occur as a result of putting it into our bodies" (p. 22)?

In fact, the libertarian view is identical to the position that Husak defends. Why, he asks, should people be punished for using drugs? To punish someone is to impose a severe disability on him; and justice requires that punishment be imposed only on someone who violates rights. The mere fact, if it is one, that drug use leads to bad social consequences does not suffice.

Husak illustrates his argument with a telling example:

> Does anyone believe that individuals should be punished for something simply because the failure to do so would cause an

---

[*] Verso Books, 2002.

[†] By "drugs" in the following I mean substances such as cocaine and heroin.

> increase in the behavior for which they are punished? This rationale fails to provide the personal justification for punishment that is needed. This is not our reason to criminalize acts like murder and rape. No one would say that we should punish such acts simply because the failure to do so might lead others to commit rape and murder. (p. 175)

To punish people simply because their acts encourage others to act in a way deemed undesirable is to use people as means, in a morally unacceptable way. If the state can imprison someone because his drug use sets a bad example to children, or helps to maintain a market in drugs associated with violent crime, is it not failing to treat the drug user as an end in himself? (Of course, much of the violent crime in the drug market stems from the fact that drug sales are illegal; but Husak is concerned in his argument only about punishment for drug use.)

"Away with such Kantian nonsense," a supporter of the consequentialist position may reply. "What we need are hard facts. If it turns out that the benefits of drug prohibition exceed its costs, we have exactly the justification needed to make the use of drugs criminal. Speculative and unprovable moral theories should not bar our way."

Husak replies to this objection in what I regard as the most brilliant passage of his book. In it, he makes an important contribution to moral theory that in scope goes far beyond the drug issue. Husak points out that our imagined objector cannot escape moral theory of the sort he dismisses as speculative. "Critics of prohibition denigrate principles of justice at their peril, for a harm-reduction approach is no less dependent on moral evaluation than the alternative they reject" (p. 177).

Our author makes good his claim with a neglected but obvious truth. How are we supposed to balance good and bad consequences, without using moral theory? "We could not hope to balance incommensurables unless we were willing to judge that some outcomes were more valuable than others. These judgments of value are moral judgments" (p. 177).

The drug prohibitionist may elect at this point to bite the bullet. He may contend that drug use not only has bad effects but also is in itself wrong, in a way that justifies punishment. But why should we accept this? The use of alcohol has similar effects to those found in drug use, yet no one proposes making the mere act of drinking a crime.

Husak has backed the drug prohibitionist into a corner. The supporter of prohibition must locate an important difference between alcohol (or tobacco) and drugs the use of which he wishes to ban. Husak has little difficulty in showing that a recent attempt by the distinguished criminologist James Q. Wilson to do this fails completely. Wilson claims that use of cocaine "alters the soul," but smoking does not. Unfortunately, Wilson fails to explain his contention in a way that can be rationally assessed. Unless he or some other prohibitionist can do so, the case for banning the use of drugs lies in ruins.

Restoring the Lost Constitution: The Presumption of Liberty*

RANDY E. BARNETT

Liberty and Obedience

October 1, 2004, *Mises Review*

THE DEDICATION OF *Restoring the Lost Constitution*, "To James Madison and Lysander Spooner," at once alerts us that we confront an unusual book. During the Constitutional Convention, Madison supported a strong national government; Spooner, by contrast, subjected to withering criticism the notion that the people of the United States had consented to the Constitution. Whom does Barnett support? The Father of the Constitution or the author of *The Constitution of No Authority*?

Barnett soon makes clear his response. He finds convincing Spooner's assault on consent theories of political obligation. But this does not lead him to question the need for a state. Quite the contrary, he aims to extricate government from Spooner's challenge: since consent does not underlie our obligation to obey the state, Barnett must locate something better that will do the job.

More specifically, why does the government established by the Constitution bind those subject to its jurisdiction? After usefully pointing out that, for the most part, the Constitution "purports to bind government officials, not private individuals," Barnett poses his fundamental question:

> The real question, then, is not whether the Constitution is binding on citizens, but whether citizens are bound by the commands

---

* Princeton University Press, 2004.

or laws issued by officials acting in its name. Does the fact that a "law" is validly enacted according to the Constitution mean that it binds one in conscience? In other words, is one morally obligated to obey any law that is enacted according to constitutional procedures? (p. 12)

Barnett does not leave his readers long in suspense: his answer is that, under the right conditions, people are indeed obligated to obey the law. So long as the government enacts laws that are "both necessary to protect the rights of others and proper insofar as they do not violate the rights of the persons whose freedom they restrict," people under the government's jurisdiction have a duty of obedience (p. 45). Barnett understands rights in a way libertarians will find congenial. Rights are negative: they forbid others from interfering with our life, liberty, and property. Barnett resolutely rejects positive rights, such as an alleged right to welfare. He holds that the Constitution, if interpreted according to its original public meaning, established a government based on adherence to rights in the proper sense. Hence, so long as the government follows the Constitution, it should be obeyed.

In like fashion, I shall not leave my readers in suspense. Although the book contains much of value, Barnett's entire project seems to me fundamentally misconceived. Suppose the government establishes a legal system, including courts and police, in order to deter violations of rights and to respond to rights violations when these occur. Let us assume further that the rights protected meet the libertarian standards that Barnett wants. Why are people under any moral duty to cooperate with such a legal system? If, e.g., the government prescribes that people pay taxes so that the system can operate, must they obey? Must they refrain from establishing competing legal systems that endeavor to compete with the government?

Individuals in their private capacities, it seems clear, stand under no parallel restraints. If someone opens a pizza parlor, in a way that violates no one's rights, you are under no duty to cooperate with him by, say, patronizing his restaurant rather than a competitor's. You are free to try to drive him out of business, if you can do so in a way that respects his rights.

Why are matters any different for the government? If, as Frédéric Bastiat argued in his great pamphlet *The Law*, the state acquires no rights that individuals do not themselves possess, where does the duty to obey the law enter the scene? How can there be a duty to obey the state if there is no duty to obey the owner of the corner grocery store? True enough, if the government is in legitimate pursuit of a criminal, we should not interfere; but why describe this obligation as a duty to obey?

Barnett might respond that I have ignored a key aspect of his proposal. Laws, to generate an obligation to obey, must not violate anyone's rights. If so, is it not open to Barnett to say that I have raised a false alarm? Why suppose that he would allow taxes as legitimate or require obedience to laws that establish a government as a monopoly agency?

But if he takes this line, he has not established the legitimacy of a government at all. It is in any case hardly likely that Barnett will take our proffered escape. The sum and substance of his book is an attempt to justify the government established by the Constitution, and this document grants the government the power to tax, among many other powers not legitimate if exercised by private individuals.

Barnett's proposal seems vulnerable on another count. He wishes to establish a duty to obey the law, but he never shows why it is desirable that people have such an obligation. (I do not think he would say that it's too bad we have the obligation, but we are stuck with it.) He seems to have "bought into" this task, a longstanding project pursued by such eminent legal philosophers as H. L. A. Hart and Lon Fuller, his own revered teacher, without question. Given the manifold invidious activities of contemporary governments, our own not least among them, finding grounds for obedience to government does not strike one as an imperative necessity. And if Barnett reiterates in reply that he has in mind only a duty to obey legitimate government, he still needs to show what, other than fashion in law schools, makes this a good thing.

Barnett is much more successful when he follows in Spooner's spirit. He raises a penetrating objection to tacit consent theories of political obligation. To those who allege that residents of a country consent to its laws by failing to leave, a response lies ready to hand, as Hume long ago pointed out. In many cases, it would be very difficult, if not impossible, for people to depart, especially if they wish to go to a place where they can avoid political obligations. How then can such constrained "consent" be held to generate an obligation to obey?

Barnett raises a deeper objection.

> For remaining in this country tacitly indicates consent only if you
> assume that the lawmakers have the initial authority to demand

> your obedience or your exit in the first place. But it is their au-
> thority that is supposed to be justified on the basis of your and
> my tacit consent. So the problem with inferring consent from
> a refusal to leave the country is that it presupposes that those
> who demand you leave already have authority over you. (p. 18)

I fear that I have given a lopsided picture of *Restoring the Lost Constitution*. I have so far devoted my entire attention to Barnett's generally wrongheaded remarks on political obligation. He devotes the bulk of the book, however, to a detailed analysis of the Constitution, in order to show that it can be
interpreted to mandate the limited government he thinks justifiable. Here he
includes much of value, including detailed accounts of the meaning of "necessary" powers and the scope of the power to regulate interstate commerce.

His discussion of judicial review makes a valuable distinction. Judicial nul-
lification, the power of the courts to declare a law unconstitutional, does not
imply that a court, even the Supreme Court, can order the other branches of
government to conform to its view of the law. "Just as the power to negate legislation does not imply the power to enact it, neither does it imply a power to
mandate that the executive branch exercise its powers in a particular mode" (p.
144). The modern view that the Supreme Court is the final authority, to which
every knee must bow, on all questions constitutional is alien to the Constitution's original intent. Barnett's case is well made, though I wish he had devoted
attention to the arguments against judicial review in that neglected classic, L.
Brent Bozell's *The Warren Revolution* (New York, 1966).

Barnett's defense of original intent and negative rights deserves much
praise, but in one area I think his discussion goes badly astray. Barnett is concerned not only to defend the original meaning of the Constitution against
those who conjure up all manner of positive rights, allegedly found in that
document's "penumbras" and "emanations." He also defends an expansive
view of the Fourteenth Amendment.

As he sees matters, the Amendment overturns the former sovereignty of
the states and subjects them to strict federal authority, should they interfere
with the "privileges or immunities" of their citizens.

> Owing to the Fourteenth Amendment . . . state governments no
> longer can claim a plenary power to restrict the liberties of the
> people subject only to their constitutions and any express restric-
> tions in the original Constitution. Rather, any state abridgment

of the privileges or immunities should be subject to challenge in federal court. (p. 321)

At first sight, this seems perfectly in order. Surely it is wrong for the states to interfere with rights, so long as these are construed in a libertarian way; and if the federal courts confine themselves to enforcing such rights, who can reasonably object?

But to argue in this way is to neglect the federal structure of government, present both in the Constitution and the Articles of Confederation. Fundamental to both the proponents of the Constitution and their Anti-Federalist opponents was a deep-seated distrust of centralized government. The national government was no more than an alliance of states, its powers confined to strictly delimited purposes. True enough, the states were free, so far as the Constitution was concerned, to violate civil liberties: the Bill of Rights limited only the national government. But a loose association of states would better protect rights than a strong central government, however libertarian it might profess to be.

Such, at any rate, is the theory of the Constitution; and the gross violations of rights that have taken place ever since Lincoln's dictatorial regime show that compelling the states to submit to a federal Leviathan is not the path to liberty.*

Barnett is blind to the virtues of federalism. He displays little sense of the importance of the Tenth Amendment in preserving liberty; instead, the "public meaning" of the Fourteenth Amendment, ratified under questionable circumstances, is treated as if it were on a par with the original intent of the Constitution's Framers. Further, even on its own terms Barnett's discussion of the Amendment is incomplete. He takes a very broad view of the aims of the Amendment, and the new powers accordingly conferred on the central government. He takes no account of critics of this interpretation, who claim that the authors of the Amendment had much more limited ends in view. Raoul Berger and M. E. Bradford might never have written on the Amendment, so far as our author is concerned.

---

* Donald Livingston has brilliantly defended the virtues of the loose confederation position, showing its basis in the thought of David Hume, in his *Philosophical Melancholy and Delirium*. Barnett's naïve reliance on the federal government to defend rights parallels the views of Clint Bolick. See his *The Affirmative Action Fraud*.

Law, Pragmatism, and Democracy[*]

Richard A. Posner

Posner (Again) Blesses Statism

April 1, 2005, *Mises Review*

RICHARD POSNER HERE ANSWERS, at least in one respect, a question that has long puzzled his critics. Posner again and again declares himself a legal pragmatist. Judges should not be bound by "formalistic" demands that they decide cases as strict deductions from laws or precedents. Quite the contrary, judges should not feel themselves irretrievably bound by a set of rules of interpretation. The question that should always guide them is, what will have the best results? "Legal pragmatism is forward-looking. Formalism is backward-looking, grounding the legitimacy of a judicial decision on its being deducible from an antecedently established rule or principle" (p. 71).

An obvious question arises: what counts as "best" in this context? Here Posner's critics find themselves baffled. Posner never manages to set out clearly the criteria for judges to use in deciding cases. Not, of course, that Posner says nothing on the topic. As always, it is impossible for Posner to shut up. But it seems a labor of Hercules to pin him down on this issue. In the present volume he fills in a few of the blanks.

Posner, a founder and principal exponent of the law-and-economics movement, has often favored wealth maximization as a decision rule for judges. He

---

[*] Harvard University Press, 2003.

makes clear, though, that he does not swear full allegiance to this rule. Indeed, he tells us that he is not a consequentialist at all.

> If a consequentialist is someone who believes that an act, such as a judicial decision, should be judged by whether it produces the best overall consequences, pragmatic adjudication is not consequentialist, at least not consistently so. That is why I prefer "reasonableness" to "best consequences" as the standard for evaluating judicial decisions pragmatically. (p. 65)

Our author explains what he has in mind by means of a bizarre example. Suppose a brother and sister wish to get married. They ask for an exception to a law banning incest because they are sterile. Clearly, Posner maintains, appeal to consequences would justify granting their request.

> It is difficult to see what good consequences the denial of such an exception . . . could have; the bad consequence would be forbidding a harmless relationship that might be indispensable to the happiness of the participants. (pp. 65–66)

But the "pragmatic judge" should be reluctant to intervene. "Horror at incest is a brute fact about present-day American society" (p. 66). Given this unfortunate circumstance, "public upset" would outweigh the benefits to the couple. Judges must not defy popular feelings, however benighted they might be, to an overly great extent.

The example, by the way, tells us a good deal about our distinguished author. The fact that incest is intrinsically immoral seems never to have entered his head. Readers of Posner's *Sex and Reason* (1992) will recall his labored attempts to show that rape should be prohibited on consequentialist grounds. The imperative demands of morality mean nothing to our master pragmatist: Kant, it seems safe to say, would not have liked Posner.

To return to Posner's hero, the pragmatic judge, is he not after all a consequentialist? Surely a consequentialist would take into account public opinion, exactly as the pragmatist would. Posner himself recognizes the point: "A complication is that almost every nonconsequentialist consideration can be recharacterized in consequentialist terms" (p. 67).

But Posner thinks that despite this point, it is not "useful" to call the pragmatist a consequentialist. Sometimes, the pragmatist will decide cases by strict interpretation of the law. If people can rely on fixed standards to guide their behavior, is this not also socially beneficial?

I shall, without reluctance, leave it to Posner to fight a battle with those who say that this too is a consequentialist consideration. A more substantive problem awaits us. Posner tells us that the pragmatist judge must be reasonable; but he refuses to specify what considerations the judge should bear in mind. We may grant his point that the reasonable judge cannot be bound by an algorithm; we might, if so minded, allow his point that he cannot offer a comprehensive list of the judge's goals. But surely he owes us something? To appeal to pragmatism avails nothing, absent an account of what one is trying to achieve.*

We are, fortunately, not left entirely in the dark. Posner makes clear one goal he very much wants to achieve. In his view, so minor a matter as civil liberties must not be allowed to impede America's crusade against terrorism. Has not September 11 changed everything?

> Suppose there were a 100-percent probability that unless prevented, a terrorist known to be loose in Manhattan would explode a nuclear bomb. No sane person would balk at abandonment of the conventional limitations on the power to search and seize and the power to extract information from suspects and even bystanders. Would he refuse to countenance an exception for a lesser threat to public safety? If the probability were 99 percent rather than 100 percent, could he sanely adhere to that position? Eventually, a rule and exception approach would dissolve into balancing, and disagreement would shrink to differing assessments of the risks and harms. (pp. 315–316)

Posner's reasoning rests on a familiar fallacy. Let us grant him that in imaginable circumstances, there are laws to which a judge might with propriety allow exceptions. It hardly follows that all cases must be decided by balancing. Suppose you think that if a policeman sees through a window a man about to detonate an atomic bomb, he may enter the man's residence without a warrant. You are not by that view forbidden to hold that torture is always wrong, without consideration of consequences. Like many conse-

---

* I have benefited greatly here from Ilya Somin, "Posner's Pragmatism," *Critical Review*, vol. 16, no. 1 (2004), pp. 1–22.

quentialists, Posner takes any recognition of emergency situations as total surrender to consequentialism.

Also on evidence in Posner's view of civil liberties is another dubious procedure. He invokes probability considerations: why, he asks, must we demand certainty before proceeding against a terrorist threat? If the danger is sufficiently great, does not even a small chance that dire consequences might impend justify drastic action? (Posner has devoted another of his innumerable books, *Catastrophe: Risk and Response*, to the importance of taking account of small chances of danger.)

Posner has moved too quickly. He does not take seriously the prospect that emergency restrictions on civil liberties will subvert our constitutional order. In his view, we have little to fear from our benign government. Once the emergency has passed, civil liberties will be restored to full standing. May we not here rely on past experience: "When the emergencies ended, civil liberties were restored, and later they were enlarged" (p. 304).

His contention seems to me disputable, but suppose that he is right. Has he not forgotten his own point about probability? Even a small chance that emergency measures will permanently subvert civil liberties needs to be considered. Must not this probability, even if one accepts Posner's view that it is small, be weighed in the "balancing" that Posner so anxiously urges on us?

Our author, avidly insistent on the need to counter threats to security, turns a blind eye to such matters. But let us put the difficulties so far raised to one side. Posner's view still must confront a severe problem. Posner says that judges must balance considerations of national security against the benefit of civil liberties; but how are the judges supposed to evaluate the dangers to security?

For this problem our author has a simple solution. Judges should accept the government's word about the severity of threats to security and what needs to be done to combat them. A mere judge, after all, is in no position to overthrow the expert knowledge that government specialists, under the supervision of the Leader, possess.

> But if lawyers are not equipped to formulate sound legal policy regarding international terrorism, who is? The President is, virtually by default. The relevant expertise is widely distributed. . . . The President has unimpeded access to this expertise. . . . In times of crises, moreover, it is natural to look to elected officials rather

than to judges to choose the response. This is the democratic approach as well as the practical one. (pp. 316–317)

So much for "balancing"; Posner's ideal judge, like his colleagues in Nazi Germany and Soviet Russia, accepts the superior wisdom of the government and its Leader. One wonders whether Posner has taken so extreme a position as a means to signal to the Bush administration that he will prove a reliable tool if nominated to the Supreme Court.

This, admittedly, is speculation. Posner is at any rate consistent in his contempt for civil liberties, as he reviews various historical episodes. Lincoln acted wisely, he thinks, in his Draconian suppression of individual rights during the Civil War. True enough, the Constitution probably does not allow the president to suspend the writ of *habeas corpus*; but who cares?

> The unconstitutional acts that Lincoln committed during the Civil War suggest that even legality must sometimes be traded off against other values. . . . Is it not vital to morale in wartime that a nation's leaders show themselves resolute, and is not brushing aside legal niceties that might [!] interfere with the determined prosecution of the war one way of showing this? (p. 301)

Though Justice Robert Jackson, "one of the greatest pragmatic Justices," is one of Posner's heroes, our author finds wanting Jackson's dissent in *Korematsu v. United States*, the case that upheld the exclusion of Japanese Americans from the west coast during World War II. Must not a good pragmatic judge defer to the military authorities in wartime?

> If the Constitution is not to be treated as a suicide pact, [a famous remark by Jackson in another case] why should military exigencies not influence the scope of the constitutional rights that the Supreme Court has manufactured from the Constitution's vague provisions? (p. 294)

I have done my best for Posner. Against the charge that his pragmatist view tells the judge nothing, I have endeavored to find a subject, national security, in which his own application of his view does yield some determinate meaning. But on the whole my quest has been fruitless. The Constitution, as Posner sees it, is a *tabula rasa* on which the pragmatist can write as he pleases.

458 ⊗ AN AUSTRO-LIBERTARIAN VIEW, VOL. 1: LAW

Does the Constitution forbid states from passing laws that impair the obligations of contract? A provision of the document says exactly this, but Posner says about the Supreme Court's decision in a famous case that upheld debtor relief:

> this is a fancy way of saying that a state *can* impair the obligation of contracts, notwithstanding the constitutional provision . . . provided it has a compelling reason to do so. The decision may have been wrong, but I would not call it usurpative. Most constitutional provisions have—or, more precisely, can be given, by judges exercising the elastic power of interpretation—enough wiggle room to accommodate an emergency. (p. 295)

For Posner, a "great decision" rises above legal argument. Speaking of a decision of John Marshall, our author has this to say:

> Pure assertion, but an assertion that in the manner of great rhetoric carried its own weight of authority, if not of "truth." The test of a great legal opinion is not its conformity to the tenets of legal formalism. It is how good a fit it makes with its social context. Often that fit is cemented by a rhetorical flourish. (p. 93)

Legal ethics must also not be allowed to interfere with the pragmatic judge, especially if he aspires to greatness. Marshall's opinion in *Marbury v. Madison* involved a conflict of interest, since it was Marshall himself who had signed the commission that had not been delivered to Marbury. "But *Marbury* is a great decision, and Marshall the greatest Chief Justice in our history" (p. 355). It passes a key test of greatness: it created new values out of nothing. "*Marbury* asserted rather than deduced the supremacy of the Supreme Court in the interpretation of the Constitution" (p. 262).

Our author, not to be denied, goes Marshall one better. Why not add provisions to the Constitution in defiance of the prescribed procedures for amendment? The Fourteenth Amendment was imposed by military force. The Radical Republican Congress dissolved the governments of Southern states that rejected the amendment. To be recognized as legitimate, a successor government had first to ratify it. This procedure clearly defies the Constitution: if a legislature does not count as a state government until after its supposed act of ratification, that act cannot count as ratification by a state. For Posner, there is no problem: "And the post-Civil War amendments to the Constitution . . . would not have been ratified had it not been for the subjugation of the Confederate states by force of arms" (p. 262).

Posner's pragmatic jurisprudence is a sorry affair, bereft of intellectual substance. Why, then, is Posner celebrated as the brightest and most scholarly of federal judges? He is able to absorb with great rapidity large quantities of information on various subjects and to deploy this material, often very effectively, in his numerous books. Readers of *Law, Pragmatism, and Democracy* will encounter discussions of the legal theories of Hans Kelsen and Friedrich Hayek, John Dewey's pragmatism, and Joseph Schumpeter's elitist theory of democracy, which Posner much prefers to the deliberative democracy in fashion nowadays.*

Faced with such abundance, even the skeptical reader seems compelled to admire Posner. Must not even opponents of pragmatism recognize his remarkable merits, just as even the staunchest Austrian economist must acknowledge that Lord Keynes possessed a scintillating intelligence?

Those who probe further, I suggest, will have reason to put aside their initial impressions. Posner's erudition is at times a contrived affair. What is one to think when Posner tells us that until preparing for a lecture in 2001, "I had never read Kelsen" (p. 250)? This is the equivalent of a specialist in Austrian economics saying, at the height of his career, that he never until recently opened *Human Action*.

In one area, in particular, Posner's pretensions fall to the ground. Posner often disparages academic philosophy; indeed, he has devoted an entire volume, *The Problematics of Moral and Legal Theory*, to his antiphilosophical enterprise. But it transpires that he has little grasp of what he presumes to condemn. Posner's account of Quine on the analytic, though "in the ballpark," misses the main point of Quine's key argument. His misrepresentation of Nelson Goodman is much more serious. Goodman did not, contrary to what Posner alleges, challenge induction; his "new riddle of induction" is not at all like Popper's inductive skepticism (p. 37). When discussing the alleged "obsession of the philosophical tradition with the conditions that make it possible (or impossible . . .) to affirm the certainty of 'obvious' propositions," he gives an example of such a proposition, a controversial opinion: "the Nuremberg Tribunal was legal" (p. 36). He recognizes elsewhere (pp. 370–371) that

---

* Naturally, Posner prefers Kelsen to Hayek. The latter's appeal to custom hardly comports well with the unlimited discretion that the pragmatist judge requires.

the tribunal was not impartial; one would have thought this a requirement of legality. I have saved the best for last. He solemnly tells us that we "now think Euclidean geometry, Ptolemaic astronomy, and Newtonian physics are all erroneous theories" (p. 39). I have at times in my remarks been unkind to Posner, but I have a suggestion for him that will win him intellectual acclaim far in excess of what he has already achieved. He has only to point out some of the alleged errors of Euclidean geometry to be recognized a great mathematician. What can have been on his mind when he wrote the sentence I have just quoted? Non-Euclidean geometry? Hilbert's standards of rigorous proof? We await further enlightenment from Judge Posner.

The Legalization of Drugs [*]

DOUGLAS HUSAK and PETER DE MARNEFFE

The Follies of the Drug War

December 1, 2005, *Mises Review*

T HIS BOOK IS PART of the valuable series For and Against, in which two philosophers debate public policy issues. Husak argues that the possession and use of so-called dangerous drugs such as heroin and cocaine should not be criminal offenses. He is also sympathetic to making legal the production and sale of these drugs, but he devotes his main attention to the former topic. By contrast, for de Marneffe the issue of legalization is primary. He maintains that production and sale of certain drugs—he concentrates on heroin—should not be legal. He does not here defend "the criminalization of heroin use, but only the criminalization of the manufacture and sale of heroin and for the possession of quantities above a certain size, a gram, say" (p. 129). I shall concentrate on de Marneffe's contribution: Husak's excellent essay summarizes and extends his *Legalize This! The Case for Decriminializing Drugs* (Verso Books, 2002), which I have addressed on another occasion.[†]

De Marneffe's argument against legalizing heroin and similar drugs depends on a plausible assumption. If drugs were legal, their prices would fall, since the heavy costs of the black market would no longer have to be borne. If so, we can expect that consumption and abuse of these drugs would rise.

---

[*] Cambridge University Press, 2005.

[†] See my review found in Volume 1, "Law."

It is a particular sort of abuse that concerns him and underlies his case for prohibition. Heroin "offers a unique and very intense form of pleasure" (p. 112). This fact generates a social problem because taking the drug "has the effect on some people of sharply depressing their motivation to achieve worthwhile goals and to meet their responsibilities and commitments to others, to go to school or go to work, for example, or to take care of their children" (p. 112).

De Marneffe has in mind especially teenagers and young adults: given the intense and immediate gratification that heroin offers they may find themselves unable to summon the willpower required to concentrate on their studies and prepare for their future lives. They may as a result "lose" a decade or more of their lives and as a result find themselves irretrievably at a disadvantage in obtaining satisfactory jobs. By no means does de Marneffe contend that all, or even most, young adults who take heroin will fall into this pattern. But a significant number will do so: and this suffices to justify prohibition of the drug.

One might at first think that de Marneffe's argument is easily turned aside. Is he not saying that the harm that taking the drug causes outweighs the pleasure that consumers of the drug obtain from it, together with the harms to those penalized for drug offenses? Regardless of whether he is right about this, one might think, is he not implicitly assuming the truth of utilitarianism? Since, in his view, the harm to the young adults counts for more than the pleasure of the users and the harm to the penalized, we maximize utility by prohibiting the drug.

But if this is de Marneffe's argument, is he not at once vulnerable to the well-known difficulties of that moral view? Utilitarianism, as Rawls famously remarked, does not take seriously the separation of persons. Well-known cases throw into question the goal of maximizing total utility. A utilitarian might have to support, e.g., killing an innocent man if this would assuage an unruly mob. De Marneffe seems caught in the same false calculus; some—the users who do not abuse the drug and drug sellers caught in the law's net—must be sacrificed so that others—the young adults at risk—can benefit.

De Marneffe responds by denying that his argument rests on utilitarianism. He knows full well the moral importance of individuals but claims that his position gives this adequate recognition. In claiming that harm of one sort outweighs benefits and harms of another, his argument does not claim that

> happiness will be maximized in the aggregate by heroin pro-
> hibition. It is an individualistic argument that claims that the

worst risk to some individual under heroin legalization is worse than the risk to some individual under prohibition, provided that the penalty structure is gradual and proportionate. (p. 125)

De Marneffe's view fails for the same reason that dooms utilitarianism. He permits some people to be harmed in order to benefit others. Those who wish to buy or sell the forbidden drugs are forbidden to do so, because de Marneffe judges that the harm to them is less severe than the harm that some drug users would suffer in a legal drug market. Though he successfully distinguishes his view from utilitarianism, he has not answered the objection at all. Libertarians think that in order to avoid unacceptably using one person for the benefit of another, coercion against those who do not themselves initiate coercion must be totally ruled out. De Marneffe obviously disagrees with this conception of individual rights, but he offers no discussion of what is wrong with it. Rothbard and Nozick might never have written a line.

De Marneffe offers no theoretical defense of his harm principle. Why does he think that state intervention is justifiable whenever this minimizes the harm to some one? He does not tell us but apparently thinks that we will find his principle intuitively evident once we learn of it. Further, he offers no basis for weighting harms: this too is a matter of case-by-case intuitions. To be fair to him, though, Husak does not offer a theoretical framework for his views either: he simply weights harms and benefits differently from de Marneffe.

Some readers may think that de Marneffe's view can be swiftly set aside. He wants us to weigh the harms to people under legalization and prohibition; but do we not know from Austrian economics that interpersonal comparisons of utility are impossible? De Marneffe has thus set a task that that cannot be fulfilled. But I do not think that this tempting refutation works. De Marneffe's judgments of harms are not value-free utility comparisons: they reflect his own opinions about what is morally worse. Austrian economics does not rule them out.

Even if we take de Marneffe's intuitionist moral methodology as it stands, though, his case for prohibition is weak. What exactly is the harm he wishes to guard against? It is not, as one might suspect, that young people will be so entrapped by the use of heroin that they cannot stop using it, or can do so only with great difficulty. Neither is the harm in question that the user's personality will suffer destruction. Quite the contrary, after a very useful discussion of various meanings of addiction, he rejects these notions:

> Some may believe ... [that] once a person uses heroin, whatever
> his age, he is "hooked" because he cannot stop using it without
> agony, and because habitual heroin use turns a person into a zom-
> bie with no capacity for genuine self-direction ... a large propor-
> tion of those who use the drug do not develop a habit ... those
> who develop a habit may nonetheless stop without great suffering
> (the discomfort involved in kicking a habit is commonly likened
> to having the flu for a few days).... Although habitual heroin use
> can be bad for a person in depressing his motivation, it does not
> turn a person into a zombie whose capacities for rational self-di-
> rection are no longer functioning at all. (p. 153)

Once more, the harm he has in mind is only that some young adults may
make poor choices for their future lives, because legalization is apt to make
heroin more readily available. They can later repent their folly but they have
wasted time; "heavy drug use during this crucial stage of a person's development will close opportunities that it will be difficult to reopen later on" (p.
117).

And it is not even all of this group that inclines our author to favor
prohibition.

> If every child were rich or highly talented, the consequences of
> increased heroin abuse among adolescents might not be so bad.
> Teenage drug abuse might set some people back a bit, but, if
> they are rich, they will always have the opportunity to reapply
> themselves to their education, and, if they are gifted, they will
> always have talents for which there is a high demand. (p. 117)

Those not in either of these favored categories may have to exert "extraordinary effort" in order to catch up. It is this inequality, then, that at bottom
drives de Marneffe's quest: everyone's liberty must be restricted because
otherwise a number of poor, untalented drug users might not have the
same chances as more fortunate users. Further, de Marneffe acknowledges
that even if drugs are prohibited, the poor and untalented who obtain
these drugs illegally may suffer the untoward consequences he fears. It is
only that he thinks there will be more of these unfortunates under a system of liberty: it is for this that everyone's freedom is to be sacrificed. This
is egalitarianism with a vengeance.

How bad is the harm that de Marneffe seeks to avert? Husak points out that little evidence supports the claim that drugs like heroin adversely affect substantial numbers of adolescents:

> How bad are drugs for underage users? . . . Longitudinal studies provide the best possible evidence about the effects of drugs on adolescents . . . these effects vary enormously. The life of most adults was relatively unaffected; that of a small number was devastated. . . . If illicit drug use were really so bad for adolescents, one would expect that those who used them would turn out to be significantly worse as adults than comparably aged individuals who abstained. But the studies do not confirm this expectation. . . . By the time they become young adults, most of these subjects have stopped using illegal drugs. (pp. 61–62, emphasis removed)

De Marneffe would probably respond that according to his principle, the harms suffered by only a few suffice to justify prohibition. I venture to suggest that our considered moral judgments, the standard by which de Marneffe operates, do not support universal prohibition to protect a small group. I exclude the views of libertarians here; I do not think that most non-libertarians would endorse a principle as restrictive as this.

Indeed our considered judgments do not support restriction even where substantial numbers are harmed when a substance is legally available. What about prohibition of alcohol? The evidence that abuse of alcohol blights certain lives is far stronger than de Marneffe's conjectures about the abuse of heroin by poor and untalented teenagers. But do not most people reject the Prohibition Amendment as an undue restriction on personal freedom? Can de Marneffe then appeal to our considered moral judgments to support his method for weighting harms? Will he say that people's rejection of prohibition does not reflect considered moral judgments? Why should we take this view of these judgments?

De Marneffe is well aware of the Prohibition Amendment, but he does not fully grasp the difficulty it presents for his argument. He suggests a number of differences between prohibiting alcohol and heroin but agrees that

> if heroin prohibition can be justified by the kind of argument
> that I [de Marneffe] have given, arguably alcohol prohibition

> is justifiable too. . . . Some may take this to constitute an objec-
> tion to this approach to rights, but, not surprisingly, I do not.
> To the contrary, if alcohol prohibition were justifiable in accor-
> dance with the individualistic principle of sufficient reason [his
> harm principle explained earlier], then, in my view, the policy
> would not violate anyone's moral rights. (p. 176)

His consistency is admirable, but he misses the essential. If de Marneffe's
harm principle fails to account for our judgment that prohibition unduly
restricts liberty, then it does not account for all of our considered moral
judgments. But just the appeal to these judgments is what is supposed to justify the principle. We are supposed to see, on reflection, that the principle is
true. In making this claim, de Marneffe is false to the moral facts.

Even if one accepted the harm principle, though, de Marneffe's argument
for prohibition is incomplete. What about severe harms to people that prohibition causes? What if these turn out to be worse than the harms to young
adults incident on ready access to drugs? Once more, our author is well aware
of these problems. He mentions, e.g., that prohibition results in a violent illegal market in drugs. Further, the illegal market has had "grave political consequences in some countries, such as Colombia and Afghanistan, where drug
lords wield tremendous political influence and inflict terrible violence on
those who oppose them" (pp. 120–121). And will not enforcement of prohibition put civil liberties at risk?

To these dangers, de Marneffe has a simple answer. We must have programs to alleviate these effects, e.g., aid to developing countries so that their
economies do not depend on illegal drugs. It is only prohibition accompanied by supplementary programs to counter the ill effects of "straight" prohibition that he favors. Yet when he considers the problems posed by freedom,
he omits consideration of anything else. Why cannot a supporter of freedom
conjure into existence programs to aid youth at risk from the malign effects
of drugs on motivation, in identical fashion to the way de Marneffe "solves"
the problems for his policy?

Victor's Justice: From Nuremberg to Baghdad*

DANILO ZOLO

Judicial Warfare

October 1, 2009, *Mises Review*

ONE WAY TO LOOK AT WAR likens it to domestic crime. If it is wrong for someone to initiate force against a person who has not violated rights, why should matters change when a group of people, acting under the command of a nation's leader, invade the territory of another country?

Further, should not war crimes, i.e., violations of rights during a war, be treated as criminal offenses as well? Proponents of this view often suggest that, just as courts punish individuals within a nation who commit crimes, so should international courts put on trial and punish political leaders and soldiers who violate rights.[†]

Hans Kelsen, the most famous European legal theorist of the 20th century, suggested in 1944 exactly such a system.

> In Kelsen's opinion, the principal cause for the failure of the
> League of Nations lay in the fact that at the summit of its power

---

* Verso, 2009.

† Jeff McMahan argues forcefully in *Killing in War* that individuals bear moral responsibility for aggressive war, but he does not endorse a punitive legal order in the style of Nuremberg. See my review found in Volume 2, "Political Theory."

structure was a Council representing a sort of worldwide political government, rather than a Court of Justice. . . . [In his
proposal] the Court was to indict individual citizens who were
guilty of war crimes, and their countries were to be held responsible for making them available to the court (p. 24).

Whatever one may think of this proposal, Danilo Zolo, a leading Italian political and legal philosopher, forcefully contends that the endeavors
at Nuremberg and elsewhere to bring to justice perpetrators of war crimes
have little to recommend them. Kelsen called for a neutral court to try all
individuals guilty of war crimes, whether from victor or vanquished nations.
What took place at Nuremberg and after was quite different: only those
from defeated nations were tried, and the winners conducted the trials.

Nothing has befallen the criminals responsible for the atomic
massacres at Hiroshima and Nagasaki in August 1945, or for the
saturation bombing which, when the war was already won by the
Western allies, killed hundreds of thousands of civilians in various German and Japanese cities. Nothing has happened to the
political and military leadership of NATO, responsible for the
"humanitarian" war of aggression against the Yugoslav Republic, which surely ranks as a "supreme" international crime. (p. xi)

In Zolo's view, international courts have not become, as Kelsen wished,
an instrument to promote peace and justice. Quite the contrary, they
have served to ensure American dominance of post-World War II politics.
Nations unfortunate enough to lose a military struggle with the United
States become subject to "victor's justice." The result is a "two-tier" structure
of justice in which opponents of America face strict scrutiny while America
and her allies are immune.

In practice, a dual-standard system of international criminal justice has come about in which a justice "made to measure" for the
major world powers and their victorious leaders operates alongside a separate justice for the defeated and downtrodden. In particular, international crimes of *jus in bello*, which are normally
considered less serious than the crime of aggression, have been
prosecuted relentlessly and in some cases punished with great
harshness, in particular by the Hague Tribunal for the former

Yugoslavia. At the same time, aggressive war, a crime predominantly committed by the political and military authorities of the major powers, has been systematically ignored. (pp. 30–31)

Kelsen, by the way, quickly repudiated the Nuremberg Tribunal. An unneutral court that operated only on the defeated powers did not conform to his conception of the rule of law.

> Kelsen argued that the trial and sentence of Nuremberg could not be allowed to stand as a legal precedent. If the principles applied at Nuremberg were to persist, then at the end of every war the victorious nations could put the governments of the vanquished on trial for committing "crimes" unilaterally and retroactively defined as such by the victors themselves . . . . In Kelsen's opinion, the punishment of war criminals should be an act of justice and not the continuation of hostilities in forms which are ostensibly legal but in reality based on the desire for revenge. (pp. 141–142)

One might object to Zolo's argument by saying that even if the two-tier system is manifestly unfair and contributes to the support of a hegemonic American foreign policy, an important consideration must be allowed its due weight on the other side. Is it not desirable that those guilty of war crimes be brought to justice? Others may be guilty as well, and the faults of the judicial procedures used need correction, but must we throw out the entire concept of individual legal guilt for war crimes?

Zolo is well prepared for this objection, and he offers a characteristically radical response. He sees little evidence that such trials lessen the incidence of war crimes or aggression. Without a deterrent effect, they merely express vengeance. Our author has little use for retribution:

> Prosecutors and judges do not seem to have given the slightest thought to the issue of the purpose of punishment or its effects on the personality and future of those convicted. The sanction—whether the death sentence, life imprisonment or a specified prison sentence—had a purely affective value. It was merely a matter of persecuting the guilty party so as to cause suffering, mortification and humiliation to the point of physical and moral annihilation. . . . The sentences handed down were

clearly designed much less to prevent any future perpetration of
crimes then to celebrate the might of the victors—themselves
responsible for grave international crimes—just as, in pre-mod-
ern times, the "splendour" of the condemned man's torment
was a celebration of the majesty of king or emperor. (p. 146)

Zolo in this connection makes apt use of the work of René Girard on the
scapegoat mechanism. (See, e.g., Girard, *The Scapegoat.*)

Even if Zolo has raised effective objections against judicial punishment of
war crimes committed by defeated nations, he must confront another objection. Is he not making very heavy weather of these trials? Whatever their
flaws, do they not occupy a minor role on the international scene? But Zolo
is after much bigger game.

A principal justification for war today is "humanitarian." In the prepara-
tory propaganda barrage that led to the Iraq War, the crimes and abuses of
Saddam Hussein played a key role. Again, Jean Bethke Elshtain and other
defenders of the American invasion of Afghanistan adduced the manifest
inequity of the Taliban's policy toward Afghan women as a reason that supported intervention.*

The trials that arouse Zolo's concern form a part of a larger ideology.
Because rights have been violated, it is argued, force must be used if this is the
only way to eradicate evil regimes. Against this line of thought, Zolo raises a
vital point. War itself will almost certainly violate rights in a horrendous way:

Finally, we must ask ourselves whether modern warfare, with its
weapons of mass destruction, can coherently be used by international institutions—or military alliances such as NATO—
charged with protecting universal values like human rights. . . .
The legitimation of "humanitarian war" is the equivalent of a
contradictory negation of all these principles. In the case of war
for Kosovo, for example, in practice the death sentence was enforced on thousands of Yugoslav citizens, in the absence of any
investigation of their personal responsibility. . . . Thousands
of simple citizens [were subjected to] lethal bombing raids, in
which . . . murderous cluster bombs and depleted uranium mis-
siles were also deployed. (pp. 60–61)

---

* See Elshtain, *Just War Against Terror.*

If at times Zolo goes too far in his skepticism about universally valid rights, he has nonetheless shown the fallacies of an all-too-common judicial model of international relations. What Isabel Paterson called "the humanitarian with the guillotine" poses a constant danger.

Morality, Political Economy, and American Constitutionalism*

Timothy P. Roth

Constitutional Economics

December 1, 2009, *Mises Review*

Timothy Roth has in earlier work offered a penetrating criticism of modern welfare economics.[†] In *Morality, Political Economy, and American Constitutionalism*, he continues and extends this criticism; but he combines this with an unusual thesis. Not only is modern welfare economics wrong, he says: it violates the principles on which the American Republic was established.

> The general theme of the book is, then, that both in its public philosophy and in its economics, our republic has strayed far from the Founders' vision. Preoccupation with preference satisfaction ... has caused us to ignore, to deny or to forget what the Founders understood. (p. viii)

At first sight, Roth's contention seems impossible. Jefferson, Madison, and the other Founding Fathers, however great their merits, were neither professional philosophers nor economists. How could their ideas be relevant to a

---

* Edward Elgar, 2007.

† See his *Equality, Rights, and the Autonomous Self: Toward a Conservative Economics* (Elgar, 2004) and *The Ethics and Economics of Minimalist Government* (Elgar, 2002).

technical branch of contemporary economic theory? Despite the initial implausibility of Roth's contention, he makes a strong case for it.

He points out that the Founders stressed, most notably in the Declaration of Independence, that each person has inherent worth:

> I [Roth] emphasize for the moment that Jefferson asserted it to be "self-evident, that all Men are created equal," and Madison averred that "the perfect equality of mankind" is "an absolute truth."

Why did the Founders think that this was true? Roth ascribes great importance to the influence of Adam Smith, particularly his notion of the "impartial spectator." Smith emphasized our natural sympathy for other people and our desire to be judged favorably by them. The criterion of morality should be the conduct that would elicit the favorable emotions of an imagined observer who had no particular interests at stake.* Roth notes that Smith was widely read by the Founders. Jefferson in correspondence appealed to a principle that recalls the impartial spectator:

> In an August 19, 1785 letter to Peter Carr, Jefferson urged that "Whenever you are to do a thing, though it can never be known but to yourself, ask yourself how you would act were all the world looking at you, and act accordingly." (p. 23)

Roth takes his argument one step further. Smith's impartial spectator theory, he thinks, bears a marked similarity to Kant's categorical imperative. This is hardly surprising, he claims, because Kant had read Smith and in his *Reflections on Anthropology* specifically mentioned the impartial spectator.

> Kant's allusion to the impartial spectator is particularly revealing because there are elements of remarkable correspondence between Smith's and Kant's construals ... the central point is that, for both Smith and Kant, the cultivation of virtue—of respect for the moral law—requires a two-person perspective. (p. 22)

Roth's argument, I must say, is rather thin. He rightly says that the Founders believed in individual rights, and it is also true that Adam Smith's *Wealth*

---

* For a discussion of Smith's moral theory, see James Otteson, *Adam Smith's Marketplace of Life* (Cambridge, 2002) and my review found in Volume 2, "Political Theory."

of Nations attracted much attention in America. It hardly follows that the Founders adopted Smith's moral theory as the basis of their own views. It does not even follow, from the undoubted parallel between his quotation from Jefferson and the idea of the impartial spectator, that Jefferson was a disciple of Smith: Jefferson had read widely and paraphrased many other writers besides Smith. It would in any case be a leap from Jefferson to the Founders as a whole.

As if this were not enough, it also does not follow from the fact that Kant referred to Smith that their respective moral theories were similar. To appeal to an impartial spectator does not suffice to tell us how the spectator would arrive at his decisions. How does Roth know that the conduct that would earn the spectator's approbation would not be closer to utilitarian than Kantian morality? Utilitarians as well as their opponents have appealed to such a detached observer: a prime instance may be found in R. M. Hare's *Moral Thinking* (Oxford, 1981).

Roth has anticipated objections to his historical reconstruction.

> My point is not that each of the Founders was, necessarily, aware either of Smith's impartial spectator or of Kant's categorical imperative. It is, to use a metaphor familiar to contemporary economists, "as if" they were familiar with both. If this means, as I shall argue below, that the contemporary politics of "wants and needs" and of economic growth and distributive justice found no place in the Founders' thinking, it also means their attention centered on just, in the sense of impartial, procedure. (p. 26)

Roth is in effect saying that the best explanation for the Founders' views is that they rejected utilitarianism in favor of a stress on following strict and impartial rules. His efforts at historical reconstruction need be taken as no more than suggestive.

The American Republic, if Roth is right, was not founded on a utilitarian basis. But should it have been? Roth clearly thinks not, and this leads us to his criticism of utilitarianism and, with it, contemporary welfare economics. He indicts utilitarianism for a familiar reason; it sometimes leads to policies that fail to respect individuals, if doing so is necessary to advance the general welfare:

> For John Rawls, at any rate, the utilitarian argument is not persuasive: "The fault of the utilitarian doctrine is that it mistakes impersonality for impartiality." (p. 68, quoting Rawls)

In other words, utilitarianism does not weight moral options from the point of view of a particular person, but this does not guarantee fairness to each person. If one objects that rule utilitarianism eliminates the problem, since rules with the greatest utility will not sacrifice individuals, Roth is ready with his response. Following David Lyons, he contends that rule utilitarianism collapses into act utilitarianism.

So much for utilitarianism; but why must welfare economics accompany it on its downfall? The Pareto criterion precludes changes that make some worse off: is not welfare economics thus immune from the objection against utilitarianism just discussed?

In response, Roth advances a formidable battery of technical objections to welfare economics. True, welfare economics has followed Lionel Robbins and does not use interpersonal comparisons of utility, but this lands it in another problem:

> Recall that [Kenneth] Arrow's Possibility Result (1951) establishes that, if interpersonal utility comparisons are ruled out, there is no possible method of aggregating individual rankings of social alternatives that meets five apparently innocuous criteria.... If the interpersonal utility comparison militates against the specification of a social welfare function, the same is true of the impossibility of a Paretian liberal. Roughly stated, the juxtaposition of meddlesome or "nosy" preferences and *respect* for minimal privacy rights prevents the emergence of *any* social choice. (pp. 122–123)

I shall leave to readers of the book the problem that Roth finds in specifying another crucial concept of welfare economics, the "efficiency frontier." Further, the theorem of second best of Kevin Lancaster and Richard Lipsey practically destroys all chance of practical application of welfare economics, even if the problems so far canvassed could be solved. Suppose, as would nearly always be the case, that the economy deviates in more than one place from Pareto optimality. A correction of some of these deviations that leaves others untouched need not move the economy toward efficiency: "[T]he point is that social welfare theory cannot, legitimately, be used to justify *either* 'market interventions' or income redistribution policies" (p. 126).

Roth also finds a deeper philosophical failing at the foundation of welfare economics. It takes people's preferences as if they reflected only self-interest:

Roth calls this the assumption of the "transcendental autonomous self." In fact, persons live their lives tightly bound up with one another. The Founders of the American Republic, along with Kant, believed that human beings had a moral sense that should guide their choices.

> Whatever else is said, the single-equation, strictly personal, intertemporally stable and exogenously determined utility function of social welfare theorists' imagination is ill-suited to accommodate any of these [communal] phenomena. (p. 115)

Modern welfare economics cannot accommodate the moral dimension of choice because it was conceived in sin. It was at its inception dominated by the false doctrines of logical positivism, which reduced ethical judgments to expressions of emotion.

If, following Roth, we reject welfare economics, what should be put in its place as a guide to policy? For him the key is a system of stable rules and institutions: the "constitutional political economy" of his mentor James Buchanan is everywhere apparent. Among the features of this approach are a stress of federalism and opposition to centralized power. Also, policies must be strictly impartial: discriminatory taxation, e.g., is not allowed. "I emphasize . . . that tax increases targeted at individual companies are patently discriminatory and, *pari passu*, immoral" (p. 146). The sum and substance of Roth's project, then, is twofold. He offers a Kantian justification for political economy in the style of Buchanan; and he maintains that this view of things is at the root of the American Republic. Readers of a libertarian bent will not be fully satisfied; but Roth's carefully argued book deserves, and rewards, close study.

The Harm in Hate Speech[*]

JEREMY WALDRON

The Harm in Restricting Free Speech

July 1, 2012, *Mises Review*

N MANY COUNTRIES, though not in the United States, laws prohibit "hate speech." Those who, in Jeremy Waldron's opinion, uncritically elevate the benefits of free speech over competing values oppose hate-speech laws; but Waldron thinks that a strong case can be made in their favor. (Waldron thinks that there are "very few First Amendment Absolutists" [p. 144] who oppose all regulation of speech; but he thinks that many other First Amendment scholars are unduly critical of hate speech regulations.) Waldron is a distinguished legal and political philosopher, but the arguments that he advances in defense of hate-speech laws, taken on their own terms, do not seem to me very substantial.[†]

Hate speech, Waldron tells, us, consists of "publications which express profound disrespect, hatred, and vilification for the members of minority groups" (p. 27). "Speech," it should be noted, is used here in an extended sense; and it is the more lasting written material, movies, posters, etc., that principally concern Waldron rather than speeches, verbal threats, or imprecations, though the latter are not excluded. Many countries ban such speech:

---

[*] Harvard University Press, 2012.

[†] His *Torture, Terror, and Trade-Offs: Philosophy for the White House* (Oxford, 2010), offers a penetrating assessment of the immorality of recent American foreign policy; and his *God, Locke, and Equality* (Cambridge, 2002) is one of the best recent books on Locke. Waldron's discussion in the present book of Locke and other Enlightenment writers on toleration is outstanding.

> The United Kingdom has long outlawed the publication of material
> calculated to stir up racial hatred. In Germany it is a serious crime
> to display the swastika or other Nazi symbols. Holocaust denial is
> punished in many countries. The British author David Irving...
> was imprisoned until recently in Austria for this offense. (p. 29)

One way to respond to this would be to assess hate-speech laws from the
Rothbardian position that I deem to be correct. This would make for a very
short review. For Rothbard, free-speech questions reduce to issues of property rights. If, for example, someone writes "Muslims get out!" on a wall, a
Rothbardian would ask, "Whose wall is it?" If the author of the message
wrote on his own wall, he acted within his rights; if, lacking permission, he
wrote on someone else's wall, he violated the owner's property rights. People have no general right of restraint against insult. Furthermore, you do
not own your reputation, since this consists of the ideas other people have
of you, and you cannot own other people's thoughts. For that reason, laws
against libel and slander are for the Rothbardian ruled out. Waldron asks, If
laws forbid libel of a person, why not laws against group libel as well? A more
un-Rothbardian argument could hardly be imagined.

I think it would be a mistake to leave matters there. Waldron— and those
like him who reject libertarianism—would be unlikely to take notice of the
foregoing criticism.* But another line of inquiry might be of more interest to
them. We can also ask how good Waldron's arguments are if judged on their
own merits rather than evaluated from an external perspective.

If we ask this question, we must first deal with a difficulty. Waldron's exact
position is rather elusive. For one thing, it is not altogether accurate to say
that he defends hate-speech laws, though this is certainly the general tenor
of his book. He sometimes confines himself to saying that there are considerations in favor of these laws: these would need to be weighed against reasons
for not restricting speech.

> My purpose in putting all this in front of you is not to persuade
> you of the wisdom and legitimacy of hate-speech laws. ... The
> point is ... to consider whether American free-speech jurispru-
> dence has really come to terms with the best that has been said
> for hate speech regulations. (p. 11)

---

* Waldron treats it as obvious that "markets ... undermine distributive justice" (p. 156).

But I do not think it admits of much doubt that for Waldron the arguments in favor of these laws are decisive.

Why, then, should we restrict hate speech? The primary consideration is that it assaults human dignity. In what Waldron, following John Rawls, calls a "well-ordered society," there is "an assurance to all the citizens that they can count on being treated justly" (p. 85). But hate speech disrupts this assurance.

> However, when a society is defaced with anti-Semitic signage, burning crosses, and defamatory racial leaflets, that sort of assurance evaporates. A vigilant police force and a Justice Department may still keep people from being attacked or excluded, but they no longer have the benefit of a general and diffuse assurance to this effect [of being treated justly], provided and enjoyed as a public good, furnished to all by each. (p. 85)

This goes altogether too fast. If you encounter a pamphlet or sign hostile to your minority group, why would you conclude anything more than that someone wishes you and those like you ill? Would not the hostile view be merely one opinion among large numbers of others? Why would it suffice to weaken your sense of assurance that you were an equal member of society?

Waldron, fully aware of this objection, responds that it neglects the effects of contagion. Even though the effect of an individual hate message may be small, the message signals to other haters that they do not hate alone. The accumulation of many such messages may indeed serve to undermine the assurance of the harassed minority.

> In a way, we are talking about an *environmental* good—the *atmosphere* of a well-ordered society—as well as the ways in which a certain ecology of respect, dignity, and assurance is maintained, and the ways in which it can be polluted and (to vary the metaphor) undermined. (p. 96)

Waldron elucidates the parallel that he draws between hate messages and environmental pollution in this way: We see that the

> tiny impacts of millions of actions—each apparently inconsiderable in itself—can produce a large-scale toxic effect that, even at the mass level, operates insidiously as a sort of slow-acting poison, and that regulations have to be aimed at individual

actions with that scale and that pace of causation in mind. An immense amount of progress has been made in consequentialist moral philosophy by taking causation of this kind, on this scale and at this pace, properly into account. (p. 97)

(Waldron refers here to the well-known treatment of "moral mathematics" in Derek Parfit's *Reasons and Persons*.)

But why does contagion operate only with bad effects? Will not the cumulative effects of a series of individual encounters in which members of minority groups are treated with equal respect generate a positive atmosphere of assurance, in precisely the same way that Waldron postulates for the amassing of hate messages? Waldron assumes without argument a quasi-Gresham's law of public opinion, in which bad opinion drives out good.

But which process, the one that produces a positive atmosphere of assurance or the one that arouses Waldron to concern, will in fact prove the stronger? One reason to think that it is the good one is this. Waldron, in response to the charge that hate-speech laws suppress legitimate issues of controversy, notes that some matters are beyond dispute; an established consensus supports them:

> Suppose someone puts up posters conveying the opinion that people from Africa are nonhuman primates. . . . Maybe there was a time when social policy generally . . . could not adequately be debated without raising the whole issue of race in this sense. But that is not our situation today. . . . In fact, the fundamental debate about race is over—won, finished. There are outlying dissenters, a few crazies who say they believe that people of African descent are an inferior form of animal; but for half a century or more, we have moved forward as a society on the premise that this is no longer a matter of serious contestation. (p. 195)

If Waldron is right, and only a "few crazies" believe the hateful doctrine, why is he so much in fear of the malign effects of allowing these people to publish their views unmolested by the state?

To be frank, I think that Waldron at times proceeds in a very unfair way. He says, in effect, to the opponents of hate-speech laws, "You say that you are willing to put up with the evils of hate speech in order to preserve the good of unhindered free speech. But you are not, in most cases, the ones who will suffer from hate speech. Why are you entitled, without evidence, to brush aside the suffering of those whom hate speech targets?"

That is not in itself an unreasonable question, but Waldron ignores one vital issue. He is endeavoring to make a case for the regulation of hate speech. He cannot then fairly shift the *onus probandi* entirely to the side of his opponents, saying to them, "prove that hate speech does not much affect its victims." It is for him to show that hate speech in fact has the dire effects he attributes to it. It is not out of the question that such speech sometimes does have bad effects, but it would seem obvious that we have here an empirical issue, one that requires the citation of evidence. Waldron so far as I can see fails to offer any, preferring instead to conjure up pictures of people who, seeing or hearing examples of hate speech, recall horrid scenes of past persecution. To what extent do people actually suffer from hate speech? Waldron evinces little interest in finding out.

If Waldron has not succeeded in making a case for hate-speech regulation, is there anything to be said against such laws—aside, of course, from the libertarian considerations that we have for this review put aside? One point seems to me of fundamental importance. Waldron presents these laws as if they limited only extreme expression of hate, e.g., suggestions that people in certain groups are subhuman or need to be forcibly expelled from society, if not done away with altogether. He rightly notes that we are not obliged to like everyone or to deem everyone equally morally worthy:

> Does this [the requirement that we treat everyone with dignity] mean that individuals are required to accord equal respect to all their fellow citizens? Does it mean they are not permitted to esteem some and despise others? That proposition seems counterintuitive. Much of our moral and political life involves differentiation of respect. (p. 86)

Hate-speech laws, Waldron says, do not ignore our rights to prefer some people to others. We further remain free to criticize minority groups, so long as we do not stray into the forbidden territory of outright hatred and denigration. Waldron claims that

> most such [hate speech] laws bend over backwards to ensure that there is a lawful way of expressing something like the propositional content of views that become objectionable

when expressed as vituperation. They try to define a legitimate mode of roughly equivalent expression. . . . Some laws
of this type also try affirmatively to define a sort of "safe haven" for the moderate expression of the view whose hateful
or hate-inciting expression is prohibited. (p. 190)

I do not doubt that Waldron has accurately quoted from the laws he mentions, but he unaccountably fails to comment on a quite well-known phenomenon. Laws of the type Waldron champions have often been used to
suppress not just vituperation but all sorts of "politically incorrect" opinions. For example, as James Kalb notes in his outstanding *The Tyranny of
Liberalism*, "the High Court in Britain [in 2004] upheld the conviction and
firing of an elderly preacher who held up a sign in a town square calling for
an end to homosexuality, lesbianism, and immorality and was thrown to the
ground and pelted with dirt and water by an angry crowd."*

Those wishing further examples of how these laws work in practice may
with profit consult the penetrating studies of Paul Gottfried, e.g., *After Liberalism: Mass Democracy in the Managerial State* and *Multiculturalism and
the Politics of Guilt*. Here we are dealing not with a matter of speculative psychology but of incontrovertible fact.

For Waldron, the state ought to watch vigilantly over us, ever alert that
some miscreant may cross the boundaries (set of course by the state itself)
of acceptable dissent from the regnant orthodoxy of multicultural society. I
cannot think that such a tutelary power has a place in a free society.

---

* I may be allowed here to refer to my review of Kalb's book in *The American Conservative*
for November 17, 2008.

The Rule of Law and the Measure of Property*

JEREMY WALDRON

An Attack on Property Rights

July 1, 2012, *Mises Review*

CLASSICAL LIBERALS like Friedrich Hayek and Richard Epstein have often claimed that the rule of law imposes strong constraints on the state's regulation of private property. If they are right, this would be a very effective argument against such regulation, as the rule of law is an ideal commanding wide respect, by no means confined to those of classical-liberal or libertarian inclinations.

Governments that arbitrarily deny legal process to groups of people or punish people for violating orders undisclosed to them obviously violate the rule of law; but how can formal requirements of proper law such as generality and nondiscrimination limit the power of the state to regulate property? The classical liberals answer that people should be able to use law to guide their behavior; interferences with private property disrupt their reasonable expectations of how they can use their property and unduly depend for their implementation on administrative discretion.

Jeremy Waldron, a distinguished legal philosopher, disagrees with this line of thought; and in this short book he deploys many arguments against it and against Lockean accounts of property rights as well.[†] I don't find what he says

---

* Cambridge University Press, 2012.

† I have recently reviewed another book by this prolific scholar, *The Harm in Hate Speech*. See my review found in Volume 1, "Law."

persuasive, but his thoughtful discussion merits the attention of everyone interested in libertarian political philosophy.

Waldron has devoted a great deal of his life as a scholar to Locke's theory of property, but his study has not led him to accept it. In this theory, people acquire property by homesteading it; once acquired, property may be transferred by exchange, gift, or bequest to others. A common objection holds that this account can have little or no application to the world we live in today. People cannot trace their property back to an original act of just appropriation, passed to them through transfers wholly legitimate.*

Waldron advances a variant of this argument. Not only cannot we trace back property titles in the way the theory needs, but we know that property titles often stem from government grants. He is a New Zealander, and he cites as an example the situation in his native country. "But mostly the land seems to have been governed by social and public legal arrangements from start to finish. It was used and cultivated first by a collective group, its original Maori owners" (p. 29). It then passed by treaty to the British government who in turn transferred it to settlers.

> The transition from indigenous tribal property to government property to leasehold property on the government's terms to individual freehold is something that was supervised by the state purportedly in the public interest at every stage. (p. 30)

What better evidence could we have that the Lockean theory cannot be used by present owners of property in New Zealand to resist government regulations as encroachments on their rights?

This argument does not succeed; it begs the question against Locke's theory. So long as the original acts of appropriation by the Maori passed the Lockean tests, which Waldron does not challenge, the process Waldron describes at no point violates Locke's theory. It is not a part of that theory that the state cannot be one of the links in the chain of transmission of property, though indeed there are excellent arguments against the justification for a state altogether. The state can, if it acquires property, then sell it to people under various conditions, but its doing so does not subject the new owners to further unspecified regulations of their property by the state. To think

---

* See the discussion of this objection in Murray Rothbard, *Ethics of Liberty*, chapter 10, "The Problem of Land Theft," especially the discussion on pp. 67 ff.

otherwise, as Waldron does, is to assume precisely what is at issue in the controversy. His account of New Zealand property leaves Locke unscathed.

Waldron has another argument against the Lockean view, and here he addresses directly the concerns about expectations used by Hayek, Epstein, and others who use the rule of law to fence in the government's interference with property rights. Do Lockean rights, he surprisingly asks, increase stability of expectations? He claims that they do not:

> The [Lockean] picture we are being sold has property rights being determined pre-politically; these are the ones that are to be respected by the legislature under this substantive constraint. (p. 38)

But the Lockean theory is controversial. Even among people who accept the basic outlines of it, disagreements over such matters as the exact nature of the principle of appropriation abound. "By insisting therefore that positive law is subject to this substantive constraint rooted in the moral reality of pre-political property rights, Locke is subjecting the legislature to a discipline of uncertainty" (p. 39).

This conclusion does not at all follow. A Lockean framework leaves many questions of detail unsettled, true enough; but then people must simply choose what to do within this framework and stick to it, in order to arrive at a stable system of property. Why must a correct theory of property resolve in advance all questions, leaving nothing to be decided by convention? Further, even if details of the theory *do* admit of correct answers, the fact that people disagree on these need not introduce instability. Those who think the arrangements in place objectively mistaken on these details may nevertheless think it more important to maintain stability than to insist that matters be changed entirely to their liking.

Although Waldron does not discuss this solution, he does address a proposal advanced by James Tully, which he acknowledges would settle the difficulty over stability. (He thinks, though, that it is a misinterpretation of Locke.) On this view, the legislature sets property rights as it wishes: it is these legislatively determined rights that are then stably established.

> On Tully's account, the property rights that are protected are themselves artifacts of public law. As such, they are clear, well known, and stable; and they are no longer at the mercy of natural law controversies. But the price of that deliverance is that

the property rights in question, being the offspring of legislation, can have very little power and status to set up against legislation (of the environmental kind). Property is no longer privileged as a special or primeval form of law. (p. 41)

Once more the conclusion does not follow. So long as stability is taken to
be of great importance, Locke's theory on this interpretation does not allow
the legislature to change property arrangements in accord with its wishes of
the moment. Waldron, anxious to pursue his environmental imperative, has
forgotten the elementary point that laws can be entrenched in a legal system
without reference to natural-law constraints.

Before turning from Waldron's discussion of the Lockean theory, I must
protest against what can only be called a gross misstatement. Concerning Robert Nozick, one of the foremost 20th-century defenders of the theory, he says,

he was never prepared to say that a Lockean theory legitimized
contemporary disparities of wealth in the United States. On the
contrary, he thought it undeniable that contemporary holdings
in America would be condemned as unjust by any remotely plausible conception of historical entitlement. (p. 33)

To this statement, he appends a reference to pages 230–231 of *Anarchy,
State, and Utopia*. It is quite true that Nozick in those pages says that schemes
of transfer payments cannot be condemned as unjust by his theory, in the
absence of information of what the principle of rectification requires. There
is nothing whatever there, though, condemning contemporary American disparities of wealth. Waldron has unaccountably attributed his own egalitarian
proclivities to Nozick.

As mentioned earlier, Waldron advances a great many arguments to challenge the connection of the rule of law with restrictions on the legislative
regulation of property, but I shall discuss only one more. Waldron has an
interesting view of the famous *Lucas* case, in which a businessman purchased
beachfront property in South Carolina, intending to build houses on the
land for commercial sale. A law passed after the sale by the South Carolina
legislature prevented him from doing so, and he suffered a large loss as a
result. He appealed to the Supreme Court, which ruled that he had been
the victim of an unlawful "taking" of his property and required that he be
granted compensation for his losses.

Waldron finds fault with the verdict. Given the many environmental regulations already enacted by the legislature, should not Lucas have anticipated that he might not have been able to use the property as he wished? How then can one rightly assert, appealing to the rule of law, that he had the right not to have overturned his reasonable expectations of how he might use the property commercially? He ought not to have assumed without warrant that he could do with the property what the legislature later determined he could not.

> True, Mr. Lucas bought his property in 1986, a year or three before the new legislation came into force. But he was not a neophyte in these matters. . . . Mr. Lucas was not exactly sand-bagged by the council's eventual intervention to safeguard the eroding beaches on and in the immediate vicinity of his property. (pp. 79–80)

In sum, Waldron thinks if someone has reason to think that the government may take from him the right to use his property for commercial use, then his reasonable expectations for use of the property have not been upset. He ought not to have formed these expectations in the first place. By analogy, someone's expectations of personal security have not been upset if he knows that he may in future be compelled to play Russian roulette. Somehow, this does not seem a satisfactory result.

Index

F

L